THE JOHN HARVARD LIBRARY

Bernard Bailyn

Editor-in-Chief

THE JOHN HARVARD LIBRARY

John Cotton on the Churches of New England

EDITED BY LARZER ZIFF

THE BELKNAP PRESS OF
HARVARD UNIVERSITY PRESS

Cambridge, Massachusetts

1968

John Harvard Library books are edited at the
Charles Warren Center for Studies in American History
Harvard University.

Contents

Introduction

IN seventeenth-century Massachusetts membership in the church was a prerequisite for citizenship. It was also a qualification for belonging to the community in a broader sense: it satisfied social and spiritual impulses that reached beyond political aspirations.[1] When the settlers debated matters of church membership they were debating an issue central to the formation of the American community.

The question of eligibility for church membership raised serious practical problems. Although the principal guides for the system were sincere and eloquent in their claims for the historicity of Congregationalism—in *The Way of Congregational Churches Cleared* John Cotton devotes a chapter to the "antiquity" of that system—they were theoretical rather than historical. To Cotton's time, all Protestants, like all Roman Catholics, had been raised in churches that admitted everyone to membership and offered the sacraments to them. Some reformed churches did deny membership to those who had lived in a demonstrably scandalous fashion, but no influential church limited membership to those whom it presumed to identify not merely as orderly in their outward behavior but also as saintly in an inward sense, because of their possession of grace. Just how such limitations on membership could become workable features of a national church was a question that more than vexed those who saw the validity of the limitations in theory.[2]

1 See, for example, Edmund S. Morgan, *The Puritan Family* (Boston, 1944), chap. vi, and Larzer Ziff, "The Social Bond of Church Covenant," *American Quarterly* 10 (Winter 1958). 454–462.
2 See, for example, Geoffrey T. Nuttall, *Visible Saints, The Congregational*

Moreover, all Christians believed there was only one church, the catholic church, and the Reformation was, for Protestants, a reform of that single catholic church. Roman Catholicism, they held, had become so corrupt over the centuries that it was now Antichristian, but the churches they established in its stead were not regarded as alternate ways to heaven. They were, rather, viewed collectively as the only way, the true Christian church descended clearly from Peter. It seemed, therefore, that even though the superintendency of individual churches by a pope or an oligarchy of bishops might not be desirable, still the individual churches should have some formal connection with one another since their individuality was merely the result of accidents of geography, language, and local history; essentially, they were one. In the church in England such connection was made through government by bishops, and when Puritanism succeeded in persuading large numbers that this was a half-way leaning towards Rome, the single most popular system offered as a replacement was Presbyterianism, government by elders who met in an hierarchical series of presbyteries, synods, and classes to administer local, regional, and national churches.

Congregationalism, however, argued not only for the limitation of membership to the saved believers but also for the integrity of the individual church and its separateness from all other churches in matters of government. Synods might be called for advice, but each church was essentially a self-contained, self-governing unit. The system therefore early gained the name of Independency, though John Cotton insisted that it be called, as eventually it was, Congregationalism.

Though Congregational theory was rapidly amplified in the

Way, 1640–1666 (Oxford, 1957), and Edmund S. Morgan, *Visible Saints; the History of a Puritan Idea* (New York, 1963).

late sixteenth and early seventeenth centuries, the only body of relevant practice that could be cited was that of the Separatist congregations. The members of these groups, insignificant in number and in social status, had become impatient with the slowness of reform of the episcopal system in the Church of England and had separated from it, most often, since such separation was patently illegal and punishable by death, by fleeing from the country. By definition, therefore, they had cut themselves off and were, willy-nilly, independent. The vast majority of Puritans, those who were to settle Massachusetts Bay and establish a Congregational system as well as those who were to control the Church of Scotland and establish a Presbyterian system, were vociferous in their condemnation of the Separatists. Though the Church of England was in need of reform, they held, it was a true church, and separation from it was schism and therefore heretical.

Reports from the Lowlands where the majority of the Separatists settled in the first decade of the seventeenth century reinforced the view that Separatism was schismatic. The Separatists seemed unable to live even with one another. John Smyth's Amsterdam group was in continuous dispute with all other English congregations; the group led by Francis Johnson and Henry Ainsworth squabbled so seriously that it broke in two; the group led by John Robinson, which was later to settle Plymouth, left Amsterdam for Leyden in 1609 because it could not maintain a tranquil course in proximity to its fellow Separatist congregations.[3]

Congregationalism, then, though it might have a respectable

---

[3] The history of these Continental Separatists is surveyed with a valuable bibliography in Henry Martyn Dexter, *The Congregationalism of the Last Three Hundred Years As Seen in its Literature* (New York, 1880).

theory, had in practice a most disputatious history. The theory affirmed that the independent, self-governing congregation was the essential unit of the true church, and that all such congregations would by the strength of grace be similar in matters of doctrine and discipline. History indicated, however, that such congregations lacked the catholic essence of the true church; their members did not communicate in other congregations and did not allow other Christians to communicate in their congregation.

Yet it was Congregationalism that the single most influential group of seventeenth-century American settlers established as their church form; it was Congregationalism that satisfied and molded their political and social aspirations as well as their spiritual longings; and it was Congregationalism that succeeded to the extent of becoming not only the orthodox way in Massachusetts but an accepted independent way within the Church of England and therefore a viable alternative to Presbyterianism in the homeland after the Revolution. How it did so makes an important chapter in American history.

In establishing Congregationalism, the American Puritans had to steer between outright separation from the Church of England and a spiral of schism on one hand, and a superintendency over congregations amounting to Presbyterianism on the other. They had to meet and adjust to strong opposition in practice from brilliant and dedicated men like Roger Williams, and to take what was practical from the avowed Separatists at Plymouth and yet not go over to separation; to continue to receive the material as well as the spiritual support of a body of English Puritans who believed them to be, at best, in partial error; and to satisfy the daily demands of a community of Englishmen struggling to keep alive on the fringe of a wilderness. That they succeeded speaks strongly for the political as well as the theological skill of a small group of ministers and magistrates.

No one man could have accomplished such a task, but it was recognized in Massachusetts, and it was a cardinal article of belief among Presbyterian polemicists in England, that if one name had to be singled out as that of the chief helmsman of the course the Massachusetts Bay Puritans were following in their churches, that name was John Cotton. It was he who had earned such a reputation for piety, learning, mildness of temper, and successful church reformation during his years in England that his reports from America were received as definitive, and it was he who preeminently possessed the scholarly powers necessary to defend the Massachusetts system in terms that would relate it historically to the true apostolic church and at the same time adjust it practically to the stresses placed upon it by Presbyterianism on one side and radicals on the other.

Now that debates over church polity have receded into a murky limbo, the works of John Cotton that are devoted to defining and justifying the Congregational way are susceptible of being seen as little more than dead words from a dead hand. And, truly, they cannot usefully be approached by a modern reader without the exercise of historical imagination. But the effort is justified by the animation that the texts readily receive from it. Cotton's *Sermon Deliver'd at Salem* becomes both eloquent and hard-headed when it is read as a lecture given in a church that had just been forced, against the will of many, to dispense with the services of Roger Williams. His *Keys of the Kingdom of Heaven* has the force of a constitution when read with a consciousness of the English political situation that led Thomas Goodwin, Philip Nye, and their friends, embattled at the Westminster Assembly, to stand behind it as a bulwark. And *The Way of Congregational Churches Cleared* is a treasury of

vital information and illuminating interpretation when read
with a sense of the magnitude of the crisis New England underwent during the Antinomian controversy.

(I)

In 1597, John Cotton, the thirteen-year-old son of a Derby
lawyer, matriculated as a sizar at Trinity College, Cambridge.[4]
His upbringing at home and at grammar school had been sympathetic to the Puritan movement, and at Cambridge he associated himself with those students and lecturers who worked
politically for a further reform of the Church of England and
who bore themselves in a restrained and sober, many would say
cheerless, fashion.

Cotton was an excellent student, especially impressive in his
mastery of the ancient tongues, but the year of his A.B., 1603,
was one in which the master of Trinity, Thomas Neville, had
committed all available funds to extensive architectural revisions
so that no fellowship money was at hand. Accordingly, young
John Cotton had to look elsewhere for continued support, and
when he accepted a fellowship at Emmanuel College under
Laurence Chaderton he not only was electing to continue his
studies but was consciously moving into a closer alliance with
the Puritan party. Trinity had been in a somewhat moderate
position with regard to ecclesiastical reforms, but Emmanuel
was a Puritan foundation—even Queen Elizabeth had referred
to it by that term—where traditional vestments had been put
aside, the prescribed form of public prayer was circumvented,
and the eucharist was received sitting. Indeed, scandalized
orthodox students noted that those at Emmanuel took supper

---

[4] The account of Cotton's life is based on Larzer Ziff, *The Career of John
Cotton* (Princeton, 1962).

on Friday and from a college kitchen that faced east although
the unconsecrated college chapel did not.

John Cotton remained at Emmanuel for nine years, receiving
his M.A. in 1606 and his ordination as a priest in 1610, before
leaving for his first vicarage in 1612. Each year at Emmanuel
his reputation grew, based at first on his learning, which led
him to keep his Divinity Act—the required reading and defense
of a thesis before an appointed opponent—in a brilliant fashion
though his opponent was the famous disputant William
Chappell, and which led him to pass with ease a Hebrew
examination based on Isaiah iii, that, in the opinion of another
learned Puritan, "hath more hard words in it, than any place
of the Bible within so short a compass."[5] He became successively
tutor, dean, lecturer, and catechist, and as he received more and
more opportunities to preach, his fame as a skillful orator grew,
and he was assured of an eager and large auditory whenever he
mounted the pulpit. Though he was associated with the Puritans, however, his was no plain style but one replete with
"invention, elegancy, purity of style, ornaments of rhetoric,
elocution, and oratorious beauty of the whole."[6] There were
degrees of Puritanism—even Laurence Chaderton, a leader in
that movement, had said, "Those who dislike the government
of the Church by bishops will substitute something far less
beneficial both to Church and State"[7]—and Cotton's did not
extend to a distrust of the pulpit eloquence most often associated
with Lancelot Andrewes, even if the doctrines he preached
differed from those of the Master of Pembroke Hall.

[5] John Norton, *Abel Being Dead Yet Speaketh* (London, 1658), p. 10.
Spelling in this and all other seventeenth-century texts has been modernized
in accordance with the principles set forth in the Note on the Text.
[6] *Ibid.*, p. 13.
[7] William Dillingham, *Laurence Chaderton, D.D.*, trans. by Evelyn S.
Shuckburgh (Cambridge, 1884), p. 10.

Though Cotton's move to Emmanuel in 1603 was, then, a signal of his engagement with the Puritan party, he later maintained that he had not become a regenerate Christian until 1609, when the sermons of Richard Sibbes brought home to him the realization that he had been building his spiritual estate on his own wit and learning rather than on a conviction of sin and a consequent detection of the movings of grace within him. He had given assent to a theology he had mastered; Sibbes led him to belief based on personal experience.

Cotton's conversion had public as well as private consequences for it resulted, among other things, in his perceiving that the elegant pulpit style that had earned him his reputation was a mere exercise of intellect. He now saw an inevitable connection between the main end of the sermon, the psychological rather than intellectual preparation of the listener for the saving experience, and the plain style. His adoption of that style affected everything he wrote. Learning was the context not the matter of his remarks, and elegance was studiously avoided as an intrusion of the self between the word of truth and its receivers. As his contemporaries phrased it, Cotton, in his preaching and writing, sought the substance of Paul rather than Plato and the manner of Moses rather than the Muses.

In July 1612 John Cotton was interviewed at Cambridge by a delegation from Boston, Lincolnshire, a town which, as a corporation, controlled the living of the Vicar of St. Botolph's Church. The delegation, headed by Thomas Wooll, the retiring vicar who had been cited several times by the bishop's court for nonconformity, was seeking another minister of reforming principles. They were particularly interested in Cotton, who had been warmly recommended by Paul Baynes and Sibbes, who was known to be an effective preacher, and whose residence at Emmanuel argued for the correctness of his ecclesiastical views.

The city council confirmed the selection of Cotton, but the Bishop of Lincoln, William Barlow, criticized the town for choosing him. He informed Cotton, then twenty-eight, that he was too young a man to be set over so turbulent a parish.

Significantly, Cotton was inclined to agree, and prepared to remain at Cambridge. But the Puritan aldermen of Boston were old hands at nonconformity, and, to quote a contemporary's report, "Understanding that one Simon Biby was to be spoken with, which was near the Bishop, they presently charmed him; and so the business went on smooth, and Mr. Cotton was a learned man with the Bishop, and he was admitted into the place, after their manner in those days." The name Simon Biby carried with it a marginal gloss, "Which some call *Simony and Bribery*."[8]

Cotton's hesitation in the face of the bishop's admonition and the aldermen's skill in meeting it were predictive of Cotton's impressively successful twenty-year career as vicar of St. Botolph's. He was able, as he reports in *The Way of Congregational Churches Cleared,* to disarm the Arminian faction in town, to identify the saints within his parish church and withdraw into a stricter communion with them, and to serve usefully as a consultant to many troubled colleagues vexed by the bishops' policies. He was effective in these activities as a result of his great learning and his equable temper. But he was able to pursue his studies and keep his temper from turning zealous under persecution because of the practical political skills of the aldermen of Boston. They fenced their vicar off from oppression effectively: when protests were lodged against Cotton's congregation within a congregation, Alderman Thomas Leverett car-

8 Samuel Whiting, "Concerning the Life of the Famous Mr. Cotton, Teacher to the Church at Boston, in New-England," *Chronicles of the First Planters of the Colony of Massachusetts Bay,* ed. Alexander Young (Boston, 1846), p. 423.

ried the appeal to the bishop's court in Lincoln, located a proctor who was susceptible to aldermanic charms, and arranged to have Cotton treated as a conformable man. When, in 1621, persons unknown shattered the stained-glass windows of St. Botolph's, destroyed the ornaments, and mutilated the statuary, the town officials convinced the royal solicitor-general that Mr. Cotton did not connive at such an anti-episcopal display. As a result of such efficient political practices, Cotton held his Puritanic course under Bishops Barlow, Monteigne, and Williams while one after another Puritan minister, in the years 1613–1632, was silenced, imprisoned, or forced to flee. Samuel Ward of Ipswich said: "Of all men in the world I envy Mr. Cotton, of Boston, most; for he doth nothing in way of conformity, and yet hath his liberty, and I do everything that way, and cannot enjoy mine."[9]

In his twenty years at St. Botolph's, Cotton received a steady flow of students from Cambridge, most of them sent by John Preston whom he had converted as Sibbes had converted him and who was now Chaderton's successor as master of Emmanuel; at Cambridge they said that Mr. Cotton was Dr. Preston's seasoning vessel. He also trained Continental ministers forced into exile by the fortunes of Protestantism in their homelands. To his Thursday afternoon and Sunday morning public lectures he had to add public lectures on Wednesday and Thursday mornings and on Sunday afternoons. A number of the disciples who attended him were to rise to positions of power at the Puritan revolution and to keep Cotton's name before the English public as the most learned and reliable of the American writers. Noblemen such as Earl Lindsey, Viscount Dorchester, and the Earl of Dorset heard Cotton preach and offered to help him

[9] *Ibid.*, p. 427.

should he need influence. Puritans of all shades of reforming principle, from Roger Williams to Archbishop Ussher, visited him or sought correspondence with him.

For those who had not had Cotton's good fortune in maintaining their posts under an increasingly restrictive episcopacy, Tattersall, near Boston, the seat of the Clintons, Earls of Lincoln, became a staging area for colonization. Cotton was in close conference with most who arrived at Tattersall and held extensive consultations with the Earl's chaplain, Samuel Skelton, immediately before Skelton left for Salem as minister to John Endicott's company in 1629. In the following year Cotton journeyed to Southampton to preach the farewell sermon to a company that included a number of people from his area and was headed by John Winthrop.

When he thought of the churches to be set up at some distance from the bishops' surveillance, Cotton was firm in his disapproval of any separateness that amounted to refusal of communion with the Church of England or Continental reformed churches. In 1629, he had praised in print the writings against Separatism of the Puritan, Arthur Hildersam;[10] and in conference with Samuel Skelton he had insisted upon the fact that any member of the true church could commune in any other church though he was not a member of the particular congregation. He maintained his insistence on the essential unity of all reformed groups in his farewell sermon, reminding Winthrop's group that England was the "Jerusalem at home" and that they must still have recourse to it.[11] Later in 1630 in a letter to Hugh Goodyear at Leyden, one of the few Puritan ministers who had chosen to ally his congregation with the Dutch Reformed

10 In his Preface to Arthur Hildersam, *Lectures Upon the Forth of Iohn* (London, 1629).
11 John Cotton, *Gods Promise to His Plantation* (London, 1630).

Church, he wrote: "What detaineth the Separatists from joining with you, I desire to know at your leisure. Unfeigned fellowship with Christ would easily admit, yea gladly seek fellowship with His members, that walk before Him in the simplicity and purity of His ordinances."[12]

He was, therefore, "grieved" to learn from Salem that the church there denied communion to newly-arrived colonists whom he knew to be "faithful servants of Christ," and he was especially disturbed that his Boston parishioner, William Coddington, could not have his child baptized "because he was no member of any particular reformed church, though of the catholic." He wrote Skelton:

> Two things herein I conceive to be erroneous, first that you think that no man may be admitted to the Sacrament, though a member of the catholic church, unless he be also a member of some particular reformed church: secondly that none of our congregations in England are particular reformed churches, but Mr. Lathrop's [a Separatist congregation] and such as his.[13]

The main part of Cotton's letter was taken up with a scriptural refutation of the policy Skelton had adopted at Salem, and since he failed to find a correspondence between what he heard about Skelton and what he knew of Skelton from their conversations in Lincolnshire, he wrote:

> You went hence of another judgment, and I am afraid your change hath sprung from New Plymouth men, whom though I much esteem as godly and loving Christians, yet their grounds which they received for this tenent from Mr. Robinson, do not satisfy me.[14]

---

[12] D. Plooij, *The Pilgrim Fathers from A Dutch Point of View* (New York, 1932), p. 87.

[13] David D. Hall, "John Cotton's Letter to Samuel Skelton," *William and Mary Quarterly*, 22 (1965), 481.

[14] *Ibid.*, p. 482.

With such misgivings about Skelton's practices, Cotton was not immediately attracted to New England as a refuge on the inevitable day in 1632 when news reached him that even his politically persuasive parishioners were powerless before the gathering strength of William Laud and that pursuivants had been sent to summon him to the High Court. He fled to London and, concealed there, was visited in his hiding place by Thomas Goodwin and John Davenport who sought to convince him that there would be no wrong attached to his conforming. But in the course of the discussions Cotton converted them to further nonconformity and propelled Goodwin onto the path that would lead him to check the Presbyterian party at the Westminster Assembly and Davenport onto the road that would lead him to found and shape the colony of New Haven along the line of Cotton's theocratic theory. The influence that Cotton could wield over the minds of such prominent men would, ten years later, mark him as the most important of the Congregational leaders and therefore a prime target for Presbyterian attack.

In his London hiding place, Cotton, having ruled out conformity, also finally ruled out flight to the Continent. Thomas Hooker, who had tried residence in Delft and Rotterdam, now secretly appeared in London to tell Cotton that he had found this an impossible experience and was going to go to New England with some of his former parishioners from Chelmsford. Migrating Boston parishioners also pressed Cotton to join them in New England, and he at last agreed. On a June morning in 1633 he boarded the *Griffin* in the Downs.

The new land that awaited John Cotton harbored churches that did not accord with his ideas on church polity. He and New England would have to come to terms with one another. Though the ultimate compromise he was to achieve came with difficulty, once devised it gave a crucial form to thought and habit in New England.

II

John Cotton was enthusiastically received in New England. As the most eminent ministerial resident he was quickly installed as teacher of the church in the principal town, Boston. He conformed with the practices he found in effect in New England, and in keeping with his scholarly habits confined his reservations to his study, pondering the relationship of the prevailing model to what he held to be ideal. This was a familiar pattern of behavior for him; he was a man who for twenty years had managed to officiate in the Church of England yet be nonconformable.

The practice of the Salem church was obviously the chief problem for Cotton. While he was still in England he had detected the taint of Separatism in Salem, and, indeed, that church, since it was the first one founded in Massachusetts Bay, had consulted with the Separatists at Plymouth Colony about its establishment and had accepted the right hand of fellowship from Plymouth once it was established.[15] Moreover, in 1634 the troublesome Roger Williams turned up at Salem once again to exaggerate those aspects of the still plastic New England way that discomfited Cotton.

Williams had first appeared in Massachusetts Bay in 1631, where, at the age of twenty-seven, he had a reputation for nonconformity and piety that gained him an invitation to minister to

15 The amount of influence Plymouth exerted upon Salem is a matter of debate. See, for example, Perry Miller, *Orthodoxy in Massachusetts* (Cambridge, 1933), and Larzer Ziff, "The Salem Puritans in the 'Free Aire of a New World,'" *Huntington Library Quarterly* 20 (1957), 373–384.

the Boston church during the temporary absence of the pastor, John Wilson. With his characteristic talent for impolitic candor, however, Williams replied that he had not come three thousand miles to associate with a church that still maintained communion with the Church of England and whose members refused to repent publicly their previous membership in that church. But this a church that regarded itself as reformed yet unseparated would not do. The Salem church, however, eagerly called Williams to serve as fellow minister to Samuel Skelton. A shocked General Court addressed John Endicott of Salem to remind him of Williams' refusal to serve at Boston and to inform Salem that Williams had "declared his opinion that the magistrate might not punish the breach of the Sabbath, nor any other offence, as it was a breach of the first table" of the ten commandments.[16] The Court marveled that Salem would act so rashly, and asked that commitment to Williams be delayed until a conference had been held. Thus early did the absence of a superintending power in the Congregational system begin to create difficulties.

Williams voluntarily settled the impending dispute, however, by setting off for Plymouth, where among avowed Separatists he hoped to find a better climate. But even they were not prepared to accept what he informed them were the logical consequences of their separation. They should maintain the purity of their separation, he said, by making it unlawful to attend services in any church that still held communion with the Church of England—which, of course, would have isolated Plymouth from Massachusetts Bay. They should not require the oath of fidelity to their commonwealth of any who were unregenerate, he said, because that oath invoked the name of the Lord and was there-

---

[16] John Winthrop, *Journal 1630–1649*, ed. James K. Hosmer (New York, 1908), I, 62.

fore a species of religious communion with those who took it—
this, of course, aimed at a clear separation of church and state
as opposed to the theocratic ideal. Plymouth was set by the ears,
and William Brewster noted with relief in 1634 that Williams
wanted once again to go to the Bay Colony. There, Brewster
felt, there was a sufficient quantity of able men to deal with
Williams' dangerously attractive doctrines.[17]

Back at Salem Williams was called to succeed the recently
deceased Samuel Skelton, and the authorities of the colony
decided they had to move against a dangerous radical who was
now adding to his previous pronouncements the claim that King
James had lied in saying he was the first Christian prince to
discover New England, had blasphemed in referring to Europe
as Christendom, and had misapplied Biblical passages to his
reign. As a first step, John Cotton was asked to review the
offensive treatise in which Williams had displayed these opinions. Cotton, as characteristically scholarly and balanced as
Williams was brilliant and headstrong, concluded that there
was room for doubt as to Williams' implications, and he became
even more convinced of it after interviews with his former
English acquaintance.

By 1635, however, the authorities felt they could no longer
wait upon the outcome of Cotton's academic debates with
Williams. The latter was insisting, with Salem's approval, that
the oath be withheld from the unregenerate, and his zealous
exponent, John Endicott, had removed the cross from the
English ensign, claiming it was idolatrous. In England, episcopal factions at court were advancing their claims to the land
occupied by the Massachusetts settlers, and the New England
magistrates could not afford to tolerate such explicit proof of
the allegation that they were anti-church and anti-king. The

17 Nathaniel Morton, *New-Englands Memoriall* (Cambridge, 1669), p. 78.

General Court, therefore, barred Endicott from serving as a magistrate for a year, and aimed at Salem's pocketbook by refusing that town's petition for further land, "because they had chosen Mr. Williams their teacher, while he stood under question of authority, and so offered contempt to the magistrates."[18] Williams, in sickbed that summer, remained firm, and informed the Salem church that not only did he refuse to communicate with the other churches in Massachusetts Bay but that unless the Salemites made the like refusal he would not communicate with them. Though incensed at the Court's vindictive action, the Salem settlers were perceptive enough to see that to follow Williams was to enter into a spiral of schismatic refinements, and they accepted his banishment and made their peace with the Court. Williams, whose courage matched his zeal, set off for Narragansett Bay—he would be heard from again in times more propitious to his ideas.

John Cotton had disagreed with Roger Williams, but he was distressed that Williams had been prosecuted so severely before he had had time to convince him in interview and written debate of his errors, and he regretted the banishment. He felt that if Williams had gone too far in his reforming notions, he himself had not gone far enough. Though it was too late to help Williams, a contribution toward peace could be made in the form of a public profession of his own inadequate understanding of the correctness of Salem's initial reformed position under Skelton. In exchange, as it were, he hoped to show Salem that it should go no further on the road to separation. Accordingly, in June 1636 he journeyed to Salem to deliver a sermon that is the first major sign of the kind of contribution he was to make in the shaping of New England. He was a conserver and consolidator rather than a founder. In the *Sermon Deliver'd at*

---

[18] Winthrop, *Journal*, I, 155.

Salem he supplied scriptural justification for the polity he had found in effect upon his arrival, but he also established its limits and showed that if it was to grow in strength it had to remain within them and not push on to further refinements that were unscriptural and that could only weaken by dividing.

That his sermon was to be extraordinary was signalled by the fact that at the outset he made a "confession" rather than beginning immediately with his text and doctrine. He admitted that Skelton was correct and he in error about the nature of a church covenant, thus contributing to the centrality in Massachusetts of the idea that regardless of a Christian's membership in the catholic church he must enter into a covenant with a particular visible church before he could enjoy the sacraments. The long-range implication of this was to strengthen the democratic element in the Massachusetts system, though Cotton himself was far from a democrat, insofar as it assured local autonomy in the most vital matters and brought all persons, however eminent or lowly in the world, to an asocial and apolitical standard: no one could presume too far on reputations earned elsewhere but had to sue again for admission into the community.

One distinguishing mark of Cotton's character, his humility, was thus revealed in the confession. In the sermon proper he also displayed at length his persuasive ability to fit scholarship to practice. For, having admitted that Skelton was correct in constituting his church anew of testifying believers, Cotton had to resolve a seeming paradox by maintaining that reformation had gone far enough and that Williams' insistence upon repudiation of the Church of England, which did not demand such testimony, was erroneous. On the surface it would seem that if one had to enter into a particular church regardless of his membership in the catholic church, Williams was correct in saying

that those in a covenanted church should surely refuse association with the Church of England, an institution that retained
corrupt practices and required no covenanting or other signs of
grace from its members.

Cotton resolved the paradox with an insistence upon grace as
the mark of the true Christian and therefore upon the preeminence of the covenant of grace over any church covenant.
Only the gracious may be admitted to church covenant; nevertheless, there were many such persons in uncovenanted churches
like the Church of England, and to pronounce them corrupt and
defiled by their membership in that church was to insist on
duties, outward practices, rather than on grace. Under Use III,
Cotton wrote:

> Suppose the church promise never to defile themselves more with any
> pollutions of the sons of men, but they do defile themselves, then
> covenant is broken; they did covenant they would not come into false
> assemblies, and that they would have no fellowship with them, that
> did allow of false assemblies; but this covenant cometh to be broken:
> if this be your covenant, it is but a covenant of works, and then no
> marvel though it do break and fail, seeing it stands upon duties, and
> keeping of duties; for being built upon the condition of duties, and
> standing upon performance of duties, and being broken upon neglect
> of duties, this is but a covenant of works.

The all-important covenant of grace was not conditional, and
Cotton in his Salem sermon emphasized its everlasting nature,
and turned the inconsistency around so that it was such as
Williams rather than he who were illogical. In separating from
the Church of England such people were making a particular
church covenant of greater importance than the invisible church,
which was the community of those who were under the covenant
of grace. Admission to a specific church covenant was not what
admitted a man to the invisible church.

His emphasis on the exclusive importance of grace is what made Cotton so popular a preacher in New England as well as England. In the tradition of Richard Sibbes he gave special encouragement to the meek and hesitant, as when, in answering an "Objection" in the sermon, he said that if

> whilst you do with patience and constancy wait, you are drawn with everlasting love; now you have Christ in you, though you do not feel him: for as the earth is hanged upon nothing, Job xxvi, 7, so now there is a place for Christ in the heart, when it is emptied of everything besides; and such a man hath Christ, and is blessed, and the covenant of grace is his, you may safely receive him into your church fellowhip . . . these kind of Christians will spring and grow, and will not profane the covenant of God, nor the covenant of the church by any unmerciful separation.

The kind of Christians who would commit an unmerciful profanation were the zealots who had "received ease from God" only to be "straitlaced towards their brethren." Let us be done with any assumption of superior holiness that leads to a wholesale renunciation of others, Cotton urged, and let us get on with the more important matter of strengthening weak Christians and recognizing our membership in the catholic church. "Admonish and reprove" your brother if you see him defiled, but do not self-righteously separate from him lest in God's eyes you prove the ungracious one, not he.

In such a manner did John Cotton knit the covenanted church to the catholic church, knit New England to England. In so doing he helped keep Massachusetts Bay in the mainstream of modern life rather than allowing it to become, as did other exiled religious groups, an enclave of contentious sectaries who alone were right and who, in isolation, were therefore dead to the larger human community.

III

The persuasiveness with which John Cotton preached his doctrine of the preeminence of grace gained him a large audience in Boston. John Winthrop noted in his *Journal:* "It pleased the Lord to give special testimony of his presence in the church of Boston, after Mr. Cotton was called to office there. More were converted and added to that church, than to all the other churches in the bay."[19]

That same doctrine, however, came close to proving Cotton's ruination in 1638 when the Antinomian controversy resulted in the trials of Anne Hutchinson. There was scarcely a doubt that the emphasis that she and her followers put on the possession of the Holy Spirit to the outright scorning of holy laws— in doctrinal terms, their insistence upon justification to the denigration of sanctification—could be found to have its roots in Cotton's magnifying of the unconditional nature of the gift of grace and his distrust of any religion that was based on external conditions that the believer had to fulfill in order to make good his salvation. He went beyond his colleagues in his insistence that man could do nothing effectual without the Spirit—even bewail his own want of belief—and he refused to accept a man's sanctified behavior as a valid sign that he was saved: "Through his mind be enlightened, sometimes to fear, sometimes to joy, to humiliation, to enlargement, to zealous reformation, yet rest in none of these, for these you may have and yet want Christ, and life in Him; common graces may and will deceive you."[20]

[19] *Ibid.,* I, 116.
[20] John Cotton, *The New Covenant* (London, 1654), pp. 14–15.

Although none of Cotton's ministerial colleagues would have asserted that morality was a certain sign of piety, they tended to be more sympathetic than he to the notion that since a saint was a good man it followed that those who conducted themselves usefully did so, in all probability, because they were inhabited by the Holy Spirit. Such a view encouraged a respect for law and fitted well with the actual fact that the state as well as the church was controlled by saved believers. Those who were labelled Antinomians, however, regarded a concern for external signs—an emphasis on fulfilling duties—as a reprehensible lingering behind in Egypt. The rapid advance on the Promised Land was to be made, they felt, only when one cast aside concern for law in his complete confidence that being possessed of the Holy Spirit he could not but act in a sanctified fashion. Anne Hutchinson and her followers were Cotton's most devoted parishioners and as opposition to them formed Cotton was slow to believe that they were dangerous. He would not recognize that a theologically defensible doctrine could have dangerous social consequences for an infant colony in desperate need of a stable code of behavior. Accordingly, in the private conferences and correspondences that took place in an ineffective effort to avoid public confrontation, he took the opinionists' side, believing that at worst they merely employed an injudicious selection of words. A public confrontation was therefore inevitable, and not until the synod called to confute the Antinomian heresies did Cotton begin to perceive that there were differences between him and the Anne Hutchinson group. His perception deepened during Anne Hutchinson's two trials and led him slowly but firmly to relinquish her and all who chose to cleave to her into the hands of their opponents. From his point of view, he had defended the doctrine that he held in common with them but had refused to follow them into doctrinal extravagances. But from the point of view of others in his day, and in this, he was either a hypocrite or a coward in his early support and ultimate abandonment of the Antinomian group.

The truth of the matter appears to be less dramatic but more in keeping with Cotton's character. A scholarly and politically unrealistic person—he was used to being sheltered by aldermen —he had adhered to doctrinal purity and in so doing had encouraged a pious but more realistic political group to begin insisting upon the consequences of his doctrine. So long as the doctrine itself was under attack he stood by them, but when it became clear to him—out of their own mouths, as he would have expressed it—that they aimed at a social revolution and were willing even to pervert doctrine to achieve it, he abandoned them. Like other men who have been caught in the middle when a fluid social situation suddenly polarized, Cotton could not escape without a trace of dishonor.[21]

Though the Presbyterians did later force Cotton into a defense of his actions and opinions in the Antinomian controversy as well as into a defense of the New England way, nevertheless his role in the controversy is not of central relevance to his writings on polity. In the short range, the New Englanders managed to keep the Antinomian difficulty to themselves; it did not become a matter of widespread knowledge among English Puritans until 1644 when Thomas Weld saw *A Short Story of the Rise, Reign, and Ruine of the Antinomians* through the press, perhaps under the mistaken belief that in publishing

---

[21] John Winthrop was satisfied with Cotton's stand at Anne Hutchinson's civil trial and checked those who were less satisfied by insisting "Mr. Cotton is not called to answer to anything but we are to deal with the party standing here before." To judge from representative works such as Edward Johnson's *Wonder Working Providences,* Winthrop's satisfaction was widely shared. But there was definitely an undercurrent of distrust of Cotton as evidenced by Thomas Shepard's diary entry, "Mr. Cotton repents not: but is hid only." Most interpreters have shared this distrust, ignoring or discounting *The Way Cleared* though it is one

Winthrop's highly partial account of the affair at that time he was offering proof of the ability of the Congregational system to check error. Before 1644, the news that Puritans sought from New England was practical information about the procedures followed in a Congregational church.

In 1642, John Cotton, Thomas Hooker, and John Davenport were invited to attend the Westminister Assembly to aid in the settling and composing of the affairs of the church. Although none of them was able to attend, interest in their ecclesiastical polity ran high at the Assembly. The overwhelming majority of the members of that Assembly were Presbyterian—indeed, so few were the opposition members that Hooker was reported to have remained in New England because he did not want "to go 3,000 miles to agree with three men."[22] The form of church government they meant to establish differed from New England's in three essential ways: they wanted to replace episcopacy with a system equally comprehensive, and therefore did not insist on regeneration as a qualification for any besides the elders; they wanted the church to be governed exclusively by the elders without participation by the members, even by way of the members' consent to the elders' rulings; and they wanted synods to be given binding power over individual congregations. Those who disagreed with them, the Independents, were less certain about the specific form of church government they wanted, but they were sure the Scots' model was unsuited for England and that some system had to be devised that would allow greater freedom for individual congregations.

Although the people of England in general and the soldiers

---

of the fullest of all primary documents on the Antinomian controversy. Rather than add another interpretation, the present editor is pleased to aid in making Cotton's own account available to all interested students.

22 Winthrop, *Journal*, II, 71.

in Cromwell's army in particular leaned far more towards the
Independent than the Presbyterian view, within the Assembly
only five ministerial members, Cotton's friend Thomas Goodwin
being one, spoke for Independency. Realizing that they were
hopelessly overwhelmed within the Assembly, they carried
their appeal to the people in *An Apologeticall Narration*
(1643), and there, because they recognized the impossibility
of staying Presbyterianism with a merely negative program, they
announced their partiality toward the New England way. In
arriving at their views of church government, they said:

> We had the example of the ways and practices (and those improved
> . . .) of those multitudes of godly men of our own nation, and among
> them some as holy and judicious divines as this kingdom hath bred;
> whose sincerity in their way hath been testified before all the world,
> and will be unto all generations to come, by the greatest undertaking
> (but that of our father Abraham out of his own country, and his seed
> after him) a transplanting themselves many thousands miles distance,
> and that by sea, into a wilderness, merely to worship God more purely,
> whither to allure them there could be no other invitement.[23]

The New Englanders' belief that they had been set in the wilds
to work out a laboratory model for the homeland—in Winthrop's words, that they were as a city upon a hill; in Cotton's,
as eyes to God's people—appeared to be justified. "Great pity
were it," said Cotton from the pulpit, "that they should want
any light which might possibly be afforded them."[24]

The immediate light the New Englanders shed was on the
actual workings of Congregationalism. The Presbyterians had
the Church of Scotland to point to as an ecclesiastical system

---

[23] Thomas Goodwin, Philip Nye, *et al., An Apologeticall Narration* (London,
1643), p. 5.
[24] John Cotton, *The Powring Out of the Seven Vialls* (London, 1642),
Sig. Bbb 4v.

successful in practice as well as sound in doctrine, and the initial questions addressed to the New England ministry were questions about how they handled specific situations within the church. Cotton had supplied several such manuals, *A Coppy of a Letter of Mr. Cotton of Boston* (1641) and *The True Constitution of a Particular Visible Church* (1642), and other New Englanders supplied other descriptions, the two most widely read being those of John Davenport and Richard Mather, both published in London in 1643 and both formulated in collaboration with other ministers in the Bay, including Cotton.[25] In these treatises the Massachusetts way was justified in pragmatic terms; the authors illustrated the smooth working of Congregationalism without specifically defending its authenticity. But after 1643, in addition to practical testimonies of Congregationalism's workability, a defense of its authentic relationship to the church founded by Jesus was required, and this task was one for which John Cotton was preeminently qualified.

Cotton supplied two such treatises, but he meant only one of them to stand as the whole of his mind on the matter. Around 1642, he had added to his sketchy descriptions of Bay procedures a justification of them based on Scripture, and had sent it to England for the edification of those sympathetic to Congregationalism. This circulated so widely in manuscript that Presbyterian attacks on it were in print before it was published, without authorization, in 1645 as *The Way of the Churches of Christ in New-england.* Cotton, though he did not disown it, did say that the printing was against his wishes and that *The Keys of the Kingdom of Heaven* (1644), published before *The Way of the Churches* but written after it, was his considered position on

---

[25] John Davenport, *An Answer of the Elders of the Severall Churches in New-England unto Nine Positions Sent Over to Them* (London, 1643); Richard Mather, *Church-government and Church-covenant Discussed* (London, 1643).

church polity, and all discrepancies between the two works were to be resolved in its favor.

That *The Keys* was a definitive statement was signalled in the introduction supplied it by Thomas Goodwin and Philip Nye who said that although they had some minor qualifications this was "that very middle way (which in our *Apology* we did in the general intimate and intend) between that which is called Brownism, and the presbyterial government, as it is practised." Independents throughout England, therefore, were invited to take their stand upon Cotton's treatise, and Presbyterians faced the task of refuting it since it was a principal support of their Independent opponents.

Three hundred years after its publication, *The Keys of the Kingdom of Heaven* presents an outmoded facade; its pages appear at first glance to be unrelieved by any element of what one might consider ordinary human interest. Here the seventeenth-century theologian, at ease in the Zion of scriptural interpretation, seems to set forth his argument in a dead language. Recalling the remote days of the apostles he seems scarcely to glance at the history of his own day. For the modern reader he seems to deal in invented rather than in documented events.

But the tensions of the times are in *The Keys*, and they drive the argument onward. Although the chief purpose of the treatise is to demonstrate that the church founded in apostolic times was indeed a Congregational one and although the chief arguments are scriptural, yet *The Keys* takes its strength from its contemporaneity. Modern scholarship has vigorously and effectively discounted the notion that the American Puritans were early democrats who farsightedly planted the love of liberty that was to flower at the American Revolution. Cotton spoke for the majority of his brethren when he wrote, "Democracy I do not conceive that ever God did ordain as a fit government either for church or commonwealth."[26] Nevertheless, *The Keys* reveals that the Congregational system was developed by men who were allied with those financial and political leaders whose ends were best served by an extension of the people's liberties. Congregationalism was an important part of the democratization of Anglo-American life.

Cotton's argument for the congregation's participation in church government is reduced to first principles in "Proposition III" in the seventh chapter:

> If the brethren of the congregation were not the first subject of their church liberty, then they derived it either from their own elders, or from other churches. But they derived it not from their own elders: for they had power and liberty to choose their own elders, as hath been showed above, and therefore they had this liberty before they had elders, and so could not derive it from them.
>
> Nor did they derive it from other particular churches. For all particular churches are of equal liberty and power within themselves, not one of them subordinate to another.

Cotton is here talking about the Christian rights of saints, not about the liberty of the people in a state of nature, a term which to him would have meant a state of damnation. But he is insisting, as others later would argue about civil authority, that all church authority initially resides in the believers, is only delegated by them, and must ultimately be referred back to them.

Liberty, in Cotton's full context, is sufficiently restricted to make it a different term from the modern one, but the kernel is there, and is pointed to by Nye and Goodwin in their opening epistle. Seeking an analogy for the model of a Congregational church as set forth by Cotton, they hit easily upon the incorporated town:

[26] Thomas Hutchinson, "Copy of a Letter from Mr. Cotton to Lord Say and Seal in the Year 1636," in *The History of Massachusetts Bay*, ed. Lawrence S. Mayo (Cambridge, 1936), I, 415.

As in some of our towns corporate, to a company of aldermen, the rulers, and a common council, a body of the people, there useth to be the like: he giving unto the elders or presbytery a binding power of rule and authority peculiar unto them; and unto the brethren, distinct and apart, an interest of power to concur with them, and that such affairs should not be transacted, but with the joint agreement of both.

The judicial system also offered Nye and Goodwin an analogy for Cotton's argument. Justifying his "dispersion of interests" within the Congregational system, and especially the elders' need to gain the consent of the congregation before passing the sentence of excommunication, they point out:

The sentencing to death of any subject in the kingdom, as it is the highest civil punishment, so of all other the nearest and exactest parallel to this in spirituals, of cutting a soul off and delivering it to Satan; yet the power of this high judgment is not put into the hands of an assembly of lawyers only, no not of all the judges themselves, men selected for wisdom, faithfulness, and gravity, who are yet by office designed to have an interest herein; but when they upon any special cause or difficulty, for council and direction in such judgment do all meet (as sometimes they do): yet they have not power to pronounce this sentence of death upon any man without the concurrence of a jury of his peers, which are of his own rank; and in corporations, as such as are inhabitants of the same place.

And they go on to appeal to the fact that Englishmen rightly consider the jury system "one of the glories of our laws, and do make boast of it," and that the same sentiment should lead Englishmen to see the need for a like system in their church.

This contemporaneity, however, though it added immediate appeal to an argument addressed to a nation in rebellion against its monarch, came close to destroying the historical bases on which the entire Congregational structure rested. If the original argument for the system was that it represented a return to the true Biblical model, then how could it also pretend to be more closely in keeping with modern municipal and judicial practices? Cotton attempts to resolve the paradox thus:

> For a mother to bear her young daughter in her arms, and not to suffer it to go on its own feet, whilest it is in the infancy, is kindly and comely: but when the damsel is grown up to riper years, for the mother still to bear her in her arms, for fear of stumbling, it were an unnecessary burden to the mother, and a reproach to the virgin; such is the case here: the community of churches (according to the Hebrew phrase) is as the mother; each particular church is as the daughter. In the Old Testament, while the church was in her nonage, it was not unseasonable to leave the whole guidance and bearing thereof in the hands of their tutors and governors . . . But now in the days of the New Testament, when the churches are grown up (or should be grown at least) to more maturity, it were meet more to give the church liberty to stand alone, and to walk upon her legs.

The days of the New Testament are not just the Biblical period but "now." Even as the church is being restored to purity it is growing up, and increasingly deserves more independence in its government. This historical theory has obvious millennial overtones, but for the present purpose it is most pertinent to note that the theory made political and social as well as Biblical models available to Cotton and those who agreed with him. *The Keys of the Kingdom of Heaven* thus has a contemporary democratic strain sinewing its scriptural arguments.

IV

John Owen became at the Restoration the leader of the Independent party, a position toward which he moved during the Commonwealth when Cromwell selected him as vice-chancellor of Oxford. But until 1644 he was an Essex rector of Presbyterian principles, and his change of mind came about when he read

The Keys. He reported: "In the pursuit and management of this work, quite beside and contrary to my expectation, at a time and season wherein I could expect nothing on that account but ruin in this world; without the knowledge or advice of, or conference with, any one person of that judgment, I was prevailed on to receive that and those principles which I had thought to have set myself in opposition to."[27]

Most other Presbyterians were not, of course, persuaded by Cotton, but they recognized the power of his arguments, and, as the pamphlet war over the nature of the church to be established in England continued to rage, no work was singled out so frequently and treated at such length by so many eminent polemicists as was *The Keys of the Kingdom of Heaven.* The years immediately following 1643, moreover, were years in which Baptists, Seekers, Familists, and a variety of other sectaries were emboldened to speak out, and in addition to Presbyterian attacks on the Massachusetts system arguments were published by the radical wing of Puritanism. When Robert Baillie, the most effective of the Presbyterian polemicists, published his *A Dissuasive from the Errours of our Time* (1645), he had available to him not only the "official" reports on Massachusetts but the complaints furnished by conservative critics such as Thomas Lechford and radical critics such as Roger Williams, as well as the description of the Antinomian crisis given in the *Short Story.*

Baillie's chief task was to prove that Congregationalism was unscriptural and unworkable, and in the latter area he received considerable support, which he worked for every advantage, from Roger Williams and the *Short Story.* Even though as a Presbyterian he was certainly as far from Williams' views as were the Congregationalists, and as an orthodox believer he

[27] John Owen, *Review of the True Nature of Schisme* (Oxford, 1657), p. 35.

would have stoutly prosecuted Anne Hutchinson, he used all
the material that pointed up weakness in Cotton's position and
in the Massachusetts way as grist for his mill. The Antinomian
controversy especially appealed to him as evidence of the shakiness of Cotton's opinions and conduct, which if they were unsound in doctrinal matters must also be suspect in matters of
ecclesiastical polity.

The tireless Baillie accumulated a great deal of evidence that
showed, he thought, the giddiness of John Cotton. In addition
to Cotton's relationship to Anne Hutchinson, as evidenced by
the *Short Story,* he used an unpublished treatise Cotton had
written over twenty years earlier in Lincolnshire that was, in
part, uncalvinistic, and copies of letters such as that Cotton
wrote in 1629 to Skelton, in order to show that Congregationalism, in spite of what its adherents said, was a patched-to-
gether, spur-of-the-moment system. He presented quotations
from his collection of material, which he called "testimonies,"
and gave them each a catalog letter for identification.

John Cotton could not very well let the *Dissuasive* pass un-
answered since his character as well as his theories were held up
to disrepute in an apparently well-documented argument. His
reply was *The Way of Congregational Churches Cleared*
(1648). The book contains two treatises: the first and longer
one attempts an almost point-by-point refutation of Baillie and
is, therefore, the most personal piece Cotton ever published; the
second answers scriptural and logical objections offered to *The
Keys* by Daniel Cawdrey in his *Vindiciae Clavium* (1645),
which was published anonymously, and by Samuel Rutherford
in his *The Due Right of Presbyteries* (1644). Cotton was also
aware that an influential attack on Independency by Thomas
Edwards, *Antapologia* (1644), was in print but he was unable
to procure a copy of it.

The second treatise, while it will continue to exist as an important document in Congregational history, does not sustain the same interest as the answer to Baillie which forced Cotton to write for the only time in his career about his life and the history of Massachusetts. Because he did so, *The Way of Congregational Churches Cleared* is a document of the first importance in seventeenth-century American history and in the history of Puritanism. Here Cotton gives his explanation of the relationship of Congregationalism to Separatism, sketches the family tree of New England theory, contrasts life under the bishops in England with life as it was led in New England, and, perhaps of greatest interest, gives his account of what happened during the Antinomian controversy. Since Baillie made the greatest use of that controversy and since Cotton, in the manner of his day, answers Baillie by following his sequence, the controversy receives extensive but never quite repetitious treatment; the reader interested principally in this part of the treatise must take care to read on beyond the obvious sections since Cotton returns to the topic time and again in response to Baillie's repeated harping on the matter.

Though the historical importance of the contents of *The Way Cleared* is self-evident, the value of its tone must also be weighed. The reader who has fellowed the political development of Congregationalism in New England and Old notes a shift in the voice in which *The Way Cleared* is presented. This shift is heralded in Nathanael Homes's introduction when he says, "If in the reign of episcopacy, those parishes were quiet where could not be found work for the hierarchy to intermeddle; surely then the classes may conveniently permit particular congregations (prostrated below them as it were at their feet) to rest in peace, whiles they meetly manage their own church affairs within their own sphere." There was, in 1648, no longer any question of Congregationalism becoming the national church system; those of that way were simply arguing for a small place in the sun. Cotton strikes this note immediately in his opening chapter: "It is one thing for Japhet and Shem to dewell together by voluntary consociation; another thing for Shem to rule over Japhet by undesired and unallowed jurisiction. . . . Let not Japhet be a servant to Shem, no more than Shem to Japhet."

Behind this attitude resides Cotton's consciousness that Presbyterians did not differ from him in any way nearly so essential as did Roger Williams, Samuel Gorton, and a host of others in New England who were, in the 1640's, demanding freedom to practice in their unorthodox fashion. Presbyterianism was as forthright as Congregationalism in its abhorrence of these opinionists. Since it appeared that Presbyterianism would never become the controlling system in the colony, and Congregationalism would never become the controlling system in the homeland, and since adherents of both polities were united in Christain essentials, the time had come to explore ways of living together so that both might turn their attention to the destroyers of doctrine. Puritanism was moving into another political phase. In one of the most incisive sections of the first treatise of *The Way Cleared,* chapter four, Cotton gives a deft demonstration of his contention that Congregationalism is as effective as Presbyterianism in countering heretics.

The second treatise is a shadow of dreary things to come in the debate on ecclesiastical polity. Although the reality now was that no single system would have unqualified dominance, the contentions and confutations went on, more and more drained of the vitality they possessed when palpably connected with wide-sweeping political consequences. Rutherford and Baillie were to respond to *The Way Cleared,* and to be answered by

Cotton in *Of the Holinesse of Church-members* (1650). And Cawdrey, dropping his anonymity, was to prepare, in *The Inconsistency of the Independent Way with the Scripture and Itself* (1651), an elaborate compilation of contradictions between Cotton's *The Way of the Churches of Christ* and his *Keys,* and between both of these and Thomas Hooker's *Survey of the Summe of Church-discipline* (1648). But the controversy, though still acrimonious, was increasingly academic.

John Cotton died in December 1652. His answer to Cawdrey was unfinished though it was subsequently completed and published by John Owen.[28] In that response he said that he discerned "no dissent at all" between other Congregationalists and himself, but added that if such did exist he was content to have his brethren qualify his work if it so pleased them. The times, not his character, had driven him into contention, and he was grateful for any opportunity to reduce its scope.

The eminence of John Cotton in his day and his significance in American history rest only in part on his writings on polity. He was undeniably the greatest preacher in the first decades of New England history, and he was, for his contemporaries, a greater theologian than he was a polemicist. Nor can his writings on polity ultimately be separated from his Christian doctrine, his millennialism, or his views on such matters as liberty of conscience.[29] But in his writings on polity, especially those reprinted in the present volume, John Cotton speaks more directly

[28] John Cotton, *A Defense of Mr. John Cotton from the Imputation of Selfe Contradiction Charged on Him by Mr. Dan: Cavvdrey* (Oxford, 1658).

[29] In connection with the issue of liberty of conscience John Cotton's reputation has suffered badly because of the brilliant response he drew from Roger Williams, though it was Williams, not he, as he pointed out at Salem, who was quick to separate from a fallen brother and act in a straitlaced fashion toward those who were less enlightened.

to twentieth-century concerns about liberty and authority than he does elsewhere, and makes clear that arguments of ecclesiastical polity in his day were not hair-splitting antiquarian squabbles but central debates about the terms on which men in England and America would live with one another.

A Note on the Texts

The intention of this edition is to present to the modern reader the complete contents of three of John Cotton's works, in pages which offer no arbitrary typographical obstacles and yet do not alter the author's meaning. Accordingly, since the principles of capitalization that are inferable from the original texts are not followed consistently in those texts, I have chosen to follow modern practice in these matters. The spelling of words, including names of people and places, also has been modernized, but modern words have not been substituted for archaic words: so, for example, "libertie" appears as "liberty," but "accompt" appears as such rather than as "account." Greek words are spelled according to modern principles rather than in duplication of the font of the seventeenth-century printer. Italics are retained when their function is to indicate emphases or quotations (indirect as well as direct), but not for the indication of proper names as in the original editions. Syntax, however, is a more subtle matter, and therefore with the single exception of marginal quotation marks the original punctuation marks have been preserved, archaic as their use may seem, in order to avoid the unconscious sacrifice of meaning and emphasis to mere tidiness.

The text of *A Sermon Preached by the Reverend Mr. John Cotton Deliver'd at Salem, 1636* (1713) is based on the copy in the library of the Massachusetts Historical Society; no known variants exist. The text of *The Keyes of the Kingdom of Heaven* (1644) is based on the copy in the Yale University Library; this is one of several variant forms, but it is, in the judgment of Henry Martyn Dexter and Julius H. Tuttle, earlier than the British Museum copy from which it differs slightly. The text of *The Way of Congregational Churches Cleared* (1648) is based on the copy in the Houghton Library of Harvard University; it does not vary in any significant way from other copies of the first edition.

All footnotes marked by superscript letters appeared as marginal notes in the original texts; those marked by superscript numbers and enclosed in square brackets have been supplied by the present editor. Since a large number of persons are named in the texts they have been identified in a single Glossary of Names at the back of the book rather than in footnotes scattered throughout.

A Sermon Delivered
at Salem, 1636

By the Reverend, Old Mr. *JOHN COTTON,*
At *Salem, June,* 1636

Having been moved by your reverend elders, and some others, to speak a word of *instruction* and *exhortation;* I thought it meet to begin with some word of *confession.*

At the first coming over of some of our honored magistrates, it so fell out, that they did arrive at this congregation, the sacrament being near to be administered, and a child being born to one of them; they themselves could neither be admitted to the Lord's Table, nor their child to baptism: When I myself heard of this, I wrote unto the pastor of this congregation[1] (now deceased) doubting of the lawfulness of that practice; thinking then, that the faithful and godly men coming where the seals were to be dispensed, and having right unto the covenant, had right also unto the seals thereof, and so that their children had right unto the former seal of baptism: something I wrote to that purpose, as I conceived, then requisite. It pleased God that He sent me a large and loving answer; but through the extremity of sickness then upon me, I could not read it;[2] and afterwards being shuffled among other papers, I could never find it to this very day: but what might have been for instruction to me from

1 [This letter to Samuel Skelton has been reprinted in David D. Hall, "John Cotton's Letter to Samuel Skelton," *William and Mary Quarterly,* 3rd ser., 23 (July, 1965), 478–485.]
2 [In 1630, Cotton and his first wife were stricken with malaria which proved fatal for her and forced him into a long period of convalescence, part of which he spent at the manor of Theophilus Clinton, fourth Earl of Lincoln.]

his letters, the Lord hath since shewed unto me by diligent search of the Scriptures.

So that however I apprehended the matter at that time, there was just reason for what was done: and now lest I should seem to alter my judgment herein without some weighty cause, let me tell you what prevailed with me, to cause me to assent to the judgment and practise of the churches here.

The Reasons are Two

Reas. 1.   The first is taken from the covenant unto whom it doth belong. I formerly conceived, that unto all the faithful the covenant did belong, and unto their seed also, not considering that which since I have learned and found, that the covenant which is made to me, and to my seed, *is not made to the right-eousness of faith at large, but to them that are righteous by the faith of the seed of Abraham; that is, to such believers as are confederate with Abraham.* And therefore it was, that though circumcision the old seal of the covenant (answerable to our baptism) was administered to all the seed of Abraham, *yet not unto those godly men that believed in his age:* For Abraham and his family were then the only visible church of God upon the face of the earth. And though Melchizedeck lived at that time, who was an heir of the righteousness of faith, yet not of the covenant of Abraham, unless he will join himself to the family of Abraham. Nor Job himself, though he was a man none like him upon the face of the earth; nor his friends; *Men fearing God,* in their generation, were yet uncapable of circumcision, unless they had joined themselves to the family of Abraham. And therefore you shall never read that the covenant belongeth to me, and to my seed, unless I be of the seed of Abraham, or joined to the family of Abraham. So we shall find it in the sanction of the Second Commandment, *That the Lord showeth mercy to thousands of the generations of such as love and fear Him:* that commandment hath respect to God's instituted ordinances. Let Jonah go to Nineveh, and by the blessing of God prevail with thousands, then the covenant of grace belongs to them; but what? to their seed also? No, verily not, unless their parents were confederate to the seed of Abraham. So that if you desire mercy to you, and to your seed, *keep then to the ordinances, and to the God of the ordinances, and so you shall keep a constant entail of the covenant to you, and to your seed; for unless men enjoy the covenant this way, it doth not belong unto their seed.* This being not considered, I fear, hath brought great mischief to all the churches that have not attended unto this principle, and hath been an occasion of much mistake to many godly parents, who plead their covenant for their seed, and many times so find little blessing; for though God hath made a covenant with them, yet it is but as a scattered stone, not laid orderly in any building; so that truly they may plead; but when God cometh to answer, He will make it appear that He did never open his mouth for a covenant with their seed until they be confederate with Abraham.

And therefore seeing my letter, as I understand, is in many of your hands, I rather make a plaister bigger than the sore, than that it should be pleaded against my practise after my departure.

Reas. 2.   The second reason is this, unto them that are not in covenant, a minister may not dispense an act of power and intrude himself, neither hath he any power until he be called; and then only over such as call him: and therefore if you should come to crave baptism for your children, or the Lord's Supper for yourselves, of a minister whom you have not called over you, he hath no power, and therefore unto you he cannot dispense an act of power: So that although the hearts of God's people might be enlarged many times, to do such things, *yet the law of the Lord's gospel doth restrain them, until men have entered into covenant, and not their own strait lacedness that keeps them back from dispensing such things.*

A Third *Reason* which is coincident with the second, and serveth to amplify the point, that they have no power over you, it will plainly appear from this ground; they that have no power to excommunicate you, they have no power to admit you to communion with them; but till you join yourselves in covenant with the church, they have no power of excommunication; therefore till then, they have no power to admit you to communion with them, for there is the like reason of both.

Now having expressed this word of *confession,* together with my acknowledgement of my dependence upon the Lord for grief and sorrow; I this desire, that if my letter remain written in any of your hands, you would not now look at it as my judgment; though sometime it was, yet now you have heard it retracted again by me, professing also, that if any thing which I have since written or spoken, God give me to see it, appear different from the truth, I will retract it also; in the mean time blame me not, if I do not retract it.

Jeremiah L, 5

Come, and let us cleave unto the Lord in a perpetual and everlasting covenant which shall never be forgotten.

Some translations reads it:[3]

---

[3] [With the exception of "not" for "never" this is the reading of the Authorized Version of 1611. Cotton's scholarship in Greek, Latin, and Hebrew was impressive, and this control led him to quote Biblical passages in his own translation as well as to paraphrase or abbreviate passages so as to cite only the relevant material. As a result, it is difficult to say with conviction that he preferred one to another of the published translations although it does appear that his citations are

Come, and let us join ourselves to the Lord in a perpetual covenant that shall never be forgotten.

These be the words which were foretold by Jeremiah, which the people of God returning out of captivity of Babel should use for the encouragement of one another to return to Zion, and there to bind themselves in church covenant with the Lord; for so you read it in the verse foregoing: *In those days (when the Lord shall destroy Babel) the Children of Israel shall come, and the children of Judah together, going, and weeping as they go; and seek the Lord their God. They shall ask the way to Zion with faces thitherward, saying, Come, and let us join ourselves to the Lord in a perpetual covenant, that shall not be forgotten.*

In these words of encouragement or exhortation, you may observe.

1. The encouragement to the work, *Come, and let us join ourselves to the Lord.*

2. This joining is set forth.

(1.) By the means of it; by a covenant.

(2.) That covenant is here amplified by a double adjunct of a double eternity.

1. Here is the covenant itself, that is perpetual.

2. Set forth not only by the durance of it, but by the report and memory of it unto all ages: *that shall never be forgotten.*

To speak to joining to the Lord at large, is neither the principal intendment of my text, nor may it be so convenient to speak only to it. I shall have occasion to open it in showing the way in which they do join to the Lord.

The doctrine which I would commend to your Christian consideration, is this;

generally closer to the Authorized Version than to the Geneva Bible. That this might be so is not surprising since he spent the first twenty years of his ministry as a vicar in an English church where the Authorized Version was used.]

Doctrine

That the church covenant, wherewith the people of Israel and Judah did join themselves to the Lord, especially after their return from Babel; and yet more especially under the days of the New Testament, was a perpetual covenant. Come, let us join ourselves to the Lord.

Israel and Judah spake this as they were a Church, and as they were about to renew church fellowship; *let us join ourselves to the Lord in a perpetual covenant that shall never be forgotten.* You read the like expression, Jer. xxxi, 31, 32, 33, 34. *This shall be my covenant with the house of Israel, saith the Lord, I will put my law in their inward parts, and write it in their hearts, and I will be their God, and they shall be my people.* And ver. 34, *I will forgive their iniquities, and remember their sins no more.* It is therefore an everlasting covenant; and He doth make the main difference between this and the former covenant to lie in this; whereas they break that covenant, ver. 32. *This covenant shall not be broken.* The Lord made a covenant with them before, but that covenant they brake; *and I regarded them not, saith the Lord:* as it is repeated, Heb. viii, 8 to 13. But in this latter covenant, He will remember their sins no more, and therefore He doth speak of the Old Testament, as of that which doth vanish away, but for the New Testament, He will establish that; according to what is written, Jer. xxxli, 40. *I will make an everlasting covenant with them, to do them good: but I will put my fear into their hearts, that they shall not depart from me.* The like we also read, Ezek. xvi, 60. *Though they have despised the oath in breaking the covenant; nevertheless, I will remember my covenant with thee in the days of thy youth, and I will establish unto thee an everlasting covenant.* And wherein doth it differ from the old covenant? I know not better how to explain it than by laying both of them together, both the old covenant and this new covenant, which he doth more renew in the days of the New Testament. In the old covenant you may observe a fourfold act of God, and a double act of the people.

First. The Lord doth prepare his people, and calleth them to Mount Sinai, and there revealeth himself in thunderings and lightnings, and flames of fire, so that the stoutest spirits amongst them quaked; and Moses though a man full of faith, yet he saith of himself, *I exceedingly tremble and fear;* and so did all the people; and when they heard the voice of the thunders, and saw the lightnings, Exod. xx, 18 to 21. they said to Moses, *Speak thou with us, and we will hear, but let not God speak with us lest we die.* Thus did the Lord prepare them by breaking, for if the Lord do intend some real and serious work, He will then shake the foundation of the stubborness of their hearts, and bring them to see their own stubborness and baseness, for else they would despise it.

Secondly. The second act of God is a Commandment which He doth put forth, wherein He doth require an exact obedience unto all the Commandments of the law, and to his statute and judgments, Exod. xix, 5. *If you will obey my voice indeed, saith the Lord, and keep my covenant; then you shall be my peculiar treasure above all people.* Now this covenant of God consisteth of moral laws, and statutes and judgments, unto all which he doth require obedience, even to all that is written in the Law, Deut. xxvii, 27.

Thirdly. The Lord doth profess unto them all that should keep covenant, that they should live by keeping covenant. And this is the grand and principal promise wrapping up all other, Lev. xviii, 5. And the apostle doth interpret the meaning of that promise, Gal. iii, 12. *The law is not of faith, but the man that doth these things shall live in them:* and this is the promise of life which God giveth to those that keep covenant.

Fourthly. The fourth act of God in making this covenant is, a heavy threatening of a curse to any that shall break these commandments, Deut. xxvii, 22; Gal. iii, 10. *Cursed is every one that continueth not in all things that are written in the law to do them.*

Now there are two acts of the people.

1. They do profess universal obedience unto all the commandments, Deut. v, 27; Exod. xix, 8. Twice they repeat it, *All that the Lord shall say unto us, we will hear it, and do it.* Only consider this, they promise it in some kind of opinion of their own insufficiency; like men under pangs of conscience, they do believe that they shall be able to keep and do all that the Lord shall say unto them. *O that there were such an heart in them!* saith the Lord, Deut. v, 29. Or as the word is in the original; *Who shall give them such a heart?* But this they promise.

2. They yield themselves to be accursed of God, if they shall not keep that covenant; and therefore when it was pronounced, *Cursed is every one that continueth not in all things that are written in the law to do them, all the people did say, Amen;* and so their faith lay upon a curse: this is the old covenant that God made with his people, and is called a covenant of works; the Lord requireth righteousness and works, He promiseth life to their works, and they say, *Amen,* to enter into a curse. Now this was a temporal covenant; this my covenant they brake, saith the Lord; and they did quickly turn aside from the ways of the Lord, and therefore Moses when he cometh and seeth the calf which they had made, he brake the tables of the covenant.

Now for the covenant that is everlasting, we may observe therein also four acts of God towards his people.

First. Look as He prepareth the other by a spirit of bondage, so he doth prepare these for his everlasting covenant, by a spirit of poverty; and they are poor and afflicted in spirit, in sense of their own unworthiness and insufficiency that which the Lord doth wish to the other, Deut. v, 29. He worketh in these, Zeph. iii, 12. *Then shall be brought home to Zion a poor and an afflicted people:* He meaneth not in respect of their civil estates, for there was not a feeble people among them; but as they stood in their spirits, they were empty, and as they thought destitute of God, and therefore should seek the Lord and his face, and his strength, like those that had lost both church and covenant; unto those the Lord will have an eye, and He will dwell with men of a contrite spirit, Isai. lvii, 15,16. And therefore with a blessing unto these, the Lord Christ doth begin his sermon in the Mount, Matt. v, 3. *Blessed are the poor in spirit.* He doth not only afflict them with a spirit of bondage; but when He cometh to make a covenant of *grace,* the people are insufficient to do all which the Lord requireth; and this is a spirit of poverty.

Secondly. When the Lord hath brought his people to be poor in spirit, He doth then promise them,

1. Christ: He giveth Him for a covenant, Isai. xlii, 6. *I have called thee in righteousness: I will give thee for a covenant unto the Gentiles.* When the Lord maketh a covenant of grace, this is the gift of God; his is the principal blessing of the covenant, Isai. xlix, 8. And the Lord will not give life in them to keep, and by them to uphold, but Jesus Christ for both.

2. In Jesus Christ He doth give everlasting communion with Him. Through Christ He will take away the stony heart, and give a heart of flesh; and He will bring with Him everlasting

righteousness, Dan. ix, 24. That is to say, such pardon of sin as He will never revoke more, that justification which He will work in Christ, He will never repent of; and therefore He saith, Jer. xxxi, 34. *He will remember their sins no more:* and for their sanctification He promiseth, Jer. xxxii, 40. *I will put my fear in their hearts, that they shall not depart from me.* And so in all the blessings of the covenant, the Lord will give an everlasting union and communion with Him, in the enjoyment of them.

Thirdly. These three things the Lord doth require.

1. *Faith:* That is to say a yielding of the soul to the Lord, as unable for this work, and yet to wait upon Him for righteousness, Ezek. xxxvi, 37. *I will be enquired for this of the house of Israel to do it for them.* Not only to be sought unto for the mercy, but I will be sought, that is, they shall seek me, they shall seek his face and his strength to do it all for them.

2. He doth require the *obedience* of faith: and this is expressly called for, Rom. xvi, 26. That is, for such righteousness, as none can work by any graces of their own; but which being wrought in them doth put life and strength into all their duties.

3. He doth require of his people that they should be of a melting frame of spirit, in regard of all their whorishness, whereby they have profaned his name; they shall wail and bemoan this: and therefore it is said of them in the verse before the text, that weeping they should go, for all the evils that they have wrought in God's sight: And this is that which we read, Ezek. vi, 9. *They that escape of you shall remember me among the nations whither they shall be carried captives, because I am broken with their whorish heart, which hath departed from me, and with their eyes which go a whoring after their idols: and they shall loathe themselves for the evils which they have committed in all their abominations.* This doth the Lord require of his people: but observe this withal, that He doth not require it

in a way of a legal command, but with an all sufficient virtue, whereby He will work in them what He doth require; so that doth He require, that they should walk holily before Him, He himself doth also work this, for in this everlasting covenant, the commandments of God are promises; for this will I be inquired, even to do all that He doth require, Zeph. iii, 12. *They shall trust in the name of the Lord.* And so for the obedience of faith, Ezek. xxxvi, 27. *I will cause you to walk in my statutes, and you shall keep my judgments and do them.* He will make us able to do it, and willing to do it, and so to do it. And this is the true meaning of all that the Lord doth require in the everlasting covenant; when He doth command He doth promise. Doth He require seeking of Him? He will put his spirit within us: Doth He require weeping and mourning? He will pour down a spirit of grace and supplication, and they shall seek Him whom they have pierced, and shall mourn for Him, Zech. xii, 10. So that this is the everlasting covenant. The Lord prepareth the heart: certain duties indeed He doth lay upon them; as to believe in his name, to yield the obedience of faith, and to mourn for Him; and He doth convey an effectual power to work them.

Fourthly. The fourth act is an act of cursing belonging to this covenant.

1. To them that do not receive it.

2. To those that do apostate from it: to them that do not receive it, Heb. ii, 2,3. If the word spoken by angels was steadfast, and every transgression and disobedience, received a just recompense of reward, how shall we escape if [we] neglect so great salvation? The neglecting of it brings desperate misery.

To those that do apostate from it, Heb. x, 29. *Of how much sorer punishment shall they be thought worthy of who have trodden under foot the Son of God, and have counted the blood of the covenant, wherewith they were sanctified, an unholy thing, and have done despite unto the spirit of grace.* This covenant is that which is spoken of, Deut. xxix, 1. beside the covenant made in Mount Horeb: and to this covenant belongeth a heavy curse, Deut. xxx, 17, 18. *If thy heart turn away that thou wilt not hear, but shalt be drawn away, and worship other gods, and serve them, I denounce unto you this day, that ye shall surely perish, and that ye shall not prolong your days upon the land wither thou passest over Jordan to possess it.* And that it is the covenant of grace, we may perceive by comparing, Deut. xxx, ver. 11 to the 14 with Rom. xvi, 6. So that we may see the Lord doth threaten a heavy curse to fall upon them that transgress this covenant.

Now for the people's part: their acts are two.

1. They fall down before the Lord confessing their unworthiness of any mercy.

2. Confessing their own inability and want of strength; and this is that which Joshua laboreth to possess the people with, Josh. xxiv, 19. There he telleth them, *Ye cannot serve the Lord your God;* that they might not trust in their own strength: and therefore when the Lord doth make this covenant with Abraham, he fell on his face, Gen. xvii, 3 in sense of his own unworthiness.

Why this covenant is such an everlasting covenant?

Reas. 1. Is from the root and fountain of it, Jer. xxxi, 3. *I have loved thee with an everlasting love, therefore with mercy have I drawn thee.* What moveth the Lord to be thus earnest and zealous in drawing men to Christ? *No man can come to me,* saith Christ, *except the Father which hath sent me draw him,* John vi, 44. How cometh this to pass? *I have loved thee with an everlasting love, therefore have I drawn thee.* Now he will carry his work an end in his with a mighty power, through all the backwardness of their own spirits: And this is the ground mentioned, Psal. lii, 4,5,9. *The Lord is merciful and full of compassion. He will be mindful of his covenant forever: He hath sent redemption to his people, and commandeth his covenant forever.* And how cometh this to pass? His redeeming love is the cause of it; as the covenant of works springeth from his justice; and hence it is that the apostle saith, Rom. vii, 12. *The commandment is holy and just and good;* if the creature keep covenant the Lord will reward; but if not He will punish; but to whom his covenant is from love and mercy, them He will draw with everlasting mercy.

2.   Another principal reason is taken from the surety; though the Israelites had Moses for a mediator, yet they had him not for a surety. Now Jesus Christ is made the surety of the covenant, Heb. iv, 6. A surety is not for a testament, but for a covenant; no need is of a surety on God's part, He never brake covenant with any; but if a surety be needful, doubtless it lieth on our part; and therefore it is said, *I will give thee for a covenant,* even Christ himself, Isai. iv, 2,3. *I will make an everlasting covenant with thee, even the sure mercies of David: behold, I have given him for a witness to the people.* And hence it is that all the promises of this covenant are made directly to Jesus Christ; the old covenant was made to the people, but this is made to Christ. To Abraham and to his seed were promises made, He speaketh not of his seeds, as of many, but as of one even Christ, Gal. iii, 16. And in Him the promises are yea and amen to us; yea, that is affirmed, *amen;* that is, confirmed: so long therefore as this church keepeth her to Christ, and holdeth Christ for her head and husband, the Lord doth keep covenant; and He hath promised to the elect seed, that they shall keep covenant, for He hath said, they shall not depart from Christ, and then they can never depart from the covenant, and though they break covenant, yet if they keep close unto Christ, they have the covenant,

although they break it. And though you read of a temporary faith, that doth endure for a season, Matt. xiii, 20, 21. And so in the parallel place, Luke iii, 13. you shall read that they are of the stony soil, that receive the word with joy, and for a time believe; and so for a time receive sundry spiritual gifts, and that with joy; and some with fear and trembling also, as the thorny soil, for they want not depth of earth, but are deeply humbled, and yet bring forth no fruit unto perfection, because they are not brought to that faith in Jesus Christ by which they are sanctified. Now therefore so long as this covenant is kept, and so long as the members of the church keep close to Christ, so long this covenant is not broken. And hence it is that when the Jews had committed the greatest sin that ever was committed upon the face of the earth, yet the apostles did not break communion with them, notwithstanding that fearful injury of putting to death the Lord of life; because they might have done it of ignorance, and therefore, Acts iii, 1. they went and joined with him in prayer; why did not they know that they had crucified a just man? and is not this a horrible profanation of the covenant? No, no, brethren, this will not break an everlasting covenant. *Father, forgive them, they know not what they do;* our Saviour prayeth for them, the apostles keep communion with them; here is the spirit of a Saviour, and of his blessed apostles: but when they do put away known Christ, Acts xiii, 45, 46, when they contradicted and blasphemed, then what says the apostles? *It was necessary the word of God should first have been spoken unto you, but seeing ye put it from you, and judge yourselves unworthy of everlasting life, lo, we turn to the Gentiles.* And so also it was a dreadful proceeding which they use in this case: Acts xix, 7, 8, 9. *He went into the synagogue, and spake boldly for the space of three months, disputing and persuading the things concerning the kingdom of God. But when divers were*

hardened, and believed not, but spake evil of that way before the
multitude, he departed from them, and separated the disciples,
—So mark you what it is that doth dissolve this everlasting
covenant; not this that they kill the Messias; it was a horrible
murder; but yet they may not separate for murder: What! if it
be the eternal Son of God! You may not separate for that neither
so long as you do not sin against knowledge; but when they do
sin against knowledge, and after they have been taught and convinced, do yet rebel, then is this everlasting covenant broken,
else it is not broken till they come to this desperate extremity.

USE I.   The use of this point in the first place, may shew us
from hence, a ground of that which some of us (yet but few)
saw the truth of, in our native country, namely the necessity of
a *church covenant* to the institution of a church, *Come, and let*
us join ourselves to the Lord: that which doth make a people a
joined people with God, that doth make a church: What is that?
The covenant of grace doth make a people, a joined people with
God, and therefore a church of God: and therefore you shall
find that when the Lord establishes Israel for a church unto
himself, He maketh this covenant; not only that in Mount
Horeb, but He doth make another covenant with them in the
plains of Moab, Deut. xxix, 10, 17. And so by this means they
come to be established to be a church unto the living God.

For further clearing of this, consider this one argument.

That whereby a church is at first established to be a church;
that whereby being fallen, a church is restored, that which being
broken, a church is broken; that giveth being to a church.

But by this a church is at first established, and by this it is
restored when it is fallen, and by breaking this, the church is
broken. This therefore giveth the being to a church. By this
a church is at first established. You are here this day that the
Lord might establish you to be his people, Deut. xxviii, 12, 13.

And how was the church renewed, but by renewing of this covenant in the days of Asa, 2 Chron. xv, 12. And so in the days of Ezra and Nehemiah, *chap.* ix, 38, *chap.* x, 29. And afterwards when the Lord would cast off his people, Zech. xi, 10, 14. *He brake the staff of beauty, and the staff of bands:* This now followeth, that so many of us, as have come to the ordinances of God, and have partaken of the seals of the covenant, and have not entered into a covenant, have violated the seals of the covenant which have not been given to the elect of God in general, but to the church of God; and therefore look at the covenant by which you have entered here, as the ability of your state, which by no changes you are forever to be removed from, but may foreever keep it by fellowship with Jesus Christ.

USE II.   In the Second Place, let me provoke myself, and all my brethren, and all the churches to consider, what kind of covenant you have entered, or will enter into: if you shall come hither into this country, and shall here confess your sins, that you have profaned the name of God withal, if you take Christ for your king, and priest and prophet, and if you shall profess to walk in all his ways, this may all be but a covenant of works.

The elders of the church propound it, will you renounce all your sinful pollutions? Will you keep covenant? And enter into a covenant with the church, and take Christ, and promise to walk after all God's ordinances? You answer, all this we will do; all this is no more than the old covenant: for you are much deceived if you think there was no speech of Christ in the covenant of works. What were the ceremonies but shadows of Christ? What was the laying the hand on the head of the sacrifice, but the laying hold upon Christ Jesus? What was the blood of the sacrifice? Was it not the blood of Christ? And what was the atonement by that blood? Was it not the atonement which is by Christ? All the understanding Israelites did see that these things did point at Christ. Now, if we do enter into a covenant to keep the ordinances of the law, of the gospel, and of the civil state, (for that was the tripartive covenant) all this may be but a covenant of works. What then must we do? We must fall down before the Lord in our spirits, and profess ourselves insufficient to keep any covenant, and profess ourselves unworthy that the Lord should keep any covenant with us; as to say, *Lord! who am I? Or what is my father's house, that the Lord should ever look upon such a poor soul as I am?* What doth the church lay hold upon duties, and there's an end? No, no, there are no true servants of Jesus Christ, but they must be drawn out of themselves by a spirit of bondage, and unto Christ by a spirit of poverty; and then a soul seeth there is much in Christ, but he cannot hope there is anything for him: now the Lord doth draw a man on to Christ Jesus, and calleth him to believe in Christ, but yet he is not able to reach Him. Now then, if the Lord draw the soul to depend upon Christ, and shall go forth, and not undertake anything in his own strength; so you will keep it by the strength of the Lord also; now the Lord will have peace with you, and the gates of Hell shall never prevail against you. Build a church upon any other foundation but faith, and the profession of faith, and it will break into manifold distempers. But if the church be built upon this rock; storms and winds will not so much as shake it, it being built upon faith, and faith upon Christ Jesus: by this means the covenant will keep us constantly, sweetly, and fruitfully, in an everlasting kind of serviceable usefulness one to another.

USE III. The use in the third place, is of direction, upon what terms you may separate. Suppose the church promise never to defile themselves more with any pollutions of the sons of men, but they do defile themselves, then covenant is broken; they did covenant they would not come into false assemblies, and that they would have no fellowship with them, that did allow of false assemblies; but this covenant cometh to be broken: if this be your covenant, it is but a covenant of works, and then no marvel though it do break and fail, seeing it stands upon duties, and keeping of duties; for being built upon the condition of duties, and standing upon performance of duties, and being broken upon neglect of duties, this is but a covenant of works; and yet you may be married to Christ in this. You come and resolve to walk in all ordinances, and undertake to reform both church and commonwealth; in such a covenant the Lord is content to take you by the hand and become a husband to you, Jer. xxxi, 32. And what will a husband do, he will rejoice with you, and you will find comfort in duties; your heart hath been refreshed that you may see you have Jesus Christ in your bosom. He will also reveal secrets unto you, He will cast in seeds of sundry good things among you, so that you shall prophecy in his name, and have a seed of prayer, and many good things, and yet may want everlasting love; you may find much comfort, and yet you will find some or other to give offence, or some or other to take offence, and you will break with breaking upon breaking until you be like sheep without a shepherd. This is not the covenant, therefore brother, upon which thou and I must live in church-fellowship everlastingly, though herein thou hast had comfort, and that unspeakable; such thou mayest have and yet run upon a covenant of works.

2. A second branch of this use may be to teach us whereupon a man may build separation. Not upon breach of duty though they transgress; and prostrate their sabbaths, defiling themselves with unclean devices of men. Is the covenant of grace broken? It is not broken until you have convinced this people of their sin, Acts iii, 17. Because, if the covenant be a covenant of grace, Jesus Christ doth step in, and all the breaches are fastened

upon Him. When then is the church of Christ broken from
Him? Not when she doth crucify Him, nor when she doth
pluck the crown of sovereignty from his head; these things she
may do of ignorance: but when they are convinced that they
have broken his will, and transgressed the rule of his gospel:
now, if out of haughtiness of spirit, they will not see an error,
but will have their own ways still; now it is no sin of ignorance,
no sin of infirmity. Now when men sin not in infirmity, not in
pang of a passion, as Peter denied his master, nor in pang of a
lust, as David when he committed adultery, but when in cool
blood, men do reject the word of life. Now, since they have
put the word of God from them, you may break off from them
and the blessing of Him that dwelt in the bush will be on your
heads. When it cometh to this that the church doth separate
from Christ, not from Christ but from known Christ, and not
from known Christ in weakness of passion, or lust, but in cool
blood; now the Lord in heaven will speak a blessing to your
separation; but if you will separate upon any other ground, you
go upon a covenant of works: and if there have been any transgression of this nature, return, and return again unto the church.
And this let me further commend unto you, let the church look
to her covenant, and let no member come in but he that *knoweth
Christ,* and that knoweth he is a *Child of Wrath;* and let him
go on, not in his own strength, but in a depending frame upon
Jesus Christ, and then all the world will know that you have
made an everlasting covenant: hold Christ, and hold the covenant and promises and blessings of the covenant.

USE IV.   The fourth use may serve, to teach any private
Christian, whether thou beest joined to the Lord in an everlasting covenant. If thou buildeth upon a covenant of works, the
end of all thy faith will be to say *amen* to a curse, Deut. xxvii,
21. If thou hast entered into a covenant of grace, the end of thy

faith will be the salvation of thy soul, and this is the faith of the gospel, I Pet. i, 8,9.

Quest. *But how shall I know whether I have built upon an everlasting covenant, or no?*

Ans. 1. The Lord hath drawn thee to make this everlasting covenant, thou did'st not take up upon thy own accord: mind therefore what I say, The Lord draweth partly by a spirit of bondage, partly by a spirit of adoption: If you never found yourself a fire-brand of Hell, if your conscience were never afflicted with your dangerous estate by nature, you were never yet in Jesus Christ. You will say, *I trust in Christ, and look to be saved by his righteousness.* Were you ever afflicted with sense of your own unrighteousness? If you say, no, I pray you read, John viii, 30. *As He spake these things, many believed on Him.* They trusted on Him for salvation. Did you then take the covenant? See what followeth: *Jesus saith unto them, If you continue in my word, then are ye my disciples indeed. And you shall know the truth, and the truth shall make you free. They answered him, We be Abraham's seed, and were never in bondage to any man:* they were never acquainted with bondage; they hoped bondage belonged to any rather than to them, and was more fit for Gentiles than for Jews. But what saith Christ? *Whosoever committeth sin, the same is the servant of sin. If the Son shall make you free, then shall you be free indeed.* And afterwards he telleth them, *You are of your Father the Devil.* For if a soul were never yet bruised with sin, and with the sense of sin, he never yet laid hold upon Christ, with true justifying faith; such an one will not continue in God's house forever.

Object. *You will say, those that are brought under Christian parents, they are not affected with such terrors as others are, that have lived in roaring distempers of them, it is great reason that God should so bring them on by showing them their fearful misery; but these have been well trained up, and I for my part, saith one, cannot tell whether ever God did work this upon me?*

Ans. If the state of such persons be good, I profess, I do not know how to interpret the speech of Christ. These men are the children of Abraham, and yet if they do not see their bondage, they are not free by the Son; there is difference in the measure of the spirit of bondage; as there is difference betwixt the lancing and pricking of a boil, and yet both let out the corruption, the one with a lesser, the other with a greater issue: therefore if the Lord doth not cut thee off from all thy good education, believe it, thou art not yet in Christ, this faith of thine will fail thee, if thou so livest, and so diest.

Object. But thou wilt say, I know the pangs of conscience, and the terrors of it, and I have seen the error of my way, and have cast off my lewd company; and since I know that the Lord requireth that I should seek Him in church estate; I have come some thousands of miles for that end, and I could not endure to see such things as are done by the devices of men: will not this hold?

Ans. I beseech you consider it, you have fallen upon this reformation, you have undertaken a covenant, yet now you have failed, and what then have you done? I go to Christ, and desire Him to sprinkle me with the blood of his covenant. Is not this a safe estate? Truly this is no more than the very covenant of works, which the people of Israel entered into at Horeb, the Lord shook the foundations of their hearts; upon it they entered into a covenant; *All that God commandeth us, we will hear it and do it:* and if they did offend, they then go to the appointed sacrifice; and what, saith the soul in such a case? *I thank God, I find some peace to my conscience.* All this you may do, you may reform yourselves and families, and churches; and when you fail at any time, you may return to Christ, and He may give you some remorse, as he did to the Israelites, Psal. lxxviii, 34, 35, 36. All this may be by a spirit of bondage: *He in mercy forgave their iniquities, and destroyed them not.* So they may come to have their sins pardoned, but this kind of pardon is but a reprievement; it is not in everlasting righteousness and mercy: they pray for Christ, and mercy, and He doth sprinkle them, and then they see and find, that the Lord hath been merciful unto them: but this will not do, the Lord will soon call back such pardon, as may plainly appear: Matt. xviii, 28. A certain man owed his Lord ten thousand talents, but when he had nothing to pay, he fell down at his master's feet, and said, *Have patience with me, and I will pay thee all;* his master had compassion on him, and loosed him, and let him go; was this in everlasting mercy? See what followeth. This fellow would pay all; and thus it is with these men, that have been under a spirit of bondage, they will cry hard for mercy, and promise to pay all in time; and now in their dealings with their brethren they are full of censoriousness, and will not bate an inch of any covenant; and they will take a man by the throat, though it be but for an hundred pence: and then what saith the Lord of such a servant? Oh! thou wicked servant, I forgave thee that great debt, shouldest not thou have had compassion of thy fellow servant? He is then wroth, and delivers him up to the tormentors, until he hath paid the utmost farthing; even so shall my heavenly Father do unto you. When men have received ease from God, and then are strait laced towards their brethren, then doth the Lord revoke his pardon. So that reformation is no assurance that God hath made an everlasting covenant with us. And mind you further, all the graces that you have laid hold upon, have sprung from your own righteousness. Thou hast taken a promise, did it belong to thee? If not it will fail you; you say you have been humbled, and come to Christ, and He hath refreshed you, mark whereupon it is built; upon your humaliation? No, but I come to Christ. Do you so? Who brought you to Christ? He saith, *No man can come to me except the Father draw him.* Now, come to such an one, and say, go to prayer; saith the poor soul, I cannot pray; be humbled, I cannot be humbled; apply promises, they belong to any rather than to me: Such a frame of spirit there is in every one whom the Father draweth: if you come to Christ by virtue of anything which is in you, it is but a legal work. And I pray consider, what it will amount unto, you will find, that these men will breed distraction in your churches, such members will make no choice how they hear, or how they deal with their brethren; look to it therefore carefully, when they come into the church, for otherwise you will find everlasting confusion, rather than an everlasting covenant.

2. Now then, doth the Lord draw you to Christ, when you are broken in the sense of your own sins, and of your own righteousness? When you look at duties you are not able to do them, not able to hear or pray aright. If the Lord do thus draw you by his everlasting arm, He will put a spirit into you, that will cause you to wait for Christ, and to wait for Him until He doth shew mercy upon you; and if you may but find mercy at the last, you will be quiet and contented with it. And whilst you do with patience and constancy wait, you are drawn with everlasting love; now you have Christ in you, though you do not feel Him: for as the earth is hanged upon nothing, Job xxvi, 7, so now there is a place for Christ in the heart, when it is emptied of everything besides; and such a man hath Christ, and is blessed, and the covenant of grace is his, you may safely receive him into your church fellowship; and though he do neither know Christ nor his covenant to be his, yet he will wait for Him, knowing there is none in heaven but Him, or in earth in comparison of Him. And you shall find such meek in spirit and merciful, and

mourning for sin: these kind of Christians will spring and grow, and will not profane the covenant of God, nor the covenant of the church by any unmerciful separation. Such neither stray on the right hand nor on the left; but when you convince them, that they have sinned against Christ and his church, they will go and complain bitterly of all the wrong they have done to Christ, and his church or covenant, and mourn for all the profanation of his name: and for the grief that they have put upon the spirits of his brethren; and these are true Israelites indeed, in whom there is no guile. Now cometh the Son with his personal work, (as He saith, John vi, 44. *No man knows the Father but the Son, and he to whom the Son reveals Him:*) in which He doth show the soul, that all this former work was the mighty hand of God, whereby He hath drawn the soul unto Jesus Christ, and afterwards doth assure and clear it unto the soul in some measure, that this way is the way wherein God leadeth all his elect ones. Now where the Son leadeth, the Holy Ghost beginneth to work his proper work in the soul, and sealeth all this to the soul; for the soul will not rest in a weak hope that Jesus Christ is his, but doth seek for more and better security of Jesus Christ. If he have a promise never so clear, yet it doth not quiet his spirit fully, it doth stay him from sinking, but not from searching. When Nathan told David, 2 Sam. xii, 13. *The Lord hath put away thy sin, thou shalt not die;* as plain a promise as any could be, and David knew that he spake it from the word of the Lord. And what doth he now? Doth that satisfy? No verily. But many men who had run upon a covenant of works, would have took it to themselves: if they had been humbled, and after received; but a child of God, though a minister should so convince him, that he could not deny but the promise belongs to him, yet he searches further. And so David, Psal. li, 1, doth still beg for mercy, *Have mercy upon me, O Lord,* etc. Why, had not David been told that the Lord had put away his sins, (for this psalm

was penned when Nathan had spoken to him, as appears by the
title:) What would he have? Surely he saw need of further
mercy. *Make me to hear the voice of joy and gladness, and
establish me with thy free spirit:* And thus he wrestles with God
and prays for it; according to what the apostle speaks, Ephes.
i, 13. *In whom after ye believed, ye were sealed with the holy
spirit of promise.* And when the soul hath received this, then
doth he sleep in quietness, and hath full contentment, and still
he doth yet depend on Christ Jesus, fearing lest he should grieve
and quench the spirit; and such a soul it is unto whom the Lord
hath made an everlasting covenant.

If this man have broken any law of God, you shall soon bring
him about to see his errors; and all this doth show a man, he is
a poor empty creature; and this soul is brought lower and lower,
and nearer and nearer to Jesus Christ. So if we do wisely consider this, it may serve to give us a taste of discerning whether
we be in an everlasting covenant, or no.

USE V. The use in the fifth place, is of consolation unto all
the faithful servants of God, whom God hath made this everlasting covenant withal: you will find that this will never be
forgotten. You have entered into such a covenant, wherein
Christ is yours, and the covenant yours, and all the promises
yours, and all the blessings yours, and the whole world yours;
and that which is the strength of the consolation, they are yours
everlastingly, if the Lord bring you out of yourselves, by a spirit
of bondage, and unto Christ by a spirit of poverty; so that you
wait upon Him and cannot rest, until Christ hath revealed himself to you by his spirit: here is your comfort, the Lord hath
made with you an everlasting covenant which shall never be
forgotten. This was David's comfort, 2 Sam. xxiii, 5. *Although
my house be not so with God, yet He hath made with me an
everlasting covenant, ordered in all things, and sure; for that is
all my salvation, and all my desire, although He make it not to*

grow. Though my house do not flourish with ordinances, not in ruling justly, as the Lord requires; though my house be out of order, and commonwealth out of order, yet He hath made an everlasting covenant. God hath laid hold upon Christ, and Christ hath laid hold upon me, and this is his stay and comfort, although God make it not to grow. And I beseech you consider it, all those that have temptations to separation, and some that have conceits of too much liberty. It is not hearing that makes a man clean, as we may see, Acts xvii, 32, 33, 34. When they heard the apostles speak of the resurrection from the dead, some mocked, and some said, we will hear thee again of this matter, and some clave to him and believed; all that heard him did not cleave to him, but only some of them. And if you have heard in England, you do thereby neither cleave unto your covenant, nor order, unless you partake of the seals of the covenant, then indeed you join unto them. Now, this is the nature of the comfort of an everlasting covenant, though we fail in families, and in churches, yet if Christ be ours, the everlasting covenant is ours. Indeed when Moses came and saw the Israelites worshipping the golden calf, Exod. xxxii, 19, because he saw they had broken covenant with God, therefore he brake the tables of the covenant; to show the Lord would have no fellowship with them; and if the covenant had not been renewed, they had perished. But come you to David's covenant, Psal. lxxxix, 28 to the 34 verse. *My covenant,* saith the Lord, *shall stand fast forever: if his children forsake my law, I will visit their transgressions with a rod; but my loving kindness will I not take from them.* This covenant doth not stand on keeping commandments, but this is all our delight, that the Lord will not break covenant with us, nor alter the thing that is gone out of his lips. Consider therefore, for here is a great deal of difference, your covenant is not a point of order only, but the foundation of all your comfort; and therefore look not at it as a complement, for it is the well-ordered covenant of God, even the security of your souls.

Object. But some will say, this would indeed much comfort me, that hath been delivered, but if a man touch any unclean thing, he is defiled, and if I touch him that hath touched any unclean thing, I am defiled also, Num. xix, 13,14. *Therefore sadness is upon me night and day for the sins of the church, and this doth eat up all my comfort?*

Ans. I pray you to consider it. I will but interpret what it is to touch a dead man, and to touch dead ordinances. I cannot give you a better interpretation than by that expression, which the apostle useth, 2 Cor. vii, 1. *It is good for a man not to touch a woman.* If so be a man touch a strange woman, so as to be familiar to plead for her, and to connive with her, this man is defiled; and if I now touch this man so as to be familiar with him, and to keep fellowship with him, I am also defiled. So in case the church do tolerate these, that do defile themselves with any sinful pollution, do not I make myself unclean now by touching this church? God forbid, unless it be by touching them with familiar connivance. But if I do now touch them, with a sharp reproof, this doth indeed touch the church, but it is so far from defiling, as that it doth hold forth the purity of his heart that toucheth them: and if you do forbear communion with the church when you know the church hath defiled herself, if you shall not come home to the church, and bewail your separation, your not touching the church hath defiled you, Lev. xix, 17. You see the church lie in sin, you will not touch her, then you sin against her, and have broken your covenant. Will you suffer your brother's ox to lie in the mire? and will not pluck it out? And are not brethren more than oxen. And I beseech you consider another place of Scripture, (and the Lord be merciful to those that have perverted the sense of it:) in Hag. ii, 12,13. where it is said, *They were all unclean, as by the touch of a dead man, both prince and priest, and people were unclean.* Very godly men they were, yet so busy with the world, that temple work was neglected, expressly against the commandment of God; for they did not only leave it off when the king restrained them with a strong hand, but in the days of Darius also (the successor of Artaxerxes) they did forbear and cease from temple work; and therefore now they are neither accepted of God, nor prospered in the outward man, they were all unclean, as by the touch of a dead man: but do Haggai and Zechariah now separate from them? No, no, brethren, they touch them to the quick, and so recover their brethren, and deliver their souls, though they be dead and defiled; yet it is not for the people of God to say, we will touch them; you shall be unclean if you touch them not: touch them, how? With dalliance, and familiarity and closeth with them: not so, for that was the sin of old Eli that he did bear with his children too much, and touched them no more sharply. But herein stood the faithfulness of these two holy prophets, that they did touch their brethren, and that thoroughly, so that the Lord did stir them up to set about temple work; and then He doth promise all that they went about should be clean and pure. I pray you therefore consider it: I am marvellously afraid of separation from churches upon any breach of duty; they who do separate for such causes, think they are sprinkled with the water of separation: but believe it, they are separated from Christ Jesus forever, if they so live and so die. Therefore if you belong to Christ, He will shew you it is not the water of separation that will serve your turn, but getting Christ Jesus, and sitting closer to Him, and to your brethren, by admonishing and reproving them, if you see them defiled. This will keep you clean, and your hearts clean, and your souls comfortable: That the Lord hath made an everlasting covenant with you that shall never be *forgotten.*

The Keys of the Kingdom
of Heaven, 1644

TO THE READER

The greatest commotions in kingdoms have for the most part been raised and maintained for and about power, *and* liberties *of the* rulers *and the* ruled, *together with the due bounds and limits of either: and the like hath fallen out in churches, and is continued to this day in the sharpest contentions* (*though now the seat of the war is changed*) *who should be the first adequate and complete* subject *of that* church-power, *which Christ hath left on earth;* how bounded, *and* to whom committed. *This controversy is in a special manner the lot of these present times: and now that most parties* (*that can pretend any thing towards it*) *have in several ages had their turns and vicissitudes of so long a possession of it, and their pleas for their several pretenses, have been so much and so long heard, it may well be hoped it is near determining; and that Christ will shortly settle this power upon the right heirs to whom He primitively did bequeath it.*

In those former darker times, this golden ball was thrown up by the clergy (*so called*) *alone to run for among themselves: and as they quietly possessed the name* Κληϱὸς, *the* clergy, *and of the* church, *appropriated to themselves; so answerably all manner of interest in power or cognisance of matters of the* church, *was wholly left and quitted to them: whilst the* people that *then* knew not the law, *having given up their souls to an implicit faith in what was to be believed, did much more suffer themselves to be deprived of all liberties in church affairs. This royal donation bestowed by Christ upon his church, was taken up and*[1] *placed in so high thrones of bishops, popes, general councils, etc. not only* far above these things on earth, *the people; but* things in heaven *also, we mean the* angels *and* ministers *of the churches themselves; in so great a remoteness from the people, that the least right or interest therein, was not so much as suspected to belong to them. But towards these latter times, after many removals of it down again, and this as the issue of many suits again and again renewed and removed, and upon the sentence (even of whole states) as oft reversed, it hath now in these our days been brought so near unto the people, that they also have begun to plead and sue for a portion, and legacy bequeathed them in it. The* saints (*in these knowing times*) *finding that the* key of knowledge *hath so far opened their hearts, that they see with their own eyes into the substantials of godliness, and that through the instruction and guidance of their teachers, they are enabled to understand for themselves such other things as they are to join in the practise of, they do therefore further (many of them) begin more than to suspect, that some share in the* key of power *should likewise appertain unto them.*

It was the unhappiness of those, who first in these latter times revived this plea of the people's right, to err on the other extreme (as it hath ever been the fate of truth, when it first ariseth in the church from under that long night of darkness which Antichrist had brought upon the world to have a long shadow of error to accompany it) by laying the plea and claim on their behalf unto the whole power; and that the elders set over them did but exercise the power for them, which was properly theirs, and which Christ had (as they contended) radically and originally estated in the people only.

But after that all titles have been pleaded, of those that are

---

1 [A superfluous "and" omitted.]

content with nothing but the whole, the final judgment and sentence may (possibly) fall to be a suitable and due proportioned distribution and disperson of this power *into several interests, and the whole to neither part. In commonwealths, it is a dispersion of several portions of power and rights into several hands, jointly to concur and agree in acts and process of weight and moment, which causeth that healthful* Κρᾶσις[2] *and constitution of them, which makes them lasting and preserves their peace, when none of all sorts find they are excluded, but as they have a share of concernment, so that a fit measure of power or privilege is left and betrusted to them. And accordingly the wisdom of the first constitutors of commonwealths is most seen in such a just balancing of power and privileges, and besides also in setting the exact limits of that which is committed unto each; yea and is more admired by us in this than in their other laws; and in experience, a clear and distinct definement and confinement of all such parcels of power, both for the kind and extent of them, is judged to be as essentially necessary (if not more) than what ever other statutes, that set out the kinds and degrees of crimes or penalties.*

So in that polity or government by which Christ would have *his* churches ordered, the right disposal of the power therein *(we humbly suppose)* may lie in a due and proportioned allotment and dispersion *(though not in the same measure and degree) into divers hands, according unto the several concernments and interests that each rank in his church may have; rather than in an entire and sole trust committed to any one man (though never so able) or any sort or kind of men or officers, although diversified into never so many subordinations under one another. And in like manner, we cannot but imagine that Christ hath been as exact in setting forth the true bounds*

---

2 [Mixture.]

and limits of what ever portion of power He hath imparted unto any (if we of this age could attain rightly to discern it) as He hath been in ordering what kind of censures, and for what sins and what degrees of proceedings unto those censures, which we find He hath been punctual in.

Now the scope which this grave and judicious author in this treatise doth pursue, is to lay forth the just lines and terriers of this division of church *power, unto all the several subjects of it; to the end to allay the contentions now on foot, about it. And in general he lays this fundamental* maxim, *that holds in common true of all the particulars, to whom any portion of power can be supposed to be committed:* that look whatever power or right any of the possessors and subjects thereof may have, they have it each, alike immediately *(that is, in respect of a mediation of delegation or dependence on each other)* from Christ, *and so are* each, the first subjects of that power that is alloted to them. *And for the particular subjects themselves, he follows that division (in the handling of them) which the controversy itself hath made unto his hands; to wit,* 1. What power each *single* congregation *(which is endowed with a charter to be a body-politic to Christ) hath granted to it to exercise within it-self: and* 2. What measure, or *rather,* kind of power *Christ hath placed in* neighbor churches *without it, and in* association *with it.*

For the first. As he supposeth, each congregation, such as to have the privilege of enjoying a presbytery, or company of more or less elders, proper unto itself; so being thus presbyterated, he asserteth this incorporate body or society to be the first *and* primary *subject of a complete and entire power within itself over its own members; yea, and the* sole native subject *of the power of* ordination *and* excommunication, *which is the highest censure. And whereas this corporation consisteth both of* elders *and* brethren, *(for as for women and children, there is a special exception by a* statute-law *of Christ against their enjoyment of any part of this public power;) his scope is to demonstrate a distinct and several share and interest of power, in matters of common concernment, vouchsafed to each of these, and dispersed among both, by charter from the Lord: as in some of our* towns corporate, *to a company of* aldermen, *the rulers, and a* common council, *a body of the people, there useth to be the like*[3]: *he giving unto the* elders *or* presbytery *a binding power of* rule *and* authority *proper and peculiar unto them; and unto the* brethren, *distinct and apart, an interest of* power *and* privilege *to concur with them, and that such affairs should not be transacted, but with the joint agreement of both, though out of a different right: so that as a church of* brethren *only, could not proceed to any public censures, without they have* elders *over them, so nor in the church have the* elders *power to censure without the concurrence of the people; and likewise so, as each alone hath not power of excommunicating the whole of either, though* together *they have power over any particular person or persons in each.*

And because these particular congregations, both elders *and* people, *may disagree and miscarry, and abuse this power committed to them; he therefore,* secondly, *asserteth an association or communion of churches, sending their* elders *and* messengers *into a* synod, *(so he purposely chooseth to style those* assemblies *of* elders *which the* reformed churches *do call* classes *or* presbyteries, *that so he might distinguish them from those* presbyteries *of* congregations *before mentioned) and acknowledges that it is an* ordinance *of Christ, unto whom Christ hath (in*

[3] [The model was also followed in civil polity in New England where the General Court was made up of magistrates, analagous to aldermen in England or to elders in Congregational church polity, and deputies, analagous to members of the common council in England or church members in Congregational polity.]

relation to rectifying maladministrations *and* healing dissentions
in particular congregations, *and the like cases) committed a*
due and just measure of power, suited and proportioned to those
ends; and furnished them, not only with ability *to give* counsel
and advice, *but further upon such occasions with a* ministerial
power *and* authority *to* determine, declare *and* enjoin *such*
things as may tend to the reducing such congregations *to right*
and peace. Only in his bounding and defining this power, *he*
affirms it to be[4] *first for the* kind *and* quality *of it, but a* dog-
matical *or* doctrinal power, (*though stamped with authority*
ministerial as an ordinance *of Christ) whether in judging of*
controversies of faith (when they disturb the peace of particular
congregations, *and which themselves find too difficult for them)*
or in discerning matters of fact and what censures they do de-
serve: but not armed with authority and power of excommunicating *or* delivering unto Satan, *either the* congregations *or the*
members *of them: but they in such cases, having declared and*
judged the nature of the offense, and admonished the peccant
churches, *and discerned what they ought to do with their*
offending members; they are to leave the formal act *of this*
censure to that authority which can only execute it, placed by
Christ in those churches *themselves; which if they deny to do,*
or persist in their miscarriage, then to determine to withdraw
communion from them. *And also for the* extent *of this power*
in such assemblies *and* association *of* churches, *he limits and*
confines that *also unto cases, and with cautions (which will*
appear in the discourse) *to wit, they they should not entrench or*
impair the privilege of entire jurisdiction committed unto each
congregation (*as a liberty purchased them by Christ's blood)*
but to leave them free to the exercise and use thereof, until
they abuse that power, or are unable to manage it; and in this

---

[4] [Period omitted.]

*case only to assist, guide, and direct them, and not take on them
to administer it for them, but with them, and by them.*

*As for ourselves, we are yet, neither afraid, nor ashamed to
make profession (in the midst of all the high waves on both
sides dashing on us) that the substance of this brief* extract
from the author's *larger* discourse, *is that very* middle way
(*which in our Apology*[5] *we did in the general intimate and intend*) *between that which is called* Brownism, *and the* presbyterial government, *as it is practised; whereof the one doth in
effect put the chief (if not the whole) of the rule and government into the hands of the people, and drowns the* elders' *votes
(who are but a few) in the major part of theirs: and the other,
taking the chief and the principal parts of that rule (which we
conceive is the due of each* congregation, *the* elders *and* brethren) *into this jurisdiction of a common* presbytery *of several*
congregations, *doth thereby in like manner swallow up, not
only the interests of the people, but even the vote of the* elders
of that congregation *concerned in the major part thereof.*

*Neither let it seem arrogance in us, but a testimony rather to
the truth, further to remonstrate, that this very* boundary platform *and* disposement *of* church power, *as here it is (we speak
for the substance of it) set out and stated; as also that the
tenure and exercise thereof in all these subjects, should be
immediate from Christ unto them all, is not new unto our
thoughts; yea it is no other than what our own apprehensions
have been moulded unto long since: and this many of our friends
and some that are of a differing opinion having known our*

[5] [*An Apologeticall Narration* (1643), the manifesto signed by the five
dissenting members of the Westminster Assembly: Thomas Goodwin, Philip
Nye, Sidrach Simpson, Jeremiah Burroughes, and William Bridge. It was their
appeal beyond the Assembly, where they were vastly outnumbered, to Parliament
and to the English people that the English church should not pattern itself on
the Scottish model but should make allowance for independent congregations.]

private judgments long, as likewise our own notes and transcripts written long ago, can testify; besides many public professions since as occasion hath been offered: insomuch as when we first read this of this learned author (knowing what hath been the more general current both of the practise and judgment of our brethren for the Congregational way) we confess we were filled with wonderment at the divine hand, that had thus led the judgments (without the least mutual interchange or intimation of thoughts or notions in these particulars) of our brethren *there, and ourselves (unworthy to be mentioned with them) here. Only we crave leave of the reverend author and those* brethren *that had the view of it, to declare that we assent not to all expressions scattered up and down, or all and every assertion interwoven in it; yea nor to all the grounds or allegations of Scriptures; nor should we in all things perhaps have used the same terms to express the same materials by.*

For instance, we humbly conceive prophecying *(as the Scripture terms it) or speaking to the edification of the whole church, may (sometimes) be performed by brethren gifted, though not in office as elders of the church; only 1. occasionally, not in ordinary course; 2. by men of such abilities as are fit for office; and 3. not assuming this of themselves, but judged such by those that have the power, and so allowed and designed to it; and 4. so as their doctrine be subjected (for the judging of it) in an especial manner to the* teaching elders *of that church: and when it is thus cautioned, we see no more incongruity for such to speak to a point of divinity in a congregation, than for men of like abilities to speak to, and debate of matters of religion in an assembly of divines, which this reverend author allows; and here, with us, is practised.*

Again, in all humility, we yet see not that assembly of apostles, elders, and brethren, Acts xv, *to have been a* formal

synod, *of messengers, sent, out of a set and combined association
from neighbor churches;* but an assembly of *the* church of
Jersualem *and of the messengers from the* church of Antioch
*alone; that were far remote each from other, and electively now
met:* nor are we for the present convinced that the apostles *to
the end to make this a precedent of such a* formal synod, *did act
therein as ordinary* elders, *and not out of apostolical guidance
and assistance; but we rather conceive (if we would simply consider the mutual aspects which these two churches and their*
elders *stood in this conjunction, abstracting from them that influence and impression which (that superior sphere) the apostles
who were then present had in this transaction) this to have been
a* consultation (*as the learned author doth also acknowledge it to
have been in its first original, only rising up to be a general
council by the apostles' presence, they being* elders *of all the
churches*) ; *or if you will,* a reference *by way of* arbitration *for
deciding of this great controversy risen amongst them at*
Antioch, *which they found to be too difficult for themselves; and
so to be a warrant indeed for all such ways of communion between all, or any, especially neighbor churches; and upon like
occasions to be ordinances furnished with ministerial power for
such ends and purposes. Our reasons for this, we are now many
ways bound up from giving the accompt of, in this way, and at
this season; but however if it should have been so intended as
the learned author judgeth, and the apostles to have acted therein as ordinary elders, yet the lines of their proportion of power
that could be drawn from that pattern would extend no further
than a ministerial doctrinal power etc. in such assemblies, which
we willingly grant. And it may be observed with what a wary eye
and exact aim he takes the latitude and elevation of that power
there held forth, not daring to attribute the least, either for kind
or degree, than what the example warrants, which was at*

utmost but a doctrinal discernment both of the truth of that controversy they were consulted in; as also the matter of fact in those that had taught the contrary, as beliers of them and subverters of the faith; without so much as brandishing the sword and power of excommunication, against those high and gross delinquents, or others, that should not obey them by that espistle.

Only in the last place for the further clearing the difference of the peoples' interest (which the reverend author usually calleth liberty, *sometimes* power) *and the* elders' rule *and* authority (*which makes that* first distribution *of church power* in particular congregations) *as likewise for the illustration of that other allotment of* ministerial doctrinal power *in an association or communion of churches as severed from the power of* excommunication (*which is* the second). *We take the boldness to cast a weak beam of our dim light upon either of these; and to present how these have lain stated in our thoughts, to this end that we may haply prevent some reader's mistake, especially about the former. For the first, we conceive the* elders *and* brethren *in each congregation, as they are usually in the New Testament thus mentioned distinctly apart, and this when their meeting together is spoken of, so they make in each congregation two distinct interests (though meeting in one assembly) as the interest of the* common council *or body of the people, in some* corporations, *is distinct from that of the company of* aldermen; *so as without the consent and concurrence of both nothing is esteemed as a church act. But so as in this company of* elders, *this power is properly* authority; *but in the people is a* privilege *or* power. *An apparent difference between these two is evident to us by this. That two or three or more select persons should be put into an office and be trusted with an entire interest or power for a multitude, to which that multitude ought (by a command from Christ) to be subject and obedient as to an ordinance to guide them in their consent, and in whose sentence the ultimate formal ministerial act of binding or loosing should consist: this power must needs be esteemed and acknowledged in these few to have the proper notion and character of* authority, *in comparison of that power* (*which must yet concur with theirs*) *that is in a whole body or multitude of men, who have a greater and nearer interest and concernment in those affairs, over which the few are set as rulers.*

This difference of power, doth easily appear in comparing the several interest of father *and* child, *in his disposement of her in marriage, and her concurrence with him therein,* (*although we intend not the parallel between the things themselves.*) *A* virgin daughter *hath a* power *truly and properly so called,* yea *and a power ultimately to dissent upon an unsatisfied dislike, yea and it must be an act of her consent, that maketh the marriage valid: but yet for her* parents *to have a power to guide her in her choice* (*which she ought in duty to obey*) *and a power which must also concur to bestow her, or the marriage is invalid, this* (*comparing her interest* (*wherein she is more nearly and intimately concerned*) *with theirs*) *doth arise to the notion of an* extrinsical authority, *whereas that power which is in her, is but simply the power of her own act, in which her own concernment doth interest her free by an* intrinsical right. *The like difference would appear if we had seen a government tempered of an* aristocracy *and* democracy; *in which, suppose the people have a share, and their actual consent is necessary to all laws and sentences, whereas a few nobles that are set over them* (*whose concernment is less general*) *in whom the formal* sanction *of all should lie, in these it were* rule *and* authority, *in that multitude but* power *and* interest; *and such an authority is to be given to a presbytery of* elders *in a particular congregation, or else* (*as we have long since been resolved*) *all that is said in the* New Testa-

ment about their rule, *and of the peoples' obedience to them, is to be looked upon but as metaphors, and to hold no proportion with any substantial reality of rule and government.*

And in this distribution of power, Christ hath had a suitable and due regard unto the estate and condition of his church; as now under the New Testament, He hath qualified and dignified it. Under the Old Testament, it was in its infancy, but it is comparatively come forth of its nonage, and grown up to a riper age (both as the tenure of the covenant of grace in difference from the old, runs in the prophets, and as Paul *to the* Galatians *expresseth it). They are therefore more generally able, if visible saints (which is to be the subject matter of churches under the New Testament) to join with their guides and leaders in judging and discerning what concern their own and their* brethren's *consciences; and therefore Christ hath not now lodged the sole power of all church matters solely and entirely in the churches'* tutors *and* governors *as of old when it was under age He did: but yet because of their weakness and unskillfulness (for the generality of them) in comparison to those who He hath ascended to give gifts unto, on purpose for their guidance and the government of them; He hath therefore placed a rule and authority in the officers over them, not directing only but binding: so as not only nothing (in an ordinary way of church government) should be done without them, but not esteemed validly done unless done by them. And thus by means of this due and golden balancing and poising of power and interest, authority and privilege, in* elders *and the* brethren, *this government might neither degenerate into lordliness and oppression in rulers over the flock, as not having all power in their hands alone; nor yet into anarchy and confusion in the flock among themselves; and so as all things belonging to men's consciences might be, transacted to common edification and satisfaction.*

For the second, let it not seem a paradox that a ministerial doctrine *authority should be found severed from that power of* excommunication, *to second it, if not obeyed. Every minister and pastor hath in himself, alone, a ministerial doctrinal authority over the whole church that is his charge, and every person in it, to* instruct, rebuke, exhort with all authority: *by reason of which those under him are bound to obey him in the Lord, not only* vi materiæ *by virtue of the matter of the commands, in that they are the commands of Christ (for so he should speak with no more authority than any other man, yea* a child, *who speaking a truth out of the word, should* lead us, *as the prophet speaks;) but further, by reason of that ministerial authority which Christ hath endowed him withal, he is to be looked at by them as an ordinance of* his, *and over them and towards them: and yet he alone hath the authority of excommunication* in him, *to enforce his doctrine if any do gainsay it: neither therefore is this authority (as in him considered) to be judged vain and fruitless and ineffectual, to draw men to obedience.*

Neither let it seem strange, that the power of the censure, of cutting men off, and delivering them to Satan *(in which the positive part* (and indeed the controversy betwixt us and others) *of* excommunication *lies) should be inseparably linked by Christ unto a particular congregation, as the proper native privilege hereof, so as that no assembly or company of* elders *justly presumed and granted to be more wise and judicious should assume it to themselves, or sever the formal power thereof from the particular congregations. For though it be hard to give the reason of Christ's institutions,*[6] *yet there is usually in the ways of humane wisdom and reason something analogous thereunto, which may serve to illustrate, if not to justify this* dispersion of interests: *and so (if we mistake not) there may be found even*

---

6 [Comma for the period in the original.]

of this in the wisdom of our ancestors, in the constitutions of this kingdom. The sentencing to death *of any subject in the kingdom, as it is the highest civil punishment, so of all other the nearest and exactest parallel to this in spirituals, of cutting a soul off and delivering it to Satan; yet the power of this high judgment is not put into the hands of an assembly of lawyers only, no not of all the judges themselves, men selected for wisdom, faithfulness, and gravity, who are yet by office designed to have an interest herein; but when they upon any special cause or difficulty, for council and direction in such judgments do all meet (as sometimes they do): yet they have not power to pronounce this sentence of death upon any man without the concurrence of a jury of his peers, which are of his own rank; and in corporations, of such as are inhabitants of the same place: and with a jury of these (men of themselves not supposed to be so skillful in the laws, etc.) two judges, yea one, with other justices on the bench hath power to adjudge and pronounce that which all of them, and all the lawyers in this kingdom together, have not without a jury. And we of this nation use to admire the care and wisdom of our ancestors herein, and do esteem this privilege of the subjects in that particular (peculiar to our nation) as one of the glories of our laws, and do make boast of it as such a liberty and security to each person's life, as (we think) no nation about us can show the like. And what should be the reason of such a constitution but this (which in the beginning we insisted on) the dispersion of power into several hands, which in capital matters, every man's trial should run through; whereof the one should have the tie of like common interest to oblige them unto faithfulness; as the other should have skill and wisdom to guide them and direct therein.*

And besides that interest that is in any kind of association, fraternity, yea or neighborhood, or likewise, that which is from

*the common case of men alike subjected to an authority set over
them to sentence them, there is also the special advantage of an
exact knowledge of the fact in the heinous circumstances thereof, yea, and (in these cases) of the ordinary conversation of the
person offending.*

We need not enlarge in the application of this: although a
greater assembly of elders *are to be reverenced as more wise and
able than a* few elders *with their single* congregations, *and
accordingly may have an higher doctrinal power, (a power
properly, and peculiarly suited to their abilities) in cases of
difficulty, to determine and direct congregations in their way;
yet Christ hath not betrusted them with that power He hath done
the congregations; because they are abstracted from the people:
and so one* tribe *of men concerned in all the forementioned
respects is* wanting, *which Christ would have personally concurring, not by delegation or representation alone, not to the*
execution *only, but even to the* legal sentence *also of* cutting
men off, *as in the former parallel and instance may be observed.
Yea, and the higher and the greater the association of the*
presbyteries are, *the further are they removed from* the people,
and although you might have thereby a greater help, in that
judicial *knowledge of the* rule, *to be proceeded by: yet they are
in a further distance (and disenabled thereby) from that precise*
practique *knowledge of the* fact *and frame of* spirit *in the person
transgressing. And cases may be as truly difficult and hard to be
decided from obscurity and want of light into the circumstantia-
tion of the fact, and person: in which it was committed, and by
him obstinately persisted in; as the law itself.*

*Other considerations of like weight might here be added, if
not for the proof (which we do not here intend) yet the clearing
of this particular; as also to demonstrate that that other way of
proceeding by* withdrawing communion *is most suitable to the*

relation, that by Christ's endowment all churches stand in one towards another, yea and wherein the least (being a body to Christ) doth stand unto all: but we should too much exceed the bounds of an epistle, and too long detain the reader from the fruitful and pregnant labors of the worthy author.

The God of peace and truth, sanctify all the truth in it, to all those holy ends (and through his grace much more) which the holy and peacable spirit of the author did intend.

THO. GOODWIN
PHILIP NYE

CHAPTER I

What the keys of the kingdom of heaven be, and what their power

The keys of the kingdom of heaven are promised by the Lord Jesus (the head and king of his church) unto Peter, Matt. xvi, 19. *To thee* (saith Christ) *will I give the keys of the kingdom of Heaven: and whatsoever thou shalt bind on earth, shall be bound in heaven; and whatsoever thou shalt loose on earth, shall be loosed in heaven.* The words being allegorical, are therefore somewhat obscure: and holding forth honor and power in the church, are therefore controversial; for where there is no honor (nor pride to pursue it) there is no contention.[a] It will not therefore be amiss, for opening of the doctrine of the power of the keys; somewhat to open the words of this text, whereon that power is built. Five words require a little clearing.

1. What is here meant by the kingdom of heaven?
2. What are the keys of this kingdom, and the giving of them?
3. What are the acts of these keys, which are said to be binding and loosing?
4. What is the object of these acts to be bound or loosed, here put under a general name, whatsoever?
5. Who is the subject recipient of this power, or to whom is this power given? To thee will I give the keys, etc.

1. For the first: by the kingdom of heaven is here meant both the kingdom of grace, which is the church; and the kingdom of

[a] Prov. xv,1.

glory, which is in the highest heavens: for Christ giving to Peter the keys of the kingdom of heaven, conveyeth therewith not only this power to bind on earth (that is, in the church on earth; for He gave him no power at all to bind in the world; the kingdom of Christ is not of this world:) but He gives him also this privilege; that what be bound on earth, should be bound in heaven. And heaven being distinguished from the church on earth, must needs be meant the kingdom of glory.

2. For the second: what the keys of the kingdom of heaven be?

The keys of the kingdom are the ordinances which Christ hath instituted, to be administered in his church; as the preaching of the word, (which is the opening and applying of it) also the administering of the seals and censures: for by the opening and applying of these, both the gates of the church here, and of heaven hereafter, are opened or shut to the sons of men.

And the giving of these keys, implieth, that Christ investeth those to whom He giveth them, with a power to open, and shut the gates of both. And this power lieth partly in their spiritual calling (whether it be their office, or their place and order in the church:) and partly in the concourse and cooperation of the Spirit of Christ, accompanying the right dispensation of these keys; that is, of these ordinances according to his will.

Moreover, these keys are neither sword nor scepter; no sword, for they convey not civil power of bodily life and death; nor scepter, for they convey not sovereign or legislative power over the church, but stewardly and ministerial. As the key of the house of David was given to Hilkiah, Isai. xxii, 22, who succeeded Shebna in his office; and his office was עַל בּוִית over the house, ver. 15, and the same word over the house, is translated steward in the house, Gen. xliii, 19.

3. Touching the third thing, what are the acts of these keys?

The acts of these keys, are said here to be binding and loosing, which are not the proper acts of material keys; for their acts be opening and shutting, which argueth the keys here spoken of be not material keys, but metaphorical; and yet being keys; they have a power also of opening and shutting: for Christ who hath the sovereign power of these keys, He is said to have the key of David, to open, and no man to shut; to shut, and no man to open, Rev. iii, 7, which implieth, that these keys of Christ's kingdom, have such a power of opening and shutting, as that they do thereby, bind and loose, retain and remit; in opening, they loose, and remit; in shutting they bind, and retain: which will more appear in opening the fourth point.

4. The fourth point then is, what is the subject to be bound and loosed?

The text in Matt. xvi, 9, saith, *whatsoever,* which reacheth not (so far as the papists would stretch it) to whatsoever oaths, or covenants, or contracts, or counsels, or laws; as if whatsoever oaths of allegiance, covenants of lease or marriage, etc. the Pope ratifieth or dissolveth on earth, should be ratified or dissolved in heaven: no, this is not the key of the kingdom of heaven, but the key of the bottomless pit, Rev. ix, 1. But this word *whatsoever,* is here put in the neuter gender, (not in the masculine, *whomsoever*) to imply both things and persons; things, as sins; persons, as those that commit them. For so when our Saviour speaketh of the same acts of the same keys, John xx, 21, He explaineth himself thus: *Whose sins soever ye remit, they are remitted, and whose sins soever ye retain, they are retained.* Whatsoever you bind on earth, is as much therefore, as whose sins soever you retain on earth; and whatsoever you loose on earth, is as much as whose sins soever you loose on earth.

Now this binding and loosing of whatsoever sins, in whosever commit them, is partly in the conscience of the sinner, and partly in his outward estate in the church, which is wont to be expressed in other terms, either *in foro interiori,* or *in foro exteriori.*[7] As when in the dispensation of the ordinances of God, a sinner is convinced to lie under the guilt of sin, then his sin is retained, his conscience is bound under the guilt of it, and himself bound under some church-censure, according to the quality and desert of his offense; and if his sin be the more heinous, himself is shut out from the communion of the church; but when a sinner repenteth of his sin, and confesseth it before the Lord, and (if it be known) before his people also, and then in the ministry of the doctrine and discipline of the Gospel, his sin is remitted, and his conscience loosed from the guilt of it, and himself hath open and free entrance, both unto the promise of the Gospel, and into the gates of the holy communion of the church.

5. The fifth point to be explained, is, to whom is this power of the keys given? The text saith, to thee Simon Peter, the son of Jonah, whom Christ blesseth, and pronounceth blessed upon his holy confession of Christ, the Son of the living God, and upon the same occasion promiseth both to use him and his confession, as an instrument to lay the foundation of his church; and also to give him the keys of his church, for the well ordering and governing of it. But it hath proved a busy question, how Peter is to be considered in receiving this power of the keys, whether as an apostle, or as an elder, (for an elder also he was, I Pet. v, 1) or as a believer professing his faith before the Lord Jesus, and his fellow brethren. Now because we are as well studious of peace, as of truth, we will not lean to one of these interpretations, more than to another. Take any of them,

7 [In the inner forum or in the outer forum.]

it will not hinder our purpose in this ensuing discourse, though (to speak ingenuously and without offense what we conceive) the sense of the words will be most full, if all the several considerations be taken jointly together. Take Peter considered not only as an apostle, but an elder also, yea, and a believer too, professing his faith, all may well stand together. For there is a different power given to all these, to an apostle, to an elder, to a believer, and Peter was all these, and received all the power, which was given by Christ to any of these, or to all of these together. For as the Father sent Christ, so Christ sent Peter (as well as any Apostle) *cum amplitudine, et plenitudine potestatis*,[8] (so far as either any church-officer, or the whole church itself, was capable of it), John xx, 21. So that Austin did not mistake when he said Peter received the keys in the name of the church. Nevertheless, we from this place in Matt. xvi, 19. will challenge no further power, either to the presbytery, or to the fraternity of the Church, than is more expressly granted to them in other Scriptures. Now in other Scriptures it appeareth; first, that Christ gave the power of retaining or remitting of sins (that is, the power of binding and loosing, the whole power of the keys) to all the apostles as well as to Peter, John xx, 21,23. Secondly, it appeareth also that the apostles commended the rule and government of every particular church to the elders (the presbytery) of that church, Heb. xiii, 17; I Tim. v, 17. And therefore Christ gave the power of the keys to them also. Thirdly, it appeareth farther that Christ gave the power of the keys to the body likewise of the church, even to the fraternity with the presbytery. For the Lord Jesus communicateth the power of binding and loosing, to the apostles, or elders, together with the whole church, when they are met in his name, and agree together in the censure of an offender, Matt. xviii, 17,18. If

8 [With greatness and abundance of power.]

an offender (saith He) neglect to hear the church, let him be to thee as an heathen or a publican, that is, let him be excommunicated. Which censure administered by them, with the whole church, He ratifieth with this promise of the power of the keys, *Verily, I say unto you, whatsoever you shall bind on earth, shall be bound in heaven, and whatsoever you shall loose on earth, shall be loosed in heaven.* In which place, howsoever there be some difference between classical and congregational divines, what should be meant by the *church* (*tell the church*) whether the presbytery or the congregation: yet all agree in this (and it is agreement in the truth, which we seek for) that no offender is to be excommunicated, but with some concurse of the congregation, at least by way 1. Of consent to the sentence. 2. Of actual execution of it by withdrawing themselves from the offender so convicted and censured. Now this consent and concurse of the congregation, which is requisite to the power and validity of the censure, we conceive is some part of the exercise of the power of the keys.

So that when Christ said to Peter, *To thee will I give the keys of the kingdom of heaven:* if Peter then received the whole power of the keys, then he stood in the room and name of all such, as have received any part of the power of the keys, whether apostles, or elders, or churches. Or if he stood in the room of an apostle only, yet that hindereth not, but that as he there received the power of an apostle, so the rest of the apostles received the same power, either there or elsewhere: and the presbytery of each church received, if not there, yet elsewhere, the power belonging to their office: and in like sort each church or congregation of professed believers, received that portion also of church power which belonged to them.

CHAPTER II

Of the distribution of the keys, and their power,
or of the several sorts thereof

The ordinary distribution of the keys is wont to be thus delivered. There is *clavis* { 1. *Scientiæ,* A key of knowledge, and a 2. *Potestatis,* key of power: and the key of power is { 1. *Ordinis,* Either a key of order, or a key of 2. *Jurisdictionis,* Jurisdiction.

This distribution though it go for current both among Protestants and Papists, yet we crave leave to express, what in it doth not fully satisfy us. Four things in it seem defective to us: 1. that any key of the kingdom of heaven should be left without power. For here in this distribution, the key of knowledge is contradistinguished from a key of power.

2. There is a real defect in omitting an integral part of the keys, which is the key of church liberty. But no marvel, though the popish clergy omitted it, who have oppressed all church liberty: and Protestant churches, having recovered the liberty of preaching the Gospel, and ministry of the sacraments, some of them have looked no farther, nor so much as discerned their defect of church liberty in point of discipline: and others finding themselves wronged in withholding a key or power, which belongs to them, have wrested to themselves an undue power, which belongs not to them, the key of authority.

3. There is another defect in the distribution, in dividing the key of order from the key of jurisdiction: of purpose to make way for the power of chancellors and commissaries *in foro exteriori:* who though they want the key of order (having never entered into holy orders, as they are called, or at most into the order of deacons only, whereof our Lord spake nothing

touching jurisdiction) yet they have been invested with jurisdiction, yea, and more than ministerial authority, even above those elders who labor in word and doctrine: by this sacrilegious breach of order (which hath been as it were the breaking of the files and ranks in an army) Satan hath routed and ruined a great part of the liberty and purity of churches, and of all the ordinances of Christ in them.

4. A fourth defect (but yet the least, which we observe in this distribution) is, that order is appropriated to the officers of the church only. For though we be far from allowing that sacrilegious usurpation of the minister's office, which we hear of (to our grief) to be practised in some places, that private Christians ordinarily take upon them to preach the Gospel publicly, and to minister sacraments: yet we put a difference between office and order. Office we look at as peculiar to those, who are set apart for some peculiar function in the church, who are either elders or deacons. But order (speaking of church order properly taken) is common to all the members of the church, whether officers or private brethren. There is an order as well in them that are subject, as in them that rule. There is a Τάξις as well Τ ῶν ὑποτακτικῶν, as τῶν ἐπιτακτικῶν. The maid in Athenaeus is said θεραπαίνης ταξὶν ἐπιλάβουσα, as well as her mistress.[9] Yet if any man be willing to make office and order equipollent, we will not contend about words, so there be no erroneous apprehension wrapped into the matter.

To come therefore to such a distribution of the keys as is more suitable to Scripture phrase. For it becomes true Israelites rather to speak the language of Canaan, than the language of Ashdod.

When Paul beheld, and rejoiced to behold, how the church of

---

[9] [There is an order as well of those who come second as of the ones in command. The maid in Athenaeus is said to be occupying the position of a female slave . . .]

Colosse had received the Lord Jesus, and walked in Him; he summeth up all their church estate, to wit, their beauty and power, in these two, faith and order, Col. ii, 5, 6.

There is therefore a key of faith, and a key of order.

The key of faith, is the same which the Lord Jesus calleth the key of knowledge, Luke xi, 52, and which he complaineth, the lawyers had taken away. Now that key of knowledge Christ speaketh of, was such, that if it had not been taken away, they that had it, had power by it to enter the kingdom of heaven themselves, and it may be to open the door to others, to enter also. Now such a knowledge, whereby a man hath power to enter into heaven, is only faith, which is often therefore called knowledge, as Isai. liii, 11. *By the knowledge of him shall my righteous servant justify many:* that is, by the faith of Christ. And John xvii, 3. *This is eternal life to know thee:* that is, to believe on thee. This key therefore, the key of knowledge, (saving knowledge) or which is all one, the key of faith, is common to all believers. A faithful soul knowing the Scriptures, and Christ in them, receiveth Christ, and entereth through Him into the kingdom of heaven, both here, and hereafter. Here he entereth into a state of grace through faith: and by the profession of his faith, he entereth also into the fellowship of the church (which is the kingdom of heaven upon earth:) and by the same faith, as he believeth to justification, so he maketh confession to salvation, which is perfected in the kingdom of glory, Rom. x, 10.

The key of order is the power whereby every member of the church walketh orderly himself, according to his place in the church, and helpeth his brethren, to walk orderly also.

It was that which the apostles and elders called upon Paul, so to carry himself before the Jews in the temple, that he might make it appear to all men that he walked orderly, Acts xxi, 18,

24. Orderly, to wit, according to the orders of the Jewish church, with whom he then conversed. And it was the commandment which Paul gave to the whole church of Thessalonica, and to all the members of it, to *withdraw themselves from every brother that walketh disorderly,* 2 Thes. iii, 6. This their withdrawing from him that walked disorderly, was the exercise of their key of order. And it was a like exercise of the same key of order, when he requireth the brethren to warn the unruly, which is, (in the original) the same word, to admonish the disorderly, 1 Thes. v, 14. And this key of order (to wit, order understood in this sense) is common to all the members of the church, whether elders or brethren.

Furthermore, of *order* there be *two keys:* a key of *power,* or *interest:* and the key of *authority* or *rule.* The first of these is termed in the Scriptures, *liberty:* so distinguishing it from that part of *rule* and *authority* in the officers of the church. We speak not here of that spiritual liberty, whether of *impunity,* whereby the children of God are set free by the blood of Christ from Satan, hell, bondage of sin, curse of the moral law, and service of the ceremonial law: nor of *immunity* whereby we have *power to be called the sons of God,* to come boldly unto the throne of grace in prayer, and as heirs of glory, to look for our inheritance in light: but of that *external liberty,* or *interest* which Christ also hath purchased for his people, as liberty to enter into the fellowship of his church, liberty to choose and call well gifted men to office in that his church: liberty to partake in sacraments, or seals of the covenant of the church, liberty and interest to join with officers in the due censure of offenders, and the like. This liberty and the acts thereof, are often exemplified in the Acts of the apostles: and the apostle Paul calleth it expressly by the name of liberty. *Brethren* (saith he) *you have been called unto* LIBERTY, *only use not your liberty as an occasion to the flesh, but by love serve one another.* Gal. v, 13, that the apostle by that liberty meaneth church liberty or power in ordering church affairs, will evidently appear, if we consult with the context, rather than with commenters. For the apostle having spent the former part of the epistle, partly in the confirmation of his calling, partly in disputation against justification by the works of the law, to the end of ver. 8 of chap. 5 in the ninth verse he descendeth not to exhort unto *bones mores*[10] in general, (as usually commenters take it) but to instruct in church discipline, in which he giveth three or four directions to the tenth ver. of chap. 6.

1. Touching the censure of those corrupt teachers, who had perverted and troubled them with that corrupt doctrine of justification by works, chap. 5, ver. 9. to the end of the chapter.

2. Touching the gentle admonition and restoring of a brother fallen by infirmity, chap. 6, ver. 1 to 5.

3. Touching the maintenance of their ministers, ver. 6,7,8 and beneficence to others, ver. 9, 10.

Touching the first, the censure of their corrupt teachers. 1. He layeth for the ground of it (that which himself gave for the ground of the excommunication of the incestuous Corinth, I Cor. v, 6.) *A little leaven leaveneth the whole lump.* ver. 9. 2. He presumeth the church will be of the same mind with him, and concur in the censure of him that troubled them with corrupt doctrine, ver. 10. (from fellowship with which corrupt doctrine he cleareth himself, ver. 11). 3. He proceedeth to declare, what censure he wisheth might be dispensed against him, and the rest of those corrupt teachers. *I would* (saith he) *they were even cut off that trouble you:* cut off, to wit, by excommunication, ver. 12. Now lest it should be objected by the brethren of the church: but what power have we to cut them off? The apostle answereth,

10 [Good conduct.]

they have a power and liberty (to wit, to join with the sounder part of the presbytery, in casting them out, or cutting them off:) *For brethren* (saith he) *you are called unto liberty.*

If it should be further objected, yea, but give the people this power and liberty in some cases, either to cast off their teachers, or to cut them off, the people will soon take advantage to abuse this liberty unto much carnal licentiousness. The apostle preventeth that with a word of wholesome counsel: *Brethren* (saith he) *you have been called unto liberty: only use not your liberty as an occasion to the flesh, but by love serve one another,* ver. 13, and thereupon seasonably pursueth this counsel with a caveat to beware of abusing this liberty to carnal contention, (an usual disease of popular liberty) and withal dehorteth them from all other fruits of the flesh, to the end of the chapter.

Evident therefore it is, that there is a key of power or liberty given to the church (to the brethren with the elders) as to open a door of entrance to the minister's calling: so to shut the door of entrance against them in some cases, as when through corrupt and pernicious doctrine, they turn from shepherds to become ravenous wolves.

Having spoken then of that first key of order, namely, the key of *power,* (in a more large sense) or liberty in *the church,* there remaineth the other *key of order,* which is the key of *authority* or of *rule,* in a more strict sense, which is in the *elders* of the church.

Authority is a moral power, in a superior order (or state) *binding or releasing an inferior in point of subjection.*

This key when it was promised to Peter, Matt. xvi, 19, and given to him with the rest of the apostles, John xx, 23. they thereby had power to bind and loose: and it is the same authority which is given to their successors the elders whereby they

are called to feed and rule the church of God, as the apostles
had done before them, Act xx, 28. And indeed by opening and
applying the law (the spirit of bondage accompanying the
same) they bind sinners under the curse, and their consciences
under guilt of sin, and fear of wrath, and shut the kingdom of
heaven against them. And by opening and applying the Gospel
(the spirit of adoption accompanying same) they remit sin, and
loose the consciences of believing repenting souls from guilt of
sin, and open to them the doors of heaven. By virtue of this key,
as they preach *with all authority,* not only the doctrine of the
law, but also the covenant of the Gospel; so they administer the
seals thereof, baptism, and the Lord's Supper. By virtue also of
this key, they with the church do bind an obstinate offender
under excommunication, Matt. xviii, 17,18 and release, and forgive him his repentance, 2 Cor. ii, 7.

   This distribution of the *keys,* and so of *spiritual power,* in
the things of Christ's kingdom we have received from the Scripture. But if any men out of love to antiquity, do rather affect to
keep to the terms of the former more ancient distribution (as
there be who are as loath to change: *antiquos terminos ver-
borum,* as *agrorum*) [11] we would not stick upon the words
rightly explained, out of desire both to judge and speak the
same things with follow brethren. Only then let them allow
some spiritual power to the key of knowledge, though not
church power. And in church power let them put in as well a
key of liberty, that is, a power and privilege *of interest,* as a
key of authority. And by their key of order, as they do understand the key of office, so let them not divide from it the key of
jurisdiction (for Christ hath given no jurisdiction, but to whom
He hath given office) and so we willingly consent with them.

11 [The ancient terms as the ancient boundaries of the fields.]

CHAPTER III

Of the subject of the power of the keys, to whom
they are committed: and first of the key
of knowledge, and order

As the keys of the kingdom of heaven be divers, so are the
subjects to whom they are committed, divers: as in the natural
body, diversity of functions belongeth to diversity of members.

1. The *key of knowledge* (or which is all one, the key of
faith) belongeth to all the faithful, whether joined to any particular church or no. As in the primitive times, men of grown
years were first called and converted to the faith, before they
were received into the church: and even now an Indian or pagan
may not be received into the church, till he have first received
the faith, and have made profession of it before the Lord, and
the church: which argueth, that the key of knowledge is given
not only to the church, but to some before they enter into the
church. And yet to Christians for the church's sake: that they
who receive this grace of faith, by it may receive Christ and his
benefits, and therewith may receive also this privilege, to find an
open door set before them, to enter into the fellowship of the
church.

2. The *key of order* (speaking as we do of church order, as
Paul doth, Col. ii, 5) belongeth to all such, who are in church
order, whether *elders* or *brethren*. For though elders be in a
superior order, by reason of their office, yet the brethren (over
whom the elders are made overseers and rulers) they stand also
in an order, even in orderly subjection, according to the order
of the Gospel. It is true, every faithful soul that hath received
a key of knowledge, is bound to watch over his neighbor's soul,
as his own, and to admonish him of his sin, unless he be a

scorner: but this he doth, *Non ratione ordinis, sed intuitu charitatis:* not by virtue of a state of order which he is in (till in church fellowship) but as of common Christian love and charity. But every faithful Christian who standeth in church order is bound to do the same, as well *respectu ordinis,* as *intuitu charitatis,* by virtue of that royal law, not only of love, but of church order, Matt. xviii, 15,16,17, whereby if his brother who offended him, do not hearken to his conviction and admonition, he is then according to order, to proceed further, taking one or two with him: and if the offender refuse to hear them also, then he is by order to tell the church, and afterwards walk towards him, as God shall direct the church to order it.

CHAPTER IV

Of the subject to whom the key of church privilege, power, or liberty is given

This key is given to the brethren of the church: for so saith the apostle, in Gal. v, 13 (in the place quoted and opened before) *Brethren, you have been called to liberty.*

And indeed, as it is the εὖ εἶναι, εὐεξία and εὐπραξία of a commonwealth, the right and due establishment and balancing of the *liberties* or *privileges* of the people (which is in a true sense, may be called a *power*) and the *authority* of the magistrate: so it is the safety of church estate, the right and due settling and ordering of the holy *power* of the *privileges* and *liberties* of the brethren, and the ministerial authority of the elders. The Gospel alloweth no church authority (or rule properly so called) to the brethren, but reserveth that wholly to the elders; and yet preventeth the tyranny and oligarchy, and exorbitancy of the elders, by the large and firm establishment of the liberties of the brethren, which ariseth to a *power* in them. Bucer's axiom is here

notable; *Potestas penes omnem Ecclesiam est; Authoritas ministerii penes Presbyteros et Episcopos.*[12] In Matt. xvi, 19, where
potestas, or power being contradistinguished from *authoritas,*
authority is nothing else but a liberty or privilege.

The liberties of the brethren, or the church consisting of them,
are many and great.

1. The church of brethren hath the *power, privileges* and
liberty to choose their officers. In the choice of an apostle into
the place of Judas, the people went as far as humane vote and
suffrage could go. Out of 120 persons (ver. 15) they chose out,
and presented two; out of which two (because an apostle was
to be designed immediately by God) God by lot chose one; and
yet this one so chosen of God, συγκατεψηφίσθη, *communibus
omnium suffragiis inter duodecim Apostolos allectus est,* ver.
26.[13] was counted amongst the apostles by the common suffrages
of them all. And this place Cyprian presseth amongst others, to
confirm the power (that is ἐξουσίαν, or *privilege,* or *liberty*) of
the people, in choosing or refusing their ministers. *Plebs Chris-
tiana* (saith he) *vel maxime potestatem habet, vel dignos sacerdotes eligendi, vel indignos recusandi,* Epistol. 4, lib. 1.[14]

The like, or greater liberty is generally approved by the best
of our divines (studious of reformation) from Acts xiv, 23.
They *ordained them elders, chosen by lifting up of hands.*

The same power is clearly expressed in the choice of deacons,
Acts vi, 3,5,6. The apostles did not choose the deacons, but
called the multitude together, and said unto them, *Brethren,
look you out seven men amongst you whom we may appoint*

12 [The power belongs to all the church; the authority of the ministry belongs
to the elders and the bishops.]
13 [Gr: to be reckoned along with [the others]; Lat: by vote of all present he
was elected to be one of the twelve apostles.]
14 [The Christian people assuredly have the fullest power, either to choose
worthy priests or to refuse unworthy ones.]

over this business: And the saying pleased the whole multitude, and they chose Stephen, etc.

2. It is a *privilege,* or a *liberty* the church hath received, to send forth one or more of their elders, as the public service of Christ and of the church may require. Thus Epaphroditus was a *messenger* or *apostle* of the church of Philippi unto Paul, Phil. ii, 25.

3. The brethren of the church have *power* and *liberty* of propounding any just exception against such as offer themselves to be admitted unto their communion, or unto the seals of it: hence Saul, when he offered himself to the communion of the church at Jerusalem was not at first admitted thereto, upon an exception taken against him by the disciples till that exception was removed, Acts ix, 26,27. and Peter did not admit the family of Cornelius to baptism, till he had inquired of the brethren, if any of them had any exception against it, Acts x, 47.

4. As the brethren have a *power* of order, and the *privilege* to expostulate with their brethren in case of private scandals, according to the rule, Matt. xviii, 15,16. So in case of public scandal, the whole church of brethren have *power* and *privilege* to join with the elders, in inquiring, hearing, judging of public scandals; so as to bind notorious offenders and impenitents under censure, and to forgive the repentant: for when Christ commandeth a brother, in case that offense cannot be healed privately, then to *tell the church,* Matt. xviii, 17. it necessarily implieth that the church must hear him, and inquire into the offense complained of, and judge of the offense as they find it upon inquiry. When the brethren that were of the circumcision expostulated with Peter about his communion with Cornelius, and his uncircumcised family, Peter did not reject them, and their complaint against him, as transgressing the bounds of their just power and privilege, but readily addressed himself

to give satisfaction to them all, Acts xi, 2 to 18. The *brethren of the Church of Corinth* being gathered together with their elders, *in the name of the Lord Jesus,* and *with his power, did deliver the incestuous person to Satan,* I Cor. v, 4,5. And Paul reproveth them all, brethren as well as elders, that they had no sooner put him away from amongst them, ver. 2, and expressly he alloweth to them all power *to judge* them that are within, ver. 22. Yea, and from thence argueth, in all the saints, even in the meanest of the saints, an ability to judge between brethren, in the things of this life, as those that have received such a spirit of discerning from Christ, by which they shall one day judge the world, even angels, so in the next chapter, the 6, of that I Cor. i, 2,3,4,5. And the same brethren of the same church, as well as the elders, he entreateth *to forgive* the same incestuous Corinthian, upon his repentance, 2 Cor. ii, 7,8.

If it be said, to *judge* is an act of rule; and to be rulers of the church, is not given to all the brethren, but to the elders only: *Ans.* All judgment is not an act of authority or rule; for there is a judgment of discretion, by way of *privilege,* as well as of authority by way of sentence: that of discretion is common to all the brethren, as well as that of authority belongeth to the presbytery of that church. In England, the jury by their verdict, as well as the judge by his sentence, do both of them judge the same malefactor; yet in the jury their verdict is but an act of their popular liberty: in the judge it is an act of his judicial authority.

If it be demanded, what difference is there between these two?

The answer is ready, great is the difference: for though the jury have given up their judgment and verdict, yet the male-factor is not thereupon legally condemned, much less executed, but upon the sentence of the judge: in like sort here, though the brethren of the church do with one accord give up their vote and judgment for the censure of an offender, yet he is not thereby censured, till upon the sentence of the presbytery.

If it be said again; yea, but it is an act of authority to bind and loose, and the power to bind and loose, Christ gave to the whole church, Matt. xviii, 18.

Ans. The whole church may be said to bind and loose, in that the brethren consent, and concur with the elders, both before the censure in discerning it to be just and equal, and in declaring their discernment, by lifting up of their hands, or by silence: and after the censure, in rejecting the offender censured from their wonted communion. And yet their discerning or approving of the justice of the censure beforehand, is not a preventing of the elders in their work. For the elders before that have not only privately examined the offender and his offense, and the proofs thereof, to prepare the matter and ripen it for the church's cognizance: but do also publicly revise the heads of all the material passages thereof before the church: and do withal declare to the church the counsel and will of God therein, that they may rightly discern and approve what censure the Lord requireth to be administered in such a case. So that the people's discerning and approving the justice of the censure before it be administered, ariseth from the elder's former instruction and direction of them therein: whereunto the people give consent, in obedience to the will and rule of Christ. Hence is that speech of the apostle; *We have in readiness to revenge all disobedience, when your* OBEDIENCE IS FULFILLED, 2 Cor. x, 6. The apostles' revenge of disobedience by way of reproof in preaching, doth not follow the people's obedience, but proceedeth whether the people obey it or no. It was therefore their revenge of disobedience by way of censure in discipline, which they had in readiness, when the obedience of the church is fulfilled in discerning and approving the equity of the censure, which the apostles or elders have declared to them from the word.

This power or privilege of the church in dealing in this sort with a scandalous offender, may not be limited only to a private brother offending, but may reach also to an offensive elder. For (as hath been touched already) it is plain that the brethren of the circumcision, supposing Peter to have given an offense in eating with men uncircumcised, they openly expostulated with him about his offense: and he stood not with them upon terms of his apostleship, much less of his eldership, but willingly submitted himself to give satisfaction to them all, Acts xi, 2 to 18. And Paul writeth to the church of Colosse, to deal with Archippus, warning him to see to the fulfilling of his ministry, Col. iv, 17. And very pregnant is his direction to the Galatians, for their proceeding to the utmost with their corrupt and scandalous false teachers. *I would* (saith he) *they were even cut off that trouble you;* and that upon this very ground of their liberty, Gal. v, 12,13, as hath been opened above in Chapter II.

But whether the church hath power or liberty for proceeding to the utmost censure of their whole presbytery, is a question of more difficulty.

For 1. it cannot well be conceived that the whole presbytery should be proceeded against, but that by reason of their strong influence into the hearts of many of the brethren, a strong party of the brethren will be ready to side with them: and in case of finding dissention and opposition, the church ought not to proceed without consulting with the synod. As there arose dissention in the church at Antioch, and SIDING, (or as the word is στάσις) they sent up to the apostles and elders at Jerusalem, who in way of synod determined the business, Acts xv, 2 to 23. A precedent and pattern of due church proceedings in case of dissention, when some take with one side, some with another. But of that more hereafter.

2. *Excommunication* is one of the *highest* acts of *rule* in the church, and therefore cannot be performed but by some rulers. Now where all the elders are culpable, there be no rulers left in that church to censure them. As therefore the presbytery cannot excommunicate the whole church, (though apostate) for they must tell the church, and join with the church in that censure: so neither can the church excommunicate the whole presbytery, because they have not received from Christ an office of rule, without their officers.

If it be said, the *twenty-four elders* (who represent the private members of the church, as the *four living creatures* do the four officers) had all of them crowns upon their heads, and *sat* upon *thrones,* Rev. iv, 4, which are signs of regal authority: the answer is, the crowns and thrones argue them to be kings, no more than their *white raiments* argue them to be priests, ver. 4, but neither priests nor kings by office, but by liberty to perform like spiritual duties by grace, which the other do by grace and office: as priests they offer up spiritual sacrifices: and as kings they rule their lusts, passions, themselves, and their families, yea, the world and church also after a sort: the world, by improving it to spiritual advantage: and the church, by appointing their own officers, and likewise in censuring their offenders, not only by their officers, (which is as much as kings are wont to do) but also by their own royal assent, which kings are not wont to do, but only in the execution of nobles.

But nevertheless, though the church want authority to excommunicate their presbytery, yet they want not liberty to withdraw from them: for so Paul instructeth and beseecheth the church of Rome (whom the Holy Ghost foresaw would most stand in need of this counsel) to make use of this liberty: *I beseech you* (saith he) *mark such as cause divisions and offenses, contrary to the* DOCTRINE *you have received,* καὶ ἐκκλίνατε ἀπ'αὐτῶν, WITHDRAW *from them.*

So then, by the agitation of this objection, there appear two liberties of the church more to be added to the former.

One is this (which is the fifth liberty in members) the church hath liberty in case of dissension amongst themselves to resort to a synod, Acts xv, 1,2. Where also it appeareth the brethren enjoyed this libetry, to dispute their doubts till they were satisfied, ver. 7, 12, to join with the apostles and elders in the definitive sentence, and in the promulgation of the same, ver. 22,23.

The sixth liberty of the church is, to withdraw from the communion of those, whom they want authority to excommunicate. For as they set up the presbytery, by professing their subjection to them in the Lord: so they avoid them by professed withdrawing their subjection from them according to God.

A seventh and last liberty of the church, is, liberty of communion with other churches. Communion we say: for it is a great liberty, that no particular church standeth in subjection to another particular church, no, not to a cathedral church: but that all the churches enjoy mutual brotherly communion amongst themselves: which communion is mutually exercised amongst them seven ways, which for brevity and memory sake, we sum up in seven words. 1. By way of participation. 2. Of recommendation. 3. Of consultation. 4. Of congregation into a synod. 5. Of contribution. 6. Of admonition. 7. Of propagation or multiplication of churches.

1. By way of participation, the members of one church, occasionally coming to another church, where the Lord's Supper cometh to be administered, are willingly admitted to partake

with them at the Lord's Supper, in case that neither themselves, nor the churches from whence they came, do lie under any public offense. For we receive the Lord's Supper, not only as a seal of our communion with the Lord Jesus, and with his members in our own church, but also in all the churches of the saints.

2. By way of recommendation; letters are sent from one church to another, recommending to their watchfulness and communion, any of their members, who by occasion of business, are for a time to reside amongst them. As Paul sent letters of recommendation to the Church of Rome, in the behalf of Phoebe, a deaconess of the church at Cenchrea, Rom. xvi, 1,2. And of these kind of letters he speaketh to the church of Corinth also, though not as needful to himself (who was well known to them) yet for others, 2 Cor. iii, 1.

But if a member of one church have just occasion to remove himself, and his family, to take up his settled habitation in another church, then the letters written by the church in his behalf, do recommend him to their perpetual watchfulness and communion. And if the other church have no just cause to refuse him, they of his own church do by those letters wholly dismiss him from themselves; whereupon the letters (for distinction sake) are called letters of dismission; which indeed do not differ from the other, but in the durance of the recommendation, the one recommending him for a time, the other for ever.

3. By way of consultation, one church hath liberty of communicating with another to require their judgment and counsel, touching any persons or cause, wherewith they may be better acquainted than themselves. Thus the church of Antioch by their messengers consulted with the church at Jerusalem, touching the necessity of circumcision, Acts xv, 3, although the consultation brought forth a further effect of communion with churches;

to wit, their congregation into a synod. Which is the fourth way
of communion of churches: all of the churches have the like
liberty of sending their messengers to debate and determine in
a synod, such matters as do concern them all; as the church of
Antioch sent messengers to Jerusalem for resolution and satisfaction in a doubt that troubled them: the like liberty by
proportion might any other church have taken; yea, many
churches together; yea, all the churches in the world, in any
case that might concern them all. What authority these synods
have received, and may put forth, will come to be considered
in the sequel.

A fifth way of communion of churches is, the liberty of
giving and receiving mutual supplies and succors one from
another. The church of Jerusalem communicated to the churches
of the Gentiles, their spiritual treasures of gifts of grace; and
the churches of the Gentiles ministered back again to them,
liberal oblations of outward beneficence, Rom. xv, 26,27; Acts
xi, 29,30. When the church of Antioch aboundeth with more
variety of spiritual gifted men than the state of their own church
stood in need of; they fasted and prayed; as for other ends, so
for the enlargement of Christ's kingdom in the improvement of
them. And the Holy Ghost opened them a door for the succor
of many countries about them, by the sending forth of some of
them, Acts xiii, 1,2,3.

A sixth way of communion of churches is by way of mutual
admonition, when a public offense is found amongst any of
them: for as Paul had liberty to admonish Peter before the
whole church at Antioch, when he saw him walk not with a right
foot (and yet Paul had no authority over Peter, but only both
of them had equal mutual interest one in another), Gal. ii, 11
to 14. So by the same proportion, one church hath liberty to

admonish another, though they be both of them of equal
authority; seeing one church hath as much interest in another,
as one apostle in another. And if by the royal law of love, one
brother hath liberty to admonish his brother in the same church,
Matt. xviii, 15,16, then by the same rule of brotherly love and
mutual watchfulness one church hath power to admonish
another, in faithfulness to the Lord, and unto them. The church
in the Canticles took care not only for her own members, but
for her little sister, which she thought had no breast, yea, and
consulteth with other churches what to do for her, Cant. viii,
8. And would she not then have taken like care, in case their
little sister having breasts, her breasts had been distempered,
and given corrupt matter instead of milk?

A seventh way of communion of churches may be by way of
propagation and multiplication of churches: as when a particular church of Christ shall grow so full of members, as all of
them cannot hear the voice of their ministers; then as an hive
full of bees swarmeth forth, so is the church occasioned to send
forth a sufficient number of her members, fit to enter into a
church state, and to carry along church work amongst themselves. And for that end they either send forth some one or
other of their elders with them, or direct them where to procure
such to come unto them. The like course is wont to be taken,
when sundry Christians coming over from one country to
another; such as are come over first, and are themselves full of
company, direct those that come after them, and assist them in
like sort, in the combination of themselves into church order,
according to the rule of the Gospel. Though the apostles be
dead, whose office it was to plant and gather and multiply
churches; yet the work is not dead, but the same power of the
keys is left with the churches in common, and with each par-

ticular church for her part, according to their measure, to propagate and enlarge the kingdom of Christ (as God shall give opportunity) throughout all generations.

CHAPTER V

Of the subject to whom the key of authority is committed

The key of authority or rule, is committed to the elders of the church, and so the act of rule is made the proper act of their office. *The Elders that rule well, etc.,* 1 Tim v, 17, Heb. xiii, 7.17.

The special acts of this rule are many.

The first and principal is that which the *elders who labor in the word and doctrine,* are chiefly to attend unto, that is, the *preaching of the word with all authority,* and that which is annexed thereto, the administration of the sacraments or seals. *Speak, rebuke and exhort* (saith Paul to Titus) *with all authority,* Tit. ii, 15. And that the administration of the seals is annexed thereto, is plain from Matt. xxviii, 19,20. *Go* (saith Christ to the apostles) *make disciples, and baptize them, etc.*

If it be objected, private members may all of them prophecy publicly, 1 Cor. xiv, 31, and therefore also baptize: and so this act of authority is not peculiar to preaching elders.

Ans. 1. The place in the Corinths doth not speak of ordinary private members, but of men furnished with extraordinary gifts. Kings at the time of their first coronation give many extraordinary large gifts, which they do not daily pour out in like sort in their ordinary government. Christ soon after his ascension poured out a larger measure of his spirit than in times succeeding. The members of the church of Corinth (as of many other in those primitive times) were *enriched with all knowledge, and in all utterance,* 1 Cor. i, 5. And the same persons that had the *gift of prophecy* in the church of Corinth, had also *the gift of tongues,* which put upon the apostle a necessity to take them off from their frequent speaking with tongues, by preferring prophecy before it, 1 Cor. xiv, 2 to 24. So that though all they might prophecy (as having extraordinary gifts for it) yet the like liberty is not allowed to them that want the like gifts. In the church of Israel, none besides the priests and Levites, did ordinarily prophecy, either in the temple, or in the synagogues, unless they were either furnished with extraordinary gifts of prophecy, (as the prophets of Israel) or were set apart, and trained up, to prepare for such a calling, *as the sons of the prophets.* When Amos was forbidden by the high priest of Bethel, to prophecy at Bethel, Amos doth not allege nor plead the liberty of any Israelite to prophecy in the holy assemblies, but allegeth only his extraordinary calling, Amos vii, 14, 15. It appeareth also that the *sons of the prophets,* that is, men set apart, and trained up to prepare for that calling, were allowed the like liberty, 1 Sam. xix, 20.

Ans. 2. But neither the sons of the prophets, nor the prophets themselves, were wont to offer sacrifices in Israel, (except Samuel and Eliah by special direction) nor did the extraordinary prophets in Corinth take upon them to administer sacraments.

If any reply, that if the prophets in the church at Corinth had been endued with extraordinary gifts of prophecy, they had not been *subject* to the *judgment of the prophets,* which these are directed to be, 1 Cor. xiv, 22.

Ans. It followeth not. For the people of God were to examine all prophecies, *by the law* and *testimony,* and not to receive them but according to that rule, Psal. viii, 20. Yea, and Paul himself referreth all his doctrine *to the law* and *prophets,* Acts xxvi, 22. And the Bereans are commended for examining Paul's doctrine according to the Scriptures, Acts xvii, 11,12.

2. A second act of authority common to the elders, is, they have power, as any weighty occasion shall require, *to call the church* together, as the *apostles called the church together* for the election of deacons, Acts vi, 2. And in like sort are the priests of the Old Testament stirred up to call a *solemn assembly,* to gather the elders, and all the inhabitants of the land, to *sanctify a fast,* Joel i, 13,14.

3. It is an act of their power, to examine, if apostles, then any others (whether officers or members) before they be received of the church, Rev. ii, 2.

A fourth act of their rule is, the *ordination of officers* (whom the people have chosen) whether elders or deacons, 1 Tim. iv, 14; Acts vi, 6.

5. It is an act of the *key of authority,* that the elders *open the door of speech and silence* in the assembly. They were the *rulers of the synagogue,* who sent to Paul and Barnabas to open their mouths in a *word of exhortation,* Acts xiii, 15. and it is the same power which calleth men to speak, to put men to silence when they speak amiss. And yet when the elders themselves do lie under offense, or under suspicion of it, the brethren have liberty to require satisfaction, in a modest manner, concerning any public breach of rule, as hath been mentioned above out of Acts xi, 2,3, etc.

6. It belongeth to the elders to *prepare matters beforehand,* which are to be transacted by themselves, or others in the face of the congregation, as the apostles and elders being met at the house of James, gave direction to Paul, how to carry himself, that he might prevent the offense of the church, when he should appear before them, Acts xxi, 28. Hence when the offense of a

brother is (according to the rule in Matt. xviii, 17) to be
brought to the church, they are beforehand to consider and inquire whether the offense be really given or no, whether duly
proved, and orderly proceeded in by the brethren, according to
rule, and not duly satisfied by the offender: lest themselves and
the church, be openly cumbered with unnecessary and tedious
agitations: but that all things transacted before the church, be
carried along with most expedition and best edification. In
which respect they have power to reject causeless and disorderly
complaints, as well as to propound and handle just complaints
before the congregation.

7. In the handling of an offense before the church, the elders
have authority both *Jus dicere,* and *Sententiam ferre;*[15] when
the offense appeareth truly scandalous; the elders have power
from God to inform the church, what the *law* (or *rule* and
will) of Christ is for the censure of such an offense: and when
the church discerns the same, and hath no just exception against
it, but condescendeth thereto, it is a further act of the elders'
power, to give sentence against the offender. Both these acts
of power in the ministers of the Gospel, are foretold by Ezek.,
xliv, 23,24. *They shall teach my people the difference between
holy and profane, and cause them to discern between the unclean and the clean.* And in *controversy they shall stand in judgment,* and *they shall judge it according to my judgment, etc.*

8. The elders have power *to dismiss the church,* with a
blessing in the name of the Lord, Num. vi, 23 to 26; Heb.
vii, 7.

9. The elders have received power, to *charge* any of the
people in *private,* that none of them live either *inordinately*
without a calling, or *idly* in their calling, or *scandalously* in any
sort, 2 Thes. iii.6 and vers. 8,10,11,12. The apostles' command

---

[15] [To pronounce judgment and to give the sentence.]

argueth a power in the elders, to charge these duties upon the people effectually.

10. What power belongeth to the elders in a synod, is more fitly to be spoken to in the chapter of synods.

11. In case the church should fall away to blasphemy against Christ, and obstinate rejection and persecution of the way of grace, and either no synod to be hoped for, or no help by a synod, the elders have power to *withdraw* (or *separate*) the disciples from them, and to carry away the ordinances with them, and therewithal sadly to denounce the just judgment of God against them, Acts xix, 9; Exod. xxxiii, 7; Mark vi, 11; Luke x, 11; Acts xiii, 46.

Object. But if elders have all this power to exercise all these acts of rule, partly over the private members, partly over the whole church, how are they then called the *servants of the Church?* 2 Cor.iv.5.

Ans. The elders to be both servants and rulers of the church, may both of them stand well together. For their rule is not lordly, as if they ruled of themselves, or for themselves, but stewardly and ministerial, as ruling the church from Christ, and also from their call: and withal, ruling the church for Christ; and for the church, even for their spiritual everlasting good. A queen may call her servants, her mariners, to pilot and conduct her over the sea to such an haven: yet they being called by her to such an office, she must not rule them in steering their course, but submit herself to be ruled by them, till they have brought her to her desired haven. So is the case between the church and her elders.

CHAPTER VI

Of the power and authority given to synods

Synods we acknowledge, being rightly ordered, as an ordinance of Christ. Of their assembly we find three just causes in Scripture. 1. When a church wanting light or peace at home, desireth the counsel and help of other churches, few or more. Thus the church of Antioch being annoyed with corrupt teachers, who darkened the light of the truth, and bred no small dissention amongst them in the church; they sent Paul and Barnabas and *other messengers* unto the apostles and elders at Jerusalem, for the establishment of truth and peace. In joining the elders to the apostles (and that doubtless by the advice of Paul and Barnabas) it argueth that they sent not to the apostles as extraordinary and infallible, and authentical oracles of God, (for then what need the advice and help of elders?) but as wise and holy guides of the church, who might not only relieve them by some wise counsel, and holy order, but also set a precedent to succeeding ages, how errors and dissentions in churches might be removed and healed. And the course which the apostles and elders took for clearing the matter, was not by publishing the counsel of God with apostolic authority, from immediate revelation, but by searching out the truth in an ordinary way of free disputation, Acts xv, ver. 7, which is as fit a course for imitation in after ages, as it was seasonable for practice then.

2. Just consequences from Scripture giveth us another ground for the assembly of many churches, or of their messengers, into a synod, when any church lieth under scandal, through corruption in doctrine and practice, and will not be healed by more private advertisements of their own members, or of their neighbor ministers, or brethren. For there is a brotherly communion,

as between the members of the same church, so between the churches. *We have a little sister* (saith one church to another, Cant. viii, 8) therefore churches have a brotherly communion amongst themselves. Look then as one brother being offended with another, and not able to heal him by the mouth of two or three brethren privately, it behooveth him to carry it to the whole church; so by proportion, if one church see matter of offense in another, and be not able to heal it in a more private way, it will behoove them to procure the assembly of many churches, that the offense may be orderly heard, and judged and removed.

3. It may so fall out, that the state of all the churches in the country may be corrupted; and beginning to discern their corruption, may desire the concurse and counsel of one another, for a speedy, and safe, and general reformation. And then so meeting and conferring together, may renew their covenant with God, and conclude and determine upon a course, that may tend to the public healing, and salvation of them all. This was a frequent practice in the Old Testament, in the time of Asa, 2 Cron. xv, 10 to 15, in the time of Hezekiah, 2 Chron. xxix, 4 to 19. In the time of Josiah, 2 Chron. xxxiv, 29 to 33, and in the time of Ezra, Ezra x, 1 to 5. These and the like examples were not peculiar to the Israelites, as one entire *national church:* for in that respect they appealed from every synagogue and court in Israel, to the *national high priest,* and court at Jerusalem, as being all of them subordinate thereunto (and therefore that precedent is usually waived by our best divines, as not appliable to Christian churches:) but these examples hold forth no superiority in one church or court over another, but all of them in an equal manner, give advice in common, and take one common course for redress of all. And therefore such examples are fit precedents for churches of equal power within themselves, to

assemble together, and take order with one accord, for the reformation of them all.

Now a synod being assembled; three questions arise about
their power: 1. *What* is that *power* they have received? 2. How
far the *fraternity concurreth* with the presbytery in it; the
brotherhood with the eldership? 3. Whether the power they
have received reacheth to the enjoining of things, both in their
nature, and in their use indifferent?

For the first; we dare not say that their power reacheth no
farther than giving counsel: for such as their ends be, for which
according to God, they do assemble, such is the power given
them of God, as may attain those ends. As they meet to minister
light and peace to such churches, as through want of light and
peace lie in error (or doubt at least) and variance; so they have
power by the grace of Christ, not only to give light and counsel
in matter of truth and practice; but also to command and enjoin
the things to be believed and done. The express words of the
synodal letter imply no less; *It seemed good to the Holy Ghost,
and unto us, to lay upon you no other burthen,* Acts xv, 27. This
burthen therefore, to observe those necessary things which they
speak of, they had power to impose. It is an act of the binding
power of the keys, to *bind burthens.* And this *binding power*
ariseth not only *materially* from the weight of the matters imposed, (which are necessary *necessitate praecepti* from the
word) but also *formally,* from the authority of the synod, which
being an ordinance of Christ, bindeth the more for the synod's
sake. As a truth of the Gospel taught by a minister of the
Gospel, it bindeth to faith and obedience, not only because it is
Gospel, but also because it is taught by a minister for his calling's
sake, seeing Christ hath said, *Whoso receiveth you receiveth me.*
And seeing also a synod sometime meeteth to convince, and
admonish an offending church or presbytery; they have *power*

therefore, (if they cannot heal the offenders) *to determine to withdraw communion from them.* And further, seeing they meet likewise sometimes for general reformation; they have power to *decree* and publish such *ordinances,* as may conduce according to God, unto such reformation: examples whereof we read, Neh. x, 32 to 39; 2 Chron. xv, 12,13.

For the second question; how far the *fraternity,* or the brethren of the church, may *concur* with the elders in exercising the power of the synod?

The answer is; the power which they have received, is a power of liberty: As 1. They have liberty to *dispute their doubts* modestly and Christianly amongst the elders: For in that synod at Jerusalem, as there was *much disputation,* Acts xv, 7 so the multitude had a part in the disputation, ver. 12. For after Peter's speech, it is said, *the whole multitude kept silence,* and silence from what? to wit, from the speech last in hand amongst them, and that was, from disputation. 2. The brethren of the church had liberty to join with the apostles and elders, in approving of the *sentence of James,* and *determining* the same as the common sentence of them all. 3. They had liberty to join with the apostles and elders in *choosing* and *sending messengers,* and in *writing synodal* letters in the names of all, for the publishing of the sentence of the synod. Both these points are expressed in the text, vers. 22,23 to 29. Then pleased *it the apostles and elders, with the whole church, to send chosen men, and to write letters by them.* See the whole church distinguished from the *apostles* and *elders;* and those whom he called the *whole Church,* ver. 22. *he calleth the brethren,* ver. 23. *the apostles, and elders, and brethren, etc.*

But though it may not be denied, that the brethren of the church present in the synod, had all this power of liberty, to join with the *apostles* and *elders* in all these acts of the synod;

yet the *authority of the decrees* lay chiefly (if not only) in the apostles and elders. And therefore it is said, Acts xvi, 4, *that Paul and* Silas *delivered to the churches for to keep the decrees that were ordained of the apostles and elders:* so then it will be most safe to preserve to the church of brethren their due liberties, and to reserve to the elders their due authority.

If it be said, the elders assembled in a synod, have no authority to determine or conclude any act that shall bind the churches, but according to the instructions which before they have received from the churches.

Ans. We do not so apprehend it; for what need churches send to a synod for light and direction in ways of truth and peace, if they be resolved aforehand how far they will go? It is true, if the elders of churches shall conclude in a synod any thing prejudicial to the truth and peace of the Gospel, they may justly expostulate with them at their return, and refuse such sanctions as the Lord hath not sancited.[16] But if the elders be gathered in the name of Christ in a synod, and proceed according to the rule (the word) of Christ, they may consider and conclude sundry points expedient for the estate of their churches, which the churches were either ignorant or doubtful of before.

As for the third question, whether the synod have power to enjoin such things as are both in their nature and their use indifferent? We should answer it negatively, and our reasons be:

1. From the pattern of that precedent of synods, Acts xv, 18. They laid upon the churches no *other burthen,* but those *necessary things:* necessary, though not all of them in their own nature, yet for present use, to *avoid the offense* both of Jew and Gentile: of the Jew, by *eating things strangled and blood;* of the Gentile and Jew both, by *eating things sacrificed to idols,* as Paul expoundeth that article of the synod, 1 Cor. viii, 10,11,12 and x,

---

16 [A rare form of "sanctioned."]

28. This eating with offense was a murder of a weak brother's soul, and a sin against Christ, 1 Cor. viii, 11,12, and therefore *necessary* to be forborn, *necessitate præcepti,* by the necessity of God's commandment.

2. A second reason may be from the latitude of the apostolical commission, which was given to them, Matt. xxviii, 19,20. where the apostles are commanded to *teach the people to observe all things which Christ had commanded.* If then the apostles teach the people to observe more than Christ hath commanded, they go beyond the bounds of their commission and a larger commission than that given to the apostles, nor elders, nor synods, nor churches can challenge.

If it be said, Christ speaketh only of teaching such things which He had commended, as necessary to salvation.

Ans. If the apostles or their successors should hereupon usurp an authority to teach the people things indifferent, they must plead this their authority from some other commission given them elsewhere: for in this place there is no footstep for any such power. That much urged and much abused place in 1 Cor. xiv, 40, will not reach it. For though Paul requiring in that place, all the duties of God's worship, whether prayer or prophecying, or psalms, or tongues, etc. that they should be performed *decently* and *orderly,* he thereby forbiddeth any performance thereof undecently; as for men with long hair, and women to speak in open assemblies, especially to pray with their hair loose about them. And though he forbiddeth also men *speaking two or three at once,* which to do, were not *order,* but *confusion;* yet he doth not at all, neither himself enjoin, nor allow the church of Corinth to enjoin such things as decent, whose want, or whose contrary is not undecent; nor such orders, whose want or contrary would be no disorder. Suppose the church of Corinth, (or any other church or synod) should enjoin their ministers to preach in a gown. A gown is a decent garment to preach in: yet such an injunction is not grounded upon that text of the apostle. For then a minister in neglecting to preach in a gown should neglect the commandment of the apostle, which yet indeed he doth not. For if he preach in a cloak, he preacheth decently enough, and that is all which the apostle's canon reacheth to. In these things Christ never provided for *uniformity,* but only for *unity.*

For a third reason of this point, (and to add no more) it is taken from the nature of the ministerial office, whether in a church or synod. Their office is *stewardly,* not *lordly:* they are ambassadors from Christ, and for Christ. Of a steward it is required he be found *faithful,* 1 Cor. iv, 1,2, and therefore he may dispense no more injunctions to God's house, than Christ hath appointed him: neither may an ambassador proceed to do any act of his office, further than what he hath received in his commission from his prince. If he go further, he maketh himself a prevaricator, not an ambassador.

But if it be enquired, *whether a synod hath power of ordination and excommunication;* we would not take upon us hastily to censure the many notable precedents of ancient and later synods, who have put forth acts of power in both these kinds. Only we doubt that *from the beginning it was not so:* and for our own parts, if any occasion of using this power should arise amongst ourselves (which hitherto through preventing mercy it hath not) we (in a synod) should rather choose to *determine,* and to *publish* and *declare* our determination. That the ordination of such as we find fit for it, and the excommunication of such as we find do deserve it, would be an acceptable service both to the Lord, and to his churches: but the *administration* of both these acts we should refer to the *presbytery* of the *several churches,* whereto the person to be ordained is called, and

whereof the person to be excommunicated is a member: and both
acts to be performed in the presence, and with the consent of the
several churches, to whom the matter appertaineth. For in the
beginning of the Gospel in that precedent of synods, Acts xv,
we find the false teachers *declared* to be *disturbers* and *troublers*
of the churches, and *subverters of their souls,* Acts, xv, 24, but
no condign censure dispensed against them by the synod. An
evident argument to us, that they left the censure of such
offenders (in case they repented not) to the particular churches,
to whom they did appertain. And for synodical ordination, although Act. i be alleged, where Matthias was called to be an
apostle, yet it doth not appear that they acted then in a synodical way: no more than the church of Antioch did, when with
fasting and prayer they by their presbyters *imposed hands* on
Paul and Barnabas, and thereby *separated* them to the work of
the apostleship, whereto the Holy Ghost had called them, Acts
xiii, 1,2,3. Whence as the Holy *Ghost then said,* 'Αφορίσατε δὲ
μοὶ τὸν τε βαρνάβαν καὶ τὸν Σαῦλον: so thereupon Paul styleth
himself 'Απόστολος ἀφωρισμένος,[17] Rom. i, 1. And this was done
in a particular church, not in a synod.

CHAPTER VII
Touching the first subject of all the forementioned power of the keys. And an explanation of Independency

What that church is, which is the first subject of the power
of the keys, and whether this church have an independent power
in the exercise thereof, though they be made two distinct ques-

[17] [Separate indeed to me both Barnabas and Paul: so thereupon Paul styleth
himself a called apostle.]

tions, yet (if candidly interpreted) they are but one. For whatsoever is the first subject of any accident or adjunct, the same is independent in the enjoyment of it, that is, in respect of deriving it from any other subject like itself. As if fire be the first subject of heat, then it dependeth upon no other subject for heat. Now in the first subject of any power, three things concur. 1. It first receiveth that power whereof it is the first subject, and that reciprocally. 2. It first addeth and putteth forth the exercise of that power. 3. It first communicateth that power to others. As we see in fire, which is the first subject of heat: it first receiveth heat, and that reciprocally. All fire is hot, and whatsoever is hot is fire, or hath fire in it. Again, fire first putteth forth heat itself, and also first communicateth heat, to whatsoever things else are hot. To come then to the first subject of church power, or of the power of the keys. The substance of the doctrine thereof, may be conceived and declared in a few propositions. Church power is either supreme and *sovereign,* or subordinate and *ministerial.* Touching the former, take this proposition.

The Lord Jesus Christ, the *head* of his church, is the Πρῶτον Δεκτικὸν,[18] the first proper subject of the *sovereign power* of the keys. *He hath the key of David: He openeth, and no man shutteth; He shutteth, and no man openeth,* Rev. iii, 7. *The government is upon his shoulder,* Isai. ix, 6. And himself declareth the same to his apostles, as the ground of his granting to them apostolical power. *All power* (saith He) *is given to me in heaven and earth,* Matt. xxviii, 18. *Go ye therefore, etc.*

Hence 1. *All legislative power* (power of making of laws) in the church is in Him, and not from Him derived to any other, Jam. iv, 12, Isai. xxxiii, 22. The power derived to others, is only to publish and execute his laws and ordinances, and to see them

18 [First recipient.]

observed, Matt. xxviii, 20. His *laws are perfect,* Psal. xix, 9.
and do *make the men of God perfect* to every *good work,* 2 Tim.
iii, 17, and need no addition.

2.   From his sovereign power it proceedeth, that He only can
erect and ordain a true constitution of a church estate, Heb. iii,
3 to 6. *He buildeth his own house,* and setteth the pattern of it,
as God gave to David the pattern of Solomon's temple, 1 Chron.
xxviii, 19. None hath power to erect any other church frame,
than as this master-builder hath left us a pattern thereof in the
Gospel. In the Old Testament the church set up by Him was
national, in the New, congregational; yet so as that in sundry
cases it is ordered by him, many congregations or their messengers, may be assembled into a synod. Acts. xv.

3.   It is from the same sovereign power, that all the offices,
or ministeries in the church are ordained by Him, 1 Cor. xii, 5,
yea and all the *members are set in the body by Him,* together
with all the power belonging to their offices and places: as in
the natural body, so in the church, 1 Cor. xii, 18.

4.   From this sovereign power in like sort it is, that all gifts
to discharge any office, by the officers, or any duty by the members, are from Him, 1 Cor. xii, 11. All *treasures of wisdom,* and
knowledge, and grace, and the fulness thereof are in Him for
that end, Col. ii, 3 and ver. 9,10; John i, 16.

5.   From this sovereign power it is, that all the spiritual
power, and efficacy, and blessing, in the administration of these
gifts in these offices and places, for the gathering, and edifying,
and perfecting of all the churches, and of all the saints in them
is from Him, Matt. xxviii, 20. *Lo I am with you always, etc.* Col.
i, 29; 1 Cor. xv, 9.

The good pleasure of the Father, the personal union of the
humane nature with the eternal Son of God, his purchase of his

church with his own blood, and his deep humiliation of himself unto the death of the cross, have all of them obtained to Him this his highest exaltation, to be *head over all things unto the church,* and to enjoy as king thereof this sovereign power, Col. i, 19; Col. ii, 2,9,10; Acts xx, 28; Phil. ii, 8 to 11.

But of this sovereign power of Christ, there is no question amongst Protestants, especially studious of reformation. Now as concerning the *ministerial* power, we give these following *propositions.*

I. *Propos. A particular church or congregation of saints, professing the faith,* TAKEN INDEFINITELY FOR ANY CHURCH (one as well as another) *is the first subject of all the church offices, with all their spiritual gifts and power,* which Christ hath given to be executed amongst them; *whether it be* Paul, *or* Apollos, *or* Cephas, *all are yours,* (speaking to the church of Corinth, 1 Cor. iii, 22) not as a peculiar privilege unto them, but common to them with any other particular church. And theirs was such a church, of whom it is said; *that they came all together into one place,* for the communication of their spiritual gifts, 1 Cor. xiv, 23. And Paul telleth the same church, that *God hath set the officers,* and their gifts, and all variety of members, and their functions in *his church,* 1 Cor. xiv, 28, where it is not so well translated [*some*] God hath *set some* in his church, for He hath set all; but speaking of the members of the church, ver. 27, he proceedeth to exemplify those members in ver. 28. καὶ οὓς μὲν ἔθετο ὁ θεὸς ἐν τῇ ἐκκλησίᾳ, *and which God hath set in his church;* that is, which members, *apostles, prophets, etc.* For though the relative be not of the same gender with the antecedent before, yet it is an usual thing with the penmen of the New Testament, to respect the sense of the words, and so the person intended, rather than the gender of their name, and to render the relative of the same gender and case with the substantive following: so here, οὓς μὲν 'Αποστόλους, προφήτας,[19] etc.

In the New Testament, it is not a new observation that we never read of any national church, nor of any national officers given to them by Christ. In the Old Testament indeed, we read of a national church. All the tribes of Israel were three times in a year to appear before the Lord in Jerusalem, Deut. xvi, 16. And He appointed them there an high priest of the whole nation, and certain solemn sacrifices by him to be administered, Lev. xvi, 1 to 29, and together with him other priests and elders, and judges, to whom all appeals should be brought, and who should judge all difficult and transcendent cases, Deut. xvii, 8 to 11, but we read of no such national church or high priest, or court in the New Testament; and yet we willingly grant that particular churches of equal power, may in some cases appointed by Christ, meet together by themselves, or by their messengers in a synod, and may perform sundry acts of power there, as hath been showed above. But the officers themselves, and all the brethren members of the synod; yea, and the synods themselves, and all the power they put forth, they are all of them primarily given to the several churches of particular congregations, either as the first subject in whom they are resident, or as the first object about whom they are conversant, and for whose sake they are gathered and employed.

II. *Propos.* *The apostles of Christ were the first subject of apostolical power;* apostolical power stood chiefly in two things: first, in that each apostle had in him all ministerial power of all the officers of the church. They by virtue of their office might *exhort as pastors,* 1 Tim. ii, 1; *teach as teachers,* 1 Tim. ii, 7; *rule as rulers,* 2 Tim. iv, 1; *receive* and *distribute* the oblations of the church as deacons, Acts. iv, 35; yea, any one apostle or

---

[19] [Whom as apostles and prophets.]

evangelist carried about with him the liberty and power of the whole church; and therefore might *baptize;* yea, and censure an offender too, as if he had the presence and concurrence of the whole church with him. For we read that Philip baptized the eunuch without the presence of any church, Acts viii, 38. And that Paul himself excommunicated Alexander, 1 Tim. i, 20, and it is not mentioned that he took the consent of any church or presbytery in it. It is true indeed, where he could have the consent and concurse of the church and presbytery in exercise of any act of church power, he willingly took it, and joined with it, as in the ordination of Timothy, 2 Tim. i, 6 with 1 Tim. iv, 14, and in the excommunication of the incestuous Corinthian, 1 Cor. v, 4,5. But when both himself and the person to be baptized, or ordained, or excommunicated, were absent and distant from all churches, the apostles might proceed to put forth their power in the administration of any church act without them. The amplitude and plenitude of power, which they received immediately from Christ, would bear them out in it. *As my Father sent me* (saith Christ) to wit, with amplitude and plenitude of sovereign power, *so send I you* (with like amplitude and plenitude of ministerial power), John xx, 21.

2. Apostolical power extended itself to all churches, as much as to any one. *Their line went out into all the world,* Psal. xix, 4 compared with Rom. x. And as they received commission to preach and baptize in all the world, Matt. xxviii, 19. So they received charge to feed the flock of Christ's *sheep and lambs* (which implieth all acts of pastoral government over all the *sheep* and *lambs* of Christ) John xxi, 15,16,17. Now this apostolical power, centering all church power into one man, and extending itself forth to the circumference of all churches, as the apostles were the first subject of it, so were they also the last; nevertheless that ample and universal latitude of power, which

was conjoined in them, is now divided even by themselves amongst all the churches, and all the officers of the churches respectively, the officers of each church attending the charge of the particular church committed to them, by virtue of their office, and yet none of them neglecting the good of other churches,—so far as they may be mutually helpful to one another in the Lord.

III. *Propos.* When the church of a particular congregation walketh together in the truth and peace, the brethren of the church are the *first subject of church liberty,* and the elders thereof of *church authority;* and *both* of them together are the first subject of *all church power* needful to be exercised within themselves, whether in the election and ordination of officers, or in the censure of offenders in their own body.

Of this *proposition* there be three *branches:* 1. that the brethren of a particular church of a congregation, are the first subjects of church liberty: 2. that the elders of a particular church, are the first subjects of church authority: 3. that both the elders and brethren, walking and joining together in truth and peace, are the first subjects of all church power, needful to be exercised in their own body.

Now that the key of church privilege or liberty is given to the brethren of the church, and the key of rule and authority to the elders of the church, hath been declared above, in chap. 3. But that these are the first subjects of these keys; and first the church, the first subject of liberty, may appear thus.

From the removal of any former subject of this power or liberty, from whence they might derive it. If the brethren of the congregation were not the first subject of their church liberty, then they derived it either from their own elders, or from other churches. But they derived it not from their own elders: for they had power and liberty to choose their own elders, as hath been showed above, and therefore they had this liberty before they had elders, and so could not derive it from them.

Nor did they derive it from other particular churches. For all particular churches are of equal liberty and power within themselves, not one of them subordinate to another. We read not in Scripture, that the church of Corinth, was subject to that of Ephesus, nor that of Ephesus to Corinth; no, nor that of Cenchrea to Corinth, though it was a church situated in their vicinity.

Nor did they derive their liberty from a synod of churches. For we found no footstep in the pattern of synods, Acts xv, that the church of Antioch borrowed any of their liberties from the synod at Jerusalem. They borrowed indeed light from them, and decrees, tending to the establishment of truth and peace. For upon the publishing of the decrees of that synod, the churches were established in the faith (or truth), Acts xvi 4,5, and also in consolation and peace, Acts xv, 31,32, but they did not borrow from them any church liberty at all.

2. Now, the *second branch* of the *proposition* was, that the elders of the church of a particular congregation, are the first subject of rule or authority, in that church (or congregation) over which the Holy Ghost hath made them overseers.

1. From the charge of rule over the church committed to them immediately from Christ: for though the elders be chosen to their office by the church of brethren, yet the office itself is ordained immediately by Christ, and the rule annexed to the office, is limited by Christ only. If the brethren of the church should elect a presbytery to be called by them in the Lord, this will not excuse the presbyters in their neglect of rule, either before the Lord, or to their own consciences. For thus runneth

the apostle's charge to the elders of Ephesus, Acts xx, 28. *Take heed to yourselves, and to the whole flock, over which the Holy Ghost hath made you overseers.*

2. The same appeareth from the gift of rule, required especially in an elder, without which they are not capable of election to that office in the church, 1 Tim. iii, 4,5. He must be one that is able to rule well his own house, or else how shall he order the church of God? The like gift of rule is not necessary to the admission of a member into the church, as to the election of an elder: if a private brother be not so well able (through weakness in prudence or courage) to rule his own house, it will not justly debar him from entrance into the church; but the like defect will justly debar a man from election to the office of an elder. Neither hath God given a spirit of rule and government ordinarily to the greater part of the body of the brethren: and therefore neither hath he given them the first receipt of the key of authority, to whom he hath not given the gift to employ it.

If it be objected; how can the brethren of the church invest an elder with rule over them, if they had not power of rule in themselves to communicate to him?

Ans. They invest him with rule, partly by choosing him to the office which God hath invested with rule, partly by professing their own subjection to him in the Lord: we by the rule of relatives doth necessarily infer, and prefer the authority of the elders over them. For in yielding subjection, they either set up, or acknowledge authority in him, to whom they yield subjection.

Object 2. The body of the church is the spouse of Christ, the lamb's wife, and ought not the wife to rule the servants and stewards in the house, rather than they her? Is it not meet that the keys of authority should hang at her girdle rather than at theirs?

Ans. There is a difference to be put between queens, princesses, ladies of great honor, (such as the church is to Christ, Psal. xlv 9) and country housewives, poor men's wives. Queens and great persons have several offices and officers for every business and service about the house, as chamberlains, stewards, treasurers, comptrollers, ushers, bailiffs, grooms, and porters, who have all the authority of ordering the affairs of their lord's house in their hands. There is not a key left in the queen's hand of any office, but only of power and liberty to call for what she wanteth according to the king's royal allowance: which if she exceed, the officers have power to refrain her by order from the king. But country housewives, and poor men's wives, whose husbands have no officers, bailiffs or stewards, to oversee and order their estates, they may carry the keys of any office at their own girdles, which the husband keepeth not in his own hand. Not because poor housewives have greater authority in the house than queens; but because of their poverty and mean estate, they are fain to be in stead of many servants to their husbands.

Object 3.   The whole body natural, is the first subject of all the natural power of any member in the body; as the faculty of sight is first in the body, before in the eye.

Ans.   It is not in the mystical body (the church) in all respects alike, as in the natural body. In the natural body there be all the faculties of each part actually inexistent, though not exerting or putting forth themselves, till each member be articulated and formed. But in the body of the church of brethren it is not so. All the several functions of church power, are not actually inexistent in the body of brethren, unless some of them have the gifts of all the officers, which often they have not, having neither presbyters, nor men fit to be presbyters. Now if the power of the presbytery were given to a particular church of brethren, as such, *primo et per se,* than it would be found in every particular church of brethren. For a *Quatenus ad omnia valet consequentia.*[20]

Object 4. But it is an usual tenent in many of our best divines, that the government of the church is mixed of a monarchy, an aristocracy, and a democracy. In regard of Christ the head, the government of the church is sovereign and monarchical. In regard of the rule by the presbytery, it is stewardly and aristocratical: in regard of the people's power in elections and censures, it is democratical: which argueth, the people have some stock of ϰράτος,[21] power and authority in the government of the church.

Ans. In a large sense, authority after a sort, may be acnowledged in the people. As 1. when a man acteth by counsel according to his own discerning freely, he is then said to be αὐτεξούσιος,[22] *Dominus sui actus.* So the people in all the acts of liberty which they put forth are *Domini sui actus,* Lords of their own action.

2. The people by their acts of liberty, as in election of officers, and concurrency in censure of offenders, and in the determination and promulgation of synodal acts; they have a great stroke or power in the ordering of church affairs, which may be called ϰράτος, or *potestas,* a POWER, which many times goeth under the name of rule or authority, but in proper speech it is rather a privilege or liberty than authority, as hath been opened above in Chapter 3. For no act of the people's power or liberty doth properly bind, unless the authority of the presbytery concur with it.

3. A third argument whereby it may appear that the elders of a particular church are the first subject of authority in that

---

[20] [Seeing that consequently it is applicable for all.]
[21] [Power.]
[22] [Free (literally, in his own power).]

church, is taken from the like removal of other subjects, from whence they might be thought to derive their authority, as was used before to prove the church of brethren was the first subject of their own liberty in their own congregation. The elders of churches are never found in Scripture to derive their authority which they exercise in their own congregation, either from the elders of other churches, or from any synod of churches. All particular churches and all the elders of them are of equal power, each of them respectively in their own congregations. None of them call others their rabbis, or masters, or fathers (in respect of any authority over them) but all of them own and acknowledge one another as fellow brethren, Matt. xxiii, 8,9,10.

And though in a synod they have received power from Christ, and from his presence in the synod, to exercise authority in imposing burthens (such as the Holy Ghost layeth) upon all churches whose elders are present with them, Acts xv, 28 (for the apostles were elders in all churches) yet the elders of every particular church, when they walk with the brethren of their own church in light and peace, they need not to derive from the synod any power to impose the same, or the like burthens upon their own churches. For they have received a power and charge from Christ, to teach and command with all authority the whole counsel of God unto their people. And the people discerning the light of the truth delivered, and walking in peace with their elders, they readily yield obedience to their overseers, in whatsoever they see and hear by them commended to them from the Lord.

3. Now we come to the *third branch* of the third proposition, which was this. That the church of a particular congregation, elders and brethren walking and joining together in truth and peace, are the first subject of all church power, needful to be exercised within themselves, whether in the election or ordina-

tion of officers, or in the censure of offenders in their own body.

The truth hereof may appear by these arguments. 1. In point of *ordination.* From the complete integrity of a minister's calling (even to the satisfaction of his own and the people's conscience) when both the brethren and the elders of the particular church whereto he is called have put forth the power which belongeth to them about him. As, when the brethren of the church have chosen him to office, and the presbytery of the church have laid their hands upon him: and both of them in their several acts have due respect to the inward ministerial gifts whereunto God hath furnished him: he may then look at himself as called by the Holy Ghost to exercise his talents in that office amongst them, and the people may and ought to receive him, as sent of God to them.

What defect may be found in such a call, when the brethren exercise their lawful liberty, and the elders their lawful authority, in his ordination, and nothing more is required to the complete integrity of a minister's calling? If it be said there wanted imposition of hands by the bishop, who succeedeth in the place of Timothy and Titus, whom the apostle Paul left the one in Ephesus, the other in Crete, to ordain elders in many churches, Tit. i, 5.

Ans. Touching ordination by Timothy, and Titus, and (upon pretense of them) by bishops, enough hath been said by many godly learned heretofore, especially of later times.

The sum cometh to these conclusions. 1. That Timothy and Titus did not ordain elders in many churches, as bishops, but as evangelists. Timothy is expressly termed an evangelist, 2 Tim. iv, 5. And Titus is as clearly deciphered to be an evangelist as Timothy, by the characters of an evangelist, which either Scripture holdeth forth, or Eusebius noteth in his *Ecclesiast. histor., lib.* 3, *cap.* 37, *Gr. cap.* 31, *Lat.* Not to be limited to a certain church, but to follow the apostles, finishing their work in planting and watering churches, where they came. They did indeed ordain officers where they wanted, and exercised jurisdiction (as the apostles did) in several churches; yet with the rest of the presbytery, and in the presence of the whole church, 1 Tim. v. But for the continuance of this office of an evangelist in the church, there is no direction in the epistles either to Timothy or Titus, or anywhere else in Scripture.

2. *Conclus.* Those bishops whose callings or offices in the church, are set forth in those epistles to be continued; they are altogether synonyma with presbyters, Tit, i, 5,7, 1 Tim. iii, 1 to 7.

3. *Conclus.* We read of many bishops to one church, Phil. i, 1, Acts xiv, 23 chap. xx, 17, 28. Tit. i, 5,7 but not of many churches (much less all the churches in a large diocese) to one bishop.

4. *Conclus.* There is no transcendent proper work, cut out, or reserved for such a transcendent officer as a diocesan bishop throughout the New Testament. The transcendent acts reserved to him by the advocates of episcopacy, are ordination and jurisdiction. Now both these are acts of rule. And Paul to Timothy acknowledgeth no rulers in the church above pastors and teachers, who labor in word and doctrine, but rather pastors and teachers above them. The elders (saith he) that rule well, are worthy of double honor, but especially they that labor in word and doctrine, 1 Tim. v, 17.

5. *Conclus.* When after the apostles' times, one of the pastors by way of eminency was called bishop for order sake, yet for many years he did no act of power, but 1. With consent of the presbytery. 2. With consent, and in the presence of the

people. As is noted out of Eusebius, *Ecclesiast. Histor., lib.* 6, *ca.* 43, *Gr. ca.* 35, *Lat.* Cyprian *Epist., lib.* 3, *Epist.* 10 *and lib.* 1, *Epist.* 3, Casaub. *adversus Baronium, exercitat.* 15, *num.* 28.

When it is alleged out of Jerome to confirm the same, that in the primitive times, *communi presbyterorum consilio, ecclesiæ gubernabantur.*[23] It is a weak and poor evasion, to put it off with observing, that he saith, *communi presbyterorum consilio,* not *authoritate.* For. 1. No authority is due to presbyters over the bishop or pastor, no more than to the pastor over them. They are συμπρεσβύτερος, fellow-elders, and coequal in authority. And 2. when Jerome saith, the churches were governed by the common counsel of them all; it argueth, nothing was done against their counsel, but all with it, else it might be said, the bishop governed the churches with the common counsel of presbyters, to wit, asked, but not followed. And that would imply a contradiction to Jerome's testimony, to say the churches were governed by the sole authority of bishops, and yet not without asking the common counsel of the presbyters. For in asking their counsel, and not following it, the bishop should order and govern the churches against their counsel. Now that the churches were governed by the common counsel of presbyters, and against the common counsel of presbyters, are flat contradictories.

2. For a second argument, to prove that the brethren of the church of a particular congregation, walking with their elders in truth and peace, are the first subject of all that church power which is needful to be exercised in their own body: it is taken

From their indispensable and independent power in church censures. The censure that is ratified in heaven cannot be dispensed withal, nor reversed by any power on earth. Now the censure that is administered by the church of a particular congregation, is ratified in heaven. For so saith the Lord Jesus touch-

23 [The churches were governed with the common consent of the elders.]

ing the power of church censures, Matt. xviii, 17, 18. *If the
offender refuse to hear the church, let him be to thee as a
heathen and a publican. Verily I say unto you, whatsoever ye
shall bind on earth, shall be bound in heaven; and whatsoever
ye shall loose on earth, shall be loosed in heaven.*

Against this argument from this text many objections are
wont to be made, but none that will hold.

Object. 1. By *church* in Matt. xviii, 17 is not mean the
Christian church (for it was not yet extant, nor could the
apostles then have understood Christ if He had so meant) but
the Jewish church, and so He delivereth their censure, in a
Jewish phrase; to account a man as *an heathen and a publican.*

Ans. 1. The Christian church, though it was not then extant,
yet the apostles knew as well what He meant by church in Matt.
xviii, 17 as they understood what He meant by building his
church upon the rock in Matt. xvi, 18. It was enough the apostles
looked for a church which Christ would gather, and build upon
the confession of Peter's faith; and being built, should be endued with heavenly power in their censures, which they more
fully understood afterwards, when having received the Holy
Ghost, they came to put these things in practice.

Ans. 2 The allusion in the church censure to the Jewish
custom, in accounting a man as an heathen and publican, doth
not argue that Christ directeth his disciples to complain of
scandals to the Jewish synagogues; but only directeth them how
to walk towards obstinate offenders, excommunicate by the
Christian church, to wit, to walk towards them, as the Jews walk
towards heathens, (to wit, denying to them religious communion) and as toward publicans, withholding from them
familiar civil communion; for so the Jews said to Christ's disciples, *Why eateth your master with publicans and sinners?*

Ans. 3. It is not credible, that Christ would send his disciples to make complaint of their offenses to the Jewish synagogues:

For, first is it likely He would send his lambs and sheep, for right and healing, unto wolves and tigers? Both their Sanhedrim, and most of their synagogues were no better. And if here and there some elders of their synagogues were better affected, yet how may it appear that so it was, where any of themselves dwelt? And if that might appear too yet had not the Jews already agreed; *that if any man did confess Christ, he should be cast out of the synagogues,* John ix, 22.

Object. 2.   Against the argument from this text, it is objected; that by the church is meant the bishop, or his commissary?

Ans. 1.   One man is not the church.

If it be said, one man may represent a church; the reply is ready: one man cannot represent the church, unless he be sent forth by the church; but so is neither the bishop nor his commissary. They send not for them, but they come unsent for, (like water into a ship) chiefly for the terror of the servants of Christ, and for the encouragement of the profane. And though some of Christ's servants have found some favor from some few of bishops, (men of more learning and ingenuity) yet those bishops have found the less favor themselves from their fellow bishops.

Ans. 2.   The bishop ordinarily is no member of the church of that congregation, where the offense is committed, and what is his satisfaction to the removal of the offense given to the church?

Ans. 3.   The New Testament acknowledgeth no such ruler in the church, as claimeth honor above the elders that labor in word and doctrine, 1 Tim. v, 17.

Object. 3.   To tell the church, is to tell the presbytery of the church.

Ans. 1.   We deny not, The offense is to be told to the presbytery; yet not to them as the church, but as the guides of the church, who, if upon hearing the cause, and examining the witnesses, they find it ripe for public censure, they are then to propound it to the church, and to try and clear the state of the cause before the church, that so the church discerning fully the nature and quality of the offense may consent to the judgment and sentence of the elders against it, to the confusion of the offender; and the public edification of them all, who hearing and fearing, will learn to beware of the like wickedness.

Ans. 2.   The church is never put for the presbytery alone (throughout the New Testament) though sometime it be put expressly for the fraternity alone, as they are distinguished from the elders and officers, Acts xv, 22, and therefore tell the church, cannot be meant tell the presbytery alone.

Object.   In the Old Testament, the congregation is often put for the elders and rulers of the congregation.

Ans.   Let all the places alleged be examined, and it will appear that in matters of judgment, where the congregation is put for the elders and rulers, it is never meant (for ought we can find) of the elders and rulers alone, sitting apart, and retired from the congregation; but sitting in the presence of the congregation, and hearing and judging causes before them: in which case, if a sentence have passed from a ruler, with the dislike of the congregation, they have not stuck to show their dislike, sometime by protesting openly against it as 1 Sam. xiv, 44, 45, sometime by refusing to execute it, 1 Sam. xxii, 16, 17. And what the people of the congregation lawfully did in some cases, at some times, in waving and counterpoising the sentence of their rulers, the same they might and ought to have done in the like cases at any time. The whole host or congregation of Israel might protest against an unrighteous illegal sentence; and a part of the congregation, who discerned the iniquity of a sentence, might justly withdraw themselves from the execution of it.

Object. 4. When Christ said *Tell the church,* He meant a synodical or classical assembly of the presbyters of many churches. For it was his meaning and purpose in this place, to prescribe a rule for the removing of all scandals out of the church, which cannot be done by telling the church of one congregation; for what if an elder offend; yea, what if the whole presbytery offend? The people or brethren have not power to judge their judges, to rule their rulers. Yea, what if the whole congregation fall under an offense (as they may do, Lev. iv, 13) a synod of many presbyters may reform them, but so cannot any one congregation alone; if the congregation that gave the offense stand out in it.

Ans. 1. Reserving due honor to synods rightly ordered, or (which is all one) a *classic* or *convention* of presbyters of particular churches, we do not find that a church is anywhere put for a synod of presbyteries. And it were very incongruous in this place: for though it be said a particular congregation cannot reach the removal of all offenses; so it may be as truly said, that it were unmeet to trouble synods with every offense that falleth out in a congregation; offenses fall out often, synods meet but seldom; and when they do meet, they find many more weighty employments, than to attend to every offense of every private brother. Besides, as an whole particular congregation may offend, so may a general assembly of all the presbyters in a nation also: for general councils have erred; and what remedy shall be found to remove such errors and offenses out of this text? Moreover, if an offense be found in a brother of a congregation, and the congregation be found faithful and willing to remove it by due censure; why should the offense be called up to more public judicature, and the plaister made broader than the sore?

Again, if an elder offend, the rest of the presbytery with the congregation joining together, may proceed against him, (if they cannot otherwise heal him) and so remove the offense from amongst them. If the whole presbytery offend, or such, a part as will draw a party and a faction in the church with them their readiest course is, to bring the matter then to a synod. For though this place in Matthew direct not to that; yet the Holy Ghost leaveth us not without direction in such a case, but giveth us a pattern in the church of Antioch, to repair to a synod. And the like course is to be taken in the offense of a whole congregation, if it be persisted in with obstinacy. Neither is it true which was said, that it was the purpose of Christ in Matt. xviii, 17 to prescribe a rule for the removal of all offenses out of the church; but only of such private and less heinous offenses, as grow public and notorious only by obstinacy of the offenders: for if offenses be heinous and public at first, the Holy Ghost doth not direct us to proceed in such a general course from a private admonition by one brother alone, and then to a second, by one or two more, and at last, to tell it to the church. But in such a case the apostle giveth another rule, 1 Cor. v, 11, to cast an heinous notorious offender, both out of church communion, and private familar communion also.

Object. 5. The church here spoken of, Matt. xviii, 17, is such an one, as whereto a complaint may orderly be made: but a complaint cannot be orderly made to a multitude, such as an whole congregation is.

Ans. And why may not a complaint be orderly made to a

whole multitude? The Levite made an orderly complaint to a greater multitude, than four hundred particular congregations are wont to amount to, Jud. xx, 1, 2, 3, 4, etc.

Object. 6.   The church here to be complained of meeteth with authority, (for censures are administered with authority) but the church of a particular congregation meeteth with humility, to seek the face and favor of God.

Ans.   Humility to God may well stand with authority to men. The twenty-four elders (who represent the grown heirs of the church of the New Testament) they are said in church assemblies to sit upon thrones with crowns on their heads, Rev. iv, 4, yet when they fall down to worship God and the Lamb, they cast down their crown at his feet, ver. 10.

Object. 7.   In the church of a particular congregation, a woman may not speak: but in this church here spoken of, they may speak; for they may be offenders, and offenders must give an account of their offenses.

Ans.   When the apostle forbiddeth woman to speak in the church, he meaneth, speaking partly by way of authority, as in public praying or prophecying in the church, 1 Tim. ii, 12, partly by way of bold inquiry, in asking questions publicly of the prophets in the face of the church, 1 Cor. xiv, 34. But to answer it: if the whole congregation have taken just offense at the open sin of a woman, she is bound as much to give satisfaction to the whole congregation, as well as to the presbytery.

Object. 8.   When schisms grew to be scandalous in the church of Corinth, the household of Chloe told not the whole congregation of it, but Paul, 1 Cor. i, 1.

Ans.   The contentions in the church of Corinth were not the offense of a private brother, but of the whole church. And who can tell whether they had not spoken of it to the church before? But whether they had or no, the example only argueth, that brethren offended with the sins of their brethren, may tell an elder of the church of it, that he may tell it to the church, which no man denieth. Paul was an elder of every church of Christ, as the other apostles were, as having the government of all the churches committed to them all.

Having thus (by the help of Christ) cleared this text in Matt. xviii, 17 from variety of misconstructions, (which not the obscurity of the words, but the eminency of the gifts, and worth of expositors hath made difficult) let us add an argument or two more to the same purpose, to prove, that the church of a particular congregation, fully furnished with officers, and rightly walking in judgment and peace, is the first subject of all church authority, needful to be exercised within their own body.

3. A third argument to prove this, is usually and justly taken from the practice and example of the church of Corinth in the excommunication of the incestuous Corinthian, 1 Cor. v, 1 to 5.

Object. 1. The excommunication of the incestuous Corinthian, was not an act of judicial authority in the church of Corinth, whether elders or brethren, but rather an act of subjection to the apostle, publishing the sentence, which the apostle had before decreed and judged: for (saith the apostle) I though absent in body, yet present in spirit, have judged already, concerning him that hath done this deed, etc.

Ans. 1. Though Paul (as a chief officer of every church) judged beforehand the excommunication of the incestuous Corinthian: yet his judgment was not a judicial sentence, delivering him to Satan, but a judicious doctrine and instruction, teaching the church what they ought to do in that case.

2. The act of the church in Corinth in censuring the incestuous person, was indeed an act of subjection to the apostle's divine doctrine and direction (as all church censures, by whom-

soever administered, ought to be acts of subjection to the word of Christ) but yet their act was a complete act of just power, (even an act of all that liberty and authority which is to be put forth in any censure). For, first they delivered him to Satan, in the name of the Lord Jesus, and with the power of the Lord Jesus, ver. 4, and that is the highest power in the church. Secondly, the spirit of Paul, that is, his apostolic spirit was gathered together with them, in delivering and publishing the sentence; which argueth, both his power and theirs was coincident and concurrent in this sentence. Thirdly, the holy end and use of this sentence argueth the heavenly power from whence it proceeded. They delivered him to Satan for the destruction of the flesh (that is, for the mortifying of his corruption) that his soul might be saved in the day of the Lord Jesus. Fourthly, when his soul came to be humble and penitent by the means of this sentence; Paul entreated the church to release and forgive him, 2 Cor. ii, 6 to 10. Now *ejusdem potestatis est ligare et solvere, claudere et aperire.*[24]

Object. 2.   All this argueth no more, but that some in the church of Corinth had this power (to wit, the presbytery of the church, but not the whole body of the people) to excommunicate the offender.

Ans. 1.   If the presbytery alone had put forth this power, yet that sufficeth to make good the proposition, that every church furnished with a presbytery, and proceeding righteously and peaceably, they have within themselves so much power as is requisite, to be exercised within their own body.

Ans. 2.   It is apparent by the text, that the brethren concurred also in this sentence, and that with *some act of power,* to wit, such power as the want of putting it forth, retarded the

---

24 [It has the same power to bind and to loose, to close and to open.]

sentence, and the putting of it forth was requisite to the administration of the sentence.

For, first, the reproof for not proceeding to sentence sooner, is directed to the whole church, as well as to the presbytery; *They are all blamed for not mourning, for not putting him away, for being puffed up rather,* 1 Cor. v, 2.

2. The commandment is directed to them all, *when they are gathered together,* (and what is that but to a church meeting?) to proceed against him, 1 Cor. v, 5. In like sort, in the end of the chapter he commandeth them all, *Put away therefore among you that wicked person,* ver. 13.

3. He declareth this act of theirs in putting him out, to be a judicial act, ver. 12. *Do you not judge them that are within?* Say that the judgment of authority be proper only to the presbytery, yet the judgment of discretion (which as concurring in this act with the presbytery hath a power in it (as was said) may not be denied to the brethren: for here is an act of judgment ascribed to them all: which judgment in the brethren he esteemeth of it so highly, that from thence he taketh occasion to advise the members of the church, to refer their differences even in civil matters, to the judgment of the saints or brethren. *Know ye not* (saith he) that *the saints shall judge the world? yea the angels?* 1 Cor. vi, 1, 2, 3, how much more the things of this life? Yea rather than they should go to law, and that before infidels, in any case depending between brethren, he adviseth them rather to set up the means in the church to hear and judge between them, 1 Cor. vi, 4.

4. When the apostle directeth them upon the repentance of an offender, to forgive him, 2 Cor. ii, 4 to 10, he speaketh to the brethren, as well as to their elders to *forgive him.* As they were all (the brethren as well as the elders) offended with his sin:

so it was meet they should all alike be satisfied, and being satisfied should forgive him: the brethren in a way of brotherly love and church consent, as well as the elders, by sentencing his absolution and restitution to the church.

3. *Object.* But was not this church of Corinth (who had all this power) a *metropolis,* a *mother church* of Achaia, in which many presbyteries, from many churches in the villages were assembled to administer this censure?

Ans. No such thing appeareth from the story of the church of Corinth, neither in the Acts, Acts, xviii, nor from either of the Epistles to the Corinthians. True it is, Corinth was a *mother city,* but not a *mother church* to all Achaia: and yet it is not unlikely that other churches in that region, might borrow much light from their gifts; for they abounded, and were enriched with variety of all *gifts,* 1 Cor. i, 5, 7. But yet that which the apostle calleth the church of Corinth, even the *whole church* was no larger, than was wont to *meet together in one place, one congregation,* 1 Cor. xiv, 23.

A fourth and last *argument* to prove the *proposition,* that every church so furnished with officers (as hath been said) and so carried on in truth and peace, hath all church power needful to be exercised within themselves, is taken from the guilt of offense, which lieth upon every church, when any offense committed by their members lieth uncensured and unremoved. Christ hath something against the church of Pergamus, for *suffering* Balaam and the Nicolaitans, Rev. ii, 14, 15, and something against the church of Thyatira, for *suffering* Jezabel. Now if these churches had not either of them sufficient power to purge out their own offenders, why are they blamed for toleration of them? Yea, why are not the neighbor churches blamed for the sins of these churches? But we see, neither is Pergamus blamed for tolerating Jezabel, nor Thyatira for tolerating Balaam, nor Smyrna for tolerating either. Indeed what Christ writeth to any one church, his *Spirit* calleth *all the churches* to hearken unto, and so He doth our churches also at this day: not because He blamed them for the toleration of sins in other churches, but because He would have them beware of the like remissness in tolerating the like offenses amongst themselves: and also would provoke them to observe notorious offenses amongst their sister churches, and with brotherly love and faithfulness to admonish them thereof.

It is an unsound body that wanteth strength to purge out his own vicious and malignant humors. And every church of a particular congregation, being a body, even a body of Christ in itself, it were not for the honor of Christ, nor of his body, if when it were in a sound and athletic constitution, it should not have power to purge itself of its own superfluous and noisome humors.

IV. *Propos.* *In case a particular church be disturbed with error or scandal, and the same maintained by a faction amongst them. Now a synod of churches, or of their messengers, is the first subject of that power and authority, whereby error is judicially convinced and condemned, the truth searched out,* and determined, and the way of truth and peace declared and imposed upon the churches.

The truth of this proposition may appear by two arguments.

1. *Argum.* From the want of power in such a particular church to pass a binding sentence, where error or scandal is maintained by a faction; for the promise of binding and loosing which is made to a particular church, Matt. xviii, 18, is not given to the church, when it is leavened with error and variance. It is a received maxim, *Clavis errans non ligat;* and it is as true,

Ecclesia litigans non ligat:[25] and the ground of both ariseth from the estate of the church, to which the promise of binding and loosing is made, Matt. xviii, 17, 18. which, though it be a particular church (as hath been showed) yet it is *a church* AGREE-ING *together in the name of Christ,* Matt. xviii, 19, 20. *If there want agreement amongst them the promise of binding and loosing is not given to them:* or if they should agree and yet in an error, or in a scandal, they do not then agree in the name of Christ; for to meet in the name of Christ, implieth, they meet not only by his command and authority, but also that they proceed according to his laws and will, and that to his service and glory. If then the church, or a considerable part of it fall into error through ignorance, or into faction by variance, they cannot expect the presence of Christ with them, according to his promise to pass a binding sentence. And then as they fall under the conviction and admonition of any other sister church, in a way of brotherly love, by virtue of communion of churches; so their errors and variance, and whatsoever scandals else do accompany the same; they are justly subject to the condemnation of a synod of churches.

2. A second argument to prove that a synod is the first sub-ject of power, to determine and judge errors and variances in particular churches, is taken from the pattern set before us in that case, Acts xv, 1 to 28, when certain false teachers, having taught in the church of Antioch, a necessity of circumcision to salvation, and having gotten a faction to take part with them, (as appeareth by the στάσις and συζήτησις;[26] of Paul and Barna-bas against them) the church did not determine the case them-selves, but referred the whole matter to the apostles and elders

25 [A broken key has no fastening power . . . a church that quarrels has no binding power.]

26 [Dissension and disputation.]

at Jerusalem, Acts xv, 1, 2. Not to the apostles alone, but to the apostles and elders. The apostles were as the elders and rulers of all churches; and the elders there were not a few, the believers in Jerusalem being many thousands. Neither did the apostles determine the matter (as hath been said) by apostolical authority from immediate revelation; but they assembled together with the elders, to *consider of the matter,* ver. 6, and a *multitude of brethren* together with them, vers. 12, 22, 23, and after, searching out the cause by an ordinary means of *disputation,* ver. 7. Peter cleared it by the witness of the Spirit to his ministry in Cornelius his family; Paul and Barnabas by the like effect of their ministry among the Gentiles: James confirmed the same by the testimony of the prophets, wherewith the whole synod being satisfied, they determine of a judicial sentence, and of a way to publish it by letters and messengers; in which they *censure the false teachers, as troublers of their church, and subverters of their souls;* they reject the imposition of *circumcision, as a yoke which neither they nor their fathers were able to bear;* they impose upon the churches none but some *necessary* observations, and them by way of that authority which the Lord had given them, ver. 28. Which pattern clearly showeth us to whom the *key of authority* is committed, when there groweth offense and difference in a church. Look as in the case of the offense of a faithful brother persisted in, the matter is at last judged and determined in a church, which is a congregation of the faithful: so in the case of the offense of the church or congregation, the matter is at last judged in a congregation of churches, a church of churches: for what is a synod else but a church of churches?

Now, from all these former *propositions* which tend to clear the *first subject* of the power of the keys, it may be easy to deduce certain *corollaries* from thence, tending to clear a parallel question to this; to wit, *in what sense it may, and ought to be admitted that a church of a particular congregation is independent in the use of the power of the keys, and in what sense not?* For in what sense the church of a particular congregation is the first subject of the power of the keys, in the same sense it is independent, and in none other. We taking the first subject and the independent subject to be all one.

1. *Corollary.* The church is not independent on Christ, but dependent on Him for all church power.

The reason is plain, because He is the first subject of all church power by way of sovereign eminency, as hath been said. And therefore the church and all the officers thereof; yea, and a synod of churches is dependent upon Him, for all ministerial church power. *Ministry is dependent upon sovereignty;* yea, the more dependent they be upon Christ, in all the exercise of their church power; the more powerful is all their power in all their administrations.

2. *Corollary.* The first subject of the ministerial power of the keys, though it be independent in respect of derivation of power from the power of the sword to the performance of any spiritual administration, yet it is subject to the power of the sword in matters which concern the civil peace.

The matters which concern the civil peace, wherein church subjection is chiefly attended, are of four sorts.

1. The first sort be *civil matters,* τὰ βιοτικὰ, *the things of this life,* as is the disposing of men's goods or lands, lives, or liberties, tributes, customs, worldly honors, and inheritances. In these the church submitteth, and referreth itself to the civil state. Christ as minister of the circumcision, refused to take upon Him the dividing of inheritances amongst brethren, as impertinent to his calling, Luke xii, 13, 14. *His kingdom* (He acknowledgeth)

is not of this world, John xviii, 36. Himself payed tribute to Caesar, Matt. xvii, 27, for himself and his disciples.

2. The second sort of things which concern civil peace, is, the *establishment of pure religion, in doctrine, worship, and government,* according to the word of God: as also the reformation of all corruptions in any of these. On this ground the good kings of Judah, commanded *Judah to seek the Lord God of their fathers,* and to worship Him, according to his own statutes and commandments: and the contrary corruptions of strange gods, high places, images, and groves, they removed, and are commended of God, and obeyed by the priests and people in so doing, 2 Chron. xiv, 3, 4, 5; 2 Chron. xv, 8 to 16; 2 Chron. xvii, 6 to 9; 2 Chron. xix, 3, 4; 2 Chron. xxiv, 4, 5, 6, 8, 9, 10; 2 Chron xxix, 3 to 35; 2 Chron. xxx, 1 to 12; 2 Chron. xxxiv, 3 to 33. The establishment of pure religion, and the reformation of corruptions in religion, do much concern the civil peace. If religion be corrupted, there will be *war in the gates,* Judg. v, 8. *and no peace to him that cometh in, or goeth out,* 2 Chron. xv, 3, 5, 6. But where religion rejoiceth, the civil state flourisheth, Hag. ii, 15 to 19. It is true, the establishment of pure religion, and reformation of corruptions pertain also to the churches and synodical assemblies. But they go about it only with spiritual weapons, ministry of the word, and church censures upon such as are under church power. But magistrates address themselves thereto, partly by commanding, and stirring up the churches and ministers thereof to go about it in their spiritual way: partly also by civil punishments upon the wilfull opposers, and disturbers of the same. As Jehoshaphat sent priests and Levites (and them accompanied and countenanced with princes and nobles) to *preach and teach in the cities of Judah,* 2 Chron. xvii, 7, 8, 9. So Josiah put to death the idolatrous

priests of the high places, 2 King. xxii, 20. Nor was that a peculiar duty or privilege of the kings of Judah, but attended to also by *heathen princes,* and that to prevent the wrath of God, against the realm *of the king and his sons,* Ezra vii, 23, yea, and of the times of the New Testament it is prophesied, that in some cases, capital punishment shall proceed against *false prophets,* and that by the procurement of their nearest kindred, Zech. xiii, 3. And the execution thereof is described, Rev. xvi, 4 to 7, where the *rivers and fountains of waters* (that is, the priests and Jesuits, that convey the religion of the sea of Rome throughout the countries) *are turned to blood,* that is, have *blood given them to drink,* by the civil magistrate.

Nevertheless, though we willingly acknowledge a power in the civil magistrate, to establish and reform religion, according to the word of God: yet we would not be so understood, as if we judged it to belong to the civil power, to compel all men to come and sit down at the Lord's table, or to enter into the communion of the church, before they be in some measure prepared of God for such fellowship. For this is not a *reformation,* but a *deformation* of the church, and is not according to the word of God, but against it, as we shall show (God willing) in the sequel, when we come to speak of the disposition or qualifications of church members.

3. There is a third sort of things which concern the civil peace, wherein the church is not to refuse subjection to the civil magistrate, in the exercise of some public spiritual administrations, which may advance and help forward the public good of civil state according to God. In time of war, or pestilence, or any public calamity or danger lying upon a commonwealth, the magistrate may lawfully *proclaim a fast as Jehoshaphat did,* 2 Chron. xx, 3, and the churches ought not to neglect such an administration, upon such a just occasion. Neither doth it im-

peach the power of the church to call a fast, when themselves
see God calling them to public humiliation. For as Jehoshaphat
called a fast: so the prophet Joel stirreth up the priests to call a
fast in time of a famine threatening the want of holy sacrifices,
Joel i, 13, 14.

It may fall out also, that in undertaking a war, or in making
a league with a foreign state, there may arise such cases of
conscience, as may require the consultation of a synod. In which
case, or the like, if the magistrate call for a synod, the churches
are to yield him ready subjection herein in the Lord. Jehoshaphat
though he was out of his place, when he was in Samaria visiting
an idolatrous king: yet he was not out of his way, when in case
of undertaking the war against Syria, he called for counsel from
the mouth of the Lord, by a council or synod of priests and
prophets, I King. xxii, 5, 6, 7.

4. A fourth sort of things, wherein the church is not to
refuse subjection to the *civil magistrate,* is in patient suffering
their unjust persecutions without hostile or rebellious resistance.
For though persecution of the churches and servants of Christ
will not advance the civil peace, but overthrow it; yet for the
church to take up the sword in her own defense, is not a lawful
means of preserving the church peace, but a disturbance of it
rather. In this case, when Peter drew his sword in defense of his
master, (the Lord Jesus) against an attachment served upon
Him, by the officers of the high priests and elders of the people:
our Saviour bade him *put up his sword into his sheath again;* for
(saith He) *all they that take the sword, shall perish by the
sword,* Matt. xxvii, 50, 51, 52, where He speaketh of Peter,
either as a private disciple, or a church officer, to whom, though
the power of the keys was committed, yet the power of the
sword was not committed. And for such to take up the sword,
though in the cause of Christ, it is forbidden by Christ; and

such is the case of any particular church or of a synod of churches. As they have received the power of the keys, not of the sword, to the power of the keys they may, and ought to administer, but not of the sword. Wherein nevertheless, we speak of churches and synods, as such, that is, as church members, or church assemblies, acting in a church way, by the power of the keys received from Christ. But if some of the same persons be also be trusted by the civil state, with the preservation and protection of the laws and liberties, peace and safety of the same state, and shall meet together in a public civil assembly (whether in council or camp) they may there provide by civil power (according to the wholesome laws and liberties of the country) *Ne quid Ecclesia, ne quid Respublica detrimenti capiat.*[27] If King Saul swear to put Jonathan to death, the leaders of the people may by strong hands rescue him from his father's unjust and illegal fury, I Sam. xiv, 44, 45. But if Saul persecute David (though as unjustly as Jonathan) yet if the princes and leaders of the people will not rescue him from the wrath of the king, David (a private man) will not draw out his sword in his own defense, so much as to *touch the Lord' anointed,* I Sam. xxiv, 4 to 7.

To conclude this *corollary,* touching the subjection of churches to the civil state, in matters which concern the civil peace, this may not be omitted, that as the church is subject to the sword of the magistrate in things which concern the civil peace: so the magistrate (if Christian) is subject to the keys of the church, in matters which concern the peace of his conscience and the kindom of heaven. Hence it is prophesied by Isaiah, that kings and queens, who are nursing fathers and mothers to the church, *shall bow down to the church, with their faces to the earth,* Isa. xlix, 23, that is, they shall walk in professed subjection to

---

[27] [That neither the church nor the state might suffer any loss.]

the ordinances of Christ in his church. Hence also it is, that David prophesieth of *a two-edged sword,* (that is, the sword of the Spirit, the word of Christ) put *into the hands of the saints* (who are by calling the members of the church) as to subdue the nations by the ministry of the word, to the obedience of the Gospel, Psal. cxlix, 6, 7, so *to bind their kings with chains, and their nobles with fetters of iron, to execute upon them the judgment written,* (that is, written in the word), Psal. cxlix, ver. 8, 9.

3. A *third corollary* touching the independency of churches is this, that a church of a particular congregation, consisting of elders and brethren, and walking in the truth and peace of the Gospel, as it is the first subject of all church power, needful to be exercised within itself, so it is independent upon any other (church or synod) for the exercise of the same.

That such a church is the first subject of all church power, hath been cleared above in the opening the third proposition of the first subject of the power of the keys. And such a church being the first subject of church power, is unavoidably independent upon any other church or body for the exercise thereof, for as hath been said afore, the first subject of any accident or adjunct, is independent upon any other either for the enjoying, or for the employing (the having or the using) of the same.

4. A *fourth corollary* touching the independency of churches is, that a church fallen into any offense (whether it be the whole church, or a strong party in it) is not independent in the exercise of church power, but is subject both to the admonition of any other church, and to the *determination and judicial sentence* of a synod for *direction into a way of truth and peace.*

And this also ariseth from the former discourse. For, if *clavis errans non ligat, et Ecclesia litigans non ligat;*[28] that is, if Christ

28 [A broken key has no fastening powers and a church that quarrels has no binding power.]

hath not given to a particular church a promise to bind and loose in heaven, what they bind and loose on earth, unless they agree together, and agree in his name, then such a church is not independent in their proceedings, as do fail in either. For all the independency that can be claimed is founded upon that promise, *What ye bind on earth, shall be bound in heaven: what ye loose on earth, shall be loosed in heaven,* Matt. xviii, 18. On that promise is founded both the independency and *security* and *parity* also of all churches. But if that promise be cut off from them, they are like Samson when his hair was cut off, weak, and subject to fall under other men; and yet they fall softer than he did: he fell into the hands of his enemies, but they fall under the censure of their friends. As the false prophet, recanting his error did acknowledge, so may they: *Thus was I wounded in the house of my friends,* Zech. xiii, 6. In the house of a neighbor church or two, I was friendly smitten with a brotherly admonition, which (like a *precious oil*) did *not break mine head:* and in the house of a synod of churches, I was friendly, yea, brotherly censured and healed.

5. A *fifth* and last *corollary* arising from the former discourse, touching the independency of churches, may be this; though the church of a particular congregation, consisting of elders and brethren, and walking with a right foot in the truth and peace of the Gospel, be the first subject of all church power needful to be exercised within itself; and consequently be independent from any other church or synod in the use of it; yet it is a safe and wholesome, and holy ordinance of Christ, for such particular churches to join together in holy covenant or communion, and consolation amongst themselves, to administer all their church affairs, (which are of weighty, and difficult and common concernment) not without common consultation and consent of other churches about them. Now church affairs of

weighty and difficult and common concernment, we account to
be the *election and ordination of elders, excommunication of an
elder,* or any *person of public note,* and employment: the *translation of an elder* from one church to another, or the like. In
which case we conceive it safe and wholesome, and in holy
ordinance to proceed with common consultation and consent.
Safe, for *in multitude of counsellors there is safety* (as in civil,
so in church affairs), Prov. xi, 14. And though this or that
church may be of a good and strong constitution, and walk with
a right foot in the truth, and peace of the Gospel: yet all
churches are not in a like athletic plight, and they will be loath
to call in, or look out for help as much or more than others,
though they have more need than others: yea, and the best
churches may soon degenerate, and stand in as much need of
help as others, and for want of it may sink and fall into deep
apostasy, which other churches might have prevented, had they
discerned it at first.

It is also wholesome, as tending to maintain brotherly love,
and soundness of doctrine in churches, and to prevent many
offenses, which may grow up in this or that particular church,
when it transacteth all such things within itself without consent.

It is likewise an holy ordinance of Christ, as having just warrant from a like precedent. The apostles were as much independent from one another, and stood in as little need of one
another's help, as churches do one of another. And yet Paul
went up to Jerusalem to confer with Peter, James, and John,
lest he *should run in vain* in the course of his ministry, Gal. ii, 2.
And though in conference the chief apostles added nothing to
Paul, ver. 6, yet when they perceived *the Gospel of the un-
circumcision was committed to Paul and Barnabas, as that of the
circumcision to Peter, James, and John, they gave* unto one another *the right hand of fellowship.* ver. 9. Now then it will

follow by just proportion, that if the apostles who are each of them independent one of another, had need to consult and confer together about the work of their ministry, to procure the freer passage to their calling, and to their doctrine: then surely churches, and elders of churches, though independent one of another, had need to communicate their sources and proceedings in such cases one with another, to procure the freer passage to the same. And if the apostles, giving right hand of fellowship one to another, did mutually strengthen their hands in the work of the ministry: then the elders of churches, giving right hand of fellowship to one another in their ordination, or upon any fit occasion, cannot but much encourage and strengthen the hearts and hands of one another in the Lord's work.

Again, something might be added, if not for confirmation, yet for illustration of this point, by comparing the dimensions of *the new Jerusalem,* which is a perfect platform of a pure church, as it shall be constituted in the Jewish church state, at their last conversion. The dimensions of this church as they are described by Ezekiel, chap. xlviii, 30, are (according to Junius) *twelve furlongs,* which after the measure of the sanctuary (which is double to the common) is about *three miles* in length, and as much in breadth. But the dimensions of the same church of the Jews, in Rev. xxi, 16, is said to be *twelve thousand furlongs.* Now how can these two dimensions of the same church stand together, which are so far discrepant one from another? For there be a *thousand times twelve* furlongs, in *twelve thousand furlongs.* The fittest and fairest reconciliation seemeth plainly to be this, that Ezekiel speaketh of the dimensions of any ordinary Jewish church of one particular congregation. But John speaketh of the dimensions of many particular Jewish churches, combining together in some cases, even to the communion of a thousand churches. Not that the church of the Jews will be constituted in a *national* and *diocesan* frame, with *national* officers, and *diocesan* bishops, or the like: but that sometimes a thousand of them will be gathered into a synod, and all of them will have such mutual care, and yield such mutual brotherly help and communion one to another, as if they were all but one body.

If any man say, *Theologia symbolica,* or *parabolica non est argumentativa,* that arguments from such parables and mystical resemblances in Scripture are not valid, let him enjoy his own apprehension: and (if he can yield a better interpretation of the place) let him waive this collection. Nevertheless, if there were no argumentative power in parables, why did the Lord Jesus so much delight in that kind of teaching? and why did John and Daniel, and Ezekiel deliver a great part of their prophecies in parables, if we must take them for riddles, and not for documents nor arguments? Surely if they serve not for argument, they serve not for document.

But furthermore, touching this great work of communion and consociation of churches, give us leave to add this caution[b], to see that this consociation of churches be not perverted, either to the oppression or diminution of the just liberty and authority of each particular church within itself: who being well supplied with a faithful and expert presbytery of their own, do walk in their integrity according to the truth and peace of the Gospel. Let synods have their just authority in all churches, how pure soever, in determining such Διατάξεις[29] as are requisite for the edification of all Christ's churches according to God. *But in the election and ordination of officers, and censure of offenders, let it suffice the churches consociate to assist one another, with their counsel, and right hand of fellowship, when they see*

b A Caution.
29 [Arrangements.]

*a particular church to use their liberty and power aright. But
let them not put forth the power of their community, either
to take such church acts out of their hands, or to hinder them in
their lawful course, unless they see them (through ignorance or
weakness) to abuse their liberty and authority in the Gospel.*
All the liberties of churches were purchased to them by the
precious blood of the Lord Jesus: and therefore neither may the
churches give them away, nor many churches take them out of
the hands of one. They may indeed prevent the abuse of their
liberties, and direct in the lawful use of them, but not take
them away, though themselves should be willing. The Lord
Jesus having given equal power to all the apostles, it was not
lawful for eleven of them to forbid the twelfth to do any act
of his office without their intervention. Neither was it lawful
for the nine who were of inferior gifts, to commit the guidance
and command of all their apostolic administrations unto Peter,
James, and John, *who seemed to be pillars.* And that, not only
because they were all (one as well as another) immediately
guided by the Holy Ghost: but because they were all equal in
office, and every one to give account for himself unto God.

It is the like case (in some measure) of particular churches;
yea, there is moreover a three-fold further inconvenience, which
seemeth to us, to attend the translation of the power of particular churches in these ordinary administrations, into the hands of
a synod of presbyters, commonly called a *classis.*

1. The promise of *binding and loosing,* in way of discipline,
which Christ gave to every particular church (as hath been
shewed) is by this means not received, nor enjoined, nor practiced by themselves immediately, but by their deputies or overseers.

2. The same promise which was not given to synods in acts

of that nature (as hath been showed in the chapter of synods) but in acts of another kind, is hereby received, and enjoined, and practiced by them, and by them only, which ought not to be.

And which is a third inconvenience, the practice of this power of the keys only by a synod of presbyters, still keepeth the church as under nonage, as if they were not grown up to the full fruition of the just liberty of their riper years in the days of the Gospel. For a mother to bear her young daughter in her arms, and not to suffer it to go on its own feet, whilest it is in the infancy, is kindly and comely: but when the damosell is grown up to riper years, for the mother still to bear her in her arms, for fear of stumbling, it were an unnecessary burden to the mother, and a reproach to the virgin; such is the case here: the community of churches (according to the Hebrew phrase) is as the mother; each particular church is as the daughter. In the Old Testament, while the church was in her nonage, it was not unseasonable to leave the whole guidance and bearing thereof in the hands of their *tutors and governors, the priests and Levites,* and in the community of the national courts. But now in the days of the New Testament, when the churches are grown up (or should be grown at least) to more maturity, it were meet more to give the church liberty to stand alone, and to walk upon her own legs; and yet in any such part of her way, as may be more hard to hit right upon, as in her elections, and ordinances, and censures of eminent persons, in office; it is a safe and holy and faithful office of the vigilancy of the community of churches, to be present with them, and helpful to them in the Lord. And at all times when a particular church shall wander out of the way, (whether out of the way of truth, or of peace) the community of churches may by no means be excused from reforming them again into their right way, according to the authority which the Lord hath given them for the public edification of all the several churches within their covenant.

Soli Christo, τῷ A, καὶ τῷ Ω[30]

---

[30] [In Christ alone, Who is our Alpha and our Omega.]

*The Way of Congregational
Churches Cleared, 1648*

An Epistle PACIFICATORY *To the* BRETHREN
dissenting from this way

Here (reverend brethren) is presented unto you in print, that
very copy, which the worthy author (Mr. John Cotton, teacher
of the church at Boston in New England) sent together with
his letter under his own hand unto me. His honoring me therein
(upon my real account) deserved his request, *that I would assist
the press,* which with the greatest diligence opportunity put into
my hands I have performed. And the worth of the subject, and
the author's sweet and solid handling of it, hath richly rewarded
my labor, *legendo, perlegendoq;* in the usal and perusal thereof.
The *man,* most patient towards a sharp *antagonist,* (you yourselves being judges.) The *manner of handling,* gracious; meek
words, playing the champion of verity and innocency, with arguments of steel, unsheathed and shining with an amiable plainess
of speech, and a free and sincere openness of heart. The *matter*
partly *apologetical,* partly *controversial.* In the former part you
will meet with: 1. A true and terse history of the purer churches
in later puddled times: the blots aspersed upon them, clearly
pumiced and sponged off: and divers precious saints for learning
and religion (through whose sides Christ's ways by opponents
have been sorely wounded) εὐτόνως καὶ ἀναπολογητῶς[1] evidently
and unrepliably vindicated. 2. A very good account of many
singular doctrinal points, not only of more speculative theology,
ventilating the chaff from the wheat, error from truth, but of

---

[1] [Vigorously and inexcusably.]

most practical soul-searching, soul-saving, and soul-solacing divinity. I might give golden instances, glaring gloriously upon my spirit, but for falling under a leaden retarding of dispatch; fearing lest the press tarry for me; for it even treads on my heel. In the latter part of this book, being controversial, you have a fair *additional* to the[a] models (afore printed) of the church way (so much called for by you;) not magisterially laid down, but friendly debated by Scripture, and argumentatively disputed out to the utmost inch of ground, and defended *cap a pie* (as they speak) from the head to the heel, of every branch of truth essential to the controversy.[2]

Now then (worthy brethren) consider and view over what ye gain to your design, whiles some among you endeavor by pen to blot the fair copy of truth; (because *you* at *present*[b] stoop not low enough to see it a truth) and to cross out the book of men's memory and esteem the names of them whom God will honor, though you will not? Surely the copy is written out fairer and fuller; books are multiplied; more men read them; and by reason of the late mists hovering over truth, and cords of bondage straitening men's consciences; all men of conscience are more eager to search out, and having found, to stand to, and sit down by those truths that clear their minds, and set free their spirits. Mists mantling and masking, the sun ascending, are soon

---

[a] 1 Church government and Church Covenant. 2 The way of the Churches in N. England. 3 The Apologet. Narrat. 4 The Keyes of the Kingdom of Heaven. 5 The model of the Church way by M. Bartlet. 6 Answer to 32 Quest. [The first- and the last-named works in this list are the same book, by Richard Mather, which published in London in 1643 under the title of *Church-government and Church-covenant Discussed* answered thirty-two questions sent to New England. The other works are, respectively, by John Cotton (1645); Thomas Goodwin, Philip Nye, *et. al.* (1643); John Cotton (1644); and William Bartlet (1647).]

[2] [The latter part is a distinct treatise. In the original edition it is separate in pagination and signature.]

[b] I. Pet. i,12. Εἰς ἃ ἐπιθυμοῦσιν ἄγγελοι παρακύψαι. The Angels desire earnestly to stoop down to look into the things of the Gospel.

cast off, and dispelled by its beams, being near his zenith. We grasp with men of rising parts, and high places, for free speaking, about text proof points, to our loss. By an antiperistatical opposition, the zeal of godly learned writers, (before concealedly clouded with more silence) is set on fire; the cloud breaks, the voice of their thunder (as the historian speaks of that Greek commander Pericles his fulminating oratory) awakens the world, the flame burns up *the hay and stubble*.[c] Truth is like camomile; the more it is trodden, the more it spreads. Like the walnut tree, the more it is beaten for its fruit this year, the more it fructifies the next. Eclipses cause men more to stare after the sun, and more joy in the enjoying of its light, when got free. The Jews crying up Mosaical ceremonies, and humane traditions; Stephen, Peter, Paul dispute, preach, apologize for the spirituality and liberty of the Gospel.[d] What succeeds? Thousands are converted, ten thousand are convinced, and the world is *overrun with the knowledge of the truth, as the waters cover the sea*. The Gentiles likewise, (especially the Roman Empire) take the next turn to dedignify the Christians, scandalize their religious practises, and to persecute both (witness the ten persecutions.) What was the income, the return of gain upon that adventure? Up start those might giants in religion, awakened with an holy inflammation of zeal, Aristides, Justinus, Melito Apollinaris, Athenagoras, Apollonius, Tertullanus, etc. And gloriously apologize for the truth: James, Thomas, Andrew, Matthew, Philip, Mark, and others of the apostles;[e] Simon and Parmenas of the seven deacons; Simeon, Zenon, Polycarp, and millions more in ensuing ages by succession, die for Christ, and

---

[c] I. Cor. iii, 12, 13, 14, etc.

[d] Acts ii. Acts iv.

[e] *Sanguine fundata est ecclesia, sanguine crevit, sanguine succrevit, sanguine finis erit.* [The church was established in bloodshed; it grew and thrived on blood; it was renewed by blood; and its end will be in blood.]

seal to the certainty of the truth with their bloods, making glorious confessions of it, whereby many martyrizers, become martyrs. *Sanguis martyrum semen ecclesiæ*.[3] Whiles the persecutors marred (as they thought) martyrs, they made martyrs: and by their opposition they increased shrill and conspicuous confessions and professions of the truth of Jesus. In so much that Pliny a great statesman to the emperor, writes to him a persuasive to stay the persecution. At last, an emperor himself Constantine the Great, becomes a Christian, and then down went Barrabas, and Christ was exalted. The sun of the Gospel shone out once again over the face of the whole earth.

Therefore my humble request to you my reverend brethren, is, that ye more study peace, and stir up love, among brethren, and less controversy in these unparalleled times of universal contention, totally polemical, both scholastically, and civilly. And to this end let us be warned (by that good account this book renders unto us) of facile credulity, either to reports, or letters, or books, unless they be handed to us from the authors themselves, with whom ye have to do. Otherwise (as this book bears notable witness) our eyes and ears shall be abused, and our judgments warped from the simplicity and straitness of truth. Suppose any real difference should be between us; if we agree in *foundation doctrinals,* yea, and in the main principals of the *constitution* and *jurisdiction,* or power of a *particular congregational church:* as that it should consist of *saints in union,* invested with *power* to take in and cast out; I wonder it should amount to so high a contest, about degrees (which alter not the kind) of *forming* and *reforming* such a church. *You* say SAINTS in *outward profession* is the *matter* of such a church; and an implicit uniting, *viz.* a walking and communicating with you is a sufficient *evidencing of the form. We* judge that *real*

---

[3] [Martyrs' blood is the seed of the church.]

SAINTS uttering in discourse the breathings of the Holy Spirit, and experiences of conversion, witnessed in a stricter conversation, to be the *matter;* and their *solemn confession* of their faith, and *express open covenanting* with the Lord to walk with such a body of saints in all the ways of Christ to their light and power for reciprocal edification, to be the *manifest form.* How is it now that only *a going before one another in degree of reformation, according to the national solemn league and covenant,*[4] should breed in you as it were a *specifical* opposition against us? If you have a mind to ascend up higher to fetch down differences from above, about *appeals:* nor here hence is there just cause to build up such bulwarks of hostility between brethren. If in the reign of *episcopacy,* those parishes were quiet where could not be found work for the *hierarchy* to intermeddle; surely then the *classes* may conveniently permit particular congregations, (prostrated below them as it were at their feet) to rest in peace, whiles they meetly manage their own church affairs within their own sphere. If *we* need advice, we shall willingly look on a company of godly elder and brethren of other churches, called together for counsel by our, and other churches (be the assembly of them smaller, greater, or greatest) as upon an ordinance of Christ, and as bound by the truth of Christ as readily to receive, as they are to give counsel to us according to the truth. Only we

[4] [In 1643 the House of Commons strongly felt the need of Scottish help in its battle with the king, but the Scots would aid only a Presbyterian England. Accordingly, in September the Solemn League and Covenant was signed by the members of Parliament, binding them to an attempt to bring the religion of England, Scotland, and Ireland into conformity, and this Covenant was offered widely as a test of fidelity to the parliamentary cause. It did, however, contain the qualification that religion would be reformed "according to the word of God, and the example of the best reformed churches," a condition put there, it is said, by Sir Henry Vane, John Cotton's erstwhile friend and lodger when he was governor of Massachusetts Bay. This qualification allowed the dissenters to maneuver in the Westminster Assembly, and was used to justify Congregationalism, as Holmes here does, as well as to introduce New England church models.]

cannot be contented to look absolutely upon all their advice
(without exception) as *authoritative* dictates, and *magisterial
canons,* necessarily to be obeyed *sub pœna* under a penalty, how
much soever our consciences remain unsatisfied the mean whiles.

The case standing hereabouts (as near as I could rough-draw
the state of it in this instantaneous haste) let us I beseech you
be rather Irenei than Cassandri.[f] As we do, ὀρθοπολεῖν Gal. ii,14,
walk even *with the right foot in the Gospel;* so let's in discipline
(whiles the difference in the *thing* is no wider) give one another
(as the apostle speaks, Gal. ii,9), the *right hand of fellowship.*
A learned Scot well observeth,[g] that *there is a kind of justice
among thieves, else their society would soon be disbanded.* And
shall it not be among brethren, saints, ministers, least we dissolve churches, yea, ordinary communion of saints? Let *Idol
Dagon* be half fish and half man, but let not Christ be divided,
nor the profession of his truth be set at odds. If our hearts
grudge (and let that be our sorrow) yet let us not[h] gnash the
teeth and saw one another's repute a two, with the teeth of keen
words. Let not anger[i] קצף boil up into a foam, to throw the scum
upon one another. Hereby else we slay both the souls of
thousands, and the charity of 10000 to their sin, and our dis-
comfort. O it is a sad thought on my spirit, that we should
pretend to have the Paraclete (so called in many languages[j] for
its comprehensive signification of *friend, comforter, doctor,
advocate, intercessor,* etc.) that is, the *spirit* to be our *comforter,*
and yet it should appear so little in us, to *teach us* and *convince
us* of vilipending, or to work in us *love, friendship,* and *beseech-*

[f] Peace-makers, not Breach-makers.
[g] Weems. Pourtrait p.1. [John Weemes, *The Pourtraiture of the Image of
God in Man* (London, 1632).]
[h] Acts vii,54.
[i] Esther i,18. [The word signifies to be angry and to foam.]
[j] Chalde. Job xvi,20. פרקליטי/Syriac. John xvi v.7. פרקליטא Gr. παρακλητος
In N.T. often/Vet. Lat. *Paraclitus,* in N.T. often.

ings towards one another. Now that the Lord would by his Spirit, with a second conversion (as the Scripture calls the progress of mortification of some special corruption) transform our rugged hearts into love, charity, yea dilection, is the prayer of yours to serve you in the Lord, and for the Lord,

NATHANAEL HOLMES

PART I
Treatise I

CHAPTER I

Of the title inscribed to Mr. Baylie, his book,
A Dissuasive from the Errors of the Time

Noah gave it for a blessing to his son Japhet (in a word both of prophecy and prayer) *God persuade Japhet to dwell in the tents of Shem,* Gen. ix,27. And if a persuasive to dwell in the tents of Shem were a blessing; then a dissuasive from the errors of the time (rightly so called) is a blessing also. But when Mr. Baylie is pleased amongst the errors of the time to reckon (that which he calleth) Independency; he may do well to consider, whether he bring not upon his credulous reader a curse instead of a blessing.

The supposed errors found in those who are called Independent Churches, are chiefly two, upon which all the rest do depend: and both of them such as may well be cleared by Noah's blessing.

For, 1. they hold that Cham and Chanaan, whilst they are such, (that is, graceless persons, and scorners at the falls and infirmities of the saints) they are not to dwell in the tents of Shem. Noah did not pray for such a blessing to them; yea, it had been a curse both to them and Shem (if he had so prayed) and not a blessing.

2. They hold also, that Japhet himself should not be brought to dwell in the tents of Shem till God persuade him. They would

not have Shem to enlarge his tents, to compass or compel Japhet
to live under his shadow. It is one thing for Japhet and Shem to
dwell together by voluntary consociation; another thing for
Shem to rule over Japhet by undesired and unallowed jurisdiction. Let Cham and Chanaan be as servants unto Shem and to
Japhet too, (for so Noah prophesied) but let not Japhet be a
servant to Shem, no more than Shem to Japhet. But though these
be the principal tenents of Independents (as they are called;)
and indeed blessed truths in the blessing of Noah: yet Mr.
Baylie reckoneth these amongst the errors of the times; and the
Independents themselves amongst the wanderers on the right
hand, together with the Brownists, (as he calleth them,)
Anabaptists, Antinomians, Seekers: as on the left hand, he reckoneth Prelates, Papists, Arminians, Socinians, Erastians.[5] And it

---

[5] [If they were given their modern political meaning, the words "right" and
"left" would here be reversed, because those groups designated by Cotton as to
the right are the more radical ones. Independents were those who though they
did not conform with the established church yet did not separate from it but
attempted to practice a form of church government in which each congregation
accepted to membership only visible saints, and chose and ordained its own
presbytery independent of any ecclesiastical hierarchy. Brownists practiced essentially the same form of church government but separated from communion with
the Church of England. Anabaptists denied that infant baptism was true baptism,
and were severely denounced by the New England orthodoxy as well as by the
established church; this belief gained its first English adherents within the Separatist congregations. Antinomians believed that Christians are set free by grace
from the need to observe the moral law, and the term was loosely applied to many
extremists who seemed to explain their behavior by attributing it to the Holy
Spirit within them. The Seekers were a small sect who believed that the true
church had ceased to exist when the spirit of Antichrist became dominant in
history, and that God would eventually send the way to a new church through
new apostles and prophets so that man must passively await their appearance, a
quietistic view which gives them a certain kinship with the Quakers. Prelates
were, in effect, those who accepted the episcopal form of the church as it crystal-
lized under Whitgift and was defended by Richard Hooker's *Of Laws of Ecclesiastical Polity* (London, 1594–1597). Papists were Roman Catholics. Arminianism
within the Church of England opposed the determinism of Calvinist theology,
insisting that divine sovereignty and human free will were compatible and that
Jesus died for all men, not just for the elect. Socinians denied the essential
divinity of Christ. Erastians maintained the supremacy of the state over the
church, even in such matters as excommunication, and were men strongly opposed

should seem, he taketh Independents to be one of the most dangerous sects of them all, (at least, as the state of the times now standeth:) or else he would not have addressed all the whole force of his discourse against them: only taking up Brownists (as he styleth them) by the way, to usher in the other with the greater prejudice. But for my part, I dislike not Mr. Baylie's zeal against errors where it is rightly placed; only let him allow the like liberty to us, which he taketh to himself, that as he publisheth a dissuasive against errors, so we may have leave to bear witness to the truth.

CHAPTER II
Of those whom the Dissuader styleth Brownists

SECTION I

Master Baylie rightly observeth, that in our departure and flight from Rome, some took up their stand too soon, before they had passed the lines (he meaneth all the lines) of communication with the whore: and others ran on too long (or too far) beyond the bounds of truth and love. The former of these sorts he maketh the Lutherans, in respect of some defects in their reformation. The latter, he maketh to be the Anabaptists in Germany. The successors of the former, he maketh to be Cranmer, Ridley, and those other confessors and martyrs who settled episcopacy and ceremonies in England. The successors of the latter sort, (the Anabaptists) he maketh to be those whom he styleth Brownists.

But as there is a vast difference between the episcopacy of

to Independency. As can be seen, the groups listed are by no means mutually exclusive since some are theological and others political so that, for instance, one could belong to two or more. Still, they tended to join into automatic couplings, so that, for instance, Anabaptists were mainly Brownists and Prelates were frequently Erastians.]

England and the superintendency of Germany, (the one ruling
by monarchical power, the other by the consent of the aristocratical presbytery:) so neither is there such correspondency
between the German Anabaptism, and the English Brownism,
as to make Brownism a native branch of Anabaptism.

Yes, (saith the Dissuader) that Brownism is a native branch
of Anabaptism, is evidenced, by the frequent transition of the
one to the other. The dissolution of ice and snow into water,
argueth strongly their original from that element; so the ordinary running over of the Separatists to the Anabaptists.

Ans. The dissolution of ice and snow into water, doth indeed argue strongly their original from water, because they are
easily resolved into it without putrefaction or corruption. But
so is not the Separatist resolved into a German Anabaptist,
without a further degree of corruption and putrefaction. It is
no argument a man is bred of worms, because he is next resolved
into worms; for he is not so resolved without putrefaction. Say
not, a man is resolved at last into dust from whence he was first
taken; and yet the resolution is not made without putrefaction.
For a man is not made of dust naturally, but by a transcendent
creating power above nature. But the Dissuader maketh the
Separation a native branch of Anabaptism.

Besides, I suppose, it is not an obvious thing to hear of an
Anabaptist turn Separatist, though some Separatists have turned
Anabaptists; which argueth there is not such a mutual frequent
transition from the one to the other, as is yearly found of ice
and snow into water, and of water into ice or snow again.

SECTION II

The first Separatist, which the Dissuader saith he hath read
of, was one Bolton, who was a minister of an old separate congregation, and afterwards felt the sense of his errors so grievous

to his soul, (by the finger of God's justice stirring in his conscience) that he did not only publicly at Paul's Cross recant them, but thereafter was so dogged with a desperate remorse, that he rested not till he had hanged himself.

Ans. 1.   Though Bolton may have been the first Separatist that the Dissuader hath read of; yet he might have read of others before him. For in the book called The Register of memorable matters touching Reformation,[6] there is recorded a story of an hundred persons, who refused the common liturgy, and the congregations attending thereunto, and used prayers and preachings, and sacraments amongst themselves; whereof fourteen or fifteen were sent to prison: of whom the chiefest was Mr. Smith, with Mr. Nixon, James Ireland, Robert Hawkins, Thomas Boweland, and Richard Morecroft. And these pleaded their separation before the Lord Mayor, Bishop Sands, and other commissioners on June 20 in the year 1567, which is about fourscore years ago; and this as it seemeth was many years before Bolton; for Mr. Baylie reckoneth the wandering of the Separatists to be about fifty years standing, (page 59) but this Smith and his company was thirty years before.

Ans. 2.   Old Mr. Brewster (the reverend elder of the church of Plymouth, a man of long-approved piety, gravity, integrity) his testimony of this Bolton may take off the prejudice which the fearful fall of Bolton seemeth to Mr. Baylie to cast upon Separation:[7] which I will recite, not to justify that way of his separation, but to take off unjust scandals. "This Bolton (saith he) partly by the terrors of bishops, and partly by flattery, was brought indeed to recant. But afterwards they sleighting him, the terrors of the Almighty fell upon him, and considering how

6 [*A Parte of a Register, Contayninge Sundrie Memorable Matters* (London, 1593).]

7 [Apparently in an unpublished letter or in conversation.]

he had sinned against his conscience, he (Judas-like) laid violent hands upon himself."

But the Dissuader may be pleased to consider, that apostasy from the way of Separation, and terror of conscience even to desperation, and self-murder following thereupon, are no just exceptions against Separation: no more than Judas his apostasy from Christ, and terror of conscience even to desperation and self-hanging following thereupon, were any just exceptions against Christianity.

SECTION III   *Of Mr. Brown, and Barrow*

Of Mr. Brown and Mr. Barrow, it is far from me to make any defense either of their persons, or of their way of rigid Separation: the hand of God upon their spirit, giving them up, one to a spirit of inconstancy and profaneness, the other to a spirit of bitterness and rashness. Though it is no just conviction of the errors of their way of Separation: yet it is a shrewd argument that either their way was not right, or their hearts not upright in it.

But this let me say, be it so, that Brown did revolt from his way, and took a parsonage from the bishop, and that in a town by name called Achurch in Northamptonshire, (a real check to his error, who formerly counted every church in England no church) yet this backsliding of Brown from that way of Separation, is a just reason why the Separatists may disclaim denomination from him, and refuse to be called after his name, Brownists. If Judas, or Julian, or Ecebolius do apostate from Christianity, no reason is there that all that profess the way of Christianity should be called Judaites, or Julianists, or Ecebolians. In Ecclesiastical History,[8] though Photinus was the disciple of Marcellus

---

8 [*Ecclesiastical History*, by Eusebius (ca. 260–ca. 340) is the principal source for the history of Christianity from the apostles to the time of its composition.]

in an heretical opinion touching Christ: yet the followers of
them both, when Marcellus had revoked his error, were not
called Marcellini but Photiniani. To speak with reason, if any
be justly to be called Brownists, it is only such as revolt from
Separation to formality, and from thence to profaneness. For
Mr. Barrow, though I neither excuse the unsoundness of his
judgment, nor the bitterness of his style: yet I doubt the Dissuader is deceived, when he saith that Queen Elizabeth was so
impatient of his contumelies, that she caused him in a morning
to be hanged on the Tower-hill. For there be grave professors
(who lived nearer those occurences) who speak of Queen
Elizabeth as ignorant of Barrow's execution, and Greenwood's,
and displeased at it, when she heard of it afterwards: neither
was their execution on Tower-hill but at Tyburn, long after the
sentence of death passed against them.

SECTION IV   *Of Mr. Johnson and Mr. Ainsworth*

The Dissuader is deceived when he saith, Mr. Ainsworth
with his half, did excommunicate Mr. Johnson and his half.
For as I am informed by some judicious professors who lived
in those parts, Mr. Ainsworth and his company did not excommunicate Mr. Johnson and his, but only withdrew from them,
when they could no longer live peaceably with them. Mr. Johnson his last book[9] argueth he had learned more moderation of
spirit, then he did put forth in his former times.

Mr. Ainsworth, a man of a more modest and humble spirit,
and diligently studious of the Hebrew text, hath not been unuse-
ful to the church in his Exposition of the Pentateuch,[10] especially

9 [Henry Ainsworth and Francis Johnson, *A Christian Plea* (Amsterdam,
1604).]

10 [Henry Ainsworth's annotations on the Five Books of Moses began appearing in London in 1616, all five books being annotated by 1619 with the Psalms
and the Song of Songs added in some editions after 1627. Each of the forms of
his annotations had frequent reprintings.]

of Moses his rituals, notwithstanding some uncircumcised, and ungrounded rabbinical observations recited, but not refuted.

But when the Dissuader saith, that Mr. Ainsworth's company after his death, remained long without all officers;

There be sundry living that know the contrary. For when he died he left two elders over the church, Mr. Delacluse, and Mr. May.

And therefore I do not see any ground of that speech,

That the weight and evidence of God's hand against Ainsworth had so far disgraced that sect, as the Dissuader expresseth. For though in simplicity of heart, in some things he went astray: yet the way he walked in, did not suffer disgrace by him, nor by the weight and evidence of God's hand upon him, for ought I have ever heard or read of him, save in Mr. Baylie. The Lord knoweth how to be merciful to such as seek him in simplicity of heart, according to light revealed, though he do observe and chasten some error in their way.

SECTION V   *Of Mr. Smith and Mr. Robinson*

The fall indeed of Mr. Smith, and the spirit of errors and instability that fell upon him, was more observable: and a dreadful warning from heaven, against αὐθάδεια self-fulness, and self-pleasing. For though the tyranny of the ecclesiastical courts was harsh towards him, and the yokes put upon him in his ministry, too grievous to be borne: yet neither was he alone in suffering: nor were those that suffered with him at that time, (Mr. Clifton, and Mr. Robinson) such inconsiderable persons, that he should affect to go alone from them. It is true, he had found help by the conference (which himself had requested) with Mr. Dod, Mr. Hildersam, and Mr. Barbon, before he left England; yea and such helps, that he thought he could have gained his tutor Johnson, from the errors of his rigid separation. But he had promised them, not to go over to him, without their consents: and they utterly dissuaded him therefrom, as fearing his instability. And yet contrary to his promise he went over to him, yea, and that contrary to his own pretense and offer of another conference with them before his going. Though the way of rigid separation had been less heterodoxall than it is, yet to venture upon it in such breach of manifest rules, no marvel, if it led him into manifest temptations and aberrations.

The Dissuader is misinformed when he saith (page 16) he moved a great company to follow him to Leyden in Holland. For as I understand by such as lived in those parts at that time, he lived at Amsterdam and there died, and at Ley in Holland he never came.

Of Mr. Robinson, the Dissuader doth rightly observe, that he was a man of the most learned, polished, and modest spirit of that way, and withal he might have said, so piously studious and conscientiously inquisitive after the truth, that (as the Dissuader rightly observeth) it had been truly a marvel, if such a man as he, had gone on to the end a rigid Separatist.

As a fruit of his studious inquisition after the truth, he resorted (as I have understood) to many judicious divines in England for the clearing of his scruples, which inclined him to separation: and when he came into Holland, he addressed himself to Dr. Ames, and Mr. Parker: rather preventing them with seeking counsel and satisfaction, than waiting for their compassion. But as they excelled in learning and godliness, so in compassion and brotherly love also; and therefore as they discerned his weanedness from self-fulness, so did they more freely communicate light to him, and received also some things from him. The fruit of which was (through the grace of Christ) that the Dissuader himself confesseth, he came back indeed the one half of the way: acknowledging the lawfulness of communicating with the Church of England, in the word and prayer; but not in the sacraments and discipline, which was (saith he) a fair bridge, at least a fair arch of a bridge for union. But when he saith, he came on to communicate with the Church of England in the word and prayer, it must not be understood of the Common Prayer Book, but of the prayers conceived by the preacher before and after sermon: and yet in coming on so far as he did, he came more than half way of any just distance.

For though he stuck at the common liturgy, sacraments and discipline: yet since then it hath appeared, there was no just ground of coming on to them. The honorable Parliament, and reverend Assembly of Divines have (by the grace of Christ) seen just cause to remove the liturgy, to abolish the hierarchy (which was the discipline he chiefly stuck at) and to give order for restraint of ignorant and scandalous persons from the sacrament, which may well make up two or three arches more (as Mr. Baylie calleth it) of that fair bridge for union, far more than the half way.

It is true, Mr. Robinson did not acknowledge a national church governed by the episcopacy to be a church of divine institution. But though he acknowledged the style and privileges of a church in the New Testament to belong to a particular congregation of visible saints; yet such national churches, French or Dutch, as were governed by presbyters, and separate from the world at the Lord's Table, he did not disclaim communion with them, I have been given to understand, that when a reverend and godly Scottish minister came that way, (it seemeth to have been Mr. John Tarbes) he offered him communion at the Lord's Table: though the other for fear of offense to the Scottish churches at home, excused himself. Yea when some English men that offered themselves to become members of his church, would sometimes in their confessions profess their separation from the Church of England, Mr. Robinson would bear witness against such profession: avouching, they required no such professions of separation from this or that, or any church, but only from the world. All which do argue, that his coming on to Protestant churches, was more than the half way. But (saith the Dissuader) this new doctrine (or way) of Mr. Robinson, though it was destructive to his old sect; yet it became an occasion of a new one, not very good. It was the womb and seed of that lamentable Independency in Old and New England, which hath been the fountain of many evils already though no more should ensue, as anon shall be declared.

Ans. When this cometh to be declared, I hope it will come to be declared also, that the way of Independency hath been bred in the womb of the New Testament of the immortal seed of the word of truth, and received in the times of purest primitive antiquity, many hundreds of years before Mr. Robinson was born: and that it hath not been the fountain of any evils at all, much less of such evils, as to deserve the style of lamentable Independency.

SECTION VI *Of the contempt and contumely said to be put upon the old Brownists by the Independents*

To shut up this chapter, the Dissuader telleth us, That the way of the old Brownists is become contemptible not only to all the rest of the world, but to their own children also; even they begin to heap coals of contumelies upon their parents' heads; as may be seen in the elegies which both Mr. Cotton, and the five apologists[11] are pleased to give them in print; yea, so much are

11 [The five authors of *An Apologeticall Narration*: Thomas Goodwin, Philip Nye, Sidrach Simpson, Jeremiah Burroughes, and William Bridge.]

these children ashamed of their fathers, that they usually take it for a contumely to be called after their name. No Independent will take it well at any man's hand to be called a Brownist either in whole, or in the smallest part.

Ans. 1.   No marvel, if Independents take it ill to be called Brownists, in whole or in part. For neither in whole, nor in part do we partake in his schism. He separated from churches and from saints; we only from the world, and that which is of the world. He turned apostate from the Separation which he had professed: and it is absurd to denominate either sect or right way, from such as apostate from it. If he had stood constant in his way, and his way had been the same with ours, yet we were not baptized into his name; and why should we then be called after his name? If schism be a manifest fruit of the flesh, then they that give nicknames tending to the reproach and division of brethren, they walk after the flesh; for they sow variance and schism amongst brethren.

2.   It is an unjust and unworthy calumny, to call either Cotton or the Apologers, the children of their fathers, whom he styleth Brownists. They never begot us, either to God, or to the church, or to their schism: a schism, which as we have lamented in them (as a fruit of misguided ignorant zeal) so we have ever born witness against it, since our first knowledge of it.

3.   Though we put not such honor upon those he calleth Brownists, as to own them for our fathers; yet neither do we put so much dishonor upon them, as to heap coals of contumely upon their heads. We look not at them with contempt, but compassion: neither do we bear witness against their schism in any words of contempt and reproach, (which are the characters of contumely) but in words of spiritual and just reproof; even in such terms, not which scornful wit, but which holy Scripture suggesteth.

CHAPTER III

An answer to the Dissuader's 3 chap. touching the
original and progress of the Independents
in New England

SECTION I   *Of the title put upon us of* $\begin{cases} A \ Sect, \\ Independents \end{cases}$

The way of the churches in New England is neither justly
called a sect, nor fitly called Independency. Not a sect; for we
profess the orthodox doctrine of faith, the same with all Protestant churches; we celebrate the same sacraments; and submit to
the spiritual government of the same lawful guides, so far as
Christ and our own choice hath set them over us. And though
we do not subject ourselves to the government of the elders of
other churches, (as many great churches do,) yet we acknowledge and reverence such churches in the Lord, as true churches
of Christ, and are willing to make use of their brotherly counsel
and help as need shall require.

And though we do not open the doors of our churches so
wide, as to receive all the inhabitants of a nation, or of every
town, into the fellowship of our churches; yet we do not
separate from such Protestant churches as do take that liberty:
but only we separate from the world, that is, from the worldly
sort of them, who either live in open scandal, or at least do not
openly hold forth any spiritual discerning of the Lord's body,
and are therefore unmeet to communicate at the Lord's Table.

Nor is Independency a fit name of the way of our churches.
For in some respects it is too strait, and in others too large; it is
too strait, in that it confineth us within ourselves, and holdeth
us forth as Independent from all others: whereas indeed we do
profess dependence upon magistrates for civil government and
protection; dependence upon Christ and his word, for the

sovereign government and rule of our administrations: dependence upon the counsel of other churches and synods; when
our own variance or ignorance may stand in need of such help
from them. And therefore this title of Independency straitneth
us, and restraineth us from our necessary duty, and due liberty.

Again, in other respects, Independency stretcheth itself too
largely, and more generally, than that it can single out us. For
it is compatible to a national church, as well as to a Congregational. The national church of Scotland is independent from the
government of the national church of England; and so is England independent from Scotland. Nor is there any sect at this
day extant, but shroudeth themselves under the title of Independency. The Antipedobaptists, Antinomians, Familists, yea,
and the Seekers too, do all of them style themselves Independents.[12] Nay, even the Pope himself, (who exalteth himself
above all civil and church-power) yet even he also arrogateth
the title of Independency; *prima sedes à nemine judicatur;* that
is, the See of Rome is independent. Why then should Independency be appropriated to us, as a character of our way, which
neither truly describeth us, nor faithfully distinguisheth us
from many others? Wherefore if there must needs be some note
of difference to decipher our estate, and to distinguish our way
from a national church way, I know none fitter, then to denominate theirs Classical, and ours Congregational.

SECTION II *Of the number of the Congregational
regiment, and of the wisdom threaped upon them,
in engaging persons of note to them*

The Dissuader acknowledgeth, we are not numerous, but the
fewest in number of the noted sects, and not to consist of above

---

12 [Familists were members of a sect called the Family of Love who maintained a mystic pantheism mixed with Antinomianism. Antipedobaptists are
Anabaptists, for which, as for Seekers, see note 5, p.175]

one thousand persons within the lines of the cities' communication.

Ans. 1.   If we be the fewest of noted sects, it was sometime the lot of God's Israel to be the fewest of all people, Deut. vii,7.

Ans. 2.   If there be a thousand of our way within the lines of the cities' communication, I hope there want not divers more to be added to them in other parts of England, besides some thousands more in New England. But it is not for us to follow David's sin in numbering the people of the Lord; only the Lord increase their number an hundreth fold, (yea, a thousand fold) and make them as the stars of heaven for multitude.

But for the quality of the persons, the Dissuader telleth us, they have been so wise, as to engage to their party some of chief note in both Houses of Parliament, in the Assembly of Divines, in the Army, in the City, and Country Committees.

But in so saying, the Dissuader putteth a dishonor both upon God, and upon those persons of chief note. It is a dishonor to God, to attribute that to the wisdom of man, which is the mighty and gracious work of the wisdom of God. And it is a dishonor to such men, to hold them forth as engaged to this way by the wisdom and industry of men, who have been well known (and some of them for many years) not to have engaged themselves or others any further, than the grace of Christ, and the conscience of his word hath engaged them to do and suffer, according to the will of God.

SECTION III   *Touching the line of the pedigree of the Independents in New England*

The Separatists (saith the Dissuader) were their fathers. This is demonstrable not only by the consanguinity of their tenents (the one having borrowed all their chief doctrines and practices from the other), but also by deduction of their pedigree in this clear line. Mr. Robinson did derive his way to his Separate congregation at Leyden; a part of them did carry it over to Plymouth in New England: here Mr. Cotton took it up, and did transmit it to Mr. Goodwin, who did help to propagate it to sundry others in Old England first, and after to more in Holland; till now by many hands it is sown thick in divers parts of the kingdom.

Ans. That the Separatists were our fathers, we have justly denied it above; seeing they neither begat us to God, nor to the church, nor to their schism. That we are (through grace) begotten to God, and to his church, we received (many of us) from the blessing of Christ upon the ministry of England. That we grew weary of the burden of episcopacy and conformity, we received from the word of God by the help of the nonconformists there. That we laid aside the Book of Common Prayer, we received from the serious meditation of the second commandment, and not from the writings of the Separatists, though they also had taken up the same conclusion upon other premises. The particular visible church of a congregation to be the first subject of the power of the keys, we received by the light of the word from Mr. Parker, Mr. Baynes, and Dr. Ames: from whom also (from two of them at least) we received light out of the word, for the matter of the visible church to be visible saints; and for the form of it, to be a mutual covenant, whether an explicit or implict profession of faith, and subjection to the Gospel of Christ in the society of the church, or presbytery thereof. And these be the chief doctrines and practices of our way, so far as it differeth from other reformed churches. And having received these, not from the Separatists, but from the Lord Jesus, by gracious saints, and faithful witnesses of Jesus; the consanguinity of our tenents with any the like found amongst the Separatists, will not demonstrate the Separatists to be our fathers.

It is very likely (and by the fruits of some of them, it is very evident) that the church of Plymouth in New England received very much light and life, by the blessing of Christ upon Mr. Robinson his ministry, whilst he lived with them in Holland: nor need we to be ashamed, to learn any truth of God from him, or them, or from any other saints of God, of far meaner gifts, than he or they had received. But I must confess ingenuously, that his denial of the parishional congregations in England to be true churches (either by reason of their mixed and corrupt matter, or for defect in their covenant, or for excess of their episcopal government) was never received into any heart, from thence to infer a nullity of their church-estate. Neither was our departure from them even in those evil times, a separation from them as no churches; but rather a secession from the corruptions found amongst them, unto which also we must have been forced to conform, even in our own practice through the rigor of the times, unless we had timely departed from them. In which case, Doctor Ames will excuse us (yea and the Holy Ghost also) from aspersion of schism or any other sin, in so doing. *De Conscientia, lib.* 4, *cap.* 24, *numero* 16, *in responsione* 7 *ad quæst.* 3.

The Dissuader is mistaken (when he saith page 54) that after the death of Ainsworth, there remained only a small handful of Separatists at Amsterdam, and another small company at Leyden, under Mr. Robinson's ministry, and besides them, no other at that time were known in the world of that religion.

For Mr. Jacob, whom Mr. Lothrop succeeded and after him Mr. Barbon being an elder governed the same separate church in Leyden which held communion with Mr. Robinson's church,

as appeareth by their letters published in print. And that church
as it began before Mr. Robinson, so it continued after him, and
still doth. And it is no less a mistake, when the Dissuader
maketh the divisions in Mr. Robinson's church, or his desertion
of many of their principles to be an occasion of well-near bring-
ing that church to nought: till some of them went over to New
England, and persuaded their neighbors who sate down with
them in New Plymouth to erect with them a congregation after
their separate way.

For the church at Leyden was in peace, and free from any
division, when they took up thoughts of transporting themselves
into America with common consent. Themselves do declare it,
that the proposition of removal, was set on foot and prosecuted
by the elders upon just and weighty grounds. For (to use their
own words) though they did quietly and sweetly enjoy their
Christian and church liberties under the States; yet they foresaw
Holland would be no place for their church, and their posterity
to continue there comfortably: at least in that measure, which
they hoped to find abroad, and that for these reasons, which I
shall recite, as I received them from themselves.

1. Because themselves were of a different language from
the Dutch where they lived, and the Dutch were settled in their
way; in so much that in ten years' space, whilst their church
sojourned amongst them, they could not bring them to reform
the neglect of the Lord's Day, or any other thing amiss amongst
them.

2. Because their countrymen who came over to join with
them, by reason of the hardness, and chargeableness of the
country, soon spent their estates, and then were forced either to
return back for England, or to live very meanly.

3. Because the country was a place of so great liberty to

children, that they could not educate their children, as their parents had educated them: nor could they give them due correction, without reproof and reproach from their neighbors.

4.   Because their posterity would in a few generations become Dutch, and so lose their interest in the English nation, name and language.

These being debated at first in private, and thought weighty, were afterwards propounded in public, and after solemn days of humiliation both in public and private, it was agreed that part of the church should go before their brethren into America to prepare for the rest: and in case the major part of the church did choose to go over with the first, then the pastor to go along with them. But if the major part stayed, then he to stay with them: and to follow afterwards, when they should hear out of America of their safety and health, and possibility of subsistence: but the Lord translated him to himself, before the rest could prepare to go along to their brethren. Notwithstanding when the first company embarked themselves for America, their brethren accompanied them to the sea, and took their leaves with such abundant expressions of brotherly love, as drew the neighbor Dutch to much observation, yea and some admiration of them, at Delph-Shoven in Holland. Their departure therefore was not in a way of division among themselves, but with mutual consent, and common intendment of peaceable cohabitation.[13]

13 [John Cotton's explanation of the history and rationale of the Plymouth colony raises a problem. On one hand, Walter H. Burgess, the biographer of John Robinson, appears to be accurate when he says that John Cotton received the story of John Robinson's relation to other Puritan ministers in Holland from the lips of his parishioners and that his presentation of the matter is "a very fair summary." On the other hand, Cotton relies not only on oral testimony but, it appears, on unpublished manuscripts. The startling fact is that his summary of the reasons for the Pilgrims' migration to America is an abbreviated but verbatim report of the reasons as they were listed in Nathaniel Morton's *New Englands Memoriall*, which was not published until 1669 (Cambridge). For his

Neither did that company which came over to Plymouth erect here a new church (as the Dissuader taketh it,) for by consent of the church which they left, they came over in church estate, and only renewed their covenant when they came hither.

Neither did the church of Plymouth (as the Dissuader reporteth them) incontinently leaven all the vicinity.

For (as themselves say) at the first coming there was no vicinity of Christian habitation. They came over in the year 1620. Mr. Endicott, (the captain with his company) came not over till the year 1628 and sat down at Salem, eight years after Plymouth. The year following, Mr. Skelton, and Mr. Higginson came over, and sitting down with Mr. Endicott at Salem, entered into a church there. How far they of Salem took up any practice from them at Plymouth, I do not know; sure I am, Mr. Skelton (their pastor) was studious of that way, before he left Holland in Lincolnshire.

Nor was there any other church planted after Salem till Mr. Winthrop, and some other godly gentlemen, and many good Christians came over together with Mr. Wilson, and Mr. Philips, (ministers of the word:) whereof the one gathered a church at Boston, and the other at Watertown, in the year 1630.

---

book, Morton, as is well known, copied almost literally from several known sources, chief of which was Bradford's journal (which was not published until its rediscovery in the nineteenth century), so the possibility exists that Cotton was not quoting a portion of the Morton manuscript but was, rather, quoting from a now lost manuscript that Morton also used. At any rate, the wording and emphases of the reasons for migration as Cotton and Morton set them forth differ from those given them by Winslow, Bradford, and others.

As for the "letters published in print" to which Cotton refers for some of his knowledge about the Separatists while they were in Holland, these are the letters that appeared as a result of the publication by Christopher Lawne and others of *The Prophane Schisme of the Brownists* (London, 1612), a book that without their permission contained the William Ames-John Robinson correspondence. Each of these men published letters to one another in clarification of their respective positions as set forth by Lawne, and in addition further letters were published in response to Lawne's book in books written by Richard Clyfton and by Henry Ainsworth.]

The next year followed Mr. Eliot, and the year after Mr. Weld, who gathered into a church at Roxbury, as old Mr. Maverick, and Mr. Warham had done the same before at Dorchester.

It was in the year 1633 when Mr. Hooker, Mr. Stone, with myself arrived in the same ship together: and being come, we found several churches gathered, and standing in the same order, and way, wherein they now walk: at Salem, at Boston, at Watertown, at Charlestown (which issued out of Boston) at Dorchester and Roxbury. So that the Dissuader is much mistaken, when he saith, the congregation of Plymouth did incontinently leaven all the vicinity: seeing for many years there was no vicinity to be leavened. And Salem itself that was gathered into church order seven or eight years after them, was above forty miles distant from them. And though it be very likely that some of the first comers might help their theory by hearing and discerning their practice at Plymouth: yet therein the Scripture is fulfilled. The kingdom of heaven is like unto leaven, which a woman took and hid in three measures of meal, till all was leavened, Matt. xiii,13.

But yet if the Dissuader knew the spirit of those men who first came over hither, after Plymouth, (though before us) he would easily discern, they were not such as would be leavened by vicinity of neighbors, but by the divinity of the truth of God shining forth from the word. The body of the people at that time was not of such a carnal spirit, as so many of them to leave so fair accommodations, and dear relations in our native country, to come over into a wilderness, to take up a form of government, upon any such ground as the Dissuader conceiteth, because it holdeth out so much liberty, and honor to the people.

This were indeed not to seek out for liberty of conscience, but elbow-roomth of lust; and not to attend the honor, but the humor of the people. To pass such a judgment upon strangers, had need to arise from divine revelation, or else it will fall under the note of humane temerity.

But (saith the Dissuader) howsoever it was in a few years, the most who settled their habitations in the land, did agree to model themselves after Robinson's pattern.

Ans. I do not know, that they agreed upon it by any common consultation: but it is true, they did as if they had agreed (by the same spirit of truth and unity) set up (by the help of Christ) the same model of churches, one like to another. But whether it was after Mr. Robinson's pattern, is spoken *gratis;* for I believe most of them knew not what it was, if any at all. And if any did know it, the men were such as were not wont to attend to the patterns of men in matters of religion (for against that many of them had suffered in our native country) but to the pattern of the Scriptures.

SECTION IV   *Of Cotton's pretended former dislike of the New English way, and after closing with it*

In pursuing this pedigree and descent of New English discipline, the Dissuader is pleased to present me to the world, to be the first who appeared in displeasure against it, though afterwards to have fallen into a liking of it.

But how doth he make it appear, that I did appear in displeasure against it? His proof is from a private letter of mine to Mr. Skelton, where I call it an error, (whether in Mr. Skelton, or some of his people) to conceive, that our congregations in England are none of them particular reformed churches. Surely, if that be all the proof, I willingly acknowledge, I did appear against that error. But neither was I the first that did appear against it, (but divers godly English ministers before me:) neither have I fallen to the liking of the contrary opinion since.

But the Dissuader is much deceived, if he take that error to be the judgment of the churches of New England, howsoever some particular persons may lean that way.

Nor will it yield any better proof, of that which he allegeth out of my Preface to Mr. Hildersam's Sermon upon John.[14] For that which I wrote, concerneth the way of the rigid Separation, which renounceth the churches of England as antichristian, and the godly members thereof, as no visible saints. Neither is my judgment altered at all in this point to this day: which also I have lately maintained in my reply to Mr. Williams his answer of my letter, and in a treatise concerning the baptism of children.[15] And what I have written in this point is suitable to the judgment of the body of the churches and elders in New England, and not at all repugnant to the way wherein we walk.

But I marvel, what should move the Dissuader to report of me, that though in England I fell off from the practice of some ceremonies, and but of some of them, and was distasted with episcopal government: yet so long as I abode in England, I minded no more than the old nonconformity: for in this one sentence he giveth a double misreport of me.

First, that in England I fell off but from some of the ceremonies. For (by the grace of Christ) I forbore all the ceremonies alike at once, many years before I left England. The first grounds which prevailed with me to forbear one ceremony, would not allow me to practice any. The grounds I well remember were two: 1. the significancy and efficacy put upon them in the Preface to the Book of Common Prayer. That they were neither dumb nor dark, but apt to stir up the dull mind of man to the remembrance of his duty to God, by some notable and

---

[14] [Arthur Hildersam, *Lectures upon the Forth of John* (London, 1629).]
[15] [The reply to Williams was printed as *A Reply to Mr. Williams His Examination* and bound with *The Bloudy Tenent Washed and Made White in the Bloud of the Lambe* (London, 1647). The treatise on baptism is *The Grounds and Ends of the Baptisme of the Children of the Faithful* (London, 1647).]

special signification, whereby he may be edified, or words to the like purpose.

The second was the limitation of church power, (even of the highest apostolical commission) to the observation of the commandments of Christ, Matt. xxviii,20, which made it appear to me utterly unlawful for any church power to enjoin the observation of indifferent ceremonies which Christ had not commanded. And all the ceremonies were alike destitute of the commandment of Christ, though they had been indifferent otherwise, which indeed others have justly pleaded they were not.

What favor I was offered not only for connivance, but for preferment, if I would have conformed to any one of the ceremonies, I forbear to mention. Yea, when I was suspended upon special complaint made against me to the king that then was, and all hope of restitution denied to me, without yielding to some conformity, at least in one ceremony at least once; yet the good hand of the Lord so kept me, that I durst not buy my ministry so dear: and yet (I thank the Lord) my ministry was dearer to me (to speak the least) than any preferment.

When the Bishop of Lincoln Diocese (Dr. Mountaigne) offered me liberty upon once kneeling at sacrament with him the next Lord's Day after: or else to give some reason, why (in conscience I could not) unto Dr. Davenant (then Bishop-elect of Salisbury, who was at that time present with him at Westminster) I durst not accept his offer of liberty upon once kneeling; but I gave them this reason for my excuse and defense,

Cultus non institutus, non est acceptus:
Genuflexio in perceptione eucharistiæ est cultus non institutus;
Ergo, non est acceptus.[16]

16 [A form of reverence that is not appointed is not sanctioned. Genuflection in receipt of the Eucharist is an unappointed form of reverence. Therefore it is not sanctioned.]

The second misreport which the Dissuader maketh of me in his former sentence, is, that howsoever when I was in England, I was then distasted with episcopal government; yet so long as I abode in England, I minded no more than the old nonconformity.

I pass by his unsavory metaphor of my distaste of episcopal government. Conscientious judgment in matters of religion is not led by taste or distaste; will he say, that both the Parliaments of England and Scotland have abolished episcopal government upon a distaste?

But when he saith, I minded no more than the old nonconformity whilst I abode in England, he must be more privy to my mind than any mortal man is, and than myself too, to make it good. There were some scores of godly persons in Boston in Lincolnshire, (whereof some are there still, and some here, and some are fallen asleep) who can witness, that we entered into a covenant with the Lord, and one with another, to follow after the Lord in the purity of his worship; which though it was defective, yet it was more than the old nonconformity. Besides, I had then learned of Mr. Parker, and Mr. Baynes, (and soon after of Dr. Ames) that the ministers of Christ, and the keys of the government of his church are given to each particular congregational church respectively: and therefore neither ministers nor congregations subject to the ecclesiastical jurisdiction of cathedral churches, no, nor of classical assemblies neither, but by voluntary consociation, and that in some cases; and those falling short of that which is properly called subjection to their jurisdiction. Which made me then to mind not only a neglect of the censures of commissary courts (which bred not a little offense to them, and disturbance to myself) but also to breathe after greater liberty and purity not only of God's worship, but of church estate. But suppose that I had then minded no more

than the old way of nonconformity; yet the experience of the
godly will easily acknowledge, that the way of the Lord is light
and strength to the upright, and giveth more and more understanding and enlargement to them that walk in it.

Nay, the Dissuader's own words might convince him, that I
minded more than the old nonconformity, whilst I abode in
England. For if Mr. Cotton, and those brethren who went along
with me, came over to New England, to join ourselves with
those American churches, (as he saith) it argueth plainly we
did not upon our coming hither, go contrary to our former judgment, and fall into a liking of this way. For then we would never
have taken so long and hazardous a voyage to join to churches
whose way was contrary to our judgments all the while of our
abode in England. Rational charity would conceive that Christian
men, who chose rather to forfeit our ministry, and maintenance,
and all our dear relations in our native country, than to submit to
a course contrary to our judgments, would never transport ourselves to America, to run a contrary course to our judgments in
a land of liberty. But thus in heat of pursuit of an adversary
(whether cause or person) men will not stick to suffer their
tongues and pens to run over, though for haste one word inter-
fere with another.

SECTION V   *Of the pretended danger of the New English
way unto the world, after Cotton and others
closing with it*

But to proceed, why should the Dissuader conceive, that our
coming over into these parts, and joining with these American
churches, should cause this new way (as he calleth it) to begin
to grow dangerous to the rest of the world?

To which world (I pray you) hath this way grown dangerous? to the Christian world? or to the antichristian world? or to the pagan world?

The pagan world of Indians here will acknowledge our sitting down by them, hath prevented the danger either of their dissolution or servitude. For the Indians in these parts being by the hand of God swept away (many multitudes of them) by the plague, the manner of the neighbor Indians is either to destroy the weaker countries, or to make them tributary: which danger ready to fall upon their heads in these parts, the coming of the English hither prevented. And of late (through the grace of Christ) one of our fellow elders, Mr. Eliot, teacher of Roxbury, having gotten the knowledge of the Indian language preacheth to them every week: one week to one congregation on the fourth day, to the other on the sixth the week following. And to him they willingly give ear, and reform their vicious living according to his doctrine, and some of them offer themselves to be trained up in English families, and in our schools: and there be of them that give good hope of coming on to the acknowledgement of the grace of Christ. To them therefore our way is not dangerous.

To the antichristian world, the more dangerous it is; I doubt not, it is the more acceptable to God, and I hope, it is not the less safe in Mr. Baylie's eye. Some of the Jesuits at Lisbon, and others in the Western Islands have professed to some of our merchants and mariners, they look at our plantations, (and at some of us by name) as dangerous supplanters of the Catholic cause. If that be the greatest danger, I presume Mr. Baylie will not *ab hoc dicto secundum quid,* pronounce us dangerous (*simpliciter*) to the rest of the world.[17]

To the Christian world, what danger hath accrued by our means? Many that knew both our magistrates and elders, and

17 [By what follows from what is said here, pronounce us dangerous (utterly) to the rest of the world.]

the chief sort of our people, and knew how little we affected
to travel into foreign countries to see fashions; they upon our
departure grew more inquisitive into the cause of our voluntary
exile; and thereupon, more jealous of corruptions at home in
the worship of God, and in church discipline; more sensible of
the burden and danger of episcopal tyranny, and consequently
more ready to follow the good example of the churches and
commonwealth of Scotland, in rejecting and shaking off episcopal usurpations and intrusions of liturgies. And hath this
been so dangerous to the rest of the world?

Besides, if books and letters do not delude us with false
intelligence, the great salvation and glorious victories which
the Lord hath wrought for England these late years by any
English power, his own right hand hath brought to pass chiefly
by such despised instruments as are surnamed Independents.
And are then the witnesses of that way so dangerous to the rest
of the world?

Wherein then lieth the danger of this way?

It seemeth the Dissuader conceiveth (as some others have
done) that this way hath been a double danger to those
churches: 1. In becoming a dangerous inlet to all kind of sects,
who shroud themselves under the name of Independents, and
claim impunity under their shadow. 2. In retarding the establishment and free passage of the work of reformation.

But for the former, if the devil come and sow tares, yea
briars and thorns, where Christ hath sown wheat, is therefore
the wheat a dangerous grain? And if thereupon not only tares,
but briars and thorns plead for freedom from eradication, must
therefore the wheat be plucked up, to root out the rest? Surely
the way which is practised in New England cannot justly be
taxed for too much connivance to all kind of sects: we here do
rather hear ill for too much rigor, which evidently argueth, our

way is of itself no inlet at all to all kind of sects, unless it be
merely by accident; as Christianity hath been an inlet to all
kinds of heresy; for where there is no Christianity, there is no
heresy.

As for the latter, the retarding of the work of reformation,
surely we find it here the readiest way to a speedy reformation.
The common disorders obvious and ordinary in other plantations, are here either not found, or soon reformed. The retarding
of reformation in England springeth rather, partly from such
as would have no reformation at all, but affect elbow-roomth
to their own lusts; partly from such as will have no reformation,
but in their own way. But if it might please the Lord to bow the
hearts, both of the Presbyterians, and of the Congregationals,
so far as both of them are come, to walk by the same rule and
mind the same thing, (both of them to mind reformation
according to the rule of the word, as they conceive it; both of
them to redress abuses, the Presbyterians, the abuses found in
their churches, and the Congregationals in theirs,) doubtless it
need not to be feared the work of reformation will speedily find
(by the blessing of Christ) a free and mighty passage throughout the three kingdoms.

S E C T I O N V I   *Of Cotton's pretended misleading* $\begin{cases} Mr.\ Davenp \\ Mr.\ Goodw \end{cases}$

If it be true which the Dissuader relateth from Mr. Edwards,[k]
that before my departure from England, I had by conference
in London brought off Mr. Davenport, and Mr. Goodwin,
from some of the English ceremonies.

Why doth he note me in his margin to be a misleader of Mr.
Goodwin and others? Is it a misleading to lead men away from

---

[k] Page 56 [In *Antapologia* (London, 1644) by Thomas Edwards].

the English ceremonies? Were they misleaders, who led the honorable Houses of Parliament to fall off from the ceremonies? Or did the Parliament mislead the people of England to the disuse of them?

But Mr. Baylie knoweth not Mr. Davenport, nor Mr. Goodwin, if he think the ablest divines in Christendom, much less such a poor weak thing as myself could bring them off to forsake their public ministry, wherein they were notable instruments of good service to God and man, unless they saw the light of the word and spirit of grace to go before them in such ways. Virgin souls are wont to follow the lamb, wheresoever he goeth, Rev. xiv,4. And the sons of God are led by the spirit of God, Rom. viii,14. And therefore let Mr. Baylie be entreated not so much to undervalue his holy brethren, as to think they were rather misled by me, than led by the spirit and word of grace in their own judgments and consciences. It is true, Mr. Davenport, Mr. Goodwin, with some other godly brethren had some conference with me at London, about the cause of my sufferings, and of my purpose to leave the land; which they said, they desired the rather, because they did not look at me as a passionate man, though the Dissuader (who knoweth me not) be pleased so to represent me to the world in this paragraph. And upon their motion two points were chiefly debated: 1. touching the limitation of church power, to matters of commandment, not of indifferency, (which I touched before). 2. touching the office of bishops, whether the Scripture bishops be appointed to rule a diocese, or a particular congregation. Now both these being agreed upon amongst us, Mr. Edwards is much mistaken, and Mr. Baylie too, when they say, that neither Mr. Davenport, nor Mr. Goodwin, nor myself did mind any further than the leaving of some few ceremonies. For grant the former principle, of the limitation of church power to matters of commandment, and all the ceremonies must be left off at once. And grant the latter, touching the limitation of bishops to a particular congregation; and it will necessarily infer an unavoidable separation from under the shadow of diocesan-episcopal government.

Besides, presently after, I received letters from Mr. Goodwin, (and as I take it, before I left England) signifying, that as in our former conferences, we had debated much of the negative part of the 2. Commandment, so he had since meditated much, and seriously of the affirmative part of it, the positive institutions of God's divine worship in opposition to humane inventions. Whereby I plainly discerned, (England as the state of it stood then) could not hold him long. It is an usual thing with God, in times of reformation to enlighten his servants, though far distant one from another, with the same beams of light of divine truth, which the world interpreteth, they have learned one from another; but indeed all from the same Spirit, who distributeth to every one, even as He will. But whether Mr. Davenport, and Mr. Goodwin received ought from me, I do not know, sure I am, I have received much from them. The members of the body of Christ, are wont to minister supply one to another, according to the effectual working of the spirit of grace in every part, to the mutual edifying of themselves, and of the whole body in love, Ephes. iv,16. And why should mutual edification be made a matter of exprobration?

SECTION VII *Of Cotton's pretended sudden change to the passionate affecting of the New English way, and the conversion of Mr. Goodwin to it*

It seemeth to me a strange speech of the Dissuader, and as far from truth, as from ingenuity, that as soon as I had tasted of the

New English air, I fell into a passionate affection with the religion I found there.

For I knew their religion before I came into New England, and himself said above, that I came with a purpose to join with their churches: which argueth, *I did not fall into an affection to their religion, by tasting of New English air.* Nor hath his speech any reasonable construction, that with *tasting the New English air, I soon fell into a passionate affection to their religion,* unless he take me for one of those children, who are tossed to and fro, and carried about with every wind (or air) of doctrine, Ephes. iv,14. Nor do I yet understand why he should account the religion of New England another religion, than that of England and Scotland and other reformed churches. Difference in some external form of church administrations is not wont in the writings of judicious divines, to make up the note and name of a different religion.

Neither can I imagine what should move him to say, that I fell into a passionate affection with the religion here. A passionate affection, is a strong, yea a violent, and inordinate affection. Did the Dissuader ever read, or hear me, to express any such violent or inordinate affection to the religion here professed?

How Mr. Goodwin cometh to be accounted, and called of the Dissuader, my convert, I do not know. It is not good to take liberty to use Scripture idioms, but in Scripture sense. The Scripture speaketh not of conversions, but in the sense of regeneration begun, or renewed: neither doth it style one man, another man's convert, but reserveth that solely and solidly to the Lord.

But I marvel why the Dissuader should say, that Mr. Goodwin with little ado was brought by my letters from New England to follow in this step of my progress.

For first, I do not remember that ever I wrote letter to him
from New England about our way. And my letter, which Mr.
Baylie quoteth amongst his testimonies (in G) was not written
to him, but to a brother of mine (by marriage) in Boston. Men
that have been bred and brought up under a form of doctrine,
or worship, or government, and never saw ground to scruple it,
they may with little ado receive it, and embrace, and follow it:
which, it may be, hath been the case of many thousands in
England, and usually falleth out in settled churches. But for
Mr. Goodwin to take up a way not only contrary to that wherein
he hath been bred and brought up, but also discrepant from the
judgments of so many godly learned brethren, to the hazard of
his ministry, and to the smothering of himself in a cloud of
calumny and obloquy, believe it who will, I cannot easily believe it, that he took up such a way with very little ado. I cannot
but believe, it cost him many prayers, and sighs, and groans,
much study, meditation, and conference, before he could satisfy
himself in such a course; he being especially (as Mr. Baylie
reporteth him) a man of a fine and dainty spirit, (and therefore
loving and tender:) to which sort of men, it is most unwelcome
to offend reverend brethren by dissenting from them: and with
whom it is most usual to suspect their own judgments and ways,
when they go alone. Luther was not accounted a man of a fine
and dainty spirit, but of a more resolute and stern temper; and
yet it was no small temptation even to him. *"Nunquid in solus
sapis? Quoties mihi palpitavit tremulum cor, et reprebendens
objecis fortissimum illud argumentum, tu solus sapis? Totne
errant universi?*[18] *etc. Luther. in Præfat. de Abroganda Missa
privata, etc.*

18 [Do you alone know the truth? How often has my heart trembled and
reproachfully raised against me that strongest of arguments, Do you alone know?
Are all the rest, so many of them mistaken?]

Mr. Edwards his Antapology, I have not had the opportunity to come by, much less to read: and therefore I cannot tell what sense to make of those words which Mr. Baylie quoteth out of him (in H) and wherein he saith, Mr. Goodwin was bold to boast of me in terms beyond the bounds of moderation. Sure I am, Mr. Goodwin was not wont to be accounted, either a bold man, or a boaster. I have many years known him and his modesty, and abhorrency both from boldness and boasting: and if Mr. Baylie take up a report to the contrary from Mr. Edwards (who is but one witness, and it may be prejudiced) I dare not follow Mr. Baylie herein, but must allow Mr. Goodwin the privilege of an elder, against whom no accusation is to be received under two or three witnesses, 1 Tim. v,19. By what rule therefore Mr. Baylie receiveth this testimony against Mr. Goodwin, by one single witness, he may do well to consider. Sure I am, it agreeth not with the rules either of Congregational or Classical church government.

But if Mr. Goodwin himself do acknowledge such a speech, he knoweth best in what sense he spake it. For myself, I can own it only in the same sense wherein Agur spake it of himself, Prov. xxx, 2, 3. *Surely I am more brutish than man; I have not the understanding of a man: I have not learned wisdom, nor know the holy.*

The next testimony which Mr. Baylie quoteth out of Mr. Edwards to the same purpose, speaketh not of Mr. Goodwin, but of some other whom Mr. Edwards nameth not. But such Apocrypha testimonies with judicious and equal minds, will never go for authentical evidences. For the matter of the testimony itself, I conceive, the form of church government wherein we walk doth not differ in substance from that which Mr. Cartwright pleaded for. For two things chiefly there be wherein such as are for a Congregational way, do seem to differ from

Presbyterians: 1. in the matter of their churches; they would have none allowed but visible saints. 2. In the exercise of church censure, they leave that power to the elders and brethren of the same church whereof the delinquent is a member. And in both these we find Mr. Cartwright's footsteps going plainly before us. For, 1. he taxeth in Bishop Whitgift, that speech of his; The church is full of drunkards and whoremongers, etc. Whereas Mr. Cartwright would not have scandalous persons borne withal in the church. And for the 2. he speaketh fully, in Cor. v,4. Forasmuch (saith he) as the apostle reproveth the church of Corinth, for that they had not (before his letters) excommunicated the incestuous; it is evident that the ministers, and the rest of the church there had power and authority thereunto.

The next testimony which Mr. Baylie allegeth to prove Mr. Goodwin boasting of this new light (as he calleth it) beyond the lines of moderation, is from the words of Mr. Williams in his examination of a letter of mine.[19] His words be, that some of the most eminent amongst them have affirmed, that even the apostles' churches were not so pure as the New England churches.

But what is this to Mr. Goodwin? Mr. Williams speaketh of some of the most eminent in New England, where Mr. Goodwin never came.

Besides, Mr. Williams doth not ascribe these words to any definite persons in New England. And, as I said before, Apocrypha testimonies will never go with equal minds for authentical evidences. It is no new thing for Mr. Williams to mistake both himself and others, as hath appeared in the reply both to his examination of that letter and to his *Bloody Tenent*. I never heard of any man's speech in New England so hyperbolical in the praise of New English churches, nor coming nearer

---

[19] [Roger Williams, *Mr. Cottons Letter . . . Examined and Answered* (London, 1644).]

to the words in hand, than the words reported of Mr. Williams himself *that of all the churches in the world, the churches of New England were the most pure; and of all New English churches, Salem* (whereof himself was teacher) *was the purest.* But such arrogant comparisons are as smoke in God's nostrils, Isai. lxv,5, the first born of vanity, and the first step to apostasy.

SECTION VIII   *Of Cotton's pretended rashness in the change of his mind in latter and former times*

Mr. Baylie proceedeth, and telleth us, "It had been happy for England, that Mr. Cotton had taken longer time for deliberation, before that change of his mind. He might have remembered his too precipitant rashness in former times, both to receive, and to send abroad to the world such tenents, whereof after he had cause to repent."

I should think myself a most unhappy man, if England should be the less happy for my sake. Mr. Baylie doth either undervalue England, or overvalue me; if he think the happiness or unhappiness of England doth stand or fall upon any deliberate or precipitate act of mine.

But what think ye, was that rash and precipitate act of mine, which hath impeached the happiness of England? It was, saith he, that change of my mind. What change was that? That which I mention in a letter to some friends in Boston, that if I were with them again, I durst not take that liberty which sometimes I had done: I durst not join in book-prayers: I durst not now partake in the sacrament with you: to wit, in respect of those scandalous persons who communicate with you, and will settle upon their lees with the more security by your fellowship with them.[20]

20 [If not the same letter, then a very similar one addressed by Cotton to "My Honored, Worshipfull, and worthy Friends, the Major and Justices, the

I do remember such a letter I wrote; whether to one or more in Boston I remember not: some say it is printed, but I know not, nor have I seen it: but I take the contents as Mr. Baylie reporteth them. And concerning them, I durst appeal even to Mr. Baylie himself, (though a stranger to me, and professing opposition) yet let him speak in good earnest, whether if I had taken longer time of deliberation even to this day, I should not have found just cause to have changed my mind, as I then did? Did I change my mind then to any other judgment or practice, than what the reverend Assembly of Divines, and the honorable Houses of Parliament have found (by the grace given to them) to be the truth and by public consent approved, and by public authority established? And doth he think, that it had been happy for England if the Parliament and Assembly had neither of them changed their minds, but still retained book-service, and admitted scandalous persons to the Lord's Table? How shall a poor Christian do to satisfy his brethren, that are not satisfied with their own judgment and ways; if he be of the same judgment, or speak the same thing with them? Verily, it is not good in God's sight (but even an abomination to Him) to keep a weight and a weight, a measure and a measure: to judge the same act in themselves to be weighty, which in others they judge to be light and rash. But the comfort is, the righteous God judgeth righteously, not according to acceptance of persons, but according to truth; and accepteth the work of his own spirit of truth and grace wheresoever He findeth it.

As for my too precipitant rashness in former times, which he is pleased to remember me of, let him be pleased to forbear his

---

Aldermen and *Common Councell,* together with the whole Congregation and Church at Boston," in Lincolnshire, appeared as the preface to Cotton's *Of the Holinesse of Church-members* (London, 1650), a treatise in which he responded to Baylie's and Rutherford's answers to *The Way of Congregational Churches Cleared.*]

censure a while, till I may give account thereof to Reverend
Doctor Twisse.[21] In the meantime let him know, that those
tenents which he saith I sent abroad to the world, whereof I
had cause after to repent, I neither sent them abroad to the
world, (but wrote them privately for the satisfaction of a neighbor minister) nor do I yet know, whether I have cause to repent
of them or no, it being near thirty years ago since I wrote them,
and many years ago since I read them.

But in the meantime, let Mr. Baylie be pleased to understand,
that I came hither in September in the year 1633, and that letter
of mine which I sent to Boston, was dated (as himself quoteth)
in October 1635. And surely to write my opinion of such a case,
which I had considered of for the space of two whole years,
doth not seem to be a rash and precipitate act: nor can it be
said with truth, that I did incontinent persuade to the New
English way, as soon as I had tasted of the New English air.
Two whole years and more, giveth a man more than a taste of
New English air; nor is that an act done incontinently, which is
done upon two years' deliberation.

SECTION IX   *Of Cotton's pretended known failings, and
Mr. Baylie's pretended just cause to discover
them to the world*

Mr. Baylie proceedeth to discover my evident and known
failings, (as he calleth them) and he conceiveth neither piety
nor charity will hinder him to remark them. And why so? Me-

---

[21] [In *A Treatise of Mr. Cottons Clearing Certaine Doubts Concerning Predestination, Together with an Examination Thereof* (London, 1646), William
Twisse criticized the deviations from Calvinist orthodoxy of an unpublished work
that Cotton had written when he was a minister in Lincolnshire. Cotton appears
to have come into accordance with Twisse's views prior to the publication of
Twisse's *Examination,* and he is not known ever to have written a response to it.]

thinks it should be some great and weighty cause, that himself, who is wont (as he saith) to speak liberally to the praises of men, who in his thoughts are much inferior to Mr. Cotton; should now give up himself to speak liberally to the dispraise and disgrace of him, whom yet in his entrance therein he seemeth to reckon amongst such as he calleth the dear children of God. Surely there is not the least child of God, but is ordained of God to be a vessel of honor; and to make any such a vessel of dishonor, what is it else but to endeavor to overthrow the eternal counsel of God? Nor is there the least child of God, but is a member of the body of Christ; and the natural members of the body are wont to cover the nakedness of such members as are most uncomely.

But Mr. Baylie is of opinion, as he saith, that when my gifts are turned into snares, and made inducements to others to follow me in my wanderings: then the discovery of my clear weakness may be a retractive to every prudent man, and a caveat from God, to beware of my ways. Belike then it will follow, that though it be contrary both to the counsel and commandment of God, and to the communion of his mystical body, to cast reproaches and dishonor upon the least of God's servants; yet for a good end, to keep others from idolizing of them, it may be lawful to ransack all their former lives, and to hang them up in the sight of the sun, in chains of public infamy, and obloquy. But I confess, I have not so learned Christ, as to allow myself to do evil that good may come of it. Nor do I believe it had been a way of God, when the men of Lystra so highly idolized Paul and Barnabas, as to account one of them to be Jupiter, and the other Mercurius, and to present them with divine worship, that then some godly brother of Paul's company should have stept in amongst them, and said, sirs, why do you these things? Paul hath been a bloody persecutor of the truths of God, a blasphemer, a scornful oppressor: and Barnabas is a man subject to passion and dissimulation, and both of them mortal men, subject to all kind of sinful corruption. Such zeal for the glory of God, I know not by what rule of piety or charity, it could have been justified. God hath sanctified other means, to wean his servants from idolizing their brethren. Cornelius idolized Peter even with divine honor, Acts x,25. But did Peter therefore, or any of the six brethren that went along with him, think it a just warrant, to proclaim to Cornel. Take heed what you do, this man whom you idolize hath been a liar, a perjured person, an horrible curser of himself, and renouncer of the Lord Jesus before many witnesses? God forbid. Yea of latter times, when the pregnant strength and glorious luster of many heroical and excellent gifts of Luther had been so idolized, that many and great nations followed him in some notorious errors of his way: yet Calvin thought it no just ground, why Bullinger or other divines should break forth against him, as he had done (*atroci invectiva,* to use Calvin's word) against them, but sweetly professeth, *sæpe dicere solitus sum, etiamsi me diabolum vocaret, me tamen hoc illi honoris habiturum, ut insignem Dei servum agnoscam,*[22] *Calvin, Ep.* 57, *ad Bullingerum.* The want of this spirit is *fundi Anglicani calamitas,* the unhappiness of England at this day. But what if all these heresies or errors, which Mr. Baylie chargeth upon me, be but so many errors of himself, or of his witnesses? Will he still make it an act of piety, or charity to remark them (as he calleth it) for my evident and known failings, and follies: which are either no failings, nor follies at all, or none of mine?

Let us examine the particulars.

---

[22] [With harsh invective . . . I have been accustomed to say that even if he were to call me Devil, I will hold him in such honor as to recognize him as an outstanding servant of God.]

SECTION X   *Of Cotton's prelatical tenents*

1. He instanceth in the errors of my education, and my long continuance in them: sundry of them (as he saith) I confess stuck by me all the time of my abode in England.

And this he proveth from the testimony of mine own letter (above mentioned) from New England to my friends at Boston, October 5, 1635. As joining in book-prayers and fellowship at the Lord's Table with scandalous communicants. It was but in the next foregoing page (page 56 of Mr. Baylie's book) wherein he maketh it the unhappiness of England, that I changed my mind from those very tenents, which he now calleth the errors of my education, and prelatical tenants? But if they be errors, why doth he tax me for changing from them? And why doth he say, "It had been happy for England, if Mr. Cotton had taken longer time, before he had changed his mind from such tenents?" Let Mr. Baylie choose which he will take; either these are no errors nor prelatical tenents; or if they were, it was no error in me, nor unhappiness to England that I changed from them. A considerate and equal mind should not be so far transported *studiopartium*,[23] nor so soon forget itself, as to censure it in one page for an unhappy change from such tenents, which in the next page he noteth for erroneous and prelatical tenents.

SECTION XI   *Of Cotton's pretended Pelagianism and Arminian errors*

2. My next error, he calleth, my more dangerous fall into the gulf of Pelagianism,[24] some of the Arminian errors. I did expect,

---

[23] [By partisan spirit.]

[24] [Pelagianism is the theological system built on the belief that man takes the first step toward his own salvation apart from the assistance of divine grace; it is, therefore, closely akin to Arminianism, see note 5, p. 175.]

he would have named what those Pelagian or Arminian errors
had been. But for that, he referreth me to the Antapology, a
book which I do not know that ever I have seen. Sure I am, I
have often assayed to get, but cannot yet procure it. The testimony which Mr. Baylie quoteth out of it, referreth me to the
Preface of Dr. Twisse his answer. I have read his Preface,
wherein I find no particular tenents of mine expressed as erroneous. But this testimony he is pleased to give me, (which might
somewhat allay the harshness of the scandal of my fall into the
gulf of Pelagianism and Arminianism) "Mr. Cotton (saith he)
as I have heard, is very sound and orthodox in the point of
election; and cometh to this work with a gracious intent to
clear the doctrine of predestination, (and that, in the particular
of reprobation) from such harsh consequences as seemeth to
be derived from thence."

Dr. Twisse doth indeed truly express that which (through
grace) was my true intent, to clear the orthodox doctrine of
predestination from such harsh consequences, as are wonted
to be derived from absolute reprobation. For when I was first
called to Boston in Lincolnshire, so it was, that Mr. Doctor
Baron, son of Dr. Baron, (the divinity reader at Cambridge)
who in his lectures there, first broached that which was then
called Lutheranism, since Arminianism:) this Dr. Baron, I say,
had leavened many of the chief men of the town with Arminianism; as being indeed himself learned, acute, plausible in discourse, and fit to insinuate into the hearts of his neighbors. And
though he was a physician by profession, (and of good skill in
that art) yet he spent the greatest strength of his studies in
clearing and promoting the Arminian tenents. Whence it came
to pass, that in all the great feasts of the town, the chiefest
discourse at table did ordinarily fall upon Arminian points, to
the great offense of the godly ministers both in Boston, and

neighbor-towns. I coming amongst them a young man, (as having gone to Cambridge in the beginning of the thirteenth year of my age, and tarrying there not above fourteen years in all, before I was sent for to Boston) I thought it a part both of modesty and prudence, not to speak much to the points, at the first, amongst strangers and ancients; until afterwards, after hearing of many discourses in public meetings, and much private conference with the doctor, I had learned at length where all the great strength of the doctor lay. And then observing (by the help of Christ) how to avoid such expressions, as gave him any advantage in the expressions of others, I then began publicly to preach, and in private meetings to defend the doctrine of God's eternal election before all foresight of good or evil in the creature: and the redemption (*ex gratia*) only of the elect: the effectual vocation of a sinner *per irresistibilem gratiæ vim*,[25] without all respect of the preparations of free will: and finally, the impossibility of the fall of a sincere believer either totally or finally from the estate of grace. Hereupon, when the doctor had objected many things, and heard my answers to those scruples which he was wont most plausibly to urge; presently after, our public feasts and neighborly meetings, were silent from all further debates about predestination, or any of the points which depend thereon, and all matters of religion were carried on calmly and peaceably. Insomuch, that when God opened mine eyes to see the sin of conformity, (which was soon after:) my neglect of conformity was at first tolerated without disturbance, and at length embraced in practice by the chief and greatest part of the town. But so it fell out, that a neighbor minister dwelling about sixteen miles off (and my very loving friend) hearing of some answers of mine tending to clear the doctrine of reprobation against the exceptions of Dr. Baron, he

---

25 [By grace . . . through the irresistible power of grace.]

seemed not to be satisfied therewith, but wrote to me seven or eight questions about the same; whereto I willingly gave him such answers as then came to hand, and that soon after the receipt of his questions, which is now long since, about thirty years ago. Little did I think, that a private letter of mine written to a very friend, should ever have been divulged abroad. But it seemeth some got copies of it; and in process of time, one copy multiplied another, till at length it came to Dr. Twisse his hand. None of his writings against Arminius or his followers had been then published: but he was then (by the report which went of him) of such high esteem with me, as I wrote him a thankful letter for the pains I heard he had taken in examining my answer to Mr. Bell's queries: (for that was the neighbor minister's name who sent them to me); and desired from him leave to see the copy of his answer. He lovingly granted it, only with desire after a time to return his αὐτόγραφον:[26] yet after that having got himself another copy, he sent me word, he was content I should keep his. Whereupon I took it with me to New England; but since my coming hither have found such constant diversion from such contemplative controversies, to attend practical, that I have not to this day been able to perpend the doctor's answer, which I see is now printed: I hope, God will give me opportunity ere long (after two or three other treatises perused) to consider of this his labor of love. I bless the Lord, who hath taught me to be willing to be taught of a far meaner disciple than such a doctor, whose scholastical acuteness, pregnancy of wit, solidity of judgment, and dexterity of argument, all orthodox divines do highly honor, and whom all Arminians and Jesuits do fall down before with silence. God forbid I should shut mine eyes against any light brought to me by him. Only I desire I may not be condemned as a Pelagian or

[26] [Autograph (i.e., the original copy written in the author's hand).]

Arminian, before I be heard, or be found more slow in retract-
iug an error, than in discerning it.

SECTION XII   *Of Cotton's pretended Montanism*

The next error which Mr. Baylie is pleased to threap upon
me is my old Montanism,[27] which he saith, he hath heard from
some gracious ministers; and wherein some think I remain
to this day.

Who those gracious ministers are from whom he heard this,
he doth not mention; nor what this old Montanism of mine
should be, he doth not express. But thus I must stand guilty in
Mr. Baylie's judgment, and by his relation, in the judgment of
all men that give credit to his testimony, of an horrible heresy,
but I must not know what; and by the accusation of gracious
ministers, but I must not know whom.

Augustine recordeth (in his Catalogue of Heresies) chap. 26,
the heresies of Montanus to be: 1. That Montanus and his two
harlot-prophetesses, Prisca and Maximilla, had received the
Holy Ghost not in part, as the apostles, but without measure.
2. Second marriages they condemn as whoredom. 3. The bread
in the Lord's Supper, they mingle with the blood of a yearling
infant.

Danaeus in his comment upon that book of Augustine, addeth
other heresies, out of other authors: as for a 4. that Montanus
himself was the comforter promised to the apostles. 5. That
incestuous copulations were not to be disallowed. 6. That en-
thusiasms and revelations were rather to be followed than the
word of God. 7. That they confounded the persons in trinity,
as did the Sabellians and Patropassiani.

---

[27] [Montanism was loosely used to describe an extreme commitment to the
apocalyptic expectation of a speedy outpouring of the Holy Spirit, although
technically it meant the heresy scored by Augustine as Cotton reports.]

Now amongst all these Montanistic tenents, I would entreat Mr. Baylie to tell me (in faithfulness) which of them it is he chargeth upon me, and which he calleth, my old Montanism, wherein some think I do remain to this day.

Or if he say, (as he doth) that he hath heard of my old Montanism, by some gracious ministers, let him be pleased to entreat them to declare to me those points of Montanism, which they know by me, or suspect in me. Otherwise I shall conceive, though they may be gracious ministers that so told him, yet it was no part of their graciousness so to speak; a speech that neither savored of truth, nor love, nor wisdom, nor faithfulness.

But in perusing the sequel of this discourse, I find a passage, which maketh me suspect, what tenent of Montanism it is which he aimeth at, in page 61, speaking of the vileness of the errors of the members of our churches; they did (saith he) avow openly, the personal inhabitation of the Spirit in all the godly; his immediate revelations without the word; and these as infallible as the Scripture itself. And this (saith he) is the vilest Montanism.

These two latter tenents, immediate revelations without the word, and them as infallible as the Scripture itself, I willingly confess they are vile Montanism; though I would not say (as he doth) the vilest. For the vilest is, to hold Montanus himself to be the Holy Ghost, or to have received the Holy Ghost in a more full measure than the apostles themselves.

But for the first of these tenents, touching the personal inhabitation of the Holy Ghost in the godly, it may further be considered before it be condemned. Personal inhabitation may be taken in a double sense: for, 1. it may hold forth no more but this, the indwelling not only of the gifts of the Holy Ghost, but of his person also in the regenerate. Or 2. it may hold forth further, the indwelling of the person of the Holy Ghost in the regenerate, so far forth as to make us one person with himself, or to communicate with us some personal propriety of his own.

In this latter sense, Mr. Baylie may well be allowed to call it, vile Montanism: for the errors are vile, and also wrapped up in Montanus his tenents: but for the former, the indwelling not only of the gifts, but of the person also of the Holy Ghost in the regenerate, I must profess, I neither believe the tenent to be vile nor Montanism. Not Montanism, for amongst all the errors of Montanus or his followers, I never read this imputed to them, by such as have been the more diligent recorders and refuters of ancient heresies. Neither Augustine, nor Epiphanius before him, nor Danaeus after him, did ever father this tenent upon the Montanists. Nor is the tenent vile or erroneous, but an holy truth of God delivered to us from the word of truth. As may appear,

1. From the testimony of the Lord Jesus, John. xiv, 16, 17, 26 with John xv,26. The argument standeth thus, *The comforter which proceedeth from the Father and the Son; even the spirit of truth, He dwelleth in the disciples of Christ Jesus.*

The comforter which proceedeth from the Father and the Son, even the spirit of truth, is the person of the Holy Ghost himself.

Therefore the person of the Holy Ghost himself dwelleth in the disciples of Christ Jesus.

2. From the testimony of the apostle Paul, 2 Tim. i,14. *That good thing* (saith he) *which is committed to thee, keep, by the Holy Ghost, which dwelleth in us.* That good thing is fitly understood by our best interpreters, Calvin and Beza, to be, not only the sound doctrine of the Gospel, and his ministerial office, but also the excellent gifts of the spirit of grace furnishing him

for discharge of his office, and dispensation of the Gospel. Whence the argument holdeth thus;

The Holy Ghost that keepeth the good gifts of grace in us, dwelleth in us.

The Holy Ghost that keepeth the good gifts of grace in us, is not the gifts, but the person of the Holy Ghost distinguished from them:

Therefore it is the person of the Holy Ghost, and not his gifts only that dwelleth in us.

3. From another testimony of Paul, Rom. viii,11. *If the spirit of Him that raised up Jesus from the dead, dwell in you: He that raised up Christ from the dead, shall also quicken your mortal bodies, by his spirit that dwelleth in you.* Whence the argument ariseth thus,

The Spirit that dwelleth in us, is the Spirit that raised Christ from the dead, and shall also quicken our mortal bodies;

But it is not the gifts and graces of the Spirit, but the person of the Spirit himself that raised up Christ from the dead, and shall quicken our mortal bodies:

Therefore it is the person of the Spirit that dwelleth in us.

It was not the gifts and graces of the spirit of Christ himself, much less our gifts and graces that did raise up Christ from the dead. Not the gifts and graces of Christ himself; for they were but created. And it was an act far above all created power, to raise up Christ from the dead. Much less were they our gifts and graces that raised Him up; for ours are not only created, but imperfect, and which is more, they were not then in being, when God raised up Christ from the dead.

To these three divine testimonies (which are the ground of my faith in this point) let me add one humane testimony of a learned divine, who was never tainted, nor taxed with Montan-

ism, I mean Zanchi, *de Tribus Elohim parte altera, lib. 4, cap.
1*. His testimony cometh in thus: *"Præter alia argumenta, quibus
confirmavimus Spiritum Sanctum verum esse Deum, illud etiam
non fuit minimum, quod inde deduximus, quia fideles vocantur
templum Spiritus Sancti,"* I Cor. vi,19 and iii,16.

Against this argument from the proof of the godhead of the
Holy Ghost, Ochino gave this answer amongst others: *"Dona
Dei nobis concessa, hoc eodem nomine notari; sed non tertium
suppositum, hoc est personam, a Patre et Filio distinctam, etc."*

To this Zanchi replieth: *"Non potest spiritus Ochinianus nisi
impudenter inficiari, quin Spiritus Sanctus, hoc est, tertia haec
persona (quae etiam Spiritus Dei, et Virtus Dei appellatur)
habitet in sanctis hominibus, et quin illi sint hujus templum,
quienim in iis habitat, judicio, et voluntate præditus est, et
loquitur; spiritus Patris vestri (inquit Christus) loquitur in
vobis,* Matt. x,20. *Spiritus antem Sanctus appellatur ipse Spiritus
Dei, et Spiritus Christi. Spiritus igitur Sanctus, hoc est tertia
persona, habitat in sanctis. Quod vero ait spiritus Ochinianus,
Non posse tertiam personam habitare in sanctis, quin ibi etiam
habitent reliqua, dictum est bene. Nam etiam Christus dixit,
ego et Pater ad eum veniemus, et mansionem apud cum faciemus,*
John xiv,23. *Hoc vero ideo fit, quoniam omnes sunt una et
eadem essentia, etc."*[28]

---

[28] [Zanchi: Besides other arguments by which we have confirmed that the
Holy Spirit is truly God, that also was not the least weighty which we deduced
from the fact that the faithful are called the temple of the Holy Spirit.

Ochinus: The gifts of God granted to us—this is to be designated by a common name, but not as a third principle, that is, person distinct from the Father
and the Son.

Zanchi: The Ochinian spirit cannot, except out of impudence, deny that the
Holy Spirit, that is the third person, which is also called the Spirit of God and
the Virtue of God, dwells in saints and that they are his temple, for that which
dwells in them is endowed with judgment and will, and speaks: "The Spirit of
your Father," says Christ, "speaks in you." Matt. x,20. But the Holy Spirit is
called the very Spirit of God and the Spirit of Christ. Therefore the Holy Spirit,
that is, the third person, dwells in the saints. And indeed what the Ochinian

SECTION XIII   *Of Cotton's pretended Antinomianism and Familism*

The Dissuader proceedeth to point at (as he calleth it) another more dangerous fall of mine, which in his margin, he nameth Mr. Cotton's Antinomianism and Familism:[29] and within a few lines, his wandering into the horrible errors of the Antinomians, and Familists, with his dear friend Mrs. Hutchinson, so far that he came to a resolution to side with her, and to separate from all the churches in New England, as legal synagogues.

If all this charge were true (as indeed, in all parts of it, it is false:) yet the errors of Antinomianism, and Familism, then stirring in the country, and condemned in the synod at Newtown, were not more dangerous, than the old Montanism. I confess, the Familism afterwards broached by Mr. Gorton, and his followers, the same which Calvin in his *Opuscula* refuteth (in his *Instructio adversus Libertinos*) as Calvin judgeth it more dangerous than popery, so I conceive it to be as dangerous as Montanism, though I cannot say more dangerous: for both of them overthrow all principles and foundations of Christian religion. But for the making good of this charge upon me, let Mr. Baylie be pleased to instance in those horrible errors either of Antinomianism or Familism, whereunto I either wandered or

---

Spirit says, that the third person cannot dwell in the saints unless the other persons dwell there also, is well said. For Christ actually says, "I and my Father will come to him, and we will make our dwelling in him," John xiv,23. And this comes about for the very reason that they are all of one and the same essence.]

[29] [The Familists did maintain Antinomian tenets, and although the sect of the Family of Love disappeared as such before the end of the seventeenth century, there is no doubt that it did so because its members found an outlet for their beliefs in Quakerism. In joining Familism and Antinomianism, then, Baylie is not just name-calling, but is attempting to separate out a theological streak for which there was not as yet any name though after 1650 it would be known as Quakerism.]

fell: or let him make it appear that I came to such a resolution, to side with my dear friend Mrs. Hutchinson, and to separate from all the churches in New England as legal synagogues.

Let us examine his proofs and testimonies.

1. The first is from the parties themselves, the followers of Mrs. Hutchinson, who (saith he) boast of Mr. Cotton for their master and patron.

And it is true, they professed so: just as Wightman who was burnt at Litchfield for Montanism, (avouching himself to be the Holy Ghost) professed he had received all his grounds from Mr. Hildersam. And I confess myself, being naturally (I thank God) not suspicious, hearing no more of their tenents from them, than what seemed to me orthodoxal, I believed they had been far off from such gross errors, as were bruited of them. But when some of my fellow brethren (the elders of neighbor churches) advertised me of the evil report that went abroad of their corrupt tenents, I desired to know what the tenents were, which were corrupt, and which they had vented here and there, in my name. They mentioned some to me, some of those which are published in the short story of that subject:[30] and named also to me the persons, who had uttered the same. I therefore dealt with Mrs. Hutchinson and others of them, declaring to them the erroneousness of those tenents, and the injury done to myself in fathering them upon me. Both she, and they utterly denied

---

[30] [*A Short Story of the Rise, Reign and Ruine of the Antinomians* (London, 1644) was written by John Winthrop but seen through the press and probably revised by Thomas Weld, who returned to England as the colony's agent and to whom the total authorship is sometimes erroneously ascribed. Although *Short Story* presumably indicates how the Congregational system is capable of dealing with heresy and blasphemy, 1644 was an impropitious time for the New Englanders to be washing their linen in public, and Thomas Hooker was of the opinion that the Scots "had a secret hand to provoke Mr. Weld to set forth his 'Short Story.'"]

that they held such tenents, or that they had fathered them upon
me. I returned their answer to the elders, who had spoken to me
of them: and I inquired, if any two of them, or their neighbors
could bear witness in this case. They answered me they had but
one witness of any corrupt tenent: and that one, loath to be
known to be an accuser of them. I replied, what course would
you then advise me to take? They answered, that I could not
indeed bring the matter to the church for want of witnesses: but
the best way would be, publicly and privately to bear witness
against such errors. I took their counsel, and bare witness
against the errors complained of, as well publicly as privately.
Which when some elders and brethren heard, meeting soon after
with some of these opinions: Lo, say they, now we have heard
your teacher bearing witness openly against those very points,
which you falsely father on him. No matter (say the other)
what you hear him say in public: we know what he saith to us
in private. This answer bred in some of my brethren and
friends, a jealousy that myself was a secret fomenter of this
spirit of Familism, if not leavened myself that way. Whereupon
sundry elders and brethren perceiving these errors to spread,
secretly and closely, they consulted among themselves, and with
me what I thought of a synod, whether it might be of use in
such a case for the clearing of these points, and the allaying of
the jealousies and differences in the country? I answered, yea.
Thereupon, with consent of the magistrates, a time, and place
was appointed for a synodical meeting, and sundry elders were
sent for, from other jurisdictions, and messengers from all the
churches in the country to assist in this work.

Against which time three things principally were attended for
preparation.

1. A solemn fast kept in all the churches: in which it fell

out, that Mr. Wheelwright's sermon was apprehended to give too much encouragement to the opinionists.[31] And himself hath since confessed, that being but new come into the country, having but little acquaintance but with his kindred, and their friends, (who were many of them leavened this way) he spake some things, which if he had before discerned their Familism, he would not have expressed himself as he did.

2. The thing attended to, for preparation to the synod, was the gathering up of all the corrupt and offensive opinions that were scattered up and down the country, and to commend them to public disquisition in the synod: that howsoever, the authors of them were loath to own them publicly, yet at least, they might see them publicly tried, confuted, and condemned. The which was accordingly done in the synod: and the opinions with their confutations are since printed in the short story, whence Mr. Baylie fetcheth many testimonies.

3. The thing thought needful for preparation to the synod, was, to gather out of my sermons to the people, and my conferences (in word and writing) with the elders, all such opinions of mine as were conceived by some, to be erroneous: and having gathered them together, to inquire in a brotherly conference with me, how far I would own them, or how I did understand them, that so the true state of the questions in difference might appear; and withal, if there were any aguish distemper, or disaffection grown in any of our spirits amongst ourselves, it might be healed in a private brotherly way, and mutual satisfaction given and taken on all hands. Accordingly we had such a meeting in private, wherein five questions were propounded unto

[31] [John Wheelwright, "A Sermon Preached at Boston in New England upon a Fast Day the XVIth of January 1636," *Publications of the Prince Society,* IX (Boston, 1876), 153–179.]

me, with desire of my plain and explicit answer to the same:
which also upon their demand, I gave suddenly.

QUESTION I *Whether our union with Christ be complete
before and without faith?*

Where I gave this answer, which was taken in writing: "Not
without, nor before the habit (or gift) of faith, but before the
act of faith; that is, not before Christ hath wrought faith in us
(for uniting himself to us, He worketh faith in us:) yet in order
of nature, before our faith doth put forth itself to lay hold on
Him."

For indeed I looked at union with Christ, as equipollent to
regeneration. And look as in generation we are in a passive way
united to Adam: so in regeneration we are united to Christ. And
as the soul *habet se mere passive*[32] (in the judgment of our best
divines) in regeneration, so also in union, and by the judgment
of Christ himself, who saith, without Christ abiding in us (and
so united to us) we can do nothing, not bring forth any spiritual
fruit at all: much less can we before union with Christ, unite
ourselves to Christ, which is the greatest and most solemn spiritual fruit of all. I was not ignorant, that some of the Schoolmen
(even some Dominicans) and out of them Ferius, and some
others (even of judicious Protestants) are of opinion, that
Christ doth give the soul by the almighty power of the *auxilium
efficax* of his spirit, to put forth an act of faith, to lay hold on
Christ, before He give them a habit or gift of faith. But I could
not understand how this could stand with Christ's word, that
without Christ abiding in us, we can do nothing. Which argueth,
no spiritual act can be done by us without Christ habitually
permanent in us. And as acute and judicious Baynes saith, in

[32] [Is in a completely passive state.]

Ephes. i, this were to give a man to see, without an eye to see withal: which though God can do by his almighty power, yet as the philosopher said of *entia:* so it may be much more said of *miracula* (which are extraordinary *entia*) *Miracula sine necessitate non sunt multiplicanda.*[33]

QUESTION II *Whether faith be an instrumental cause in applying Christ's righteousness to our justification?*

Whereto I answered,

"Faith is an instrument to receive the righteousness of Christ applied to us of God, for our justification: but not properly an instrumental cause."

Where I understood instrument, as the Hebrews do כלי which they indifferently put for instrument, or vessel: for faith emptying the soul of all confidence in its own righteousness, is a fit vessel or instrument to receive the righteousness of Christ offered and imputed; and so I took faith rather as a fit disposition of the subject to be justified, than as a proper instrumental cause of our justification: like the empty vessels of the prophet's widow, which whilst they were empty, the oil ran forth into them (the empty vessels being fit to receive it:) but yet the empty vessels were not properly instrumental causes of the running forth of the oil, but only instruments to receive it.

QUESTION III *Whether the Spirit of God in evidencing our justification doth bear witness in an aboslute promise of free grace, without qualification, or condition?*

My answer was,

"The Spirit in evidencing our justification doth bear witness either in an absolute promise, or in a conditional: in case, the condition be understood, or applied absolutely, not attending

---

[33] [Miracles are not to be multiplied without necessity.]

the condition as the ground or cause of the assurance, but as the effect and consequence of it: or (as I might have added, as before) as a fit disposition of the subject to receive it."

For I conceived, though the Spirit may evidence to us our justification in a qualification or condition: yet sometime the condition is not there before the promise, but freely given with the promise, as Acts x, 43, 44, where though Cornelius and his household were believers, yet many of his kindred and friends were not: who yet upon hearing the promise of remission (or justification) unto faith, they received both faith and justification, and the evidence of both, all together: as did also the jailor in the like sort, Acts xvi,31. Sometime, though the qualification or condition be there before, and the Spirit do bear witness to our justification in that condition: yet the condition is not the cause either of justification, or of the evidence of it, as in Luke vii,47. Christ beareth evident witness of the remission or justification of Mary Magdalen, in her love to Him. Nevertheless her love was not the cause, neither of her justification, nor of the assurance of it, but an affect of both. For she expressed those evidences of her love to Christ, because her sins were forgiven her, and because herself was assured of the forgiveness of them.

Sometimes the qualification or condition mentioned in the promise, though it be in the soul before, yet it is not evident there before. And then the evidence of justification springeth not from the condition, but from the grace of the promise, clearing and evidencing both the condition and the justification. Thus Christ applieth himself by his spirit, to bruised reeds, or broken hearts, Isai. lvii,15.

Lastly, if faith itself be meant to be the saving qualification or condition, and be also found, and that evidently in the soul to whom the promise of justification is made; yet the Spirit may bear witness in the promise of grace to the justification of such a soul, without either the word expressing the condition in that place, or the soul attending the condition at that time: as when Christ said to the woman, Luke vii,48. *Thy sins are forgiven thee,* He neither mentioned her faith in that word, nor doth it appear, that she did reflect upon her faith in receiving that promise at that time. Many an Israelite stung by the fiery serpents in the wilderness, might look up to the brazen serpent for healing, and yet at that time not look to their eye, nor think upon their eye by which they looked. And though afterwards Christ do make express mention of the woman's faith, to which he attributeth her salvation, (*Woman,* saith he, *thy faith hath saved thee,* ver. 50) nevertheless, that faith, though it be an evidence of assurance in the subject person of his justification: yet it is also an effect or consequence of the evidence and assurance of the object, that is, of the grace and mercy of God clearly revealed and applied to the soul in the promise, even to the begetting of faith itself, and the assurance of it. As when Christ did promise (by the ministry of Paul) salvation to the jailor in believing; the grace of Christ clearly revealed and applied in the promise did beget faith in the jailor, and the assurance of faith. And so his faith, and the assurance of it was an effect and consequence of the grace and assurance of it offered to him in the promise. Faith though it be an evidence of things not seen (with bodily eye;) yet it is an effect of a former evidence, even of the light of God's countenance shining forth through Christ in the promise of grace upon the soul, to the begetting of faith, and the assurance of it.

But howsoever, faith being always of a self humbling efficacy, it is a fit disposition of the subject to receive comfort and assurance, Isai. lvii,15.

Calvin defineth faith to be *divinæ ergo nos benevolentiæ firmam certamque cognitionem, quæ gratuitæ in Christo promissionis veritate fundata, per Spiritum Sanctum et revelatur men-*

tibus nostris et cordibus obsignatur,[34] *Institut* 1.3, *c.2,Sect.* 7.
Now when he cometh to expound what he meaneth by the free
promise of grace in Christ, upon which this knowledge (or
assurance) of faith is founded, he maketh it to be, not conditional. And he giveth this reason, *quoniam* (saith he) *condition-
alis promissio qua ad opera nostra remittimur, non aliter vitam
promittit, quam si perspiciamus esse in nobis sitam. Ergo, nisi
fidem tremere, ac vacillare volumus, illam salutis promissione
fulciamus oportet, quæ a Domino ultro ac liberaliter, potiusque
miseriæ nostræ quam dignitatis respectu offeratur;*[35] *ibidem
Sect.* 29.

But what was the occasion of this question from any speech or
writing of mine, I cannot call to mind, unless it were concerning
the first evidence of justification, which is the purport of the
next question. For otherwise, if faith and assurance be first
founded and bottomed upon a promise of free grace, I never
doubted, but that sanctification or faith, (any saving qualification) may be, (and is by the help of the Spirit) a clear and
certain evidence of justification. So that put the question *in
terminis,*

"Whether the Spirit of God in evidencing our justification
doth bear witness in an absolute promise of free grace, without
qualification or condition?"

I should answer plainly and roundly, the Spirit doth evidence
our justification in both ways, sometime in an absolute promise,
sometime in a conditional.

[34] [A firm and certain knowledge of divine good will towards us, which,
founded upon the truth of the free promise in Christ, by means of the Holy Spirit
is both revealed to our minds and impressed upon our hearts.]
[35] [Since a conditional promise, with which we are sent back to our tasks,
does not promise life on any other condition than that we perceive it to be
situated in us. Therefore, unless we want our faith to be shaken and to totter,
we must prop it up with the promise of salvation, which is offered by the Lord
spontaneously and generously, looking rather to our wretchedness than to our
worthiness to receive it.]

QUESTION IV *Whether some saving qualification may be a first evidence of justification?*

Hereto I answered,

"A man may have an argument from thence, (yea, I doubt not a firm and strong argument) but not a first evidence."

For I conceived, faith itself, which is an evidence of things not seen, and the first saving qualification that doth evidence justification, is itself founded upon a former evidence, even the free grace of God in Christ, revealed in the promise of grace, and applied to the soul effectually by the Spirit of grace, both in our effectual calling (even to the begetting of faith) and in our justification. Accordingly, the apostle reckoning the evidences that bear witness of our life in Christ, giveth the first place to the Spirit, before any fruit of the Spirit; there are three (saith he) that bear witness on earth, the Spirit, the water, and the blood, 1 John v,8. First, the Spirit, to wit, of illumination and drawing, whereby He revealeth Christ to us, and worketh faith in us, 2 Cor. iv,6.; Ephes. i, 17, 18; John vi, 44, 45. Secondly, the water of sanctification. And thirdly, the blood of atonement (or pacification) pacifying the conscience.

Calvin also is of the same judgment in this question, in 2 Pet. i,10 and in John iii, 14 and 19.

And Zanchi likewise doth at large dispute this question, and conclude it against Dr. Marbachius in his *Miscellanies,* in that part of it entitled, *Disceptatio inter Duos Theologos,* from page 598 to page 605. *Editionis in quarto.*

QUESTION V *Whether Christ and his benefits be dispensed in a covenant of works?*

Whereunto my answer was,

"Christ is dispensed to the elect in a covenant of grace: to others He may be dispensed in some sort, (to wit, in a taste of Him) either in a covenant of works, or in a covenant of grace legally applied."

To give an hint of the reason of mine answer. The covenant on Mount Sinai, (wherein Christ was dispensed in sacrifices and ceremonies) though to the faithful seed of Abraham it was a covenant of grace, (wherein they saw Christ and his benefits graciously dispensed to them, Psal. li, 7. yet to the carnal seed, it seemed to me to be a covenant of works, to prepare them for the saving benefits of that covenant of grace which was formerly given to Abraham and his seed, (but neglected by them in Egypt) and afterwards renewed in the plains of Moab, Deut. chap. xxix and chap. xxx. And so Paul maketh that covenant on Mount Sinai, to be expressly a different covenant from that of grace, to wit, a covenant gendering unto bondage, Gal. iv, 24, 25, and the other covenant, Deut. xxx, to be of grace, Rom. x, 6,7, 8. Moses also himself, having recited the covenant on Mount Sinai, Deut. v, he maketh the observation of all the commandments to be the righteousness of the people, Deut. vi,25. and their life, Levit. xviii, 4. And so Paul understandeth him, Rom. x, 5. Gal. iii, 12. Now that covenant which gendereth unto bondage, and holdeth forth righteousness and life upon obedience to all the commandments, is a covenant of works.

And so have the chiefest germane divines, as well as Piscator, and Polanus, taken the covenant on Mount Sinai to be a covenant of works. See Pisacator, Ezek. xvi. *Observat, ultima in vers.* 60,62, *et* Polanus *ibidem.*

How far there arose any consent or dissent about these questions, between my fellow brethren (the elders of these churches) and myself, it is not material now to particularize; it is enough, that upon our clear understanding of one another's minds and judgments, and upon the due proceeding of our church against convinced notorious errors and scandals, we have ever since (by the grace of Christ) much amiable and comfortable communion together in all brotherly kindness. But this short relation may suffice.

To let Mr. Baylie know, and all them that shall read his book, to consider, what slender ground he had to speak of my wandering into the horrible errors of the Antinomians, and Familists, and siding therein with Mistress Hutchinson, and therein to tell the world of a more dangerous fall of mine, than that of Montanism: and withal to clear up to him, what little ground Mistress Hutchinson had, to pretend, that she was of Mr. Cotton's judgment in all things: that so Mr. Baylie may likewise observe what ground himself had to take up such a report against me, upon her testimony. Which yet will the more fully appear, if I proceed to relate a principal passage or two in the synod, after it was assembled. It was the first act of the synod (after prayer and choice of moderators) to propound the several offensive opinions, which had been dispersed up and down the country, and briefly to argue them, and bear witness against them. The opinions were about fourscore (more or less) which being orderly propounded and argued against, I perceived that some of the members and messengers of our church, were ready to rise up, and plead in defense of sundry corrupt opinions, which I verily thought had been far from them, especially such as concerned union with Christ before faith, justification without faith, inherent righteousness, and evidencing a good estate by it at all, first or last. Whereupon as soon as I could get liberty of speech with them, "Brethren (said I) if you be of that judgment, which you plead for, all these bastardly opinions, which are justly offensive to the churches, will be fathered upon Boston." They answered me again, though they were not clear

for those opinions, which they spake for, yet neither were they
clear for condemning of them, considering the tenderness of
some consciences: I replied, if they were doubtful of the
erroneousness and danger of such opinions, they should have
dealt openly with the church at home, when they were chosen
messengers, and should have declared their judgments before
the church as knowing such points amongst others were likely
to come into agitation in the synod: whereas now look what
they speak, it is conceived by the whole country to be the
judgment of our church.

Hereupon some of the messengers of our church withdrew
themselves, and appeared no more in the synod, such as did appear, did much what forbear any prosecution of argument in
such causes. But that (to my remembrance) was the first time
of my discerning a real and broad difference, between the judgments of our brethren (who leaned to Mistress Hutchinson)
and myself. And therefore to clear myself, and the sounder
members of our church from partaking in those manifold errors
there presented, I declared my judgment openly before all the
assembly, that I esteemed some of the opinions to be blasphe-
mous: some of them, heretical, many of them, erroneous: and
almost all of them, incommodiously expressed: as intending to
except those chiefly, wherein I had declared mine own opinion,
as before.

But because I would deal openly and ingenuously with Mr.
Baylie, and hide nothing from him, that might fortify his
accusation against me, there was some color of my leaning to
one Antinomian tenent in one day of the synod. For though in
answer to the questions of the elders before the synod, I had
affirmed faith to be an instrument for the receiving the righteousness of Christ to be our justification: yet for as much as

some great divines had let fall some expressions, that seemed to favor the Antinomian party in a contrary tenent, I was desirous to hear that point a little further ventilated, and to see the difficulties a little more fully cleared. Dr. Twisse (not suspected for an Antinomian, much less for a Familist) in his *vindiciæ gratiæ, de electione, parte* 2, *section* 25, *numero* 5, bringeth in Arminius, arguing against Mr. Perkins, thus: "The righteousness of Christ wrought or performed, is not ours, as wrought or performed, but as by faith imputed to us." Whereto the Dr. answereth, "Before faith, this righteousness of Christ was ours, and in the intention of God the Father, and of Christ our Mediator, was wrought for us. And because it is wrought for us, therefore God in his own time will give it us, and grace of every kind, even faith itself amongst the rest. But faith coming, (which the Holy Ghost kindleth in our hearts) then at length this love of God to us in Christ is acknowledged and perceived. Whence it is, that the righteousness of Christ is said to be imputed to us, (by faith, because it is not discerned to be imputed to us, but by faith: and then we are said to be justified with that kind of justification, and absolution from sin, which breedeth peace in our consciences."

"And this (saith he) I confirm by two arguments. 1. Because by the righteousness of Christ, we obtain not only remission of sins, but faith itself, and repentance, as it is written, God hath blessed us with all spiritual blessings in Christ, Ephes. i,3. Therefore even before faith and repentance, the righteousness of Christ is applied to us, as for which we obtain grace effectual to believe in Christ, and to repent. 2. Because justification and absolution, as they signify an imminent act in God, are *ab eterno, etc.*"

Whereto he subjoineth the poet's ingenuous verse to the reader.

Si quid novisti rectius istis,
Candidus imperti; si non, bis utere mecum.[36]

Before Dr. Twisse, Chamier (a divine, as free as the other from suspicion of Antinomianism) denieth faith to be a cause of justification; "For if it were (saith he) justification should not be of grace, but of us. But faith is said to justify, not because it effecteth justification, but because it is effected in the justified person, and requisite to be found in him, *De Fide libr.* 13, *cap.* 6. And to the same purpose, *De Justificatione, libr.* 22, *cap.* 12, he contendeth, that faith as it doth not merit, nor bring justification, so neither doth it (*impetrare*) obtain it. For if it were so, then *tum ratione, tum tempore fides præcederet justificationem,* faith should go before justification, both in nature and time: which (saith he) in no sort may be granted. For faith is itself a part of sanctification; but there is no sanctification, but after justification, *quæ et re, et natura prior est,* which both in the thing itself, and in nature is before it.

To the like purpose doth Mr. Pemble deliver his judgments in his book of the nature and properties of grace and faith, Page 24, 26, of his edition in folio.

The discrepance of all these divines from the received expressions of the most, gave just occasion, why in such an assembly, the judgment of sundry acute and judicious elders might be enquired. Accordingly, in one day of their dispute in the synod (with Mr. Wheelwright, if I forget not) I interposed such a word as this, God may be said to justify me before the habit, or act of faith, and the habit is the effect of my justification, intending the same sense, as hath been expressed out of those divines: upon which, the next day was taken up in disputing

---

[36] [If you know anything more correct than this, share it openly; if not, adopt these principles with me.]

and arguing that point with me. And when I saw their apprehensions, that they were suitable to Scripture phrase, and the contrary difficulties might be removed *sano sensu,* I the next morning did of myself freely declare to them publicly, my consent with them in the point, which (as they professed) they gladly accepted.

Now upon all this relation (which is the substance of the whole truth in this cause) I desire Mr. Baylie might consider what ground he had, either to report me to the world as sometimes dangerously fallen into the horrible errors of Antinomianism, and Familism: or to take Mrs. Hutchinson's report in this cause, that she was of Mr. Cotten's judgment in all things. Let him please to read the short story of the errors and heresies, for which she was admonished publicly in Boston church, and let him judge of himself, whether she was of Mr. Cotton's judgment in all things.

I would not have enlarged myself so much, either to clear her testimony, or to elevate it, were it not to take off some scruples and surmises in Mr. Baylie of some dangerous guilt in me of Antinomian, and Familistical errors, which he thinks cannot be avoided by what he collecteth from other testimonies, as well as hers which may fully be prevented and avoided by this relation of the true state of things.

But before I leave speech of her, let me speak a word to Mr. Baylie of the epithet he is pleased to give her, when he styleth her, my dear friend, with whom I resolved to side and separate from all the churches in New England, as legal churches.

At her first coming, she was well respected and esteemed of me, not only because herself and family were well beloved in England at Allford in Lincolnshire (not far beyond Boston) nor only because she with her family came over hither (as was said) for conscience sake: but chiefly for that I heard, she did much good in our town, in woman's meeting at childbirth-travails, wherein she was not only skillful and helpful, but readily fell into good discourse with the women about their spiritual estates: and therein cleared it unto them, that the soul lying under a spirit of bondage, might see and sensibly feel the heinous guilt, and deep desert of sin, and thereby not only undergo affliction of spirit but also receive both restraining, and constraining grace likewise, (in some measure) restraining from all known evil (both courses, and companies) (at least for a season) and constraining to all known duties, as secret prayer, family exercises, conscience of Sabbaths, reverence of ministers, frequenting of sermons, diligence in calling, honesty in dealing and the like: yea and that the soul might find some tastes and flashes of spiritual comfort in this estate, and yet never see or feel the need of Christ, much less attain any saving union, or communion with Him, being no more but legal work, even what the law, and the spirit of bondage (breathing in it) might reach unto. By which means many of the women (and by them their husbands) were convinced, that they had gone on in a covenant of works, and were much shaken and humbled thereby, and brought to enquire more seriously after the Lord Jesus Christ, without whom all their gifts and graces would prove but common, and their duties but legal, and in the end wizen and vanish. All this was well (as is reported truly, page 31 of her story) and suited with the public ministry, which had gone along in the same way, so as these private conferences did well tend to water the seeds publicly sown. Whereupon all the faithful embraced her conference, and blessed God for her fruitful discourses. And many whose spiritual estates were not so safely laid, yet were hereby helped and awakened to discover their

sandy foundations, and to seek for better establishment in
Christ: which caused them also to bless the Lord for the good
success, which appeared to them by this discovery.

Hitherto therefore she wrought with God, and with the
ministers, the work of the Lord. No marvel therefore if at that
time, she found loving and dear, respect both from our church
elders and brethren, and so from myself also amongst the rest.

Afterwards, it is true, she turned aside not only to corrupt
opinions, but to disesteem generally the elders of the churches,
(though of them she esteemed best of Mr. Shepard) and for
myself, (in the repetitions of sermons in her house) what she
repeated and confirmed, was accounted sound, what she omitted,
was accounted Apocrypha. This change of hers was long hid
from me: and much longer the evidence of it, by any two clear
witnesses. I sent some sisters of the church on purpose to her
repetitions, that I might know the truth: but when she discerned
any such present, no speech fell from her, that could be much
excepted against. But further discourse about her course is not
pertinent to the present business. But by this Mr. Baylie may
discern, how far Mrs. Hutchinson was dear unto me, and if he
speak of her as my dear friend, till she turned aside, I refuse
it not.

But yet thus much I must profess to him, that in the times of
her best acceptance, she was not so dear unto me, but that (by
the help of Christ) I dealt faithfully with her about her spiritual
estate. Three things I told her, made her spiritual estate unclear
to me. 1. That her faith was not begotten nor (by her relation)
scarce at any time strengthened, by public ministry, but by
private meditations, or revelations only.

2. That she clearly discerned her justification (as she professed:) but little or nothing at all, her sanctification: though

(she said) she believed, such a thing there was by plain Scripture.

3. That she was more sharply censorious of other men's spiritual estates and hearts, than the servants of God are wont to be, who are more taken up with judging of themselves before the Lord, than of others.

Now a word of that other passage in Mr. Baylie's speech, touching my resolution to side with Mrs. Hutchinson, and to separate from all the churches of New England, as legal synagogues. The truth is, I did intend to remove, but not to separate; much less with Mrs. Hutchinson, and least of all from all the churches of New England: and yet less than the least of all, to separate from them as legal synagogues.

The occasion of my intent of removal was this. After the banishment of Mrs. Hutchinson and sundry others by occasion of her, the general court made an order, that none should be received to abide as inhabitants in this jurisdiction, unless they were allowed under the hand of the governor or two assistants. The assistants are our magistrates. When this law came to be put into use, I was informed that some godly passengers who hither arrived out of England, were refused to sit down amongst us, because (upon trial) they held forth such an union with Christ by the Spirit giving faith, as did precede the acting of faith upon Christ: and such an evidence of that union, by the favor of God shed abroad in their hearts by the Holy Ghost, as did precede the seeing (though not the being) of sanctification.

This took the deeper impression upon me, because I saw by this means, we should receive no more members into our church, but such as must profess themselves of a contrary judgment to what I believed to be a truth. Besides I was informed, that it was the judgment of some of place, in the country, that such a doctrine of union, and evidencing of union, as was held forth by me, was the Trojan Horse, out of which all the erroneous opinions and differences of the country did issue forth.

Hereupon, fearing this might in time breed a renewal of paroxysms, I called to mind the intent of my coming hither, which was, not to disturb, but to edify the churches here: and therefore began to entertain thoughts rather of peaceable removal than of offensive continuance. At the same time there was brought to me a writing, subscribed with about three-score hands to encourage me to removal, and offering their readiness to remove with me into some other part of this country.

I considered, if we removed, it would be matter of much various construction amongst such as knew us, both in Old England, and New; and I was loath to do any thing, (especially of importance) but what I might give account of before God, and his people; I took advice therefore of some friends here, especially Mr. Davenport, and resolved, first to clear the certainty of the grounds of the information given me of the rejections of those godly persons (of whom I had heard) for their judgment's sake in those points. 2. To see if my continuance here would certainly, or probably breed any further offensive agitation: and 3. If both those things were found clearly, then to take opportunity with common consent to remove to Quinipyack[37] whereto at that time a door was opened.

But when I came to enquire the certainty of these informations, in conference with some of our chief magistrates and others, I found, though there had speech been about such points between themselves, and some passengers: yet their refusal of such passengers was not upon those points; but (as I remember) upon denials of inherent righteousness in believers, and of any

---

[37] [Original name of New Haven, Connecticut.]

evidence of a good estate from thence, first or last. Withal, they
declared to me their minds touching such points of union, or
evidencing of union, which I had taught, that they did not look
at them to be of such fundamental concernment either to civil
or church peace, as needed to occasion any distance in heart,
(much less in place) amongst godly brethren. Which when I
heard from them, and found upon search, the misinformations
given me, were but misprisions, I then laid down all thoughts of
removal, and sat down satisfied in my abode amongst them, and
have so continued (by the help of God) to this day. By all this
may appear the truth of what I said, that though I had thoughts
of removal, yet not with Mrs. Hutchinson, she being gone to
Rhode Island, but I intending Quinipyack. Much less had I any
thoughts of separation from all the churches of New England:
for the churches in Quinipyack are in New England. And those
churches at the Bay (amongst whom I lived) it was far from my
thoughts to separate from them, whom I ever truly honored as
the holy spouses of Jesus Christ. Nor did I ever look at such
points, as any just ground of separation from any church (so
much as in place, much less in communion:) no nor any just
ground of removal from them, unless a man were compelled to
profess contrary to his judgment. And least of all durst I turn
my back upon such churches as legal synagogues, who do all of
us hold union with Christ, and evidencing of union by the same
Spirit, and the same faith and the same holiness: though some
may conceive the union wrought in giving the habit, and others
rather refer it to the act: and some may give the second place
to that, whereto others give the first.

It was therefore too much credulity in Mr. Baylie, either to
take up the former testimony from Mrs. Hutchinson, or this
latter from Mr. Williams: though if both of them had joined

in one and the same testimony, (which they do not) yet the testimony of two excommunicate persons doth not make up *idoneum testimonium*[38] in ecclesiastical causes.

No? saith Mr. Baylie, if I mistake not the humor of the man, (Mr. Williams he meaneth) he is very unwilling to report a lie of his greatest enemy.

I look not at myself, as his greatest, or least, or any enemy at all. I do not know, that I did ever walk towards him either in the affection, or action of an enemy, notwithstanding the provoking injuries, and indignities he hath put upon me.

Nor would I call it any man's humor (as Mr. Baylie calleth it, Mr. Williams his humor) to be very unwilling to report a lie of his greatest enemy.

But this I say, Mr. Williams is too too credulous of surmises and reports brought to him, and too too confident in divulging of them. Which if Mr. Baylie know not, he may (at his leisure, if he think it worth the while) peruse the reply, I have made to his answer of my letter, as also my answer to his bloody tenent.

But Mr. Baylie giveth the more credit to Mr. Williams his testimony, because Mr. Williams saith in his examination of my letter, how could I possibly (saith he) be ignorant of their estate, when being from first to last in fellowship with them, an officer amongst them, had private and public agitation concerning their estate, with all, or most of their ministers?

The answer is very easy both to Mr. Williams, and Mr. Baylie too, that Mr. Williams speaketh of the times before his banishment: then indeed he had some fellowship with us, and might have had more, but that he suspected all the *status conventus*[39] of the elders to be unwarrantable, and such as might in

38 [Proper witness.]
39 [Assemblies.]

time make way to a presbyterial government. But this testimony, which he giveth about my nearness to separation from these churches, was many years after his banishment from us, when he was in no fellowship with us, sacred nor civil, nor came any whit near any private or public agitation amongst us, nor could have any intelligence of our affairs, but by report and fame, which is *tam ficti pravique tenax, quam nuncia veri,*[40] and is indeed in this point, most false.

But yet (saith Mr. Baylie) the truth of this horrible fall (of Mr. Cotton) if you will not take it, neither from the followers of Mrs. Hutchinson, nor from the testimony of Mr. Williams: yet we may not reject the witness of Mr. Winthrop, and of Mr. Wells in their printed relations of the schisms there.

"Both these, albeit, with all care and study, they endeavor to save Mr. Cotton's credit: yet they let the truth of Mr. Cotton's seduction fall from their pens in so clear terms, as cannot be avoided: yea so clear, as no art will get Mr. Cotton cleared."

Notwithstanding all this confident charge of Mr. Baylie, there will be no need at all of any art to clear Mr. Cotton, from seduction into any such horrible fall, the naked truth (by the help of Christ) will clear both itself, and him. The testimonies of Mr. Winthrop, and Mr. Wells, are all delivered (as it seemeth) in the short story.

In the Preface, page 7, it is said, "By this time, they had to patronize them, some of the magistrates, and some men eminent for religion, parts and wit."

Ans. 1. This were something, if there were no more men eminent for religion, parts and wit, in the country but myself, who profess no eminency in any of these in respect of many of brethren. But if I were eminent, the testimony concludeth not. Let not art judge, whether the conclusion will follow from both

---

[40] [As much prone to fiction and falsehood as a messenger of the truth.]

the premises particular: but let common sense judge of such men, as then lived in the country, whether there were not many eminent persons for religion, parts, and wit, who did patronize them, though I had been out of the country.

2. I willingly confess, that I myself, though I did not patronize them, yet I did countenance them (in my measure) whilst they held forth (to my knowledge) no more than I have formerly delivered of my own tenents: which yet I hope he will not again tax, as an horrible fall into Antinomianism and Familism. When their errors were brought to me, I bare public witness against them, even before I was fully persuaded that those persons were guilty of them.

His next testimony (which he quoteth from page 25 of the short story) the former part of it concerneth Mr. Wheelwright, and not me: though I must confess I do not know how it can be collected from Mr. Wheelwright's doctrine, unless it were by a forestalled misapprehension and misapplication of those hearers, who were leavened with corrupt opinions. The latter part of the testimony, "That the former governor never stirred out, but attended by the sergeants with halberts or carabines, but the present governor was neglected:" I do not remember, that ceremony was any more than once neglected: and when I heard it, I bore witness against it. And they excused their former observance, by the eminency of the person. But sure I am, the present governor (as he well deserveth all honor from his people, so) he is seldom or never seen in public, but in like sort attended with halberts or carabines.

Next, he allegeth a testimony from the court, which (it is likely) was delivered by Mr. Winthrop, being then governor, page 35 of the short story: "They soon profited so well, as in a few months, they outwent their teacher."

Ans. This testimony is so far from taxing me of any horrible fall, that it clearly acquiteth me from the fellowship thereof. For if they outwent their teacher, as the court said (and said truly) then I went not along with them in their tenents. And teacher I was called, and their teacher, as being called to that office in that church, whereof many of them were members.

The next testimony (from page 33 of the story) expresseth, "That upon the countenance it took from some eminent persons, her opinions began to hold up their heads in courts of justice."

Ans. This might indeed argue, that some magistrates leaned more or less to that way: but it reacheth not me, who am seldom present at any courts, but when with other elders I am sent for. And let it not be forgotten, what I related above, that many held with those opinionists (as they were called) when they knew of no other opinions held forth by them, but what was publicly taught in our church: but after they were discovered to overgo not so much their teachers, as the truth, and that so evidently, as could clearly be convinced by the testimony of two or three witnesses, they were soon forsaken by those, who esteemed better of them before.

His next testimony is from the story, page 32. "It was a wonder, upon what a sudden, the whole church of Boston (some few excepted) were become her new converts, and infected with her opinions."

And Preface page 7. "Most of the seducers lived in the church of Boston."

Ans. That most of the Church of Boston consented with Mrs. Hutchinson, (whilst she openly held forth no more, than what was publicly taught) is true; but nothing to prove Mr. Cotton's horrible fall, for after she fell into any horrible, or evident errors, it may clearly appear, the whole church were not become her converts, by this undeniable evidence, that the whole body of the church (except her own son) consented with one accord, to the public censure of her, by admonition first, and excommunication after.

But (saith Mr. Baylie) "None of these erroneous persons were ever called to account by the presbytery of that church, till after the assembly, though the pastor of the church, Mr. Wilson was always exceeding zealous against them."

Ans. 1. Mr. Baylie is mistaken, when he saith, Mr. Wilson was always exceeding zealous against them. For the whole church will bear him witness, he was a long time full of much forbearance towards them, and thought well of them, and bare witness to the ways of free grace in such manner, as testified his good will to them and the truth. Afterwards in some private conference, which one or more of them had with him, and (our beloved sister) his wife, he discerned some more rottenness in them, and their way, than he suspected before: and after that time indeed, he grew more zealous against them, but the occasion of the offense was private, and (for a good space) unknown both to me and the church.

2. But why they were not called to account by the presbytery of the church, the reason was evident: because their gross errors were not confirmed into us, by two or three witnesses. And this I can truly profess, that when the elders of other churches acquainted me with some of their errors, (even when the noise of them was spread far and near:) yet they acknowledged, the erroneous persons were so cautious, that they would never vent any gross errors before two witnesses. And this I can further truly avouch, that myself dealt sadly and seriously with some chief leaders of them, both by word, and writing to recover them from the error of their way: which though they would argue for, yet they would ever excuse themselves from settling upon any such things. I dealt also with others (whom I began to suspect

might be leavened by their leaders) and earnestly charged them to beware what tenents they received from them, lest by that means they might be corrupted themselves, and their leaders hardened. But they would not be known to me, that they drunk in any such dregs, as afterwards appeared.

His next testimony is taken from Mrs. Hutchinson's speech in the open court, preferring my ministry in holding forth free grace, above some, or most of the other elders. But of the invalidity of her testimony in these things I have spoken, (I suppose) enough above. An evil spirit (which sometimes breatheth both in good and bad persons,) may give a glorious testimony to some servants of God, not so much to honor them, or their doctrine, as either to cover themselves under their shadow, or else (but that was not her aim) to bring them and their doctrine into suspicion and trouble, as the spirit of the Pythoness did to Paul and Silas, Acts xvi, 17, to 20. That speech of hers, I bore witness against it, as prejudicial and injurious both to them and me.

Another testimony he allegeth out of the story, page 50. That all the ministers consented in bearing some witness against Mr. Wheelwright, except their brother the teacher of Boston.

Ans. The story relateth those words, as the speech of the elders; that they speak of me, as their brother, to wit, the brother of the elders, lest any should misconceive of their speech, as ranking me in a brotherhood with erroneous persons.

That I did not consent with the rest of my brethren (the elders) in drawing the inference out of Mr. Wheelright's sermon, which they (being required) presented to the court, I had a twofold reason for it. 1. Because I was not present with them, when they searched Mr. Wheelwright's sermon, and gathered that inference from it.

2. Because I could not speak it of mine own knowledge, that the elders of the country did walk in or teach such a way of salvation, and evidencing thereof, as Mr. Wheelwright describeth, and accounteth to be a covenant of works.

They knew what themselves taught in that point, better than I. The elders might testify what they knew: I could not testify, what I knew not. But it seemeth any testimonies will serve turn, when such as these are thought unavoidable, to lay me under the guilt of an horrible fall.

Yet one more remaineth, from page 21, that albeit the assembly of the churches had confuted and condemned most of these new opinions, and Mr. Cotton had in public view consented with the rest: yet the leaders in those erroneous ways stood still to maintain their new light. Mr. Wheelwright also continued his preaching, and Mrs. Hutchinson her wonted meetings: and much offense was still given by her, and others in going out from the pastor's exercise.

Ans. 1. As the assembly of the churches confuted and condemned those errors, so I will not say, that the motion of confuting them (as I remember) arose from myself. And myself also had an hand in confuting such of them, as the elders committed to my hand, themselves took several likewise tasks, none of us confuted all. My consent to the confutation. I have expressed above, and in what sense. What I did in public view (as the story expresseth it) I spake before the Lord, and from the truth of my heart.

That notwithstanding this act of the assembly against the errors, the leaders still stood to maintain their way, it was because the assembly did not fasten these errors upon any persons either in our own, or other churches. And what corrupt opinions were maintained by our members, it was done in private, and not before such witnesses, as might reach to public conviction.

Mr. Wheelwright's continuance in his preaching, was eight or nine miles distance from us. And having been put into that place before by the church, whilst the farmers there belonged to our church (which by reason of the distance, we soon after dismissed into a church estate amongst themselves) we that were elders could not (if we would) discharge him from that work, without the consent of the church. But though he gave some offense in some passages at the assembly, (which he since upon further conference and consideration retracted:) yet neither the church, nor myself (notwithstanding those unsafe expressions) did ever look at him, either as an Antinomian or Familist. Many of us knew that he had taken good pains against both, and in that very place, where he was wont to preach: insomuch that one of his hearers (who since joined Mr. Gorton's society) openly contested against his doctrine as false and anti-christian. And when Mr. Wheelwright was put out of this country (though he be since restored) yet if he had cleaved to the errors which Mrs. Hutchinson's company fell into, he would never have refused their earnest invitation and call of him, to minister unto them. They sent to him, and urged him much to come to them, to a far richer soil, and richer company than where he lived: yet he constantly refused, and upon that very ground, because of the corruption of their judgments: professing often, whilst they pleaded for the covenant of grace, they took away the grace of covenant.

Mrs. Hutchinson's continuance of her weekly meetings we could not proceed to the suppression thereof, with consent of the church, before we received the conviction of her personal errors, which she still closely carried, till after her civil censure. And then she declared herself more plainly, and witnesses arose more fully, and the church proceeded against her accordingly.

The going of herself and others out of the congregation when our pastor began to exercise, though many feared it was a turning their backs upon his ministry: yet the most of them were women, and they pretended many excuses for their going out, which it was not easy to convince of falsehood in them, or of their contempt of him.

But in fine, when her Antinomian and Familistical errors were held forth by her before sufficient witnesses, our church (as I said before) proceeded without delay, first, to admonish her according to the rule, Tit. iii, 10, 11. Afterwards when upon serious pains taken with her, Mr. Davenport and myself (as we thought) had convinced her of her erroneous ways in judgment and practice, so as that under her hand, she presented a recantation before the whole church, (indeed before many churches then assembled at Boston) yet withal, (after some passages of speech) professing that she never was of any other judgment, than what she now held forth, so many witnesses forthwith rose up to convince the contrary, that with common consent both of the elders and brethren of our church, she was cast out of our communion.

And now that (by the help of Christ) I have perused all the testimonies which Mr. Baylie hath alleged to convince me of an horrible fall into Antinomianism, and Familism, I desire him in the fear of God to consider, whether any or all these testimonies severally or jointly, will amount to make good such grievous scandals as he hath charged upon me. Which if they neither will, nor can reach unto, let him remember his promise in his Epistle Dedicatory, that in all which he hath said over and above (just testimony) he will undertake to give ample satisfaction, wherein so ever he hath given the least offense to any. Meanwhile the Lord lay not this sin to his charge.

SECTION XIV. *Of Cotton's humiliation upon his former fall, as is reported by Mr. Baylie*

But yet let me add a word more, to a word of Mr. Baylie's in his entrance of this discourse of my Antinomianism, and Familism, which may else leave an impression upon the minds of some reader, as if I had acknowledged this my dangerous fall, and had been much humbled for it.

"This other more dangeous fall (saith he) as it hath already much humbled his spirit, and opened his ear to instruction, and I trust will not leave working, till it have brought him yet nearer to his brethren: so to the world's end, it cannot but be a matter of fear and trembling to all, who shall know it, and of abundant caution, to be very wary of receiving any singularity from his hand, without due trial."

Ans. 1. Suppose all this were true *in terminis,* as Mr. Baylie hath expressed it, yet this were no impeachment at all to the doctrine and practice of that (which he calleth) our Independent church way; nor is it any just ground of caution to be wary of receiving my testimony to it. Peter's dangerous and dreadful fall into the denial of Christ, (though he seemed to be a pillar) was no impeachment, but advancement to Christianity. And if my fall were so dangerous, walking in this church-way, and stumbling so foully in it, the greater grace and witness from heaven was upon his churches in this way, who by the blessing of God were instruments of recovering me out of this fall, even by a consultatory conference in a synod, which did not assume to themselves any power of church censures. Let me be accounted to have fallen, and to have fallen (as Mr. Baylie representeth it) horribly, so that the truth and ways of Christ may stand and find free passage.

Neither is this fall of mine such a just ground of caution (as he would make it) unto any, to be very wary of receiving my testimony to this church way. For the way is no singularity from my hand, but that which the body of the rest of my brethren, and of the churches in this country do walk in with me.

Ans. 2. But yet, let not Mr. Baylie make further speech or use of my humiliation, than was performed, or intended by me. For God hath not given me to this day (upon my best search) to discern any such fall into Antinomianism, or Familism, as either hath, or might much humble my spirit.

It is true, my spirit hath much cause to be humbled, (and so through mercy it was) upon many just occasions at that time. As first, that so many erroneous and heretical opinions should be broached in the country, and carried on with such arrogancy, and censoriousness, and guile of spirit.

Secondly, that the principal offenders in this kind were members of our own church, and some of them such as had near relation to myself.

Thirdly, that myself should be so sleepy and invigilant, as that these (not tares only, but briars) should be sown in our field, and myself not discern them, till sundry persons up and down the country were leavened by them.

Fourthly, that such as endeavored the healing of these distempers, did seem to me to be transported with more jealousies, and heats and paroxysms of spirit, than would well stand with brotherly love, or the rule of the Gospel.

The bitter fruits whereof do remain to this day, in the letters sent over that year from hence to England. Whence also it came to pass finally, that in the course taken for the cleansing of God's field, it seemed to me, that some good wheat was plucked up with the tares, some simple hearted honest men, and some truths of God, fared the worse for the resemblance which the tares bare to them.

Upon all which grounds, myself with our whole church thought it needful to set a day apart for public humiliation before the Lord, wherein these and the like, both in prayer and preaching, were opened more at large before the Lord and his people.

But all this will not amount to make good Mr. Baylie's word, that my dangerous fall into Antinomianism and Familism hath much humbled my spirit.

Nor can I say (as he doth) that it opened mine ears to instruction. For I do not know, that they have been shut to it, when I discerned the spirit, and word of truth breathing in it.

Nor can I say after him, that the humbling of my spirit for those dangerous errors, will not leave working till it have brought me yet nearer to my brethren.

For though I bless the Lord, who hath brought me nearer to my brethren, and them also nearer to me, which I trust will still grow whilst ourselves grow (in all the duties of brotherly love, wherein we have much sweet and frequent intercourse:) yet I do not intepret this as the fruit of my spirit's humiliation for my Antinomy, and Familism: but as the fruits of our clearer apprehension, both of the cause and of the state of our differences, and of our joint consent and concurrence in bearing witness against the common heresies, and errors of Antinomianism, and Familism, which disturbed us all.

But Mr. Baylie as he began his discourse of my dangerous fall with relation of my humiliation for it: so he shutteth it up, page 58, with a like close of my grief of mind, and confusion for it.

"I have been informed (saith he) by a gracious preacher who was present at the synod in New England, that all the brethren there, being exceedingly scandalized with Mr. Cotton's carriage, in Mistress Hutchinson's process, did so far discountenance, and so severely admonish him, that he was thereby brought to the greatest shame, confusion, and grief of mind, that ever in all his life he had endured."

Ans. 1. I conceive it is not allowable in presbyterial discipline, (sure I am, not in Congregational) that an accusation shalt be received against an elder under one witness, though he gracious and a preacher: especially when this gracious preacher is nameless, and his testimony hovereth in generalities, without instance in particular offenses: as that all the brethren were exceedingly scandalized with Mr. Cotton's carriage in Mistress Hutchinson's process, but not expressing what carriage, nor what process, wherein they were scandalized.

And that all the brethren did so far discountenance him, and severely admonish him, as that he was thereby brought to the greatest shame, and confusion, and grief of mind, that ever in all his life he endured. But no mention for what offense they did so severely admonish him, nor wherein they did so far discountenance him.

Such words of infamy, and reproach may pass for table talk (which yet moral philosophy would not approve:) but surely in orderly church discipline, such dealing could not pass without just reproof, unless there were too much prejudice or partiality, the rule is plain and obvious, and not now the first time violated in the Dissuasive, 2 Tim. v,19.

Ans. 2. I must (as justly I may) protest against that testimony, not only as violating the rule of love, but of truth also, For,

1. It is untrue, that all the brethren were scandalized with my carriage, much less exceedingly scandalized at the synod, or in any process about Mrs. Hutchinson. There were sundry godly brethren otherwise minded, and otherwise affected.

2. It is untrue also, that such as were scandalized, did so severely admonish me, or discountenance me; for I can neither

call to mind any such deep discountenance, nor any such severe admonition of brethren, and yet I had reason to know it, and to remember it well, as well as any brother at the synod: the matter so nearly concerning myself, and more nearly and deeply, than any man else.

3. It is most untrue, that I was so far discountenanced, and so severely admonished, as that I was brought to the greatest shame, confusion and grief of mind, that ever in all my life I had endured.

I should have little comfort in my own spirit, to look either God or man in the face, if the discountenance or admonition of men (especially for such carriage) were the greatest shame, and confusion, and grief of mind, that ever in all my life I had endured. The rebukes of God upon the soul for sin will put a man to far greater shame, and confusion and grief of mind, than any discountenance, or admonition from brethren, (especially for such offenses), Psal. lxxvi,7. But whatsoever discountenance, or disrespect I met withal, from one hand or other, till the true state of my judgment, and carriage was clearly manifested, I have long ago left with the Lord. But I conceive I have met with more hard measure in letters to England, and in ungrounded reports there, than ever I found from the admonition, or discountenance of any brethren here.

SECTION XV *Of the shameful absurdities said to be found in the way of Independency: notwithstanding the great helps, to prevent, or cover it: and first, of those helps*

Mr. Baylie now undertaketh to prove that which he calleth a broad assertion, and well may he so call it; for it reacheth far beyond all dimensions of truth. His assertion is, that the way (which he calleth) Independency hath in a few years (less than one week of years) flown out into more shameful absurdities, than the Brownists to this day, in all their fifty years' trial have stumbled upon.

How will Mr. Baylie (think you) make this good?

His affirmation, that the way of Brownism, and Independency (as he styleth them) are both of them really one and the same, because he saith, it will appear hereafter, I refer it therefore to his place.

But before he cometh to make his broad assertion good, yea and (as he promiseth) palpable, he maketh it also by the way, admirable, and that many ways.

1. In that Independency hath been brought to the utmost pitch of perfection, which the wit, and industry of its best patrons were able to attain: and hath been fenced with the laws of gracious magistrates, who were at our absolute devotion, and yet hath flown out, etc.

Ans. 1. We that judge that way (which he calleth Independency) to be of God, should account it blasphemy in ourselves to accept such a style put upon us, as to be the best patrons of it. We do verily believe, that though ourselves, all of us, should employ our best wits and industry to join with Mr. Baylie to subvert and deface it: yet the Lord Jesus would show himself a patron to maintain his own institutions, though with the confusion of the faces, and enterprises of us all. The word which hath gone out of his mouth for the government and ordering of his church till his second appearing, he himself as He hath spoken it, will also shew it forth in his times, who is the blessed and only potentate, the king of kings and lord of lords, 1 Tim. vi, 14, 15.

Ans. 2. We cannot but with thankfulness acknowledge the goodness of God in our gracious magistrates, and their assistance to us in the work of the Lord; but when Mr. Baylie maketh them

to be at our absolute devotion, his ὑπερβολὴ,[41] is too too injurious
in debasing them, and (in their eyes) advancing us. For neither
are they devoted to us at all, nor much less absolutely. Though
they sometimes consult with us in matters of conscience; yet
they take our counsel no further than they see it cleared from the
word. And besides, it is too vast an advancement of us, to make
them absolutely of our devotion. For devotion in matters of
religion, (or as Thomas speaketh, *in iis quæ ad Dei cultum, et
famulatum pertinent*)[42] is a divine worship due to God only;
in as much that Aquinas taketh it to be too high a worship to be
terminated in saints, 22, *quest.* 82, *art.* 2. And yet he alloweth
more divine worship to saints, than any orthodox Protestant
can excuse from idolatry.

Again secondly, it may seem to make the palpableness of our
outflowings the more admirable, in that (as he saith) much of
our way is yet in the dark.

Thirdly, in that none of ourselves have proclaimed our discords to our own shame.

Fourthly, that none who have fallen from us, have of purpose
put pen to paper, to inform the world of our ways.

Fifthly, that none of us have been willing to reply to any of
the books written against us, etc.

Ans. It were much I confess, if we had all these advantages
of concealment which he mentioneth, and yet nevertheless so
many, and so shameful absurdities of ours should fall out in so
short a time, and become so palpable as Mr. Baylie proclaimeth
them. But the truth is, neither have we had those advantages,
(he speaketh of) but the contrary disadvantages, nor yet do we
fear, that he will be able to find such absurdities to have fallen
out in our way, much less so shameful.

41 [Hyperbole.]
42 [In those matters which pertain to the worship and serving of God.]

For first, the way of the New English churches is not in the dark, but published to the view of the world, in the book so entitled (refuted by Mr. Rutherford) as also in the Apology of these churches, in the Covenant, in the answer to thirty-two questions; in another answer to nine questions; in the answer to Mr. Herle, and to Mr. Rathband.[43] Some of our most populous churches do no church act, no not of discipline, but in the presence of the whole town, (non-members, as well as members) so many of them as are pleased to be present. Ways of truth seek no corners; if any church admonish a brother privately, it is because his offense is not known to non-members.

Again, if in our discords, none of us have proclaimed our shame, whence hath Mr. Baylie gathered all our shameful absurdities? The short story, (the greatest storehouse of his testimonies) what is it, but a fruit of our discords? Besides, if none that have fallen from us, have of purpose put pen to paper to inform the world of our ways, what mean the bleatings of plain dealing, and Mr. Williams his invectives against us, which yield a further supply to Mr. Baylie's testimonies?

Moreover, if none of us have been willing to reply to the books written against us, how come it to pass that Mr. Hooker hath written a large answer to Mr. Rutherford, Mr. Davenport to Mr. Paget, Mr. Mather to Mr. Rathband, Mr. Shepard and Mr. Allen to Mr. Ball, Mr. Norton in Latin to Mr. Appollonius; myself to Mr. Williams, both to his examination of my letter,

---

[43] [These are, respectively: John Cotton, *The Way of the Churches of Christ in New England* (London, 1644); Samuel Rutherford, *The Due Right of Presbyteries* (London, 1644); Richard Mather, *Church-government*, which was frequently referred to as an apology and which answered thirty-two questions; Richard Mather and William Tompson, *A Modest and Brotherly Answer* (London, 1644), which answered Charles Herle; and Thomas Weld, *An Answer to W.R.* (London, 1644), answering William Rathband, bue see note 44, p. 261, for the authorship of this work.]

and to his bloody tenent?[44] If any of these have miscarried by the way, or in England have met with a suppression for an impression, it cannot be said, that none of us have been willing to reply to the books written against us, nor that we have been wanting in endeavors, according as the Lord hath vouchsafed us means and opportunity.

If still there be other books written against us, unto which no reply is yet made, it may be considered, our laborers (in that kind) are few, our hands feeble, our times took up with the duties of our calling, helps to ease us are wanting. Domestical questions are not wanting, and many times books are extant against us some years before they come to our hands. And yet let not Mr. Baylie take our silence for a consent to what is written against us: or for a sign of our fear to lay open the true state of our cause, or the nakedness of our way, (as it seemeth

---

[44] [The "bleatings" were those of Thomas Lechford's *Plain Dealing* (London, 1642). Williams' "invectives" were included in those works of his alluded to in the list Cotton here presents, the books being, respectively: Thomas Hooker, *A Survey of the Summe of Church-discipline* (London, 1648); Rutherford, *Due Right of Presbyteries*; John Davenport, *Answer of the Elders* (London, 1643); John Paget, *A Defence of Church-government* (London, 1641); Richard Mather, see below; William Rathband, *A Briefe Narration of Some Church Courses* (London, 1644); Thomas Shepard and John Allen, *A Defence of the Answer* (London, 1644); John Ball, *Trial of the New Church-way in New England and Old* (London, 1644); John Norton, *Responsio ad totam questionum syllogen* (London, 1648); Guillaume Apollonius, *Consideratio quarundum controversiarum* (London, 1644); John Cotton, *The Bloudy Tenent Washed* (London, 1647), which includes *A Reply to Mr. Williams His Examination*; and Roger Williams, *Mr. Cottons Letter . . . Examined and Answered* (London, 1644), and *The Bloudy Tenent of Persecution* (London, 1644). Although Richard Mather took a large part in the written debate with the Presbyterians, his *A Modest and Brotherly Answer* (London, 1644), written with William Tompson, was directed at Charles Herle rather than at Rathband. In 1644, *An Answer to W.R.* was printed, but the title page says Thomas Weld is the author. Cotton's allusion here, however, raises the suspicion that Mather may indeed have written part or all of this answer since Weld, who was the colony's agent in England, is known to have seen the writings of New Englanders through the press and is suspected to have left his own name on some of them.]

to him:) but let him consider, that if many books be written by several hands, of several subjects against any of us, he whom it concerneth, cannot reply to them all at once, but to one after another, as the Lord giveth help and opportunity.

SECTION XVI   *Of the first absurdity said to be found in our way of Independency*

But what may be those shameful absurdities, which in less than one week of years, we have flown out into more than (those he calleth) Brownists in fifty years of their trial.

The fruits of our church way, (saith he) are first, the holding out of all our churches and Christian congregation many thousands of people, who in former time have been reputed in Old England very good Christians.

And this (saith he) seemeth a grievous absurdity, a great dishonor to God, and cruelty against men to spoil so many thousand Christians, whom they dare not deny to be truly religious of all the privileges of the church, either to themselves, or to their children, or put them into the condition of pagans, etc.

Ans. 1.   If all this were true, yet it is no greater an absurdity than that wherein those whom he calleth Brownists, have not only stumbled upon, but professedly walked in: yea it may be, denying church communion to as many churches as we do to persons in this country. And this Mr. Baylie hath taxed them for, above in page 27 of his book, though here he forget it.

Ans. 2.   It is not true, that we hold out any at all, English or Indian, out of our Christian congregations. All without exception are allowed to be present, at our public prayers and psalms, at our reading of the Scriptures, and the preaching and expounding of the same, and also at the admitting of members, and dispensing of seals and censures.

Ans. 3.   It is not truly spoken, that we hold out of all our churches many thousands of people, who in former times have been reputed in Old England very good Christians, and whom ourselves dare not deny to be truly religious.

I dare be bold to speak it, we hold not out any one such; but if any such be held out, we hold not off from them, but they from us: yea we seriously invite them (publicly and privately) to join with us: unless such religious persons lie under some scandal of corrupt life, or doctrine.

How then will Mr. Baylie make good (that which he truly calleth) his broad assertion? Yes, he undertaketh to make it good by three testimonies.

1.   Saith he, "We have heard sundry to esteem the number of the English in that plantation to exceed forty thousand men and women. But when Mr. Cotton is put to it, he dareth hardly avow the one half of these to be members of any church."

And to prove this, he quoteth (in P) the answer to the twenty-three questions, page 7.

Whereto the reply is ready, 1. Mr. Baylie is mistaken, if he think the answer to the thrity-two questions was penned by me. Those questions were sent by some ministers in Lancashire or Cheshire to one of their countrymen, (a reverend brother, and fellow-elder amongst us) Mr. Mather: who to satisfy their desires returned them that answer, which (it seemeth) hath since been printed. Which I speak not, because I waive the answer, for when he wrote it, he wrote advisedly, and as his whole answer is solid, and judicious; so is his answer, to the question put to him, pertinent and full; but to Mr. Baylie's assertion, it cometh nothing near it. But Mr. Baylie should have done well, to have taken his full answer to that question. The New English plantations are scattered above two hundred miles in length upon the sea coasts: and of what they did in those remote plantations, he could not then give present account. But (saith Mr. Mather) in the churches within the Bay, where most of us are best acquainted, we may truly say, that for the heads of families those that are admitted, are far more in number than the other, besides whom there are sundry children and servants, that are admitted also.

And for the reasons (saith he) why many are not yet received to church communion, they be sundry:

1. Sundry are new come over, and so are not yet known.

2. Sundry when they come to be known are found scandalous.

3. Some godly persons forbear to join with us for a time, till they may try, which church and ministry they can best close withal.

4. Those that are known to be godly (I may add, though but in judgment of charity) they are all admitted to some church or other, presently upon their own desire, unless they have given some offense, which also is removed upon their giving due satisfaction.

This testimony will not reach (nothing near) Mr. Baylie's assertion, that we hold out of all churches many thousands of people, who were well reputed of in Old England for very good Christians, and such as ourselves dare not deny to be truly religious.

2. His second testimony is from Mr. Lechford, who styleth his book against the country, Plain Dealing. And what saith he? In his page 73, "Here are (saith he) such confessions, and professions required both of men, and women, both in private and public, before they be admitted, that three parts of the people of the country remain out of the church, so that in short time, most of the people will remain unbaptized."

Ans. The book is unfitly called Plain Dealing, which (in respect of many passages in it) might rather be called false and fraudulent. I forbear to speak of the man himself, because soon after the publishing of that book, himself was called away out of the world to give account of his book and whole life before the highest judge. He was indeed himself not received into the fellowship of the church, for his professed errors: as 1. that the Antichrist described in the Revelation was not yet come, nor any part of that prophecy yet fulfilled from the 4. chapter to the end.

2. That the apostolic function was not yet ceased: but that there still ought to be such, who should by their transcendent authority govern all churches. To reclaim him from these errors, he was seriously dealt withal both in conference, and (according to his desire) in writing. But when he saw, he could not defend the latter error, but by building again the bishops, against whom he had witnessed (as he said) in soliciting the cause of Mr. Prynne, he rather than he would revoke his present tenent, acknowledged he was then in an error, when he took part with Mr. Prynne, and Mr. Burton, and therefore he would now return to England again, to reduce those famous witnesses from the error of their way. And accordingly, away he went: but see the wise hand of God disappointing his ends; when he came to England the bishops were falling, so that he lost his friends, and hopes both in Old England and New: yet put out his book (such as it is) and soon after died. By the way, let no man think, he was kept out of our churches, for maintaining the authority of bishops. For we have in our churches some well respected brethren, who do indifferently allow either Episcopal, or Presbyterial, or Congregational government, so be it they govern according to the rules of the Gospel. Neither do we disturb such, nor they us in our communion with them. But to return to Mr. Lechford's Plain Dealing: that which he testifieth, neither is it true; neither if it were, doth it reach Mr. Baylie's assertion.

It is not true, that three parts of the country remain out of the church, if he means three parts of four, no though he should take in those remote English, who live a score of miles or more from any church.

But were his speech more true than it is, yet it will not make good Mr. Baylie's assertion, unless those three parts of the country, which (he saith) remain out of the church, were reputed in Old England for very good Christians, nor durst ourselves deny them to be truly religious, to which this testimony alleged giveth no evidence at all.

Mr. Baylie's third testimony is from Mr. Williams, whom he calleth one of us, who maketh such Protestants to be heathens and publicans, who depart from the beast in a false constitution of national churches, if the bodies of Protestant nations remain in an unregenerate estate.

Ans. I know not why Mr. Baylie should call Mr. Williams one of us, who renounceth our churches, and is himself cast out both of church fellowship, and civil cohabitation with us.

His testimony, which Mr. Baylie quoteth out of him, of the estate of all such Protestants, as live in a national church estate, as if Christ did account them heathens and publicans.

I say no more to it but this, they may be so accounted by Mr. Williams, but we do not believe they are so accounted of by Christ, but many thousands of them to be precious saints in the eyes of the Lord Jesus.

To these testimonies, Mr. Baylie interfereth his own testimony and others of his judgment, "It seemeth to us (saith he) a grievous absurdity, a great dishonor to God, and cruelty against men to spoil so many thousand Christians, whom we dare not deny to be truly religious, of all the privileges of the church," etc.

Ans. 1. It is not enough, that we dare not deny men to be truly religious: but it were meet we should know them, at least, conceive good hope they are truly religious, (at least in the judgment of charity) before we receive them into the church. And of such there are not many thousands, no nor many scores, whom we dare spoil of church privileges, unless their own offense, or choice spoil them.

Secondly, if men be not religious, no not so much as in profession, why should it be accounted a grievous absurdity, not to receive them into the church? A thing is absurd, which is ἄτοπον out of place. Are men who are not spiritual, out of their place, when they are not placed in a spiritual society? If the churches be (as Christ describeth them) golden candlesticks Rev. i,20. is tin and lead out of place, when it is not soddered into a golden vessel? Sure God himself thought otherwise, Isa. i,25. But is it not rather a grievous absurdity, and far out of place, when such are admitted to the Lord's Table, who either discern not the Lord's body, or if they be admitted to drink his blood, will be ready when they are got into the field to spill the innocent blood of those Roundheads, whom they lately partaked withal at the Lord's Table?[45]

And as for the great dishonor to God, (which Mr. Baylie imputeth to this way of ours) is it a dishonor to God, that such are withheld from the Lord's Table, by whom the name of God is dishonored either through their ignorance or scandal?

Is it not rather a great dishonor to God, to set up Christ a visible head of such members, by whom his name is evil spoken of? And what cruelty is it against men, to keep such from eating

[45] [After the defeat of his army, Charles, on May 5, 1646, entered the Scots' camp at Newark as their "guest," and for some six months thereafter tried to divide them from the Independents of Cromwell's army so that the two would come to blows and he, with the opposition divided, could again rule on his own terms. Though his plan failed and the Scots surrendered him to Parliament in January 1647, Cotton was probably writing at a time when his latest intelligence was one which emphasized that the Scots had harbored the king and that a battle between them and Cromwell's men was a possibility.]

and drinking the Lord's Supper, who would eat and drink it
unworthily, and so eat and drink their own damnation? 1 Cor.
xi,29. The Lord himself thought it no cruelty to debar our first
parents from the tree of life, who if they had found free liberty
to eat it, would have blessed themselves in a false hope of living
forever? Gen. iii, 22, 23.

SECTION XVII   *Of the second shameful absurdity said
to be found in our way of Independency*

Come we now to a second shameful absurdity, which he
maketh to be another fruit of our church way.

That it hath exceedingly hindered the conversion of the poor
pagans. The principles and practise of Independents doth cross
this work and hope of it. What have they to do with those that
are without? Their pastors preach not for conversion: their
relation is to their flock, who are church members, converted
already to their hand by the labors of other men, before they
can be admitted into their church. Of all that ever crossed the
American seas, they are noted as most neglectful of the work of
conversion. I have read of none of them, that seem to have
minded this matter.

Ans. This is indeed a shameful absurdity, if it be true: but
a sinful and shameful calumny, if it be false. As indeed false it
is in every branch of it. First, there is no principle or allowed
practise of ours that doth hinder (much less exceedingly hinder)
the work or hope of the conversion of the natives: though we
profess we have nothing to do to censure Indians, and so to
judge them that are without; yet we think it a principal (though
not the only) work and duty of our ministry to attend the work
of conversion, both of carnal English, and other nations, whether
Christian, or pagan. The neglect of it, we look at as an ungracious and uncharitable fancy. How shall men (ordinarily)

be converted to the faith without hearing? And how shall they hear without preaching? And how shall they preach, unless they be sent? And who are now sent, but pastors and teachers?

But the relation of our pastors is to their flock? What then? May there not fall out to be hypocrites in our flock? And must we not preach for their conversion? And are not the children of the members of our church, many of them such, as when they grow up stand in need of converting grace? And must we not preach for their conversion? Besides, when an infidel or un-believer cometh into the church, do not all the prophets that preach the word, (and among them, surely the pastors and teachers are not the least) do they not all apply their speech to his conviction and conversion? 1 Cor. xiv, 24, 25. What though a pastor be a feeder to his flock already begotten unto God? Yet he may (and ought to endeavor to) become a father also in Christ, to such as are yet unregenerate, whether of his flock, or out of his flock. To turn many to righteousness is prophecied of, to be the work of the המשכילים[46] of the New Testament, Dan. xii,3. But our church members are converted already to our hands by the labors of other men, before they can be admitted into our church.

So saith Mr. Baylie indeed: but if he were here, he would soon hear many of those who are admitted into our churches, openly acknowledge, the first work of saving grace to have been wrought in their hearts by the ministry of the word here, and sometime by the same, or like ministry in our native country. And the children of the faithful born, and baptized in our churches, will acknowledge no other ministry, by whom they have believed, but that which they have attended upon, here.

But (saith Mr. Baylie) I have read of none of them that seem to have minded the matter of conversion.

Ans. 1. What if he have not read, what we preach here of

---

46 [They that be wise.]

conversion? Doth he think it meet, we should print all the sermons we preach? What if any of us should say, I have not read of any Scottish minister who have published any of their labors in that argument, (save Mr. Rollock, and him in Latin, and that haply in the schools, and many have not seen him neither) shall we therefore think it credible, that so many holy faithful laborers in Christ's vineyard in that whole nation, do not seem to mind the matter of conversion?

But whether he have read of any of our books of that subject, or no, surely it is not, because none of such are extant to be read. He may read when he pleaseth Mr. Shepard's two treatises, one styled The Sincere Convert, the other The Sound Believer, besides sundry treatises of Mr. Hooker touching the soul's preparation to Christ, effectual calling, and justification, etc.[47] and when he hath read them, let him then tell the world, whether of all that have crossed the American seas (as he speaketh) the ministers of this way have been justly noted to be most neglectful of the work of conversion. Yea let me make bold in God's fear to pray Mr. Baylie, and those others, who have noted us as most neglectful of this work, to enquire and consider whether among all the servants of Christ now living in any reformed churches (put them all together) they have published so many treatises of the work of conversion, as the ministers of this way have done, in New England, and London, which I speak not (the Lord is witness to my soul) out of carnal arrogancy to boast of our labors, in so holy and weighty an argument: but out of conscience to bear witness to the way of God's truth against such an unjust and unworthy scandal. But

47 [Thomas Shepard, *The Sincere Convert* (London, 1641) and *The Sound Beleever* (London, 1645); Thomas Hooker, *The Soules Preparation for Christ* (London, 1632), *The Soules Humiliation* (London, 1637), *The Soules Vocation* (London, 1637), *The Soules Implantation* (London, 1637), *The Soules Ingrafting* (London, 1638), *The Soules Exaltation* (London, 1638).]

when I speak of these treatises of conversion, I do not include all
that are written under the glorious and fallacious styles of free
grace, and Gospel truth, which nevertheless do but indeed lay
the leaven of Arminian-universal-free grace, and Antinomiam
impenitency: but I speak of those treatises which are pure from
such leaven, as keeping the pattern of wholesome words and
sound doctrine, dividing the word of truth aright, in the right
use of the law and Gospel, wherein though they sometime declare such works of grace to be preparations to conversion,
which others do take to be the fruits of conversion: yet they all
agree in this, that such works are found in all that are under the
powerful and effectual saving work of the Spirit, and word of
Christ, and in none else, which is the light and life of the
saints in Christ Jesus.

I will not speak here of the conversion of Weaquash, which
(as I hear) is published in a little script, entitled, New England's
First Fruits.[48] Nor would I have mentioned the endeavors of
some of our fellow brethren here, to help forward the work
of conversion in Virginia, were it not that the blessing of the
Lord Jesus upon their labors doth call for acknowledgment.
Some honest minded people in Virginia discerning their want
of spiritual ministry, sent earnest letters, and one or more messengers, to the elders of these churches here for some of our
ministers to break the bread of life to them. The elders here
seeking counsel of God, and one another, we borrowed two of
the pastors of our churches, (Mr. Knowles of Watertown, and
Mr. Thomson of Braintree, the churches being either of them
supplied with two ministers apiece) and sent them forth
solemnly in the name of the Lord to that work; who as they went

---

[48] [*New Englands First Fruits* (London, 1643), a twenty-six page tract which
painted an attractive picture of the climate, the natural resources, and the opportunities for converting the heathen in New England, and which extolled the
newly-founded Harvard College. It was seen through the press by Thomas Weld.]

along took with them one Mr. James, a minister (though then
out of employment) from New Haven, to the fellowship of
that work. And for their better encouragement, our governor
here wrote a letter to the governor of Virginia to acquaint him,
and his assistants, with the occasion and end of their coming,
and expressed withal his desire of their Christian entertainment
for a time, and peaceable return, if they found any inconvenience
by their coming. What entertainment they found from the major
part of the government there, I forbear to speak. The bloody
massacre, which soon after their dismission, the Indians in those
parts executed upon the English, cried aloud from heaven, that
after a white horse, God is wont to send forth a red, Rev. vi, 2,
3, 4. But nevertheless, God so far forth followed their labors
with his blessing in the work of conversion, that sundry of them
were effectually wrought upon by the power of the Lord Jesus;
whereof some of them came along with our ministers at their
return, and are received into our churches: others of them who
could not so well dispose of their affairs there, joined with one
Mr. Harrison, a minister there (who was also mightily stirred
up by our ministers' coming:) and they with him have since
given up themselves to more holy communion and conversation
before the Lord.

Others of the Western Islands (as Barbados, Antigua, Nevis)
have desired the like help from us: but the departure of some
of our ministers since (one to heaven, others to England) have
hitherto detained us from opportunity to afford unto them the
like succor for the present.

I will not speak, what opportunity of reaching forth a blessing to the Indians in this kind, God hath lately begun to open us
a door of: in that divers of their sachems, and sagamores, (as
they call them, to wit, their governors) have submitted themselves to the government of the English, and have willingly sub-

jected themselves to the acceptance of the Ten Commandments, though some of them do most stick at the seventh commandment, as it forbiddeth polygamy. Nevertheless otherwise they willingly consent to abandon adultery and fornication, and unnatural lusts.

But though the Indians have been slow to learn our language, especially in matters of religion (howsoever in trading they soon understood us:) yet we have often offered to bring up their Indian children in our schools, that they might learn to speak to their countrymen in their own language. But because that might prove long, one of our elders (Mr. Eliot, the teacher of the church of Roxbury) hath (with the consent of the natives) preached to them first by an interpreter, but since having with much industry learned their language, he now preacheth to two congregations of them in their own language weekly. One week on the fourth day to one congregation, who sit down near Dorchester Mill, and another week, on the sixth day, to another congregation of them, who sit down in Cambridge, near Watertown Mill. To ease and encourage him in his work, the ministers of neighbor churches take off by turns his weekly lecture on the third day. The fruit hitherto hath been, the Indians resort more and more to these assemblies, hear with reverence and attention, reform (and make laws amongst themselves, for reformation of) sundry abuses, ask sundry questions for their instruction, and among the rest, an old counsellor of one of their sagamores enquired, if it might be possible that our God, and our Christ should accept an old sinner such as himself? Mr. Eliot answered him, yes, there was hope, because he never had the means of the knowledge of God offered to him before. And our Saviour Christ did sometimes call into his vineyard some to do him service, even in the last hours of the day, in the last part of their lives. And the old Indian being demanded if he under-

stood this? He answered, yea, saith he, I understand it, and believe it.

It is true, there may be doubt that for a time there will be no
great hope of any national conversion, till Antichrist be ruined,
and the Jews converted; because the church (or temple) of God,
is said to be filled with smoke, till the seven plagues (which are
to be poured upon the antichristian state) be fulfilled: And till
then, no man (that is, no considerable number of men out of
the church, as pagans be) shall be able to enter into the church,
Rev. xvi,8, yet nevertheless, that hindereth not, but that some
sprinklings, and gleanings of them may be brought home to
Christ, as now and then some proselytes were brought into the
fellowship of the church of Israel, when there was a greater
partition wall set up between Jews and Gentiles, than now there
is between Christians and pagans. And the Lord shine upon them
in mercy, in blessing the means of his grace to them in the Lord
Jesus.

The proof that none of us seem to have minded the work
of conversion, Mr. Baylie allegeth out of the book entitled
Plain Dealing, which saith, "There hath not been sent forth
any, by any church, to learn the natives' language, or to instruct
them in our religion first, because they say they have not to do
with them being without, except they come to hear and learn
English."

Ans. 1.   What if there have not been any sent forth by any
church to learn the Indian language? That will not argue our
neglect of minding the work of their conversion. For there be
of the Indians that live amongst us, and daily resort to us; and
some of them learn our language; and some of us learn theirs.
And men that love the Lord Jesus do gladly take opportunity to
instruct them in our religion, and to teach them both law and
Gospel. And of late, the word (as I have said) is publicly

preached unto them in two several Indian congregations; though
we never thought it fit to send any of our English to live amongst
them, to learn their language: for who should teach them?

Ans. 2.   When the author of Plain Dealing saith, we have
not instructed them in our religion, upon this pretense, because
we say, we have not to do with them being without, except they
come to hear and learn English.

I know not whether ever any gave him so weak an account
or no: if any so did, it was his rashness, or ignorance both of us,
and the truth. But if the author speak it, as a point of our profession or practice, that we do neglect the instruction of the
Indians, and especially upon such a reasonless reason, I will say
no more to it but this, it seemeth there are two sorts of Plain
Dealing: plain honest dealing, and plain false dealing, of
which latter sort, this speech is.

But Mr.Baylie acknowledgeth Mr. Williams his endeavors in
this kind, but doth thereby the more aggravate our corrupt
principles and practice, who have neglected so great an opportunity as to prosecute his course. Only Mr. Williams (saith he)
did assay, what could be done with those desolate souls, and by
little experience quickly found a wonderful great facility to
gain thousands of them to so much and more Christianity both
in profession and practice, than in the most of our people doth
appear.

But the unhappiness of these principles whereof we speak,
did keep him (as he professeth) from making use of that great
opportunity, and large door, which the Lord there hath opened
to all who will be zealous of propagating the Gospel.

Ans. 1.   If Mr. Williams his speech of the wonderful great
facility he had of gaining so far upon the Indians, be not too
prodigally hyperbolical (as I much fear it is) I think his sin
is so much the greater before the Lord, that he did neglect to

take the opportunity of preaching to them the word of the Lord, that they might have been brought on, not only to an antichristian conversion (such as he maketh the conversion of the common sort of Christians in Protestant churches) but to a sincere conversion unto Christ Jesus. But I confess with Mr. Baylie, his own corrupt principles, (his own I say, not ours) it seemeth have detained him from putting forth his hand to the Lord's plough in so large a field. For if he look (as it seemeth) for new apostles to be sent immediately from Christ for such a work; or if he think, no church is, or will be extant upon the face of the earth, till Antichrist be abolished out of the world, these and such like principles are enough, not only to retard him from the planting of churches amongst Indians, but also to further him in supplanting all the churches of Christ in Christendom.

Ans. 2. I said not without cause, that I feared Mr. Williams his testimony of the facility of such a conversion of the Indians was too hyperbolical. For I received advertisement from Mr. James (one of the ministers, who went to Virginia upon the Lord's work, of which I spake before) that whilst he was detained (by winds) in Maryland (a popish plantation between us and Virginia) he saw, as I remember, (for his letter is not present at hand with me) forty Indians baptized in new shirts, which the Catholics had given them for their encouragement unto baptism. But he tarried there so long for a fair wind, that before his departure, he saw the Indians (when their shirts were foul, and they knew not how to wash them) come again to make a new motion, either the Catholic English there must give them new shirts, or else they would renounce their baptism. I doubt, the Indians about Mr. Williams are not of a much better spirit. I might mention a fairer instance in these parts, yet such as may argue what kind of facility there is in the Indians to conversion, so much as to outward profession. At our first coming hither, John Sagamore was the chiefest sachem in these parts. He falling sick, our pastor Mr. Wilson hearing of it (and being of some acquaintance with him) went to visit him, taking one of the deacons of our church with him, and withal, a little mithridate, and strong water. When he came to his lodging (which they call a wigwam) hearing a noise within, he looked over the mat of the door to discern what it meant, and saw many Indians gathered together, and some powwaws amongst them, who are their priests, physicians, and witches. They by course spake earnestly to the sick sagamore, and to his disease, (in a way of charming of it and him) and one to another in a kind of antiphonies. When they had done, all kept silence, our pastor went in with the deacon, and found the man far spent, his eyes set in his head, his speech leaving him, his mother (old squaw sachem) sitting weeping at his bed's head. Well (saith our pastor) our God save Sagamore John, powwaw *cram* (that is, kill) Sagamore John: and thereupon he fell to prayer with his deacon, and after prayer, forced into the sick man's mouth with a spoon, a little mithridate dissolved in the strong water; soon after the sagamore looked up, and three days after went abroad on hunting. This providence so far prevailed with the sagamore, that he promised to look after the Englishman's God, to hear their sermons, to wear English apparel, etc. But his neighbor Indians sagamores, and powwaws hearing of this, threatened to *cram* him (that is, to kill him) if he did so degenerate from his country gods, and religion, he thereupon fell off, and took up his Indian course of life again. Whatsoever facility may seem to offer itself of the conversion of the Indians, it is not so easy a matter for them to hold out, no not in a semblance of profession of the true religion. Afterwards God struck John Sagamore again, (and as I remember with the small pox) but then when they desired like succor from our pastor, as before, he told them, now the Lord was angry with Sagamore John, and it was doubtful, He would not be so easily be entreated. The sagamore blamed himself and justified God, and confessed, he should not have been discouraged by their threats from seeking our God: for those sagamores and powwaws who did most terrify him, he had seen God sweeping them away by death, before himself, in a short time after. And therefore when he saw he must die (for he died of that sickness) he left his son to the education of our pastor, that he might keep closer to the English, and to their God, than he himself had done. But his son also died of the same disease soon after. All which I relate, to shew, that though a form of Christian religion may be professed amongst Christians with some facility; yet it is not so easy a matter to gain these pagan Indians so much as to a form of our religion, and to hold it, howsoever Mr. Williams did promise himself greater possibilities.

Ans. 3.   Mr. Baylie shall do well to consider, that Mr. Williams his speech doth not so much hold forth the facility of the Indians to any such conversion, as might fit them for church estate, but rather the hypocrisy and formality of the ordinary church members of national churches; which he professeth is so far off from true conversion, that it is the subversion of the souls of many millions in Christendom, from one false worship to another.

Ans. 4.   It is no unhappiness of any principle of ours, that hath kept Mr. Williams from making use of his great opportunity, and open door, to propagate the Gospel amongst the Indians. For though their facility to such a carnal conversion, as he describeth, gave him no just warrant, to gather them into a church estate: yet it was a just encouragement to provoke him (who understood their language) to have preached the word of God unto them, which might have been mighty through God (if sincerely dispensed) to have turned them from darkness to light, from the power of Satan unto God, and so have prepared them, both for church fellowship here, and for heaven hereafter.

But if Mr. Baylie conceive that either Mr. Williams, or else we were to be blamed, because we do not presently receive Indians into the fellowship of our churches, seeing their facility to conform their outward man to us, and to so much of our religion, as Mr. Williams mentioneth: he shall do well to consider beforehand, whether Jacob's children did well to persuade the Schechemites, Gen. xxxiv, to receive circumcision, before they better understood the convenant of Abraham, (to which circumcision was a seal) and had made some better profession of taking hold of it.

SECTION XVIII *Of the third shameful absurdity said to be found in our way of Independency*

Come we now to consider of the third shameful absurdity, which Mr. Baylie maketh the fruit of our Independency, breaking forth in the practices and profession of the most, who have been admitted as very fit, if not the fittest members of our churches.

And these evil fruits he brancheth out into five sorts:

1. (Saith he) in the vileness of their errors.
2. In the multitude of the erring persons.
3. In the hypocrisy joined with their errors.
4. In the malice against their neighbors, and contempt of their superiors, magistrates and ministers for opposition to their evil way.
5. In their singular obstinacy, stiffly sticking unto their errors, etc.

Ans. 1. Suppose all this to be true: yet this is so far from

discrediting the way of Independency, or arguing the tree to be
bad by these bad fruits, that it doth rather justify the way to be
of God, which so easily hath either healed, or removed, so
many, so vile, so general, so subtle, so headstrong corruptions,
and them that maintained them. *Non scelus, non scelerum
varietas aut atrocitas,* is *dedecus politiæ, sed scelerum impunitas.*[49] The church of Ephesus was not blamed by Christ,
because false apostles and Nicolaitans were found amongst
them: but commended, because she could not bear them, Rev.
ii, 2, 6. Nor is Thyatira blamed, that Jezabel was found amongst
them, but that they suffered her, Rev. ii,20. What if so many,
so hideous vile errors were found in our churches? What if the
number of erring persons were (as he speaketh) incredible?
Multitudes of men and women everywhere infected? almost no
society, nor family in the land free from the pest? Boston (which
he is pleased to style, the best and most famous of our churches)
so far corrupted, that few were untainted? What if they accounted the late governor[50] their true friend, and thought no
less of Mr. Cotton, and Mr. Wheelwright whom they adored?
What if they had drawn to their sides not only multitudes of the
people, but the ablest men for parts, in all trades, especially the
soldiers? What if all these evils were carried forth with pre-
sumptuous contumacy against godly magistrates, and the ortho-

---

49 [It is not crime, nor the variety and atrocity of crime that is a shame to
the state, but rather its impunity.]

50 [The late governor was Sir Henry Vane (1613–1662), son of a member of
the Privy Council, who came to Boston in 1635 where he lodged with John
Cotton with whose teachings he agreed. In 1636, in spite of his youth, he was
elected governor in deference to his station in life, and during his administration
the Antinomian controversy burst forth in full, probably because the opinionists
with reason believed they now had an ally in the governor and could proceed
less guardedly. Winthrop was elected in place of Vane in 1637, and in September
of that year Vane returned to England, distressed at the severe prosecution of
the Hutchinson group. Back in England, as a lay member of the Westminster
Assembly he proved a valuable ally for the Congregationalists.]

dox ministers? Yea, what if to all the rest, they added obstinacy against all wholesome means of redress and remedy?

Is it not therefore the more evident demonstration of the gracious presence, and mighty power of God, in the discipline of our churches, that did so effectually, so speedily, so safely, so easily, purge out all this leaven, either out of the hearts of the people, out of their families, and churches, or else out of the country?

Whence the argument seemeth to me to arise unavoidably.

Those evils, which Independency doth either heal, or remove, they are not the fruits of Independency.

But all these grievous and dangerous evils, Independency did either heal or remove.

Therefore these grievous and dangerous evils were not the fruits of Independency.

Again, that government, which by the blessing of Christ, doth safely, speedily, and effectually purge out such grievous and dangerous evils, as threaten the ruin of church and state, that government is safely allowed, and justly and wisely established in any civil state.

But Independency by the blessing of Christ doth speedily, safely, and effectually purge out such grievous and dangerous evils, as threaten the ruin of church and state: therefore Independency is safely allowed, and justly, and wisely established in any civil state.

Object. 1.   But this purging and healing of these grievous and dangerous evils was not the fruit of the Independent church government, but of their civil government. "We have oft marvelled, that the eldership of Boston did never so much, as call Mrs. Hutchinson before them, to be rebuked for any of her errors, though their general assembly had confuted them, and condemned them: yet still she was permitted to go on, till the

zeal of the new governor, and the general court did condemn
her to perpetual banishment. Then, and not till then, so far as
we can perceive by the story, did the church of Boston bring a
process against her. And when the process was brought to an
end, Mr. Cotton would by no means put it in execution; that
burden was laid upon the back of Mr. Wilson his colleague,
however not the fittest instrument, being the person to whom
Mrs. Hutchinson had professed greatest opposition. And when
the sentence was pronounced against her, they tell us, that the
great cause of it was none of her errors or heresies, but her other
practices, especially her gross lying."

Ans. 1.   Whatever assistance the civil government gave to
the purging and healing of these evils, it was the fruit of Independent church government. For whether the neighbor churches
suspected our church of Boston might be partial, and indulgent
to these erroneous persons: or whether they saw, we wanted
sufficient witnesses upon which we might proceed against them
in a church way, they took a right course (according to the
principles of the Independent government) to gather into a
synod with the consent of the civil magistrates: and in the synod
to agitate, convince and condemn the errors, and the offensive
carriages then stirring. Whereat the magistrates being present,
they saw just cause to proceed against the chief of those whom
they conceived to have bred any civil disturbance: and the
churches saw cause to proceed against their members, whom they
found to be broachers or maintainers of such heresies.

Ans. 2.   It hath been declared above, why the eldership of
Boston did not call Mrs. Hutchinson before them to rebuke her
for her errors, or to restrain her from going on, though the
general assembly had confuted and condemned her errors and
course.

For though the errors were condemned, (and by the elders

of Boston, as well as others:) yet the errors were not fastened personally upon her: nor had we any two witnesses, that would affirm to us, that she did broach or maintain such errors or heresies, till after her sentence unto banishment by the general court; and then indeed, as she was more bold and open in declaring her judgment before many witnesses: so the elders of the church of Boston called her to account before the church, and convinced her of her errors, and with the consent of the church, laid her, and one or two more of her abettors under the censure of an admonition even for those corrupt opinions, which were charged upon her, and proved against her.

Object. 1.   Yea but Mr. Cotton would by no means put the censure in execution upon her, that burden must be laid upon the back of Mr. Wilson, etc.

Ans.   The censure of admonition, because it was for matter of erroneous doctrine, it was thought meet to be dispensed and administered by Mr. Cotton, who was their teacher: which also (by the help of Christ) he did perform, setting before her both the corrupt causes of her errors, and the bitter fruits of them: and charging her solemnly before the Lord, and his angels, and churches then assembled, to return from the error of her way.

Afterwards, when upon further serious debate and conference with her by Mr. Davenport, and myself, she was convinced of all her errors in particular, she being called again before the church, did openly recant every error and heresy, and professed her repentance for every miscarriage against magistrates and elders: which far exceeded the expectation of the whole congregation, which then consisted of many churches, and strangers. But when she had done, she added withal, that she had never been of other judgment, howsoever her expressions might seem to vary. This sounded so harshly, and falsely in the ears of many witnesses, that many rose up to convice her of her falsehood and lying, in so saying. Which when she did not hearken to, she was esteemed, by the judgment of the elders, and our whole church, to be justly subject to excommunication. Which though I did not think meet to be dispensed by myself (because the offense was not in matter of doctrine but of practice, which more properly belonged to the pastor's office, or ruling elders':) yet I declared to the whole congregation the righteousness of the censure, and satisfied the scruples of some brethren, who doubted of it. But yet if the church, or other elders had put that task upon me, I should no more have refused the dispensing of the censure of excommunication upon her, than I did before of admonition. Neither was her opposition against Mr. Wilson any just reason exempting him from that duty. For she saw, we all with one accord, concurred in that sentence: it was no partial act of his, but the common vote both of the presbytery, and fraternity. And what if she had professed her opposition against us all? Had that been a just excuse to exempt any of us from performing a service due to God, and the church, yea and to herself also?

Object. 2. But when the sentence was propounded against her, they tell us, the great cause of it was none of her errors, and heresies, but for other practices, especially her gross lying.

Ans. We could not justly pronounce the cause of her sentence to be her errors and heresies, which she had openly recanted, and given her recantation under her handwriting. Neither did any of us say, that such heresies did not deserve the censure of excommunication, if she had continued obstinate in them: but we thought it needful to follow the rule of the apostle, not to reject an heretic till after once or twice admonition, Tit. iii,10, under which if the heretic relent, the church proceeding stayeth, unless some other offense set it forward, as it did in her case.

SECTION XIX *Tending to rectify some mistakes of Mr. Baylie in relating the former absurdities*

But before I leave this close of Mr. Baylie's third chapter, touching the evil fruits of Independency, let me advertise him of some few further mistakes in his narration of the same.

First, when he reckoneth in the front of vile errors, the inhabitation of the person of the Spirit in all the godly, let him weigh what hath been said above, touching that point. And if he clear it to be an error, I willingly shall acknowledge, he shall teach me that, which I yet know not. I profess myself willing to learn of a meaner man, than Mr. Baylie.

Secondly, when he maketh the number of erring persons incredible, almost no society, no family free from the pest, Boston itself so far infected, that few there were untainted: let him be pleased to consider, whether his testimony will make it good. His testimonies (recited in his marks *FF,GG*) speak to the utmost of truth, but not so much as he avoucheth. The short story in Preface, page 7, saith indeed, "They had some of all sorts and qualities in all places to patronize and defend them: and almost in every family some were ready to defend them as the apple of their own eye."

But this will not make it good, that almost in every family some were infected with the pest of their errors. It is one thing to speak in the defense of erroneous persons, another to speak in defense of errors. Multitudes there were, that thought well of the persons, who knew nothing of their errors, but heard only of their unbottoming sandy foundations of a spiritual estate, which hath been mentioned above, chap. 3.

Which may also truly be said even of Boston likewise. The body of the church, the greatest part of them were like those members of the church in Thyatira, of whom it is said, Rev.

ii,24. They knew not the depths of Satan. The truth whereof may evidently appear by this, that when those errors of Mistress Hutchinson were publicly charged upon her before the church, and proved by sufficient witnesses, the whole body of the church, and all the brethren with one accord (save only her son) consented readily to her censure: which they would not have done, if the whole church of Boston (some excepted) had become her converts, and were infected with her opinions.

Thirdly, when he saith, they adored some of their ministers, and instanceth in Mr. Cotton, and Mr. Wheelwright.

Adoration is too vast an hyperbole to be made good by just testimonies. All hyperbolical praises, though they may far exceed the bounds of truth in comparisons of men with men; yet they will not reach adoration, which is divine worship. Neither will it be made good, that they magnified either Mr. Wheelwright, or me, for the defense of their errors. Yea they soon forsook Mr. Wheelwright (as well as he them) when they saw his judgment (as well as mine) against Antinomianism, and Familism.

Fourthly, when he saith, "Mistress Hutchinson, and the late governor, kept almost every day, so private and long discourse with Mr. Cotton, that made them conclude all was their own."

I must needs profess, that cannot be made good by any witness of truth, Mistress Hutchinson seldom resorted to me: and when she did, she did seldom or never enter into any private speech between the former governor and myself. And when she did come to me, it was seldom, or never (that I can tell of) that she tarried long. I rather think she was loath to resort much to me, or to confer long with me, lest she might seem to learn somewhat from me. And withal I know (by good proof) she was very careful to prevent any jeolousy in me, that she should harbor any private opinions, differing from the course of my public ministry. Which she could not well have avoided, if she had kept almost every day so private and long discourse with me.

But what testimony, or proof doth Mr. Baylie allege for this our private and long conference almost every day? His mark [γγ] referreth us to the short story, where it is said, "They made full account the day had been theirs."

But did they make this account upon occasion of these our private, and long, and frequent conferences every day? Not a syllable of proof for this point. It is not righteous dealing, large charges, and narrow proofs.

Fourthly, that which Mr. Baylie further relateth from the testimony of Mr. Williams, is as far from truth, as the former.

Mr. Williams (saith Mr. Baylie) told me, that he was employed to buy from the savages, for their late governor, and Mr. Cotton, with their followers, a portion of land without the English plantation whither they might retire and live according to their mind, exempt from the jurisdiction of all others, whether civil or ecclesiastic, Mr. Williams was in so great friendship with the late governor, when he told me so much, that I believe he would have been loath to have spoken an untruth of him.

Ans. But this I dare be bold to say, if Mr. Williams told Mr. Baylie so much, that he was employed by me to buy any land from the savages, for me and my followers (as he calls them) he spake an untruth of me, whatsoever he did of the governor. Yet because I would not speak nor think worse of Mr. Williams than necessity constraineth, I cannot say but that he might speak as he thought, and as he was told; for it may well be, that such as abused the governor's name to him for such an end, might also more boldly abuse mine. But I must profess, I neither wrote, nor spake, nor sent to Mr. Williams for any such errand. If ever I had removed, I intended Quinipyack, and not Aquethnick. And I can hardly believe the governor would send to him for any such end, who I suppose never thought it likely, that himself should tarry longer in the country than he tarried in the Bay.

Fifthly, when Mr. Baylie objecteth the profaneness of these erroneous persons, and justifieth it by the testimonies of Mr. Weld and myself, and aggravateth the same by their profession of piety (so far, that they avow their standing loose from all reformed churches as unclean, because of their mixture with the profane multitude.)

Let him be pleased to consider; first, what was said above, *Non scelus, sed sceleris impunitas,* is the guilt of a society, whether civil or sacred.

Secondly, what Mr. Weld meant by fouler sins than pride, or lying, found in those persons, I cannot guess; nor have I heard of them: unless he meant the adultery of one, who upon his own confession was cast out of the church for that crime.

As for the testimony of mine, which he quoteth from some words in the vials,[51] wherein the sins of the people were reproved, let him not improve them further than they will bear. Such reproofs do not always argue sins of our church members: or if they did, yet not, that those sins are openly known: or if openly known, yet not, that they were tolerated. And yet all these must concur, or else the vices found amongst professors, will not argue the viciousness either of their doctrine or worship or church government.

Luther complaineth *in Postill., super Evangel., Dom. adventus, sunt nunc homines magis vindictæ cupidi, magis avari, magis ab omni misericordiâ remoti, magis immodesti, et indisciplinati, multoque deteriores, quam fuerunt sub papatu.*[52] And Chryso-

---

51 [John Cotton, *The Powring Out of the Seven Vialls* (London, 1642).]
52 [There are now men more desirous of vengeance, more covetous, more

stom, (*in opere imperfect in Matt. Hom.* 49) speaketh of
Christians as becoming like the heretics, or pagans, or worse.

Yet I suppose he that should improve the words either of
Chrysostom, to argue the discipline of Christians, worse than
that of the pagans: or of Luther, to argue the discipline of
Protestants to be worse than that of Papists, he shall doubtless
stretch their words upon the rack, far beyond the scope of their
meaning. The words I spake, were in comparison between the
godly professors in England, and ours here, and at such a time,
when episcopal persecution made them draw the nearer to God,
and to walk the more circumspectly before men. But sheep set
at liberty from the fear of wolves, will straggle further from
their shepherd, than when they resent danger.

Thirdly, it is too gross and heavy an aggravation, which Mr.
Baylie putteth upon us, if he mean it of us, that our profession
of piety is so fair that we stand aloof from all reformed churches
as unclean, because of their mixture with the profane multitude.

For it is more than he can prove, or we do profess. Though in
the bishops' time, we did not forthwith receive all the members
of the Church of England into the fellowship of our churches:
yet (for ought I know) we are not likely to stand aloof from
Presbyterial churches faithfully administered, nor from the testimony which they shall give of their members, that may have
occasion to traffic hither. And the like do I conceive of other
reformed churches in other nations of Christendom. Presbyterian
churches faithfully administered, are not wont to admit a mixed
profane multitude to the Lord's Table.

Sixthly, let me take off one instance more, which Mr. Baylie
giveth of one abomination, which to him seemeth strange. That
the midwives to our most zealous women, should not only have

---

completely removed from compassion, more unrestrained and undisciplined, and
far meaner than they were under the papacy.]

familiarity with the devil, but also in that service commit devilish malefices: which so far as they tell us, were not only passed over without punishment, but never so much as enquired after.

Ans. This accusation is indeed of some weight, because it is of a grievous, and devilish crime, and it tolerated. But how doth it appear to him, that it was tolerated? Not only passed over without punishment, but never so much as enquired after?

Why, saith he, so far as they tell us. So far as they tell us? Is the silence of a short story of this or that fact, a good argument, *a non dici, ad non esse?*[53] Yea it is a good argument on the contrary, that there was inquiry made after that midwife, and diligent search into her, or else it would have been recorded, as some close conveyance of the erroneous party. The truth is, the woman, though she offered herself to the elders of our church, yet was not received, upon discovery of some unsound principles in her judgment. Being then no member, the church had no power to deal with her. But when suspicion grew of her familiarity with the devil, especially upon that occasion, which the short story relateth, she was convented before the magistrates, and diligently examined about that, and other evils. But though no familiarity with the devil could be proved against her; yet because of some other offenses in dealing with young women, she was forbidden to stay in the country.

SECTION XX   *Tending to consider what better fruits might have been expected from Presbyterian discipline, for the removing of the like absurdities*

Having thus given account to Mr. Baylie of the inconsequence of all his discourse from the errors of this country, to argue the unsoundness of our church discipline, let me now

---

53 [Because it wasn't spoken of it doesn't exist.]

entreat him to consider, what better fruits might have been
expected in the like case from Presbyterial government. I
demand, if Presbyterian government had been established
amongst us, should we not then have received all these heretics,
and erroneous persons, into our church? Yes surely, for no
member of the commonwealth is excluded: well, therein our
Congregational discipline bringeth forth no worse fruit, than
their Presbyterian.

I demand again, if these persons should afterwards fall into
error, or heresy, which could not be proved by two witnesses,
what course would Presbyterian government have taken? Would
it not have forborne process, till sufficient testimony might be
brought to convince them? If suspicion of their unsound judgment had grown, would they not have examined them, and if
they denied it, and no sufficient testimony could be brought
against them, would not the presbyters have let them alone?
Hitherto we did the same.

I demand further, if any presbytery in a church, were suspected to be too remiss in proceeding against such delinquents,
would not the presbytery of the neighbor churches have taken
the matter in hand, and so gathering into a synod, first convinced such errors, and then condemned them, and the maintainers of them too, if they were found guilty of them and
persistent in them? Thus far also the presbytery of our neighbor
churches did proceed as to gather into a synod, and both convinced and condemned the errors. And though they did not
proceed to condemn or censure the maintainers of them; yet
when they had gotten proof thereof, they proceeded in their
own congregations to the censure of their own erroneous members (after all other means to recover them used in vain) and
besides, they dealt with the presbytery of our church to do the
same. And we hearing their complaints and their proofs, we

respectively hearkened to them, and proceeded to the like censure in our church, as they had done in theirs; and in like sort
travailed with our members for their conviction, as they had
done with theirs, even so far, that Mistress Hutchinson was
brought to a recantation, though her prevarication of it brought
her to a censure, yea the utmost censure, and that with general
consent of our whole church, and satisfaction of others. It
seemeth then, that our Independency (as it is called) doth no
more breed, nor nourish, nor tolerate errors, or heresies, than
Presbyterian discipline doth. And if there should a defect arise
in any church, there is the like remedy in the vigilancy of other
churches, and finally, obstinacy in all evils of notorious offense,
whether in judgment or practice, meeteth at length with the
same or like censure, in either government.

Let not therefore Mr. Baylie allow himself in saying as he
doth (in the close of his third chapter) that this new and
singular way, the Lord hath so manifestly cursed with more bad
fruits, and greater store of them, than ever yet did appear upon
the tree of Brownism. For though it becometh not us to make
comparisons of fruits with other churches (unless themselves
did provoke us to it) nor doth it concern us to deal with them
about any offense, unless we dwelt near them, and knew their
estate:) yet this is enough to us, to clear us unto Mr. Baylie,
and to the world, against all his exceptions, that (through the
mercy of Christ) no evil fruit at all hath sprung from our
church government. What offense soever, in judgment of practice, hath been suspected or found among us, it hath not sprung
from the government; but from personal defects, either among
the brethren or elders. And what hath been suspected, or found
in either of them, hath either been cleared, or healed, or removed
by the government. Blessed be the name of the Lord Jesus,

whose throne is in Zion and his furnace in Jerusalem, who delighteth to bless his own ordinances with power and peace.

CHAPTER IV
Of the antiquity of Congregational discipline, compared with Classical

SECTION I

Mr. Baylie speaketh of our Congregational, and (as he calleth it) our Independent way, as not having continued a week of years (that is, not seven years) when the errors brake forth in New England, page 59. Sometimes he maketh us the same in reality with the Brownists, page 58, to whom he attributeth about fifty years of continuance, page 59. Sometimes he maketh us followers of Mr. Robinson, who stepped in to support (as he speaketh) languishing Brownism, when it was ready to fall, pages 17 and 54. All which expressions tend to make the world believe, that our Congregational way, or (as he calleth it) Independent, is but of yesterday, newly sprung up, unknown and unheard of in the former ages of the church; which if it were true, were no small prejudice to the way we walk in. The way of God is the old way, Jer. vi,16, yea so old, as fetcheth his antiquity from the ancient of days, and from the Lord Jesus, who is the way of truth and of life. *Id verum, quod primum: id primum quod ab initio.*[54] There is no false way, but is an aberration from the first institution.

Give me therefore leave to profess freely without offense, what I truly believe without scruple, that though the acts of church government (in the ordination of officers, and censure of offenders) by the presbyters of neighbor churches, be very

[54] [That is true which is first; that is first which is there from the beginning.]

ancient: yet not more ancient than *Humanus Episcopatus*[55] (as Beza calleth it:) nor so ancient, as the way of our Congregational government of each church within itself, by the space of three hundred years. I will not speak here of those texts of Scripture, Matt. xviii, 15, 16, 17; I Cor. v, which convince us that Congregational discipline was instituted by Christ, and his apostles. I refer them to the sequel, wherein our particular tenents are discussed by Mr. Baylie, which will come in due place (God willing) to be reviewed and examined. But,

In the first century, whilst the apostles lived, we read of no act of church power put forth by the elders of churches over absent congregations, but only in Acts xv, 28 with chap. xvi,4. But let it be considered:

1. That this synod was not *Status Conventus,* a set monthly, or yearly assembly, the ordinary standing judicatory of the church: nor assembled for administration of ordinary church power (as ordination of officers, or censure of offenders) but called together upon urgent and unwonted occasion, the dissension of the Church of Antioch, which both craved, and needed direction in such a case, Acts xv, 1, 2. And we easily grant (what we willingly practice in a Congregational way) that neither doctrine, nor discipline can well proceed unto public edification, when the church is rent with dissension. The promise of Christ's presence with his church, is given to them met in his name, and agreeing in his name, Matt. xviii, 18, 19. But when a congregation wanteth agreement and peace amongst themselves, it is then a way of God (according to the pattern, Acts xv, 2) to consult with some other church, or churches, either by themselves or their messengers met in a synod. But then they send not to them for power to administer any ordinance amongst themselves, but for light to satisfy dissenters, and

55 [Human episcopacy (i.e., the ideal that all men are priests).]

so to remove the stumbling block of the suspicion of mal-administration of their power, out of the way.

But otherwise, when churches want not peace nor light within themselves, to exercise that power without distraction, which the Lord hath given them, Christ doth not direct his churches to gather into a synod for removing of known offenses either in doctrine or manners: but only sendeth to the pastors or presbyters of each church, to reform within themselves, what is amongst them, Rev. chap. ii and chap. iii. A plain pattern to churches, in case of public offenses tolerated in neighbor churches, not forthwith to gather into a synod (or classical meeting) for redress thereof: but by letters and messengers to admonish one another of what is behoveful; unless upon such admonition, they refuse to hearken to the wholesome counsel of their brethren. And then the dissension of this church from others hindering the free passage of the Gospel (as much as dissension amongst themselves doth) it may give just and necessary occasion of assembling a synod of elders, and messengers of neighbor churches for the conviction of their sin with common consent, and if (after long patience) they remain obstinate, to withdraw from them the right hand of fellowship in the communion of churches.

2. The synod assembled at Jerusalem, Acts xv, was not a convention or consistory of elders apart from brethren: but such a number of brethren were admitted into their assembly, as carried the name of a whole church, distinguished expressly from the apostles, and elders, Acts xv, 22, 23. The same who are called the brethren, distinct from the apostles and elders, ver. 23, are called also the whole church, ver. 22. And with them is the power communicated, which the apostles and elders put forth in those synodical letters, ver. 22 to 29. If the classis do admit the brethren of the church where they meet, to sit with

the elders, in debating and determining the matters of the synod, even such a number of brethren, as may denominate them a whole church, as then they shall come nearer to the primitive pattern, so they may expect a freer passage of the presence and blessing of the Holy Ghost with them.

3. That synod having heard and argued the whole cause in controversy, they give their judgment both of the doctrine taught at Antioch, and of the persons that taught it, as troublesome to the church, and subversive to their souls, and unwarranted by themselves, ver. 24. Nevertheless, they neither excommunicate them themselves, nor command the church to excommunicate them: but leave that to the church to exercise their own power according to the rule of the word, in case any of their members should be found to persist obstinately in such pernicious doctrine after conviction.

4. That synod laid indeed a burden (or weighty charge) not only of a doctrine to be believed, but of a duty in matter of practise to be performed (for avoiding of offense:) and lay it they did with the greater power, according to the greater measure of grace and light received, both from texts of Scriptures clearly opened, and from direction of apostles personally present. But though we dare not allow alike equal power to ordinary synods, unless they had the like equal presence and assistance of infallible guides, (such as the apostles were) yet our Congregational way doth easily allow the like power to the like orderly synods so far forth, that when they have cleared from the Scriptures any doubtful point of doctrine or practice, to be of necessary observation, they will readily submit as to a counsel and command of God, both from the word, and the word dispensed in the way of an ordinance. In such a case we acknowledge with our best divines) *potestatem in synodis* διορθωτικὴν, καὶ διατακτικὴν a power in synods to direct and appoint, what spiritual prudence from the word shall determine. But it is one

thing, to direct and charge churches from the word of the Lord, what should be done by them: another thing to do their acts of power for them. The one guideth them in the use and exercise of the power: the other taketh their power, or at least the exercise of it, out of their hand, which is more than the pattern of synods, in Act xv, doth hold forth.

SECTION II

In the second century of years, the government of the church was administered, not in a Classical, but in a Congregational way, as in the former century, of which we need no better evidence, than the evident testimony of the Magdeburgenses, in the second century, chap. 7, *tit. de consociatione ecclesiarum, cæterum* (say they) *si quis probatos authores hujus seculi perspiciat, videbit forman gubernationis propemodum* Δημοκρατίας *sim lem fuisse. Singulæ enim parem habebant postestatem, verbum Dei pure docendi, sacramenta administrandi, excommunicandi hæreticos, et sceleratos, ministros eligendi, vocandi, ordinandi, et justissimas ob causas iterum deponendi, conventus et synodos congregandi, etc.* That is, if a man search the approved authors of this age, he shall see the form of the government, to be almost like to a democracy: for every single church had equal power of preaching the word, administering sacraments, excommunicating heretics and notorious offenders, absolving penitents, choosing, calling, ordaining ministers, and upon just and weighty causes deposing them again: power also of gathering conventions and synods, etc.

What is Congregational government, and Independent from other churches, and presbyters, if this be not? Though he mentioneth conventions and synods, yet he speaketh of them, not as having power to govern the churches, but of the churches, as having power to gather them. But the synods left the power of choosing, calling, ordaining ministers, of censuring heretics and offenders, and of absolving penitents to the single churches, each one enjoying equal power within themselves. The help which neighbor churches yielded one to another, was not *cum imperio, et subjectione,* (as he speaketh in the same place) not with dominion of some, and subjection of others, but *charitatis et edificationis studio,* out of brotherly love and care and desire of mutual edification. Which made him say, their form of government was like well nigh, or almost to a democracy: like to a democracy, in regard of mutual equality of power in one church towards another: and yet but almost like to a democracy, in regard each church within itself had an aristocracy or presbytery for their guidance and government, though they did no act of church government without concourse and censure of the brethren.

The rash attempt of Victor (Bishop of Rome) in this age against the churches of Asia, to censure them for a different observation of Easter, it only argueth, that the mystery of iniquity did more early, and earnestly work in Rome, than in other churches; but doth not hold forth any received custom of that age, the officers of one church to proceed to the censure of their brethren in other churches. For this attempt of Victor was generally contested against by Irenæus, and other bishops.

SECTION III

In the third century of years, the churches enjoyed (to use the words of the Centurists,[56] *Cent.* 3, *cap.* 7) almost the like form

---

[56] [The *Historia Ecclesiae Christi* (Basle 1559–1574), a landmark in church history, traced the church from its beginnings to 1400, dividing the history into centuries. The authors, chief of whom was Matthias Flacius, were known as the Centurions of Magdeburg, and the work was frequently called "Centuries" or some variation of that term such as Cotton uses.]

of government, according to the course of the former age, though somewhat more enlarged by ambition.

For it appearth, Novatus was excommunicate by a counsel at Rome under Cornelius. And Samosatenus was excommunicate and deposed by a council at Antioch. But yet where the bishops did more attend to the rule of Scripture, and former precedents, Congregational churches did still enjoy their wonted liberty and power.

Their bishops and other officers were not chosen to their hands by a consistory of bishops (or pastors) amongst themselves in the absence of the people: but (as Cyprian telleth us) amongst them, in Carthage, and almost throughout all the provinces, "As they have received from the apostles, so they hold it, that for the orderly celebration of ordination, all the neighbor bishops, (or pastors) of the same province, where a minister is to be ordained, they come together to that people, and the bishop is chosen in the presence of the people, to whom his life is best known. As (saith he) was done amongst us in the ordination of our fellow minister Sabinus; his office was put upon him by the suffrage of the whole brotherhood, and by the judgment of all the pastors both present, and such as by letters gave testimony of him: and so hands were imposed upon him," *Cyprian Epistolarum l.* 1, *Epistola* 4. And in the same epistle he saith, "The people fearing God, and obedient to the ordinances of Christ ought to separate from a wicked ruler, *Cum ipsa maxime potestatem habeat vel eligendi dignos sacerdotes, vel indignos recusandi:* Seeing the people chiefly have the power of choosing worthy ministers, and refusing the unworthy." And as election and ordination of ministers was transacted in the presence and with the suffrage of the people, so was excommunication also: for upon this ground, Cyprian argueth and aggravateth the offense of the brotherhood in other churches, who took upon them to question and waive that censure, *post divinum judicium,* (he meaneth, the judgment of God's ministers the elders) *post populi suffragium, post coepiscoporum consensum:* after the divine judgment of their elders, after the suffrage of the people, after the consent of neighbor ministers, *Cyprian Epistolarum l.* 1, *Epistola* 3, where he giveth to each rank, their proper act in passing church censure: he assigneth to the elders of the church *judicium,* the judgment: to the people, *suffragium,* suffrage or vote: to neighbor ministers, *consensum,* consent.

And that the people had the like concourse in the absolution and admission of penitents, appeareth by Cyprian in the same epistle, *vix plebi persuadeo* (saith he) *immo extorqueo, ut tales patiantur admitti:* (*tales nempe, de quorum sincera pænitentia vix plebi constabat*) *et justior factus est fraternitatis dolor, ex eo quod unus atque alius obnitente plebe, et contradicente, mea tamen facilitate suscepti, pejores extiterunt quam prius fuerant.*

"With much ado I persuade people, and even wrest it from them, that they would suffer such to be admitted, (of whose repentance they were doubtful: and the grief of the brotherhood is so much the more just, because one or two before having been received by my facility (the people gainsaying, and striving against it) proved worse afterwards than they were before."

Where though he spake of the peoples' gainsaying and striving against his receiving of one or two: yet it evidently appeareth that in his ordinary and usual course, he was not wont to receive any without the peoples' consent. And even then when they did gainsay and strive against his act at first, yet he was not wont to proceed, till with importunate persuasions, and wrestlings with them, he had prevailed with them to give way.

But of others he speaketh (*Epistolarum lib.* 3, *Epistola* II.) *Cæteros,* saith he, *cum ingenti populi suffragio recipimus:* "The rest were received with the free and general suffrage of the people." And again, (*Epistola* 16 of the same book) he thus speaketh *ad plebem, examinabuntur singula, præsentibus, et judicantibus vobis.*

And indeed (in the end of the tenth epistle of his third book) he professeth his resolution to perform no act of church government without consent of the elders and deacons, and brethren of the church: *A primordio episcopatus mei, statui, nihil sine consilio vestro, et sine consensu plebis, mea privatim sententia gerere.*[57]

All these are express and lively lineaments of the very body of Congregational discipline, the same (for substance) wherein we walk at this day. And therefore let it not be slighted or despised, as a novel invention, of seven, or twenty, or fifty years' standing.

CHAPTER V
Of the fruits of Congregational discipline

SECTION I *Of the fruits of it in the primitive times*

We have heard of the corrupt fruits, which Mr. Baylie chargeth (but corruptly, and causelessly) upon Congregational discipline: let us now see, whether better fruits have not been found to grow upon it, even such fruits as do argue the discipline to be the plantation of the Lord Jesus.

1. Presupposing that which hath been proved, that our Congregational discipline, is the same (for substance) wherein the primitive churches walked for the first three hundred years, (to wit, during all the time of the primitive persecutions) I

---

[57] [In the presence of the people they will be examined one at a time while you are present to judge. . . . At the beginning of my episcopate I decided to do nothing privately on my own initiative without your advice and without the common will of the people.]

conceive (without arrogancy) we may acknowledge the fruits of their discipline to be the fruits of ours.

First, their exact strictness in examining and trying their *catechumeni,* before they received them into *ecclesiam fidelium,* brought forth this savory and spiritual fruit, the purity of churches. Pagans themselves could not charge them with any crime, but the name and profession of Christianity, see Pliny, *Epistolarum lib.* 10, *Epistolam* 97, Tertullian *Apologetick, chap.* 3. That which he saith of Cujus Sejus, was a general eulogy of their church members, *Bonus vir, malus tantum quod Christianus.*[58] A like fruit to that of Daniel against whom his enemies could find no occasion of complaint of error or fault, except it were for the profession of the law of his God, chap. vi, 4,5.

And as their strict examination received their members pure: so their strict censure kept them pure. For in the church, *judicabatur magno cum pondere:*—and in their feasts they were temperate and religiously fruitful in savory and gracious conference, and so departed better than they met, *Ut qui non tam cænam cænaverint, quam disciplinam,*[59] *Tertul. Apol., Cap.* 39.

2. From this purity and vigilancy of their discipline, in the admission of their members, and in the administration of their censures, there sprung forth many other gracious fruits, as their holy and constant and confident confessions of the name of Christ before judgment seats, the patient and glorious martyrdom of innumerable saints, to the conviction and astonishment of a world of persecutors.

Whence also sprung at last, the conversion of a great part of the word unto the truth, the advancement of a Christian emperor, the rooting out of paganish idolatry, and propagation of the profession of Christian religion, not only through the Roman

---

[58] [He was a good man, bad only in that he was a Christian.]
[59] [Like men who have not so much dined on dinner as on learning.]

Empire, but in many other nations exempt from the power of Roman armies, yet not from the power of the name of Christ, and of his church.

Afterwards, in the days of Constantine, when the external peace and liberty of the churches, encouraged all sorts of men (clean and unclean) to offer themselves to the fellowship of the church, and Congregational discipline began to be neglected through the usurped authority of the bishops, and presbyters, the limits of the church began to be as large as the precincts of the parish: and the church itself (which before was wont to be as a garden enclosed, Cant, iv,12.) did now become as a wilderness lying open to all the beasts of the field; who so would offer himself, might have free passage into the bosom of the church: and offer themselves they did, not from the savor of spiritual gifts (as was wont to be done in Congregational discipline:) but from respect to the countenance of higher powers, and the privileges and preferments flowing therefrom; church members being far more readily received to place of trust and honor, than men without. But this inundation of corrupt members was prevented by the vigilancy of Congregational discipline, whilst it stood in force, in the former centuries.

3. This was another good fruit of the Congregational discipline in those primitive times, that whilst it took place in the churches, there could be no place, nor way open for the advancement of Antichrist, no nor for the usurpation of episcopal prelacy. For whilst every church kept their government within their own congregation, they knew not the heavy and lordly yoke of cathedral churches, much less were they trodden down with impositions from the See of Rome. It is true, Victor, Bishop of Rome attempted a censure against the churches of Asia, but his arrogancy was speedily repressed by Irenæus, and sundry others both in Europe and Asia. And when some scandalous persons

in the African churches did appeal in Cyprian's time from those churches unto Rome, Cyprian and his fellow bishops (or presbyters)in the African churches, did easily prevent the impeachment of their church government from remote churches, and kept still their government within themselves.

SECTION II *Of the fruits of Congregational discipline in our churches in New England*

2. For the fruits of Congregational discipline, as it hath been exercised amongst us (though in much weakness) the Lord hath not left us without testimony from heaven.

First, in making these churches a little sanctuary (through his grace) to many thousands of his servants, who fled over hither to avoid the unsupportable pressures of their consciences by the episcopal tyranny.

Secondly, in blessing the ministry of our preachers here with like fruits of conversion (as in our native country) of sundry elder and younger persons, who came over hither not out of respect to conscience, or spiritual ends, but out of respect to friends, or outward enlargements: but have here found that grace, which they sought not for.

Thirdly, in discovering and suppressing those errors of Antinomians, and Familists, which brake forth here amongst us, and might have proceeded to the subversion of many souls, had not the blessing of Christ upon the vigilancy of Congregational discipline, either prevented or removed, or healed the same.

Fourthly, it hath been also a testimony from heaven of God's blessing upon our way, that many thousands in England in all the quarters of the kingdom, have been awakened to consider of the cause of church discipline, for which we have suffered this hazardous and voluntary banishment into this remote wilderness: and have therefore by letters conferred with us about it, and been (through mercy) so far enlightened, as to desire an utter subversion of episcopacy, and conformity, yea and the honorable Houses of Parliament, the Lord hath been pleased to help them so far to consider of our sufferings, and of the causes thereof, as to conclude a necessity of reformation of the ecclesiastical state, (amongst other causes, so) by reason of the necessity put upon so many English subjects to depart from all our employments, and enjoyments in our native country, for conscience sake.

SECTION III *Of the fruits of Congregational discipline in England*

3. For the fruits of Congregational discipline in England, they that walk in that way amongst you, might speak far more particularly, and largely, than I here can do at such a remote distance. But if books, and letters, and reports do not too much abuse us with false intelligence, the great, and gracious, and glorious victories, whereby the Lord hath wrought salvation for England in these late wars, have been as so many testimonies of the blessing of God upon our way. For the chiefest instruments, which God hath delighted to use herein, have been the faith and fidelity, the courage, and constancy of Independents. And when I say Independents, I mean not those corrupt sects and heresies, which shroud themselves under the vast title of Independency, and in the meantime cast off all church government, and churches too; but such as profess the kingdom of Christ in the government of each holy congregation of saints within themselves.

Far be it from me to undervalue the brotherly assistance of the Scottish churches and commonwealth in working so great a deliverance for England. Yea I account their concurrence a greater matter than assistance in this great work. Their exemplary piety and zeal, their courage and confidence in rising up, and standing out against the invasion of episcopal tyranny, and superstition, did doubtless quicken and encourage England to stand for the like liberty in the like cause: and to put forth that zeal, which the Lord had kindled in the hearts of many for reformation. And this was more than an assistance, even a guidance. Afterwards the forwardness of the Scottish nation to advance their armies into the English fields for the help of England against the common enemies of church and state, was an act of brotherly love never to be forgotten without due and thankful acknowledgement, and encouragement. But yet let the good pleasure of the Lord be acknowledged, who out of his abundant grace, hath granted the chiefest successes to the English designs by the forces of the Independents, which may not be denied without too much ingratitude both to God and man. Let all the glory thereof be wholly and solely given to the Lord: but yet let not the instruments be accounted unfruitful, by whom the Lord hath brought forth such blessed fruits of victory, and liberty, both from civil servitude, and superstitious thralldom, and withal so great an advancement of reformation both in church and state.

The inundation of sects and heresies in London, and the retarding of reformation in England, which have both of them been objected as the bitter fruits of the Congregational way, have been cleared above, to spring from other roots, not from that way. See chap. 3, sect. 5, the end of it.

THE SECOND PART

(being Doctrinal, and Controversial) Concerning
Congregational Churches and their Government

THE PREFACE

The author of the book entitled *Vindiciæ Clavium*,[60] thought good to conceal his own name, though in matters of accusation (whereof the book is full) it was the manner of the Romans (and that Roman manner was but just and equal) to have the accuser *show himself face to face,* Acts xxv, 16. And indeed the equity and equality of brotherly love would have required him either to have declared his own name, or to have concealed mine as well as his own. A little love amongst brethren would sooner heal the dissensions of brethren, than great store of books, breathing lust to contention. It is neither Presbyterians, nor those of the Congregational way (whom they call Independents) that do hinder either reformation or peace: but only the want of ἀληθεύειν ἐν ᾿Αγάπῃ, the want of following and holding forth the truth (or that which we believe to be the truth) in love, on both sides: it is love that edifieth both souls and states.

[60] [*Vindiciæ Clavium* (London, 1645) by Daniel Cawdrey (1588-1664), appeared without the author's name on the title page. Cawdry was a prolific writer against the bishops, on one hand, and the Independents on the other, in which latter category this work is to be placed. It was prompted by Cotton's *The Keys of the Kingdom of Heaven,* and in 1651, Cawdry, this time identifying himself, responded to Cotton's arguments set forth here, in *Vindiciæ Vindicarum.* Cotton died before completing his answer to this second attack of Cawdry's, but it was completed by John Owen and published as *A Defence of Mr. John Cotton from the Imputation of Selfe Contradiction Charged on Him by Mr. Dan: Cavvdrey* (Oxford, 1658).]

But since the author of *Vindiciæ* is pleased to conceal his name, I therefore think it not amiss (for brevity's sake, and to prevent a long periphrasis of the author of *Vindiciæ Clavium*) when I am occasioned to name him (which is very often) only to take leave to call him Vindex, or (in English) sometime the Assertor, sometime the Avenger; which both the title and purport of his book do hold him forth to be, acting the part of both.

The scope of his book (so far as it concerneth me) is chiefly to shew forth my weaknesses and contradictions, as his title manifesteth. But if Christ may have any glory by that, I shall willingly acknowledge (without his accusation, and much more without his conviction) that I am made up of weaknesses and contradictions. The best good in me is but weak at the best: and that which is corrupt, is weakness itself. If there be old and new man in me (as by the grace of Christ I see what I am) verily I cannot but find a bundle, not only of contradictions, but of contrafactions in myself. I believe, I doubt: I allow, I condemn: I hope, I fear: I love, I hate: I rejoice, I grieve: I would, I would not: I do, I undo: the same self, the same thing, at the same time.

Nevertheless all this will not argue that which the Avenger saith; *he hath heard, that I have often altered my judgment since I went to New England: nor that the author of the Keys does contradict the author of the Way, which is himself.*

I have not had liberty to peruse the *Way,* since it was published: but I see by the first words of it, that the publishers had not the copy which was taken hence from me, but an imperfect transcript. But I do believe what the publishers do report; *that setting aside some difference in logical terms, there is no material difference between the Keys and the Way, either in doctrine of divinity, or in church practice.*

Yes, (saith the Avenger) I find, he doth (in these) as flatly

contradict himself, as ever any man did. *Instance in one place,
(and leave the rest to the following discourse.) In the Keys,*
(page 4) he saith; *The Keys were delivered to Peter as an
apostle, as an elder, and as a believer. The sense of the words
(of Christ to Peter) will be most full, if all the several considerations be taken jointly together.* But in the *Way,* (page 27)
he saith, *The power of the keys is given to the church, to Peter
not as an apostle, not as an elder, but as a professed believer:
Is not this a flat contradiction?*

Ans. 1.   The words are not mine, but the Assertor's, which
he reporteth me to say in the *Keys; The Keys were delivered to
Peter as an apostle, as an elder, and as a believer.* I would be
loath to be found to speak so illogically, as to say, Socrates
hath a power of motion given to him, as a living creature, as a
man, as a philosopher. It is a trivial rudiment in schools, whatsoever is attributed to any as such, is given to all such universally,
and to such reciprocally and only. If the keys were delivered to
Peter as an apostle, then to all the apostles, and only to the
apostles. My words expressed by me are plain enough, and (I
thank God) not destitute of reason. *It hath proved a busy question, how Peter is to be considered in receiving this power of the
keys, whether as an apostle, or as an elder (for an elder also he
was) or as a believer, professing his faith before the Lord Jesus,
and his fellow brethren.*

I added indeed, the sense of the words of Christ to Peter, (*To
thee will I give the keys of the kingdom of heaven*) *will be most
full, if all the several considerations be taken jointly together.*

Wherein as I expound mine own meaning in the words following (in that treatise of the *Keys*) so the publishers of the
Keys do fitly express the same in their epistle [*The disposal* (say
they) *of this power, may lie in a due allotment into divers hands
according to their several concernments; rather than in an entire*

*and sole trust committed to any one man, or any sort or rank of
men, or officers.*] What saith the Avenger to this? *Herein* (saith
he) *perhaps we might agree with them, but then not with the
author, who places all the power in one sort of men alone, that
is, the brethren without officers, in the Way,* page 45. But the
Assertor taketh too much liberty, to affirm, I say that in that
place, which in the same passage I do expressly deny; my words
are express, *They,* (that is the Brethren) *may not administer
sacraments in defect of all officers, because by the appointment
of Christ, that pertaineth only to such as are called by office to
preach the Gospel,* Matt. xxviii, 19, 20.

But (saith the Avenger) in the *Way* (page 27) he saith, *The
power of the key is given to the church, to Peter, not as an
apostle, nor as an elder, but as a professed believer, in the name
of believers. Is not this a flat contradiction?* No verily, the solu-
tion is very easy and obvious, even to the Avenger himself, if he
would but have cast his eye upon the very next words in the
Keys, whence this ἐναντιόφανες[61] is fetched. The words run thus,
*The sense of the words will be most full, if all the several
considerations be taken jointly together. Take Peter considered
not only as an apostle, but withal an elder also, and a believer
too, professing his faith, all may well stand together. For there
is a different power given to all these, to an apostle, to an elder,
to a believer: and Peter was all these, and received all the power
which was given by Christ to any of these, or to all of these together.—So that Augustine did not mistake, when he said, Peter
received the keys in the name of the church.*

I cannot conceive what should move the Avenger so con-
fidently to charge *a flat contradiction in these two passages, and
that as flatly as ever man did contradict himself:* unless it were
partly through misreport of my words in the one place: whereof

---

[61] [Apparent contradiction.]

before) partly through misapprehension what the force in logic is, of a *quatenus tale:*[62] For he that knoweth that, he is not ignorant, that if Peter had received the power of the keys, *quatenus apostolus,* or *quatenus presbyter,* as an apostle, or as an elder; then only apostles, or only elders had received all church power, which all judicious divines, and (I doubt not) himself amongst them will utterly deny. But he saith Peter received the power of the keys, as standing in the room of all sorts of officers and members of the church, and so in the name of the whole church, he affirmeth that Peter received all church power, which is found in all professed believers, whether officers, or private brethren: and of officers, whether ordinary, as elders; or extraordinary, as apostles and evangelists. And is there any passage in the *Keys* which crosseth or contradicteth this? and that flatly, and so flatly, as never any man more?

Let this serve for my first answer to this contradiction: let me also add another.

Ans. 2. If there had been some difference between the *Way* and the *Keys* in some expressions: yet (as the prefacers related from a letter of mine to a friend of theirs:) it lay rather in logical terms, than in doctrine of divinity, or church practice: and such, amongst others, is this very point in hand. If there seem to be any difference in the expression of the one treatise, or of the other, about this point, it is in the first subject of the power of the keys (which is a logical notion) but the point is the same, both in doctrine of divinity, and in church practice.

As for the imputation of inconstancy, which the Avenger is pleased to put upon me, *he hath heard that I have often altered my judgment since I went to New England:* I should thank him if he would tell me either wherein I have altered my judgment,

---

[62] [Literally, "to the extent that such is so," and in this context, "in such a capacity." So *quatenus apostolus,* e.g. is in the capacity of an apostle.]

or from whom he so heard: meanwhile, he may do well to remember, that a citizen of Zion (a pure member of a pure
church) taketh not up *a reproach against his neighbor,* Psal.
xv, 3. John Baptist was surmised by some to be a *reed shaken
with the wind;* but it was a windy fancy.

3. And for a third answer, it were no just matter of calumny
if in some later tractate I should retract, or express more com-
modiously, what I wrote in a former less safely. Augustine (as
much above me, as the moon to a little star) lost no whit of his
reputation in the church, by writing two whole books of re-
tractions of his own opinions and expressions.

CHAPTER I

Of the church, to which Christ committed the power of the keys

SECTION I

Vindex doth here first enquire what I mean by this church:
whereof, though he might fully have informed himself from
the fifth point of the first chapter of the *Keys* (which he himself
had in hand:) yet in hope of some advantage, he chose rather
to fetch it from another tract of mine, touching our church way:
which though he say, it went up and down in the dark; yet its
dark walking was no intent of mine, but that it should find either
timely impression, or (by advice of friends) utter suppression.
Now in that tract I said, the church to which the Lord Jesus
committed the keys of the kingdom of heaven, Matt. xvi, 19,
is *coetus fidelium,* commonly called a particular visible church,
meeting together with common and joint consent into one congregation, for public worship and mutual edification.

But (saith the Avenger) *of all the rest this is the most im-*

*probable sense of our Saviour's words, if by the kingdom of
heaven on earth, he meaneth that church of which he spake before in ver. 18. But that was either the catholic visible church:
or rather the invisible mystical church; for that only is built
upon the rock, and against that the gates of hell shall never
prevail: whereas particular churches may fail.*

Ans. 1.   It is not a more improbable sense of our Saviour's
words, to understand the kingdom of heaven, Matt. xvi, 19, of a
particular visible church, rather than of the catholic visible
church. For I do not read that the Scripture doth anywhere acknowledge a catholic visible church at all. The catholic church
is not visible as a church: and the church that is visible, is not
catholic. Doctor Ames his judgment seems to me more orthodoxal, *ecclesia non est tota simul visibilis,*[63] *Medull, l.* 1, *c.* 32,
num. 1. For though the whole church (or which is all one, the
catholic church) may be visible in her singular members; yet so
they are not a church. Or though it may be visible in the several
particular congregations, yet none of them is catholic. Or though
all of them together may be called a catholic church, or general
assembly, if they were met together; yet I suppose, Vindex
would be loath to say, that Christ giveth the power of the keys
(all ecclesiastical power) into their hands. Such general assemblies are rare and extraordinary; and extraordinary assemblies
are not fit judicatories to hear and censure ordinary offenses, or
to administer the ordinary acts of church power.

Ans. 2.   He therefore distrusting (as it seemeth) that to be
the meaning of our Saviour's words (to understand the kingdom
of heaven of the catholic visible church) he expoundeth it
rather to be meant of the invisible mystical church. And indeed,
true it is, that Peter and other preachers of the Gospel have
received such a power of the keys, as by the ministry of the word,

63 [The church is not completely visible everywhere at once.]

to beget faith in their hearers, and so open to them a door into the invisible church: as also to convince unbelievers of their damnable estate, and so ministerially to declare them shut out from the fellowship of the invisible church. But there is also a power of the keys, to open a door unto professed believers into the visible church: and again to shut them out of the visible church, when they grow scandalous. And therefore the visible church cannot be excluded from one part of the meaning of the kingdom of heaven, whereof Peter received the keys.

Besides, certain it is, that when by the power of the keys, a believer is received into the invisible church, he can never be shut again out of that church. But the keys here given to Peter, have a power to shut out of the kingdom of heaven, even the same persons, unto whom they have opened the door before. And therefore the kingdom of heaven (whereof Peter received the keys) is not meant only of the invisible church, but of the visible church also.

Ans. 3. The reasons which Vindex objecteth to the contrary, will not prevail against this truth, no more than the gates of hell against the church.

Object. 1. *It is the invisible church only which is built upon the rock, and against that, the gates of hell shall never prevail: whereas particular churches may fail.*

Ans. It is not true, that the invisible church only is built upon a rock; for particular churches are built upon a rock also. Built they are upon divine institution, and Christ is laid for the foundation of them; or else they are not churches of Christ, which are described to be *in God our Father, and in our Lord Jesus Christ,* 1 Thes. i,1. The Apostle Paul laid Christ for the foundation of the visible church of Corinth, 1 Cor. iii, 10, 11. Christ is not the head of that church whereof He is not the foundation: and where He is the foundation, He is also the rock, on which they are built; for He is not a sandy foundation.

Yea, but particular churches may fail.

What then? So may true disciples of Christ fail (in respect of bodily subsistence) and yet the gates of hell never prevail against them; for they will be received into everlasting habitation, Luke xvi,9.

Yea, but particular churches may fail and fall away from the faith; all the churches of Asia are fallen from Christ to Mahomet: and sundry in Europe from Christ, to Antichrist.

Yet those churches that were founded upon Christ, and builded upon that rock, they neither failed, nor fell away. It was their successors, and not they, that failed, and fell in that sort. If the posterity of an holy particular church do degenerate, they were never founded upon Christ, but in an outward form. God may remove the candlestick (that is, his particular church) out of that place (say out of Corinth or Ephesus, Rev. ii,5) yet he will ever have some or other particular churches visible in one place or other; and so against that church state, the gates of hell shall never prevail. Dr. Whitaker declareth the judgment of orthodox Protestants in this point; *Nos dicimus, aliquam semper fore in mundo ecclesiam, quæ Christo pareat, eamque visibilem,*[64] *De Ecclesia, quest.* 3, *cap.* 2. Junius in his animadversions in Bellarm, Controv. 4 de Concil. and Eccles. Cap. 13 Art. 1. *Concludimus inquit, ne visibilem quidem ecclesiam, posse deficere, atque interire, adeo ut in se ipsa sit invisibilis, etc.*[65] And Doctor Ames beareth the like witness. *Ecclesia nunquam*

---

[64] [We say that there will always be some church in the world which obeys Christ, and that it will be visible.]

[65] [We conclude, he says, that not even the visible church can fail and die to such an extent that it should be in itself invisible.]

plane definit esse visibilis.[66] Medull. *l*, 1 cap. 31. And this they intend of some particular visible church or other. For a catholic visible church they dispute against, but maintain the catholic church to be invisible. Whitaker de Ecclesia Q. 2a, 10, *Dicimus ecclesiam catholicam invisibilem esse, etiam tum cum particularis quæque; ecclesia vel maxime floret.*[67]

Object 2. *The kingdom of glory is one part of the meaning of the kingdom of heaven, and it is not contradistinguished to a particular congregation, but to the general visible church on earth.*

Ans. There is not any particular congregation on earth, but may be, upon just occasion, contradistinguished from the kingdom of glory. It may truly be said, whosoever is duly bound or loosed in any one particular church, is also bound and loosed in the kingdom of glory. There is no semblance of difficulty herein.

Nevertheless, when (in the *Keys,* page 2) I spake of the power of the keys given to Peter to bind on earth, I did not mean it in any one single particular church on earth alone, but generally and indefinitely, in every particular church on earth. For every apostle had transcendent power in every particular church on earth: and every particular church on earth (being all of one common nature militant here on earth, and different from the triumphant church in heaven) may justly be contradistinguished from the kingdom of glory. But yet I never dreamed of a general visible church on earth (as Vindex expoundeth me:) unless he mean it, as visible in particular congregations. And if he so mean, it will better express the truth, and my meaning, to say, that Peter received the keys to bind and loose (as in

---

[66] [The church never absolutely ceases to be visible.]

[67] [We say that the church as a whole is invisible; even when each particular church is flourishing to the highest degree.]

the invisible church in some sort, so) in the particular visible
church indefinitely; that is, in every particular visible church on
earth. For a particular visible church is of a common and general
nature, and comprehendeth in it every singular particular visible
church, as that of Corinth, Ephesus, Philippi, and the rest.

Object. 3. *That church is meant, in Matt.* xvi, 19, *whereof
Peter was one* (*Way,* page 1). *But Peter was not a member of
such a particular congregation: for there was none such extant,
when Christ spake these words to Peter.*

Ans.   I presume Vindex is not ignorant, that in rational discourses, and propositions of art, the *copula* doth not *connotare
tempus,* but only *connectere* the *subject,* and the *prædicate:*
else he will open a way to insoluble fallacies

As in that sophism.

> *Nullus Infans fuit Juvenis:*
> *Omnis Senex fuit Infans:*
> Ergo, *Nullus Senex fuit Juvenis.*[68]

This connotation of time in the *copula,* breedeth the fallacy; let
Vindex therefore be pleased to leave such arguings to sophisters,
or make use of them when he will refresh his wit in argument
with young scholars. But amongst brethren, what if I should say,
resurrection to glory is given to the bodies of the faithful,
whereof elect infants are a part? Though the resurrection be not
yet come, nor elect infants yet come to be faithful yet the proposition is true, because the *subject* and *prædicate* have true connection in the nature of the thing, though not in the present
order of time. When Christ directed his disciples, and amongst
them, Peter, in case of private offense, and obstinacy therein, at
length, to tell the church, whether by church he meant the par-

---

[68] [No infant has been a youth. Every old man has been an infant. Therefore,
no old man has been a youth.]

ticular congregation, or the presbytery; neither of them both
were then extant, when Christ spake these words to Peter. But
will that be a good argument to prove, that Christ did not
direct the offended brother either to tell the particular church,
or to tell the presbytery, because neither of them were then
extant?

*Object. 4. That church whereof Peter received the keys, was
such whereto Peter or any offended brother might tell an offense, and have it censured. But that was never done in a church
of saints, believers without officers; nor was the church of
Corinth such a church, but had officers, who might authoritatively censure the incestuous person, etc.*

Ans. This is another passage of sophistry, but somewhat
more open.—For if the objection be cast into a true syllogism,
it will run thus: The church of which Peter received the keys,
was such to which Peter, and any offended brother might tell an
offense, and have it censured. But the church of saints and believers without officers, was not such to whom Peter, or any
offended brother might tell an offense, and have it censured.

Thus, the minor is justly denied: and therefore Vindex
chooseth rather to put his minor in other terms;

The church of saints and believers without officers, was not
such a church, to whom Peter or any offended brother did tell
an offense.

But now there is *quatuor termini*[69] in his syllogism: might
tell an offense, and did tell an offense, make two different
mediums. What if the church of Corinth when they censured
the incestuous person, were not such a church without officers?
Or, what if no church wanted presbyters in the apostles' times?
If it were so, it was the greater bounty of Christ to them in those
primitive times, when gifts of the Spirit were poured out in more

[69] [Four terms.]

abundance. But yet if a church of saints, or believers without officers, have power from Christ to elect officers, then have they power also much more to admit members. And if they have power to admit them without officers, they have like power upon just offense to exclude them out of their holy communion without officers. For it is the same power to open and to shut, *instituere, et destituere.*

Object. 5. *The church to which the keys are given, are said to be such as do all of them meet in one place for the administration of the ordinances of Christ:*

But the ordinances of Christ are not to be found, much less administered in a church of believers without officers.

Ans. This latter proposition is left naked and unguarded without proof. And I confess, *ipse dixit* may go for a warrant in Pythagorean philosophy: and *teste me ipso*[70] may go for a warrant in royal grants of favor: but not in matters of faith, nor of justice between king and subject, much less in matters of controversy amongst brethren. The truth is, though the ordinances of Christ may not all of them be administered in a church of believers without officers, and authoritative dispensing of the word and censures, and ministration of sacraments: yet some ordinances of Christ may be found and administered in a church of believers without officers. As it is an ordinance of Christ, two or three of them (much more all of them) to meet and pray together, and admonish one another in Christ's name, Matt. xviii,20. It is an ordinance of Christ, to elect officers, (deacons and elders) for this is the power and privilege of the church of brethren. Though Titus was left in Crete to ordain elders in every city, Tit. i,5, yet not to elect them: as Cyprian argueth from sundry passages of the Acts of the Apostles, and other Scriptures; and thereupon inferreth, *Plebs Dominicis*

---

70 [He himself says it . . . I myself as witness.]

praeceptis obsequens et Deum metuens—ipsa maxime potesta-
tem habet, vel eligendi dignos sacerdotes, vel indignos re-
cusandi,[71] *Cyprian. Epistolarum l.* 1, *Epistola* 4.

And if a church of believers may thus supply themselves with
officers when they want them, and if officers and brethren have
all ordinary church power, (and so all ordinances of Christ,
which are ordinarily administered, found amongst them) then
what hindereth, but that a church of believers hath in it, as some
ordinances formally, so all radically and virtually, and the same
administered, and administrable amongst them?

Object. 6. *When it is said (in the Way,* page 1) *Christ*
committed the keys to the church, that is, to a particular congre-
gation, it must be meant either subjective, *or* objective; *if it be*
meant in this latter sense, that the keys are committed to the
church, as the object of the exercise of the keys, that is, for the
good and use of the church, it is truly said, but nothing to the
purpose. In this sense, the keys are given first and more im-
mediately to the invisible mystical church (all are yours, whether
Paul, etc) *then to the general visible church for their sakes;*
then to the particular congregation, as a part and member of
that general visible church.

But if it be meant in the former sense (as it must be so meant,
or else the author of the Way *doth equivocate with us from the*
beginning throughout the whole book) then he falleth into the
extreme of the Brownists, which he so laboreth to avoid. For to
take the church, in Matt. xvi, for a particular congregation of
believers without officers, is a new, strange, and false gloss,
maintained by none but Brownists, and such like Separatists.

Ans. When I said Christ committed the keys to the church,

---

71 [The people, obeying the precepts of the Lord and fearing God, have
themselves the greatest power to elect worthy priests or to refuse unworthy
ones.]

that is, to a particular congregation, I meant it indeed *subjective,*
though not excluding *objective.* For I do not make the particular
visible church a different church from the invisible. The distribution of the church into visible and invisible, is not into divers
kind of churches, nor into divers kinds of members of the same
church, but into divers adjuncts of the same members of the
same church: who in respect of their spiritual and internal estate
(to wit, their faith) are invisible; but in respect of their external condition (to wit, the profession of faith) are visible.
The particular church (I speak of it indefinitely) receiveth the
power of the keys both *subjective* to itself, and *objective* for
itself, though the saving benefit thereof redound only to the elect
amongst them, who are also of them. Neither is this *to fall into
the extreme of (those whom you call) Brownists, to take the
church for a particular congregation without officers.*

For first, when I wrote that proposition (in the first words of
the *Way*) it was not then in my mind to understand any other
particular congregation to which Christ had committed all
ordinary church power, and the administration thereof, but to a
congregation of believers furnished with officers. For I spake
of such a church whereof Peter was one; and he was an officer.
Though I perceive Mr. Rutherford understood me otherwise,
(as you also do:) and so from thence raiseth his first controversy: *whether the church of believers destitute of the eldership, have the power of the keys?*

Which (to avoid misconstruction) I expressed more distinctly
in the tract of the *Keys.* But yet, take it as he doth, for a church
of believers without officers; they have received some part of the
power of the keys formally, as the election of officers, etc. and
the whole ordinary power of the keys, radically and virtually.
The stock of the vine (which groweth in the bulk from the root)
hath not immediate power to bring forth grapes; but yet it hath

power to produce branches, which do bring forth grapes: so the body of the church of believers, though they have not immediate power of rule authoritatively to dispense the word, or to administer sacraments at all: yet they have power to produce such officers as may perform the same.

Again secondly, Dr. Whitaker was none of them whom you call Brownists, yet he speaking of this text (which you quote in this paragraph, to prove that ministers are given to the church *objective*, for their good, not *subjective*, so as the church to have power over them, 1 Cor. iii, 22, 23. He beareth witness against your gloss: *Apostolus,* saith he, *non tantum ait ministros institutos esse propter utilitatem ecclesiæ: sed sic illos esse ecclesiæ ut ecclesia est Christi. At ecclesia Christo subjicitur non propter Christi utilitatem instituta est. Et apostolus ecclesiam esse Dei templum, affirmat: ministri in templo, non supra templum,*[72] *Whitak. Controv. 4, quest. 1, num. 11, in fine.* Neither was Parker one of those whom you call Brownists, or such like Separatists, but wrote against them. But yet he understandeth the church, Matt. xvi, of a particular congregation of believers, as distinct from officers: yea and proveth it at large. *Parker de Ecclesiastica Politia, l. 3, cap. 1, 2, 3.*

Object 7.   To conclude, the church of which our Saviour speaketh, is called here the kingdom of heaven (on earth:) But a particular congregation of believers is never called the kingdom of heaven; being but a member or corporation of that kingdom. It were as improper to call a congregation, Christ's kingdom, as to call London the kingdom of England.

Ans. 1.   It is not material whether a particular congregation

---

[72] [The apostle does not only say that ministers are appointed for the advantage of the church; but that they are of the church even as the church is of Christ. Although the church is subject to Christ, it is not instituted for the advantage of Christ. And the apostle maintains that the church is the temple of God: the ministers are in the temple, not above the temple.]

of believers be ever expressly called the kingdom of heaven or
no; it is enough it is called a church, yea as it is distinguished
from church officers. Those whom he calleth the whole church
distinguished from the apostles and elders, Act. xv,22, the same
he calleth the brethren, ver. 23. And if the brethren may be
called the church, they may justly also be called the kingdom of
heaven, seeing the style of the kingdom of heaven is usually
given to the church. You may more truly observe, that the
presbytery is never called in Scripture the kingdom of heaven:
no, nor are they called the church, unless it be in that one place,
Matt. xviii,17, which yet may sooner be presumed, than proved
to be understood of the presbytery; I mean a consistory of presbyters, distinct from the congregation of believers.

Ans. 2.   I dare not say that the particular visible church is
never called the kingdom of heaven. For when Christ went out
to hire laborers into his vineyard, it was unto this or that particular church, respectively. And this vineyard thus destitute of
laborers or officers, and distinguished from them, is called the
kingdom of heaven, Matt. xx,1.

Again, when the kingdom of heaven is compared to ten vir-
gins, five wise, and five foolish, Matt. xxv, 1, 2, this is a description of the estate of each particular church, respectively; without
respect to their officers. Besides, when the kingdom of God is
said to be within us Luke xvii, 21, and all the faithful are said
to be made kings and priests unto God, Rev. i,6. Even a kingdom of priests, 1 Pet. ii,9, can it then be termed an improper
speech to call a particular church of believers, the kingdom of
heaven?

*Yes, they are but a member, or corporation of the kingdom:
and it were improper to call London the kingdom of England.*

But every similar part of a similar body doth properly partake
both in the name and nature of the whole. Every part of water

is water, and is both cold and moist, as the whole water is. And such a part of such a body, is a particular visible church. The church of Corinth is said to be the body of Christ, and the members thereof, members in particular. And Christ hath given unto them all his officers, as well as unto other churches, 1 Cor. xi, 27, 28. But such is not the state of London. London is not a similar, but a dissimilar part of England, and different from all the corporations of England, different in power, different in privileges: how then can a comparison of unequals, be drawn to parallel a state of equals.

SECTION 11   *What the keys of the kingdom of heaven be*

In opening what the keys of the kingdom of heaven be, it was not my intent to enumerate them all distinctly and particularly in that first chapter of the description of the keys, which was but a preface and introduction to the whole tractate. I thought it enough to give an instance only in general, there, in two or three examples; reserving a more exact distribution of them to the chapters following: and referring each sort of them to their several subjects in their proper place, lest I might clog myself and the reader with needless repetitions. I therefore contented myself to say in general, *The keys are the ordinances of Christ, which He hath instituted to be administered in his church, as the preaching of the word, as also the administering of the seals and censures.*

I instanced in these, as most obvious, and of easiest apprehension to any vulgar reader. But in instancing these, I supposed no man would be of so narrow apprehension, as not to conceive those things to be included, without which, these cannot duly be performed. As, the word cannot be preached, nor the sacraments dispensed, without a vocation unto such spiritual admin-

istrations. Nor can it be doubted, that if there must be a vocation
to administer these, there must be also some, who have power
from Christ to give such a vocation.

Albeit, (if it had been of any weight for the expediting of any
controversy about the keys (which I know none:) I might
easily have given some definition of the keys; as to say, the keys
of the kingdom of heaven are spiritual powers given by Christ
to his church to dispense the treasures of his kingdom, for the
opening and shutting, binding and loosing the spiritual estates
of men in the church. By spiritual powers, I mean spiritual
callings, and spiritual gifts fitting for them, enabling to some
spiritual acts: by the treasures of the kingdom I mean the words,
seals, and censures, and the spiritual blessings laid up in them.
But callings, gifts, and treasures, are all of them ordinances. The
other parts of the definition, what be the acts, and ends, objects,
and subjects of this power, I opened formerly in the third,
fourth, and fifth paragraphs of the first chapter of the *Keys*.

But upon what I expressed in this paragraph, Vindex is
pleased to animadvert some things.

1. *In this paragraph* (saith he) *as you do clearly lay down
the state of the question: so do you strongly confute the scope of
your whole book, which is to give the people a share in the
government of the church.*

Ans.   Vindex doth clearly mistake my scope and meaning, to
think I did lay down the state of the question in this paragraph.
For I think it is no question at all, that the keys of the kingdom
of heaven, are the ordinances of Christ, which He hath instituted
to be administered in his church. Neither is it the scope of my
whole book, to give the people a share in the government of the
church: nay, it is not the scope of the greater part of the book:
nay further, there be that blame the book for the other extreme,
that it placeth the government of the church not at all in the

hands of the people, but of the presbytery. So various are the apprehensions of books by variety of readers, and by their sometime judicious, sometime cursory reading.

Least of all is there any color for this apprehension, that I do in this paragraph strongly confute the scope of my book. *Yes, (saith he) for if the keys be the ordinances of Christ, they are given indeed for the church of believers, that is, for their good and benefit, objective; but are never in all the Scripture, nor in all antiquity said to be given to the church subjective.*

Ans. What power I acknowledge given to the church of believers *subjective,* either in admission of members, or election of officers, or censure of offenders, I do allege Scriptures for it; which when Vindex taketh in hand to evade them, I shall return him (God willing) further answer, which in this place were an unseasonable prevention: but when he affirmeth that such power as I acknowledge given to the church, is not to be read in all antiquity, it maketh me to suspect, that either he hath not read all antiquity, (which yet is no crime, only he should not then have denied them all, to own this power; for it is not safe to avouch more than we know:) or if he have read them all, he hath forgotten what is recorded by the most ancient antiquity for the space of the first three hundred years, during all the time of the primitive persecution. Of which I have given account to Mr. Baylie in answer to the historical part of his *Dissuasive,* (chap. 4 sect. 1, 2, 3) whereto I refer him.

But, saith Vindex, it soundeth ill at first hearing, to say, that the people have any power to exercise ordinances, of preaching, or administering the seals or censures. The power of preaching or administering sacraments by the people, as none but Separatists do usurp; so yourself complain of it, page 6. And why you should allow them power in censures, there is very little reason.

Ans. If preaching the word, or administering the seals, were all the ordinances which Christ hath instituted, and no more but they, Vindex saith true, it would sound ill at first hearing (and if he will, at second and third hearing too) to say, the people have any power to exercise these ordinances; unless that kind of preaching be understood, which Dr. Ames approveth, *l. 4 de Casibus Conscientiæ, cap. 25, in respons. 3, ad Quæst. 1.*

But to allow the people a power in censures, I marvel it should sound so ill at first hearing, of such whose ears have been long wonted to hear of suspensions, and excommunications; not only of private Christians, but even of many ministers, by chancellors and commissaries, who generally are no ministers, and it were to be wished, that the most of them, (yea, or the best of them) were as good as brethren. But yet I somewhat wonder, that he that in this paragraph could allege all antiquity, should think it to sound ill at first hearing, that the brethren of the church should have any hand in church censures; who knoweth what reverend testimony ancient Tertullian giveth of them (*Apologetici Capite* 39) *Quum probi, cum boni coeunt, cum pii, cum casti congregantur, non factio discenda est, sed curia.*[73] And what an hand Cyprian giveth to the people in church censures, none that have read him can be ignorant. What reason there is for their power in church censures (whether little, or much) we shall further consider (God willing) in its place; for here you neither give reasons against it, nor refute our reasons for it.

2. A second thing which Vindex animadverts in the former paragraph is, *that I call the keys, ordinances, which Christ hath instituted to be administered in his church, the church of believers, a particular congregation.*

But mark it (saith he) *not by a church without officers: but by the officers instituted in the church.*

Ans. He need not have bid me to mark that, which if him-

---

[73] [When honorable men, when good men come together, when pious men, when holy men assemble, they ought not to be spoken of as a faction, but as a senate.]

self had marked, he could not but see, that I never acknowledged it to be in the power of the people to administer all ordinances, but to administer some ordinances themselves, and to elect and call such to them, as might administer all the rest.

3. His third animadversion is, *that I say, the keys are neither sword nor scepter: for they convey not sovereign power; but stewardly and ministerial: which clearly* (saith he) *excludeth the people; for they have no stewardly or ministerial power over themselves.*

Ans. As if the people were not stewards of the grace of God given to them! The apostle Peter maketh account, that, *as every man received the gift, so he should minister the same, as good stewards of the manifold grace of God,* 1 Pet. iv,10. If the people have received any gift of grace, they are either stewards of it, or lords: lords they are not, who must give account to the Lord for the employment and improvement of their gifts: what are they else then but stewards? Yea (you will say), but private men may bestow their gifts privately. But election of officers is a public gift, whatsoever else beside; and that must be dispensed publicly; and that not as lords, to elect whom they list, but as stewards and ministers to Christ, to elect whom the Lord hath chosen.

I said indeed (*in that paragraph*) *that Christ in giving the keys, investeth those to whom He giveth them, with a power to open and shut the gates both of the church and heaven; and that this power lieth partly in their spiritual calling* (*whether it be their office, or their place, and order in the church*) *and partly in the concourse and cooperation of Christ, accompanying the right dispensation of those keys or ordinances.*

But (*saith Vindex*) *I suppose the word calling, should be taken here of some special calling or office: which again would exclude the people, as having no office in the church.*

Ans. There is no reason why you should suppose, that calling here should be taken of some special calling or office; if special denote a specification of a calling distinct from other members of the church: but if it only specify a distinct calling, or state, or order different from such as are not members of the church: so it is true indeed, every member of the body hath a special calling distinct from such believers or others, as are not yet received into member-like communion with this or that particular church; yea, and every member of this or that particular church, hath a calling to put forth some acts of power in his own church, which members of another particular church have not power to put forth there, though they may put forth the same each one in his own church respectively: every member of the body of a particular church hath some function, or action, (or as the new translation termeth it) some office in the body. For that which is expressed in the protasis of the apostle's comparison, is implied in the rendition, Rom. xii, 4, 5. As we have many members in one body, and all members have not the same office: so we being many, are one body in Christ, etc. If all the members of the body have not the same office, it implieth, they have all of them some office, or function, or action, though not the same. But custom hath obtained, that they only are accounted to have a special calling or office in the church, who are set apart for the eminent administrations in the church; as the pastors, teachers, elders, deacons. And such a special calling, it is not requisite that the common brethren of the church should have, to disperse that power of the keys which is committed to them. For Christ hath neither called them to it, nor given them gifts suitable for it.

But (*saith Vindex*) *when you say the power of the keys lieth in their spiritual calling* (*whether it be their office or place, and order in the church:*) *you add this explication on purpose to steal in the interest of the people in some share of the keys.*

Ans. It is not stealth, but justice to give every man his own:

liberty, to whom liberty; power, to whom power; honor, to whom honor belongeth. The psalmist foretold it in a new song (all which new songs have special accomplishment in the New Testament) that this honor have all his saints, to wit, in the congregation of saints to execute the spiritual censures (or judgments) written, Psal. cil,9. And if the Lord have given them this honor, it is rather stealth (yea sacrilege) to take it from them, than to allow it to them.

But (saith Vindex) if place, or order in the church, do give the people out of office, any power in the keys; that is, in the ordinances; then may women and children claim an interest in those keys, for they have a place and order in the church as well as men.

Ans. It is not every place or order in the church, that giveth power to receive the ordinances administered by others, much less power, themselves to dispense ordinances. Children have not power to receive the Lord's Supper, much less to administer it. And for women, God hath expressly forbidden them all place of speech and power in the church, 1 Cor. xiv, 34 and 1 Tim. ii, 11, 12, unless it be to join with the rest of the church, in singing forth the public praises of the Lord. Let every soul enjoy such privileges and liberties, as the Lord hath given him in his place and order: and neither affect nor attempt more. The female sex, and nonage, fall short of some power, which Christ hath given to the brotherhood.

SECTION III   *Of the subject to whom the power of the keys is given*

I conceive it would be some loss of time and labor, to argue this question with Vindex alone: whose exceptions so far as they concern the point in controversy, are but collections out of the writings of others, who have more distinctly and elaborately disputed the cause. And therefore it will be requisite, in this, and the like points of controversy, rather to consider what hath been written by learned and reverend Mr. Rutherford, and Mr. Baylie, and yet by the way, not to neglect what personal exceptions Vindex hath taken of myself.

In the *Way of the Churches of New England*, chap. 1, sect. 1, it was laid down for the first proposition: *That the church which Christ in the Gospel hath instituted, and to which He hath committed the keys of his kingdom, the power of binding and loosing, the tables and seals of the covenant, the officers and censures of his church, the administration of all his public worship and ordinances, is cœtus fidelium, a company of believers, meeting in one place every Lord's Day, for the administration of the holy ordinances of God to public edification.*

Upon this proposition Mr. Rutherford (as he excelleth in acuteness and scholastical argumentativeness) hath raised four questions, though some of them more than I did intend to point at in the proposition. Let us consider of them in their order, not with a spirit of contention (which himself in his epistle to the reader, candidly professeth against) but with a spirit studious of truth and peace.

The first question he raiseth from that proposition, is this: *Whether a company of believers and saints, builded by faith upon the rock Christ, and united in a church covenant, be the only instituted visible church of the New Testament, to the which Christ hath given the keys?*

Himself understandeth the proposition, as if it held forth the affirmative. But in very truth, as the word [only] is not in the proposition: so it was far from my intendment, to exclude an organical church (a church furnished with all her officers) from being an instituted visible church of the New Testament, as well as *cœtus fidelium,* a company of Christians without officers. When the proposition speaketh of officers as given to the church, it intendeth them not as mere adjuncts given to a subject, but as integral parts given to the whole body of the church, for completing the integrity and perfection of it. And so much the very words of the proposition do imply; for it speaketh of such *a church, to whom Christ hath given the administration of all his public worship and ordinances: which is not a power given to a church of private believers, destitute of officers.* Howsoever they may be capable (more or less) of some spiritual administrations: yet doubtless they are not capable of all: and for instance, not of the administration of sacraments, without officers.

Neither was it my intendment in that proposition, to exclude lawful synods (gathered, and proceeding according to the pattern, Acts xv) from all participation in some part of the power of the keys. For they have a power to decide controversies from the word, and to appoint a course for the preventing and healing of offenses, and for agreement in the truth according to the word. But these synods are not the ordinary standing judicatories of the church: neither do they convene, nor exercise their directive power, but when the particular churches lie under variance or offense, or are not yet settled in a way of truth and peace. But my intendment simply was, that each particular church when it is organized with all his officers, and walketh in a way of truth and peace; there is no part of the power of the keys, but a particular church hath received it within itself, and may administer the same to the edification of the whole body.

Neither let it be thought (in that first proposition) that I intended to invest a church of believers (without officers) with all the power of the keys, because I speak of the election and ordination of officers afterwards. For so I speak also of the

gathering and admission of members: and yet it may not be
inferred, that I should intend a church invested with all power,
which yet is destitute both of members, and officers. But it is a
well known rule of method, to define or describe at first, *totum
integrale,* with the proper adjuncts (or passions) of it, and then
to descend to set forth the several members, and integral parts
thereof, with their several operations in due place.

So that this first question raised from this first proposition is
no question at all; and therefore it will not be needful to examine the distinctions, or conclusions raised up against it. For
they do not contradict the true meaning of the proposition, unless it be some parts of the second conclusion, which come in
their place to be considered of in the sequel.

SECTION IV   *Touching the power of the keys in the
church of believers without officers*

The second question, which Mr. Rutherford raised out of the
first proposition formerly mentioned, is

*Whether or not, Christ hath committed the keys of the king-
dom of heaven to the church of believers, which as yet wanteth
all officers, pastors, teachers, etc.*

But this question, so far as it concerneth my proposition (to
speak with leave and due reverence) is as ungrounded as the
former. For the proposition speaketh not of a church that
wanteth all officers, but of a church that having received officers
from Christ, hath power to administer all the public worship,
and ordinances of Christ. This point and my plain meaning
therein, is more fully and distinctly opened in the small treatise
of the keys. But for the present stating of the question, our
judgment is expressed in two conclusions; which so far as they
are controverted, are to be cleared.

First that the church of believers destitute of officers, hath received some part of the power of the keys: as a power to receive members, to elect officers, and to do such other church acts, as do not require office rule, or office power.

Secondly, that the church of believers, though for the present destitute of officers, hath in it a radical or virtual power, whereby it may call forth such officers, as may administer all those acts of office rule, or power, which of itself without them, it could not exercise.

Against these two assertions, I do not find any thing in his distinctions or conclusions, or arguments which doth prevail with me to depart from them, as indeed he doth not directly so much dispute against these conclusions which we hold, as against that question (which himself by mistake gathered from the proposition) which we hold not.

Though I said the keys were given to a church of believers, whereof Peter was one, yet that was only to show, that Peter in his lowest spiritual relation in the church (as a professed believer) had his share in the power of the keys: but not that he had his share in the whole power of the keys, as a professed believer: but that he had other parts of the power of the keys, as an elder, and as an apostle immediately given him by the Lord Jesus.

In his second distinction (page 7) *I do not understand the safety of that speech; that pastors and teachers are gifts, of which the church is not capable, as a subject.* For the apostle saith, Christ hath given (amongst other officers) pastors, and teachers to his church, Ephes. iv,8, 11. And if He have given them to the church, the church is the recipient subject of them. As if the eye be given to the body, the body is the recipient subject of it. And though the church cannot exercise the pastors', and teachers' place by themselves; yet they may be their pastors and teachers. As the body though it cannot see by itself, yet it may by the eye, which is given to it of God for that end: Neither is it a safe speech (as I conceive) to say, *that the church is capable of these gifts (pastors and teachers) as the object and end, because the fruit and effect of these gifts redoundeth to the good of the church; if that be meant as the only respect, in regard of which they are said to be given to the church.* For pastors and teachers are given to the church, as integral parts of the church, as the church is *totum integrale.* Now integral parts are intrinsical and essential to a *totum integrale,* and not extrinsical, as the object, and end be to a thing.

The testimony which he allegeth from Reverend Parker, and Baynes, and the Parisian School,[74] doth indeed argue, that the fruit and effect of the gifts of pastor and teacher doth redound to the good of the church (which no man denieth) but Mr. Rutherford well knoweth, that Parker and the Parisian School, do grant further (even more than I argue for) that the church is not only the object and end, but the first subject also of all church power: which though Mr. Baynes waive (in the place alleged by him) and dispute thereupon both against Mr. Parker and the Parisian School (under the name of Sorbonists;) yet he clearly closeth with Mr. Parker and us, in the conclusion; that the visible church, instituted by Christ and his apostles, to which the keys are given, is not a diocesan, or provincial, or national assembly, but a particular congregation, *Diocesans Trial, Q.* 1. But if Mr. Rutherford intend no more but this, that the church is not capable of exercise of the pastors' and doctors' place, and

[74] [The theological faculty of the University of Paris, which met regularly at the Sorbonne throughout the seventeenth century, argued as a school against the pope's dominion over things temporal and in favor of the authority of general councils, the liberties of the churches, and the revocability of papal judgments. These doctrines were summed up in 1682 as the Four Gallican Articles and represent the French clergy's claims to a wide degree of independence within Roman Catholicism.]

therefore is not the first subject of their office power; I for my part readily close with him therein, reserving due respect to others of different judgment.

In his third distinction, *which he putteth between a formal ordinary power, and a virtual or extraordinary power, I do not well reach his meaning: for when he cometh to apply this distinction in his second conclusion, he granteth a virtual power, not formal, in the church of believers to ordain pastors, or to do some such act, as may supply the defect of ordination: as in a church in an island, where the pastors are all dead, or taken away otherways; and yet he maketh not this an official, or an authoritative power properly, but a virtual, and extraordinary power, not ordinary: like that which David had to eat the show—bread. And in like case of extreme necessity, he alloweth a private man, endued with gifts and zeal to teach publicly.* But I confess, I do not well understand, how a man in case of necessity hath any virtual power to do this or that act, but he hath also a formal power to do such an act in that case of necessity. Such an act I say, either the same in kind, or the same in analogy. When David did eat the show-bread, he had a lawful not only virtual, but formal power, as an Israelite in necessity (to whom moral duties were to be preferred before ceremonial) to eat for the sustentation of life. When a free people choose a king, and crown him, though they be not endued with a formal, but a virtual sovereign power, to give kingly authority which they have not; yet they have formally a power to yield themselves unto subjection to such a person as they have chosen; and that doth virtually and analogically set up him in the throne. For he that hath formal power to make one relative, he hath an analogical power, to set up his correlative. They that can make themselves subjects, can make another to be their sovereign.

But this I willingly admit which he saith, *that the ordination*

*of pastors by the church of believers, is not an official, nor
properly an authoritative act of power.* For the election of a
pastor by the brethren of the church, is an higher act of power
than their ordination is: as the election of a king is an act of
higher power, than his coronation. And yet the election of a
pastor, is not an act of official, or authoritative power: no more
than the election of a king by a free people is an act of official,
or authoritative sovereignty.

As for the public teaching of a private man endued with gifts
and zeal, I know not why it may not be allowed, not only in case
of extreme necessity, but in some cases of expediency, as when
his gifts are to be proved, before he be called into office.

In the third conclusion, Mr. Rutherford telleth us, *that as a
reasonable man is the first, immediate, and principal subject of
aptitude to laugh, and the mediate and secondary subjects are
Peter and John, and such particular men: so it is the order of
nature to give church properties, and powers, first to the species
and common nature of the church, and not to this or that particular church.*

But this conclusion of his crosseth nothing in that first
proposition of mine, nor any other tenent of ours. For that
proposition doth not make this or that particular church (which
is indeed a singular church) the first subject of church power:
but a particular visible church, which holdeth forth the *species*
or common nature of each particular, or singular church.

It is readily admitted what he saith, *that to be builded on a
rock, victory over hell, and such like, are given principally and
immediately to the catholic and invisible church, as to the first
and principal subject.*

But we cannot so easily admit that which he subjoineth, that
the keys are given to the catholic invisible church, as the first
and principal subject (though we grant they are given for their

end and use) But we rather believe they are given to the particular visible church, wherein the power of the keys is only exercised and used. The invisible catholic church doth never convene for the administration of church power: and it were in vain to give power to such a subject, which never is called to bring it forth into act.

In his arguments, Mr. Rutherford doth chiefly aim at this conclusion; to prove that the keys are not given to a church of professed believers, destitute of pastors and teachers, etc. A conclusion which he is pleased to frame unto himself, but had not occasion to collect it from any words in my proposition; which only affirmeth, that the keys were given to such a particular visible church, whereof Peter was one, and to whom Peter in case of offense might complain, even to the congregation. I might therefore omit this question wholly, but that he so handleth it, as if there were no church power at all, but only that which he calleth official, and authoritative power: and so he maketh all the acts of the brethren of the church (who are no officers) as no acts of power at all, and consequently, no part left to the people in the power of the keys: which putteth upon me a necessity of clearing some expressions in his arguments.

1. His first argument (page 9) is, *the church to which the keys were given, is builded upon a rock, is the house of wisdom, the house of God.*

But such is not a company of professing believers, united by church covenant, and destitute of pastors and teachers, etc.

Ans. This latter proposition is justly denied.

For Mr. Rutherford himself acknowledgeth a church in an island, where the pastors are taken away by death, or otherwise, page 8. And if such be a church, then truly it is built upon a rock, the rock of divine institution, and the rock of Christ believed on, and professed. Such a church is also an house of wisdom, and an house of God; or else the wisdom, and presence, and grace of God given to the church (yea to two or three of the church) dieth and perisheth with their church officers.

Object. The church of believers gathered without pastors and teachers, though united in a church covenant, yet not being builded by pastors and teachers (who are given to gather and to edify the body) they are only the materials of the house, but not the house.

Ans. 1. The church is truly said to be builded by pastors and teachers, upon the foundation of the prophets and apostles, when by their doctrine they were first brought on to believe, and by the same doctrine taught to assemble into church fellowship. It is true, the faith which they received by the edifying ministry of pastors and teachers, doth not make them members of the visible church, but of the invisible; and so fit materials only of the visible church. But yet they being also taught to make profession of their faith before the Lord, and his people, in covenanting or professing subjection to the Lord, and one to another in the use of his ordinances (so far as they are or shall be committed to them) they thereby receive the form of a visible church upon them. For as faith is the essential form of the catholic invisible church: so is the profession of faith, and the obedience of faith to Christ in his ordinances amongst themselves, the essential form of a particular visible church, amongst themselves I say. For profession of faith, and of the obedience of faith at large, without respect of subjection to ordinances in this or that church, maketh a man no more a member of the church at York, than of the church at Edinburgh. But when such a society of believers is combined together by profession of faith, and obedience of faith to the ordinances administered, or administrable amongst themselves; they are now not only the materials of a visible church, but have the true form of church estate, notwithstanding their want of pastors and teachers. Otherwise pastors themselves should be the form of the church, by which it is, and without which it cannot be a church. As if the body of a man could not be an human body, without eyes or arms: or had only the matter of a man, (or some part of the matter) but not the form.

What though such a society of believers be not a ministerial church, without pastors and teachers? yet it is not pastors and teachers, that giveth them the form of a church, no not of a ministerial or organical church, much less of an homogeneal. For ministers (pastors, or teachers) themselves are only materials (parts, and members) of a ministerial church, not the form of it. The form of such a church, is the mutual profession (or stipulation) or (that which amounteth thereto) the agreement and consent beween ministers and people to administer and submit unto, the holy ordinances of Christ amongst themselves, according to the rule of the Gospel. Say not, *a church of believers without ministers, wanteth the power of edifying the body of Christ, which is required in a visible church,* Ephes. iv, 11.

For every member of the church hath an edifying power, received from the head Christ Jesus, to the effectual working of the increase of the body, unto the edifying of itself in love, Ephes. iv, 16.

And though neither all, nor most of the brethren of a church have ordinarily received a gift of public prophecying, or preaching: yet in defect of public ministers, it is not an unheard of novelty; that God should enlarge private men with public gifts, and that they that have received such gifts, should take liberty to dispense them unto edification. For we read that when the church at Jerusalem were all of them scattered abroad, except the apostles; yet they that were scattered went everywhere preaching the word, Acts viii, and xi, 19, 20, 21.

Neither let it be said, *that such a church (or society) of believers is not wisdom's house, because it is not builded by pastors and teachers, who are given to edify, and gather the body.* For though in a material house of wood or stone, the builders do not only prepare the materials, but do also introduce the form: yet in a spiritual house (such as a church of believers is) the form is induced not by any formal act of the ministry of pastors and teachers (though they may be instrumental, in giving a word of direction) but by the voluntary stipulation or profession of subjection of this society of believers to the Lord Jesus in the use of his ordinances. The church as it is the house of God; so it is also the spouse of Christ: ministers are the friend of the bridegroom, and of the bride. The ministers have done their work in preparing the bride for the bridegroom; as also in ministering to her when she is married. But in betrothing her to Christ, the bride in that work, must herself profess her own acceptance of the Lord Jesus, and subjection to Him; which she may do effectually, whether ministers be present and assistant or no. It is true, ministers are ordinarily present and directive in this work, and in that respect are sometimes said to espouse them to Christ, 2 Cor. xi,2, but the formal bond of their spousage lieth not in the presence or assistance of ministers, but in their own professed yielding up of themselves unto the Lord in his covenant. As in the consummation of marriage between man and wife; the bond of the espousage lieth not in the presence, or assistance of ministers or magistrates, but in the husband's open profession of his acceptance of her, and in her open profession of her acceptance of him, and subjection to him in the duties of marriage.

His second argument is taken from the stewardship of them to whom the keys are committed.

To them (saith he) *are the keys promised, who are the stewards of the mysteries of God, 1 Cor.* iv, 1, *and servants of the house by office,* 2 Cor. iv,5, *and by office to open the doors, and behave themselves aright in God's house,* 1 Tim. iii,16, *and to divide to those of the house their portion of meat in due season, Matt.* xxiv,45, *and to cut out the word.* 2 Tim., ii, 15.

But a company of professing believers, joined together in church covenant, and destitute of officers, are not stewards by office, nor servants over the house, etc.

The assumption Mr. Rutherford taketh for granted, and so he well may; unless office be taken in a large sense (as it is in Cicero's *Offices*) for a duty, which we owe to every one in his place respectively; and as he saith (*ad Terent.*) *In familia bene instituta, dicimus omnes in officio esse oportere.*[75] In which sense also the translators take it in Rom. xii,5, where they speak of all the members of the body (whether natural body or ecclesiastical) as having all of them received an office, though not all of them the same office, Rom. xii,4. And in the same sense, the apostle Peter exhorteth all the saints of God to administer the good gifts they have received, as good stewards of the manifold grace of Christ, 1 Pet. iv, 10, 11. In this sense every member of the church may be said to have an office, and a stewardly office in the church.

But take office properly, for a calling invested with power to perform special acts of public service to the church; so indeed it implieth a contradiction, that the church should be its own officer. For the very term of officer implieth subordination; and Mr. Rutherford speaketh properly; that they are servants of the

[75] [In a well-established family we say that all ought to have an office.]

house by office, whom he putteth for the officers of the house. Now the church cannot be her own servant.

But yet this giveth the more just ground of denying the *major* proposition. That to them only are the keys promised, who are the stewards and servants of the house by office. The *mater familias* in the house, hath keys of power over her children, and servants, and yet is neither steward nor servant of the house.

It is true, the keys are a symbol of power. And power is either supreme, and sovereign, or subordinate, and subservient. Sovereign power in the church belongeth to the Lord Jesus, who is therefore said to have the key of David, to open and none to shut; to shut, and none to open, Rev. iii,7.

And yet in proper speech, Christ is no church officer, no officer in the church, (unless it be to God the Father) no more than the king can be said to be an officer in the commonwealth. Officers are of an inferior rank, Deut. xvi,18. But subordinate power is two-fold: 1. οἰκονομικὴ, *officiaria potestas,* stewardly ministerial office power. And secondly, *honoraria potestas, an* honorable power: such as a king going into a far country may leave to his queen; whom though he leave her subject to the laws and officers of his court and kingdom; yet he betrusteth her with this power, that in defect of officers, she shall have power to choose new, according to the law: and together with the officers, joint power, either to admit servants into her family, or upon just cause to remove any of them out of her family. And that Christ (the king, and husband of his church) being gone himself in bodily presence into a far country, hath left this honorable power to his church, as to choose their own officers, to join in admission of members, and censure to offenders; I presume Mr. Rutherford will not gainsay. To give a touch of each; plain it is, that when deacons were to be chosen into office, the apostles referred the choice of them to the multitude of brethren, and they performed it, Acts vi, 1,2,3,5. When Saul essayed to join himself to the church at Jerusalem, he was not received till the brethren's fear of his carnal estate was removed, and themselves satisfied, that he was a disciple, Acts ix,26. Let no man except, Paul did not essay to join himself as a member to the church at Jerusalem: for he was (being an apostle) an officer, (and therefore a member) in all churches: for his call to the apostleship was at first unknown to them: and the argument holdeth so much the stronger, that if the brethren must be satisfied in the discipleship of an apostle, before he can be admitted to join with them; much more may they require probable ground of the discipleship of a brother, before he be admitted to join with them in church communion. And when the incestuous Corinthian was to be cast out of the family of the church; Paul referreth the administration of that power to the joint proceeding of the elders and brethren of that church, leaving to either sort their concourse of several power respectively.

Now then to apply this distinction of power to the argument. All the places alleged by Mr. Rutherford, do indeed prove *that the keys were promised and given to the stewards and officers, and servants in the house of God:* which we willingly acknowledge. We acknowledge also that which he affirmeth, *that a company of professing believers joined together in church covenant, and destitute of officers, are not stewards by office, nor servants in the house of God.* But this we deny, that all the keys, all kind of power in the church, is promised and given to the officers of the church, solely and solidly. All office power indeed, is given to the officers; nor do we permit the church of brethren to usurp any part of office power unto themselves. But we see the Scripture acknowledgeth other power in the church, besides office power.

I shall not need to enlarge further answer to this second argument. The testimonies which he allegeth to prove his proposition; they prove that the keys signify power, and authority, and that stewardly, or office power, is given to the officers of the church. But none of them prove, that all power is office power, or that the keys hold forth no other power but office power: or that the church of believers hath received no power at all. The text in Isa. xxii,23 speaketh not of a spiritual or ecclesiastical power, but of a civil power. The text in Isa. ix,6 and Rev. iii,7 speaks not of a ministerial, or office power, but of a sovereign power in Christ Jesus.

What Schindler speaketh of מפתח as it crosseth not us; so it concerneth not the keys spoken of in Matt. xvi where the word in the Syriac is not, מפתה but קלורה a word (as it seemeth) taken up from the Greek.

What those many other authors say of the keys in the places alleged by him, do not at all weaken our defense: which maketh me (I confess) the more to wonder, that he should conclude that troop of witnesses with this period: *that he thinks while of late, never any interpreter dreamed, that in this text, Matt. xvi, that the keys of the kingdom of heaven are given to all believers, but only to the stewards of the house.*

Mr. Rutherford knoweth well, that Bucer exponding Matt. xvi saith expressly *De potestate clavium, Hæc potestas penes ecclesiam omnem est; authoritas modo ministerii penes presbyteros et episcopos, ut Romæ olim potestas populi fuit, authoritas senatus,* Ferius: (not later than Bucer) upon Matt. xvi affirmeth; *Claves datas ecclesiæ, ut dominæ et sponsæ: Petro, ut ministro.*[76] Reverend Baynes, though in the first subject of the power of the

[76] [This power belongs to every church; only the authority of ministry belongs to the elders and the bishops, as the power of Rome once belonged to the people; the authority to the senate . . . The keys were given to the church as to a bride and mistress; to Peter as to a minister.]

keys he do somewhat dissent from us: yet he confesseth in that third conclusion of his, upon question 3 page 83, of his *Diocesans Trial: that he setteth down that conclusion against the divines of conscience against our prime divines, as Luther and Melanchthon, and against the Sorbonists.* But though all these might be said to be of late, surely Augustine is not of late, whom I think best to quote, as his testimonies are at large alleged by Doctor Whitaker against Bellarmine; the rather, that so we may take in the judicious doctor's notes upon them. *Augustine, tratat,* 50 *in Johannem, Si in Petro, inquit, non esset, ecclesiæ sacramentum, non ei diceret Dominus, tibi dabo claves regni cælorum. Si hoc Petro tantum dictum est, non facit hoc ecclesia: si autem hoc in ecclesia fit; Petrus quando claves accepit, ecclesiam sanctam significavit.*

Again, *De Agon. Christ., c.* 30, he saith, *Petrum inter omnes apostolas, ecclesiæ personam sustinuisse: et claves datas esse ecclesiæ, cum Petro datæ sunt.*[77]

On which, and some such like passages in Augustine, Doctor Whitaker giveth this exposition: this is not saith he, *that the church should receive the keys* suo quodam modo, *after a certain sort, but that in Peter they did receive them properly, truly, and more principally, than Peter himself.*

Let no man except, that by the church be understood not the brethren of the church, but only the apostles, and their successors the presbyters.

For though it be true, that office power was given to them only, yet it is clear; he acknowledgeth (as others do) a power

---

[77] [If the sacrament of the church were not in Peter's care, he says, the Lord would not have said, "To you I shall give the keys to the heavenly kingdom." If this was said to Peter only [as an individual] this does not make a church. If, however, this happens in [the framework of] a church, when Peter takes the keys that signified that the church was holy. . . . Peter among all the apostles has taken upon himself the person of the church and the keys were given to the church when they were given to Peter.]

likewise of the people in the government of the church. In stating church government, he giveth it thus for a conclusion. *Si velimus Christum ipsum respicere, fuit semper ecclesiæ regimen monarchicum: si ecclesiæ presbyteros, qui in doctrina et disciplina suas partes agebant, aristocraticum: si totum corpus ecclesiæ, quatenus in electione episcoporum et presbyterorum, suffragia serebat, democraticum. Sic partim aristocraticum, partim democraticum, partim etiam monarchicum, est, semperque fuit ecclesiæ regimen,*[78] *Whitakers, Controv. 4, Q. 1, c. 1, num. 2.*

Nor let any put off Whitaker or Augustine, with this evasion, that Peter is said to have received the keys in the person of the church, not because the church is any subject of that power, but because it is the end of that power: all the power of the keys being given to Peter, not for himself, but for the good, and utility of the church.

Such an evasion Chamier rejecteth with indignation, *Hoccine vero (inquit) est candide agere? hoccine Augustinum interpretari? Atqui Augustinus non quærit, quem in finem datæ sint claves, sed quærit cui. Hæ vero quæstiones quanto separentur intervallo, quis non videt? Sed et exemplo facile docetur. Unicuique datur declaratio Spiritus ad utilitatem, inquit Paulus,* 1 Cor. xii, *id est, in bonum ecclesiæ, ut totus sermo ostendit. An dicat aliquis, eum cui datur declaratio Spiritus, figuram gestare ecclesiæ, quum eam accipit? minime vero: est enim non publicum sed privatum donum: publicum quidem ipsa utilitate, sed privatum donatione, possessioneque. Cum igitur quærit Au-*

---

[78] [If we wish to consider Christ himself, there has always been a monarchic kind of government; if we wish to consider the elders of the church, who take part in forming the doctrine and the discipline, there has always been an aristocracy; if we consider the whole body of the church, since it has a voice in the election of bishops and elders, there has always been a democracy. So, partly aristocratic, partly democratic, and even partly monarchic it is and always has been, the church's government.]

gustinus, cui sint datæ claves, Petro soli, an toti ecclesiæ, importune inculcatur, datas esse in bonum ecclesiæ quia nihil obstaret, quo minus et datæ essent in incommune. Bonum ecclesiæ, et tamen soli Petro. At Augustinus hæc opponit, datæ sunt soli Petro, et datæ sunt ecclesiæ, ut si soli Petro, non ecclesiæ: et si ecclesiæ, non soli Petro. Si Petro inquit hoc tantum dictum est, non facit hoc ecclesia.[79]

I forbear (for brevity sake) to recite what he further disputeth against Horantius to the same purpose in the words following, *De Oecumen. Pontifice. l.* 11, *cap.* 10.

3. I come to consider of Mr. Rutherford's third argument, which he propoundeth thus:

To those, in Matt. xvi, *doth Christ give the keys, to whom He giveth warrant for the actual exercise of the keys? But this warrant is official authority of binding and loosing, Christ giveth to Peter only, as representing apostles, teachers, and elders: and not to a church of believers converted covenant wise, and destitute of officers, ergo etc.*

Ans. The proposition is not always universally safe, if it be understood of the actual exercise of the keys, (by them who

---

[79] [But is this (says he) to act honestly? Is this to interpret Augustine? For Augustine does not ask to what ends the keys were given; rather, he asks to whom they were given. But who does not see how different these questions are from one another? It will also be easily shown by an example. The revelation of the Spirit is given to each and everyone for the advantage, Paul says, I Cor. xii, that is, for the good of the church, as the whole message sets forth. Or would some one say that he to whom the Spirit is revealed, when he has received it, symbolizes the church? Not at all: for the gift is not public but private; public, to be sure, as regards its general advantage, but private as regards the gifts and the possession. Therefore when Augustine asks to whom are the keys given, to Peter alone or to the whole church, the necessary conclusion is that the gifts are for the good of the church, because nothing prevents the gifts from having been given for the common good of the church, and yet to Peter alone as an individual. But Augustine objects against saying that they were given to Peter alone and to the church, inasmuch as if to Peter alone, then not to the church, and if to the church, then not to Peter alone. If this is said, to Peter alone, then it does not make a church.]

receive them) in their own person. For Christ himself, who received from the Father the power of all church administrations: yet in the days of his flesh, He in his own person baptized no man, John iv,2. And after his ascension, though the sovereign power of the keys do still remain with Him, yet he performeth all the external exercise of church power by his ministers.

If it be said, that though Christ did not exercise all church power in his own person, yet He had warrant so to do: it may justly be replied, Christ best understood his own warrant, and He that did not exercise this or that act of the church power in his own person, surely He did not think it expedient to exercise it in his own person. And *quicquid non expedit, quatenus non expedit, non licet:* that which is not expedient, so far forth as it is not expedient, is not warrantable.

Besides it is a disputable case amongst civil, and canon lawyers, and by Covarruvias judged for the affirmative, that in some cases, the wife after her husband's death hath a just interest in some such offices as he cannot warrantably exercise in his own person.

And he instanceth in *Officio Decurionatus, Covarr. Tom.* 2, *lib.* 3, *cap.* 19, *Num.* 4.

Queen Elizabeth whilst she lived, had lawful power to punish her enemies by slaughter in war; her criminal subjects by hanging; other offenders by scourging: but it were an hard saying to affirm, that she had warrant to exercise all these acts of power in her own person.

Ans. 2. I willingly grant that Peter, in Matt. xvi, *received the promise of all office power, as representing the officers of the church, apostles, teachers, and elders: and with that power, a warrant of all official exercise of that power.*

But this I say withal, that Peter in receiving the keys (or the promise of them) he received from Christ both sorts of subordinate church power, not only *officiariam,* but *honorariam po-testatem.* And in receiving this latter, he represented the person of all professing believers. For it were not reasonable to think, that Peter receiving the keys as a reward of the profession of his faith, should receive no power at all to professing believers as such, but all power only to professing officers.

Object.   But if professing believers, as such, had received any part of the power of the keys, they had then received the power of binding and loosing, which they have not: for binding and loosing are the acts of the official power of the keys: ergo, the church of believers being destitute of officers, and governors hath not received any part of the power of the keys.

Ans.   The proof of this argument will not hold, unless binding and loosing were the *adequate* acts of the official power of the keys. But though binding and loosing, or (which is all one) opening and shutting, be indeed the *adequate* acts of the power of the keys; yet not so of their official power. The Lord Jesus hath the key of David, He bindeth and none looseth, He looseth and none bindeth, Rev. iii,7, and yet this, his binding and loosing are not the acts of the official, but of the sovereign power of the keys. The brethren of the church at Jerusalem, who were scattered upon the persecution that arose about Stephen: they preached the word of Christ to Jews and Grecians about Antioch, and by the good hand of the Lord upon them, a great number believed, and turned to the Lord, Acts xi, 19, 20, 21. These brethren in opening the door of faith to their hearers, though they wanted office, yet they wanted not the power of the keys, to open the kingdom of heaven unto them.

The brethren of the church of Corinth concurred with their officers, in delivering the incestuous person to Satan, and afterwards in the public pardon of him, and release of his censure. In both which they put forth the spiritual power of the Lord

Jesus, which is, *the power of the keys,* 1 Cor. v, 4, 5 with 2 Cor.
ii, 7 to 11. And yet they neither had the official power of the
keys, nor did they exercise it. It was also an act of church power,
which the church of brethren at Jerusalem did put forth in joining in the definitive sentence of the synod, and in sending forth
letters and messengers to the churches of Antioch, Syria, and
Cilicia, for the publishing and promulgating of the sentence.
And yet the brethren themselves neither had office power in
themselves, nor did they exercise it.

*Object. But those brethren in Corinth, and Jerusalem,
though they had not office power in themselves, yet they had it
amongst themselves in the apostles, and in the elders then
assembled: and so with them they might join in some act of
church power, which without them, they might not have been
put forth at all: or if they had, it had been of no power.*

Ans. This were indeed to make the church power in brethren
a mere cipher, yea less than a cipher. For a cipher though it be
of no number or account, unless some figure of the decad be
joined before it; yet if it be joined before it, the cipher will increase the number and account, and make it at least tenfold more
than it was before. But all the brethren of the church without
officers, are not only made as so many ciphers, as those who of
themselves can do no act of number or account at all: but also
though an officer, or a whole presbytery join with them, and go
before them, yet the act of the whole church of brethren, maketh
the act of no more account, no more value or validity, than it was
before; which seemeth to me an unworthy thing and unreason-
able. For seeing that the profession of the faith in Christ was
the original ground, (or at least the occasion) of the grant of
all church power unto Peter in the name of the church, how can
it stand either with faith or reason, that a church of believers
professing the same faith with Peter, shall receive no part of

church power at all, in respect of their profession of the faith, but only in respect of their officers that preach the faith? whereas Peter then spake not as a preacher only, but as a professor of the faith. Faith when it seeth a promise made to another in respect of this or that qualification or duty, it is apt (by the help of the spirit of grace) to apply the same blessing, or some part of it at least, unto itself in the same cause.

Again, if it were so, that a church of believers destitute of officers, should have received from Christ no part of the power of the keys, then in case the whole presbytery of a church should be removed by death, or crime, or otherwise, the church should cease to be a church. For the power of the keys comprehendeth the latitude of all church power. And *ut seres habet in esse, sic in operari.*[80] Take away all power of action, and operation from a church, and you take away the church itself. And so you will make ministers to be not only the integral parts of a church, but the essential parts also. Yea by this means, the estate of the church is in worse condition, than is the estate of any civil commonwealth. For take away all the magistrates, and governors of the commonwealth, yet still the commonwealth subsisteth in itself; it ceaseth not to be a commonwealth, nor is it left destitute of all actions of a commonwealth. The body of the people may solemnly assemble together, and choose out of themselves new magistrates: or if they want good choice among themselves, they may supply themselves from their confederates. But the church of Christ (which of all societies is the most honorable, and most completely supplied with power to attain its own end, and is built upon the most sure foundation) if it be once deprived of her officers and rulers, it straightway becometh null, both in essence and action. Time was, when David speaking to the church said, *Glorious things are spoken of thee, thou city*

[80] [As is the essence of a Chinese, so is his actions.]

of God, Psal. lxxxvii,3. And one of those glorious things were, *that her foundations are in the holy mountains,* ver. 1. *And the Lord loveth the gates of Zion, more than all the dwellings of Jacob,* ver. 2. But surely, if the church's being, did so easily vanish with the loss of their officers, this would turn their glory into shame, above all other societies.

4. Proceed we now to the fourth and last argument, whereby Mr. Rutherford goeth about to prove, that the church of believers destitute of an eldership, hath no power of the keys.

If the power of the keys lay in competition between a church of believers destitute of its own eldership, and a church of believers furnished with it (as the question might seem to import) I should easily grant more ample power to a church with its eldership, than to a church without it; or if the competition of the power of the keys lay, whether in the church without the eldership, or in the eldership without the church (especially when the greater part of the eldership consisteth of the elders of other churches), though we give not much power to a church without an eldership: yet we should give less to an eldership without the church.

But the true state of the question is, whether a Congregational church of believers furnished with officers, and walking in the truth and peace of the Gospel, have not received the power of the keys (the power of binding and loosing) within themselves? or, whether this power be first given to a classical, or provincial, or national assembly of the church officers, or presbyters: and from them derived to a Congregational church of believers with their officers?

But it may be also a second question touching a Congregational church of believers, whether no power of the keys (that is, no part of the power of the keys) be given to them without an eldership.

This hath Mr. Rutherford put for the question, and maketh it the title of every leaf of chap. 1, sect. 2. *The church of believers destitute of an eldership have no power of the keys.*

Three of his arguments in this question we have already perused: cometh we now to his fourth.

His fourth argument then is this: if Christ do not say in this place, Matt. xvi nor in Matt. xviii, *that the keys and the acts of the keys (to wit, binding and loosing) are given to a church of believers without their officers, then neither of the places prove, that the keys are given to such a church.*

But Christ doth not say it: ergo, the text cannot bear it.

Ans. 1.   If this text, in Matt. xvi, do prove that the keys are given to a church of believers with their officers, it is as much as I infer from it.

Ans. 2.   Yet two things there be in the words of the text, which do infer, that some part of the power of the keys is given to a church of believers without their officers.

The first may be collected thus; if the keys be the power of edifying the church, and the church be edified of believers by the public profession of their faith, then believers publicly professing the faith, have some part of the power of the keys given to them.

But they keys are the power of edifying the church, and the church is edified of believers, by the public profession of their faith.

Therefore believers publicly professing the faith, have some part of the power of the keys given to them.

What may here justly be denied, I see not. The major proposition is evident of itself. For no man can do any act of spiritual efficacy, but he hath received from Christ some spiritual power to do it.

And *habenti dabitur*,[81] to him that edifieth the church by any power received, to him shall the more abundant power be given to do the same.

The minor proposition is as clear: for the keys are nothing else, but the instruments of edifying the church. Though their immediate and proper work be to open and shut (and metaphorically, to bind and loose) yet both these are nothing else but acts of edifying the church. And that the church is edified or builded of believers, publicly professing their faith: the Lord himself doth acknowledge in the words of the text, when he saith, *Upon this rock,* (that is, upon this public profession of faith in me) *I will build my church.* Peter by this public profession of his faith, did edify himself, and his fellow disciples: and thereby obtained both a reward of his profession, to become the foundation of the church: and a reward to himself, of receiving the keys; that is, a power both by gift, and office to edify the church in a more settled manner, and abundant measure, not only as a believer, but as a chief elder, and apostle.

The second thing in the text, that may infer some part of the power of the keys to be given to a church of believers even without officers, may thus be taken up.

If Peter had the keys given to him as a reward, not for doing an act or duty of his office, but for doing an act or duty common to him with other believers; then believers making the same public confession of faith with him: as they do partake with him in the duty, so do they partake also (in some measure) in the reward.

But Peter had the keys given him as a reward, not for doing any act or duty of his office, but for doing an act or duty common to him with other ordinary believers.

81 [To him who has it shall be given.]

Therefore other ordinary believers making the same public confession of faith with him, they do partake with him in the duty; so do they also partake in some measure in the promised reward of the power of the keys.

The former proposition is not only the collection of many divines both ancient and modern, but it dependeth upon a principal ground of the work of our ministry. For our ministry taketh it for a sure ground of the application of Scriptures; that what promise we find given to any upon occasion of this or that qualification or condition, the same is intended by God, and easily applied by us to all others, in whom the like condition or qualification is found according to their measure.

The latter proposition is so clear, as needs no proof, unless we shall make the public confession of faith in Christ, not to be the duty of ordinary believers, and church members, but only of church officers: or unless we could find some other occasion, upon which Christ made this gracious promise of the keys to Peter, beside the public confession of his faith in Christ before the Lord and his brethren.

Object. 1. *When Christ gave the promise of the keys, he speaketh not to the church, but turneth his speech to Peter, ver. 19, saying, I will give to thee (Peter, not to the church) the keys of the kingdom of heaven. Surely none needeth to teach our Lord to speak: this change of the persons to whom the keys are promised, wanteth not a reason, etc.*

Ans. As we need not, so we do not go about, to teach the Lord to speak. Here is no changing of persons, nor turning of speech, in giving the promise of the keys. Christ began his speech to Peter, and He continueth his speech to Peter, from ver. 17 to 19. All upon occasion of Peter's confession. In ver. 17. Christ giveth to Peter a promise of blessedness from the cause of his confession. In ver. 18 He giveth a promise of reward to his confession; that upon it, as upon a rocky foundation, He will build his church in impregnable stability. In ver. 19 He giveth a promise of reward unto himself upon occasion of his gracious public confession, even a promise of the keys of the church. And the promise is more fitly given to Peter in the name of the church, than to the church by name; because it was not the church by name that made that confession, but Peter in the name of the church.

Object. 2. *If the promise were given to Peter in the name of believers, how will that stand with the judgment of the way, who will not allow every company of believers, because they are believers to be an instituted visible church; (to whom the keys are given) but they must be a company of believers professing covenantwise, faith in Christ and church communion. But then the keys are not given to believers because they are believers, and the spouse of Christ, but because they are such professors and so combined in church covenant.*

Ans. The author of the *Way* doth no where say, that the keys are given to a company of believers, only because they are believers; but because they are believers making public confession of their faith before the Lord, and their brethren. For Peter himself received not the keys merely as a believer, but as a believer publicly professing his faith before Christ, and his fellow disciples in Christ's school. If other writers speak otherwise, (that the keys were given to Peter a believer in the name of believers) they must be understood to speak of believers, not as keeping their faith to themselves, but as making profession of their faith publicly; so as they come to be received into the society of the visible church. Faith giveth a man fellowship in the invisible church, and in all the inward spiritual blessings of the church. But it is profession of faith, that giveth a man fellowship in the visible church. It is not a society of believers, as such, that maketh them a church: for a society of Christian merchants may meet together in a ship to transport themselves to Hamburrough, or Lubeck but they are not thereby a church, nor have received church power. But if they do publicly profess their faith, and their obedience of faith to the Lord Jesus in the public ordinances of his worship, which He hath committed to his church, and they are capable of; then indeed they are a professed visible church of Christ, and a body united to Him, and one to another by such profession, and do also partake in the power of the keys according to their measure.

Object. 3. I ask whether true or false profession be the nearest intervening cause of these, to whom the keys are given?

Ans. True or false profession may be attended, either in respect of the doctrine of faith in Christ professed, or in respect of the grace of faith professing it. If the profession of the doctrine of faith be true, though the grace of faith in the professor of it be uncertain, and it may be hypocritical (and so false) yet we dare not deny the nature and power of a church to such. As the church judgeth not of hidden crimes, so neither do the faithful judge of the churches by their hidden hypocrisy, but by their open scandals in doctrine, or life. God would have his people live without anxious perplexity, (as in point of marriage, 1 Cor. vii,32 so) in every society. It were an inextricable perplexity, to suspend the essence or validity of churches or church administrations, upon the hidden sincerity of churches, and of church officers, or members. It is true, that church estate and church privileges, and church power are given to believers, making public profession of their holy faith: to them are the keys given, and for them. And yet for their sakes God doth vouchsafe both the name, and style, and power of a church to such as make the like profession of the faith with them, though not with the like sincerity. The church of Sardis had a name to

live, yet was dead, Rev. iii, 2. Nevertheless, the Lord reckoneth
it amongst the golden candlesticks, and walketh amongst them,
Rev. ii,1. It appeareth there were a few names amongst them,
that were sincere, Rev. iii,4. And Dr. Ames maketh it most
probable, *that there is no particular church, wherein the profession of the true faith doth take place, but that in the same are
found some true believers, Medull. Theolog. l. 1, c. 32, num. 10.*

*Object. 1.   If a false profession be sufficient to make persons
a true visible church; then 1. the keys are not given to believers,
because they are believers, and united to Christ as his body and
spouse.*

Ans.   The keys are given to believers, because they are believers, making public confession of their faith. To hypocrites
they are given, not for their hypocrisy, but for the truth of that
faith which they do profess in common with sincere believers:
and for the sake of those true believers who do communicate
with them, and for the whose sake the whole body is united to
Christ, and his spouse, though adulterous in heart.

*Object. 2.   Then the author of the Way saith amiss, that
the church instituted by Christ, is a company of believers, faithful and godly men; for a company of hypocrites are not such.*

Ans.   The author of the Way speaketh of the church as it
ought to be, and as it is in outward visible profession. Hypocrites in outward profession and appearance, go for faithful
and godly, and such in truth they ought to be, as well as in
appearance.

*Object. 3.   Our brethren prove the keys to be a part of the
liberty of redeemed ones; but counterfeit professors are not
redeemed ones: nor have they that liberty purchased to them in
Christ.*

Ans.   It is true, the keys are a part of the liberty of redeemed
ones. For the keys hold forth an ecclesiastical power, and all

power in heaven and earth was given to Christ upon his resurrection from the dead, Matt. xxviii,18. And though counterfeit
professors be not the redeemed ones of Christ (properly so
called:) yet for the sake of the redeemed ones, counterfeit professors have that liberty purchased to them by Christ, as to partake in the power of the keys. Otherwise what can be said of
hypocritical elders, of whom Mr. Rutherford doubteth not, they
have received the power of the keys: and yet though their persons be not the redeemed ones of Christ, yet they have this
liberty, or service rather purchased to them by Christ, as to be
serviceable to the church in the administration of the power of
the keys. The spiritual gifts (though common) whereby
apostates are said to be sanctified, were purchased to them by
the blood of Christ, Heb. x,29. And yet the power whereby
hypocrites or apostates lord it over the redeemed ones of God,
is but a service, Rom. ix,12.

*Object. 4. It shall follow, that our brethren widely mistake
a supposed difference, which they devise betwixt the Jewish and
Christian churches; to wit, that to make men members of the
Jewish church, external holiness was sufficient, as to be born
Jews, to be circumcised, etc. but that the visible church of the
Gentiles after Christ, must be the bride of Christ, and by true
faith united to Him. Whereas the members of a visible Christian
church, are and may be hypocrites, though not known to be such,
as were the members of the Jewish church.*

Ans. Who it is that Mr. Rutherford meaneth, to have put
this difference between the members of the Jewish and Christian
church, I do not know: but thus far I own it, 1. that the church
of the Jews was national in their solemn assemblies, as well as
Congregational in their synagogues: and that accordingly they
had national congregations in Jerusalem; national sacrifices,
and national high priests, besides national government: but the

visible instituted churches of Christ in the New Testament, are Congregational, 1 Cor. xiv,23. 2. That we do not read of the children of Israel, who were circumcised in their infancy, to have been afterwards debarred from the Passover upon point of moral profaneness: they having many sacrifices to expiate אשמות ceremonially, which Christian churches have not, but only penitential acknowledgement after censure. In that respect, I suppose (under correction) there was more toleration of sundry moral crimes in the church fellowship of the Jews, than ought to be born in Christian churches. But otherwise I easily acknowledge, that in Christian churches, as well as in Jewish, many hypocrites creep in, and are long tolerated therein (it may be all their days) and yet without impeachment of the truth and essence of the estate of churches whereof they are members, and without infringement of the power of their church administrations (when dispensed otherwise according to rule) notwithstanding the hypocrisy of sundry members, yea, and of officers also.

To this place it belongeth (I mean to the clearing of this text, Matt. xvi) to consider of the reasons whereby Mr. Rutherford goeth about to prove, *that Christ spake to Peter, as to one representing the apostles, and not as one representing all believers.*

I suppose he understandeth apostles in a large sense, for all messengers sent of Christ for the ministry of the Gospel in the church. Otherwise, if he should mean, Christ spake to Peter, as to one representing the apostles properly so called (the twelve apostles) then the elders of churches could claim no interest in the power of the keys from Christ's words to Peter.

Nor do I maintain from this place, that Christ spake to Peter as representing all believers; but as representing believers making public profession of the name of Christ before the Lord and their brethren. Against this his arguments be.

Arg. 1. *Binding and loosing are denied of our brethren to belong to many that make Peter's confession.* [Thou art the Son of the living God] *as to believing women and children.*

Ans. 1. Women and children, though they being believers, may make Peter's confession, yet they make not public confession before the Lord and his people, as Peter did. Now it is to believers making public confession of their faith in Christ, to whom the promise of the keys is made.

Ans. 2. Women are expressly forbidden public speech in the church (and therefore public profession), 1 Cor. xiv,34. And children are not able to make public profession; and therefore both of them are justly exempted from the power of the keys.

If it be objected, that it is a new and uncouth exposition of the text, to interpret Peter's confession, of the confession which members make of their faith, when they enter into the fellowship of the church: nor were Christ and his apostles at that time in hand with any such work.

I answer, though Peter's confession of his faith at that time was not made for such an end, for his admission into the household or church of Christ: yet it is enough, that Christ rewardeth that confession of his, with such a promise of all believers into his church by such a door. It is true, the same confession may be made upon other occasions; but yet this appeareth to be one occasion and use of this confession, to receive professed believers into the fellowship of the church, and the ordinances thereof; seeing we read that Philip made it a necessary predential act unto the Eunuch to make the like confession before he would receive him unto baptism, which was the seal of his admission, as into Christ, so into the fellowship of his church. And accordingly it hath been anciently observed in the primitive churches, not to receive *competentes,* or *catechumeni* into the fellowship of the church, and unto baptism, before they had made public confession of their faith before the Lord and his church: which is a thing I doubt not, well known to Mr. Rutherford, to no man more; that I might seem to do him wrong to allege testimonies for it.

Arg. 2. *If Christ had spoke to Peter here of building a ministerial church upon his confession, and gifting it with the power of the keys, then the visible church should be made as stable and firm from defection, as the church of elect believers, against whom the gates of hell cannot prevail. Now this is most untrue, since visible churches do fall away (as the seven churches in Asia, the church of Corinth, Ephesus, etc.) and likewise this would warrant the papists to make use of this place, as they do, to prove the invincible stability of the church and their impossibility of apostacy, etc.*

Ans. 1.   Though this or that visible church do fall away, yet Christ hath ever had some or other visible church upon the face of the earth, in one country or other. Else the gates of hell had more prevailed against the visible Christian church, than ever this could do against the visible Jewish synagogue.

Ans. 2.   This or that visible church that did fall away, was not a society of such professed believers as were built upon a rock; but rather the sinful generation that rose up after them, who did degenerate from their parents' faith and profession, and so fell into the gulf of apostacy, whether Turkish or antichristian.

Ans. 3.   Though the gates of hell have sometimes prevailed against this or that particular visible church, holding fast the profession of their faith without wavering: yet they have not prevailed to their destruction, but to their dispersion only; which tendeth to the multiplication and enlargement of particular churches. The persecution raised by the gates of hell against the primitive church at Jerusalem about Stephen, it prevailed indeed to the dispersion of the whole church (save the apostles), Acts viii, 1, but that dispersion was as seed scattered out of the garner into the field, which bringeth forth a more plentiful harvest. And so did their dispersion propagate churches both in Samaria and Antioch.

Ans. 4.   Nor will this stability of visible churches promised by Christ, strengthen the popish plea of the stability of their church at Rome. For it is neither that promise of Christ, Matt. xvi, nor any other that doth promise stability to any one particular church in this city or town: nor any exposition of ours, reach forth such a thing. The woman may be in the wilderness, and fed by witnesses, (the church may be in obscure places, and fed by faithful witnesses) when yet neither herself, nor her witnesses dwell in Babylon.

Glossary of Names

All names mentioned by John Cotton are here identified except for those so widely known that desk dictionaries list them (e.g. Queen Elizabeth, John Calvin) or those few about whom little can be added to what Cotton himself says (e.g. Mr. James, the minister who went to Virginia).

AINSWORTH, Henry (1571-1623). A Puritan minister who attached himself to the Separatists shortly after he left Cambridge, went into exile with them in 1593, and, in 1596, together with Francis Johnson founded an independent church in Amsterdam. The course of the church was plagued with difficulties, Teacher Ainsworth generally being more conciliatory than Pastor Johnson, and finally, in 1610, Ainsworth's group withdrew in support of their belief that excommunication was to be approved by the whole congregation rather than just by the elders. Ainsworth produced a considerable body of controversial and exegetical literature. Cotton refers specifically to his *Annotations upon The Five Books of Moses* (1619, 1621, 1626, 1627, 1639).

ALLEN, John (1596-1671). Minister at Dedham from 1639, he collaborated with Thomas Shepard in *A Defence of the Answer* (1648), a response to Presbyterian attacks on John Davenport's answer to questions sent to New England. Allen also published other religious and polemical works.

AMES, William (1576-1633). Outstanding Puritan theologian who went beyond his Cambridge tutor, William Perkins, in the extremity of his reforming beliefs. He refused to wear the surplice, and the severity of his attack on card playing gained him a suspension from his duties as minister at Cambridge and the enmity of loyal bishops who drove him to Holland by blocking all English appointments. There he debated church polity with the Anglicans at Leyden and theology with the Arminians at Rotterdam and at the Synod of Dort (1618-19). As a result of the victory of

Calvinism at Dort, Ames became a hero of the English Puritans who were, nevertheless, unable to persuade the authorities to allow him to return home. He became successively professor of theology at Franeker, rector of that university, and, in the year of his death, President of an English college which was to be built at Rotterdam. He attracted Protestant students from all over Europe and the American Puritans were consistently hopeful that they could persuade Ames to migrate to their settlement. The two works of Ames most read and admired by the Americans were *Medulla theologicae* (1630) and *De conscientia, Ejus Jure et Causibus* (1632).

APOLLONII, or APOLLONIUS, Guillaume (d. 1655). A Protestant theologian, native of Zeeland, who is best known for his writing on the power of the sovereign in ecclesiastical affairs.

APOLLONIUS of Tyana (ca. 98). A philosopher and religious reformer whose life became so legendary that it was frequently represented as a living model of the Gospels. Anti-Christians found the exaggerated tales about him a convenient target for attack and in response to one such attack Eusebius of Caesarea gave the legend of Apollonius the value which Cotton and others of his time accepted.

ARISTIDES of Athens (2nd cent.). Known to Cotton and his contemporaries through relatively brief references made by St. Jerome and Eusebius. According to the latter, Aristides delivered a defense of Christianity to the Emperor Hadrian, maintaining that Christians had a fuller understanding of God's nature than did barbarians, Greeks, or Jews, and that only they followed his precepts.

ARMINIUS, Jacobus (1560-1609). Eminent Dutch theologian who studied at Geneva under Beza as well as at Utrecht, Marburg, Padua, and Rome, and who after entering upon his ministry at Amsterdam in 1588 began to make known his doubts about the doctrine of predestination as expounded by Calvin. The attacks upon his views (chief of which was made by William Perkins) led him to state them with greater precision. His influence increased after he became a professor at Leyden in 1603. His efforts on behalf of the views that divine sovereignty is compatible with free will in men, and that Christ died for all men not just the elect, caused both opponents and supporters to term such views Arminian although there is doubt as to how much of a specific influence he exerted on the many Protestants who, in the seventeenth century, fell away from strict predestinarian beliefs.

ATHENAEUS (2nd-3rd cent.). A Greek scholar of Egypt, he wrote on a variety of topics, and because of his habit of wide quoting preserved fragments of hundreds of otherwise unknown writings. He was known to the seventeenth century because of the monumental scholarship of Casaubon.

ATHENAGORAS (2nd cent.). He is described in his earliest manuscripts as "the Christian Philosopher." In his "Apology" (ca. 177), addressed to Marcus Aurelius and Commodus, he answered calumnies against the Christians, and in a later work defended the doctrine of the resurrection of the dead. He was the first to construct a philosophical defense of the doctrine of God as Three in One.

BALL, John (1585-1640). A Presbyterian minister, graduate of Oxford, who was a tutor in Cheshire in 1610 when he was converted to Puritan principles. His zeal gained him a series of posts in the control of the Puritans and likewise a series of terminations by the authorities; he was imprisoned several times. He was a noted scholar and engaged Separatists and Congregationalists in published debates. Cotton refers to him because of his *Trial of the New Church-way in New England and Old* (1644).

BARBON, Praise-god (1596?-1679). A leather seller and member of the independent church founded by Henry Jacob, he was elected minister of a Baptist congregation in London and wrote a justification of infant baptism. While carrying on his leather trade, he became widely known as a preacher and served as a member for the City of London at the short parliament of 1653, an assembly that because of the oddity of his name far more than the awesomeness of his contribution is now known as the Barebones Parliament. Barbon himself withdrew from politics after this brief excursion and lived to a ripe age although he was, after the Restoration, imprisoned for a time.

BARROW, Henry (d. 1593). An eminent Separatist who gave up the study of the law in favor of theology and in this connection came to know John Greenwood who introduced him to the Separatist doctrines of Robert Browne. When Greenwood was arrested in 1586 Barrow visited him at the Clink only to learn that he too was under arrest. With his fellow prisoners, Greenwood and John Penry, he wrote a full account of his treatment together with a number of other works which were smuggled out of Fleet Prison and published in Holland. Eventually he and Greenwood were indicted for these publications, and after being taken to Tyburn and having ropes placed around their necks failed to cause them to repent, they were hanged. Barrow's writings, especially *A True Description out of the Word of God* (1589), earn him a place among the founders of Congregationalism, although his association with Separatism led Cotton to disown him.

BAYLIE, Robert (1599-1662). Famous for his learning among a learned Scottish clergy, after being educated at the university in Glasgow, his native place, he accepted ordination from the bishops rather than the Church of Scotland. By 1637, however, he had broken fully with episcopalianism and was spokesman for the Scottish church interests that led to the Civil War. He attacked Arminianism and prelacy, and was with the army of covenanters at Dunse Law. In 1642 Baylie became professor of divinity at Glasgow but was frequently absent since he was a member of the Westminster Assembly. Throughout the interregnum he engaged in published attacks on the various "errors" which he thought infected English Protestantism, one such attack being *A Dissuasive from the Errors of the Time* (1645). Baylie was one of the divines appointed to wait on Charles II at the Hague after he was proclaimed in Scotland, but he turned down a bishopric at the Restoration though he did become principal of his university.

BAYNES, Paul (d. 1617). A remarkable Puritan preacher who succeeded William Perkins as lecturer at St. Andrew's Cambridge and who converted, among others, Richard Sibbes, who in turn converted Cotton. Baynes was silenced by the authorities but was warmly welcomed by a host of Puritan gentlemen who all but competed for the honor of showing him hospitality. He had a wide circle of correspondents, among them Cotton whom he recommended to the aldermen of Boston, Lincs., for the St. Botolph's vicarage Cotton subsequently held for some twenty years. His books were all published posthumously; that most relevant to Cotton's reference to him is *The Diocesans Tryall* (1621).

BELLARMINE, St. Robert (1542-1621). A priest of the Jesuit Order, he became professor of controversial theology at the Collegium Romanum in 1576 and was made a cardinal in 1599. His writings formed a prominent part of the Counter-Reformation; even James I engaged in controversy with him.

BEZA, Theodore (1519-1605). One of the great men of the Reformation, he was born of a Catholic family in Burgundy, and abandoned the study of law in favor of a pleasant life of light living and poetry writing. In 1548, however, he went first to Geneva after renouncing his Roman Catholicism and then to Lausanne where he taught Greek. In 1554 he published a treatise defending the burning of Michael Servetus; in 1556 he published an annotated Latin translation of the New Testament; and in 1558 he accepted Calvin's offer of a professorship at Geneva. After the death of Calvin he became leader of the Swiss Calvinists, and was famous for his rigid determinist views. The work of his which was best known to Cotton and the Americans was *Tractiones theologicae* (1570-82).

BOLTON, John (*fl.* 1567-1572). A member of the Plummer's Hall congregation in London, he practiced nonconformity but not separation for a time before seceding and accepting the eldership of a "privy church." He was imprisoned for his beliefs, excommunicated from the Church of England, and persuaded to recant at Paul's Cross. He hanged himself.

BREWSTER, William (1567-1644). One of the leaders of the Pilgrim fathers, he was raised at Scrooby where his father was bailiff of the manor. After some education he became the trusted retainer of William Davison and accompanied him on diplomatic missions, leaving his service in order to succeed to his father's duties at Scrooby in 1589. He gradually became the protector and then the leader of the congregation at Scrooby that finally separated from the established church in 1606, emigrated to Amsterdam in 1608, and moved to Leyden in 1609, where he became elder and teacher and supported his family by turning printer. He took the lead in the early (1617) negotiations with the Virginia Company, but in

1619 returned to England and took little part in the final plans though he was chosen leader of the church group that embarked on the *Mayflower*. As such he was barred from civil office, but he was Bradford's chief aide in all matters at Plymouth and led the church there until a minister succeeded him in 1629. His background and ability commanded the respect of the unseparated Puritans at Massachusetts Bay.

BROWNE, Robert (1550?-1633). The first and most famous Separatist, he probably lived in London as a schoolmaster and occasional preacher after being graduated from Cambridge, but in 1578 he returned to the university and, encouraged by Richard Greenham, began preaching in its vicinity. Becoming convinced that the whole ecclesiastical system was erroneous, he repudiated his ministry and was inhibited from preaching by the bishops, after which he migrated to Norwich and gathered together a congregation of Separatists who came to be known as Brownists. On complaint of nonconformists as well as Anglicans he was arrested in 1581, but after his release he returned to his interdicted ways so that he was arrested again but again released, the clemency shown him being the result of the intercessions of Lord Burghley, a kinsman, who assured the authorities Browne was zealous rather than malicious. In 1581 he migrated to Middleburg with his congregation but there promptly fell into discord with unseparated exiles. In 1583 his headstrong character led to his parting company with his own congregation and returning to Scotland where he was imprisoned before being allowed to continue on to England. There once more he was imprisoned, only to be released thanks to Burghley, and he managed to stay out of trouble until 1586 when he was cited for his preaching, and upon his ignoring the citation, was excommunicated. Amazingly this act seemed to affect a change of character in him, for in 1586 he became a grammar school master, returned to good terms with the church, and five years later accepted Lord Burghley's benefice, the rectory at Achurch, where he continued in office for more than forty uneventful years. But at the end, when he was over eighty years of age, Browne's old temper flared and he struck a constable who had come to collect the rates and spurned a justice of the peace who was anxious to placate him.

As a result he was imprisoned, though he had to be carried off to jail in a cart with his feather bed. His Separatist career was well over by the time John Cotton was in grammar school and fourteen years before Robert Baylie was born.

BUCER, Martin (1491-1551). One of the eminent leaders of the Reformation, he was a member of the Dominican Order who, in 1518, began corresponding with Luther and in 1522 became one of the first German reform priests. He was excommunicated in 1523 for preaching Lutheranism, and as his reform views developed he attempted to mediate between Luther and Zwingli, and, after the death of the latter, became leader of the reformed churches in Switzerland and southern Germany. With religious peace constantly breaking down on the continent, Bucer migrated to England in 1549 where he was received with honor and made Regius professor of divinity at Cambridge. Six years after his death, however, and one year after the execution of his friend Cranmer, Bucer's body was exhumed and publicly burned by the Marian authorities.

BULLINGER, Johann Heinrich (1504-1575). A Reformation leader who joined the movement after reading Luther and Zwingli and in 1531 succeeded the latter as chief pastor at Zurich. He collaborated with Calvin, corresponded widely with English reformers, and was hospitable to many Marian exiles as the result of which he had great prestige among English Puritans. Nevertheless, he was not so extreme in reform as Calvin and it was he whom Elizabeth consulted in making her reply to the papacy in 1570 when Pius V declared the breach between Rome and the Church of England to be final.

BURTON, Henry (1578-1648). Prominent Puritan minister who tutored in the house of Sir Robert Carey after leaving Cambridge and through his interest became clerk of the closet to Prince Henry, and in 1612, at Henry's death, to Prince Charles. After Charles's accession he received the rectory of St. Matthew's Friday Street and from that post in pulpit and in print he began a vigorous assault on the bishops which led to his apprehension for sedition in 1637. He was imprisoned with Prynne and Bastwick and after a stormy trial deprived of his benefice, degraded from the ministry, fined five thousand pounds, and set in the pillory where his ears were cut off.

When he was conveyed northward to Lancaster for perpetual imprisonment so sympathetic were the mobs that greeted him that his progress resembled a triumphal procession, one which was actually realized when he was released by Parliament in 1640 and entered London with Prynne. He then established a congregation on the Independent model, for which form he was a constant polemicist.

CARTWRIGHT, Thomas (1535-1603). Considered by most of his contemporaries to be the leader and most learned of the Puritans of his day, he was forced out of his post at Cambridge in Mary's day but returned on the accession of Elizabeth to lead the fight on behalf of the Geneva discipline. In 1569 he was made Lady Margaret professor of divinity. He engaged in vigorous debates with John Whitgift in which he denounced the hierarchy and for which he was eventually deprived of his office and forced to leave for Geneva in 1571. Returning to England in the following year, Cartwright entered the "Admonition Controversy" in opposition to Whitgift, and, as a result, was again forced into exile in 1573. When he returned to England without royal assent in 1585 he was imprisoned, but Elizabeth deemed it prudent to release him and friends procured him a post at Warwick which he held until being again imprisoned in 1591 for refusing the ex officio oath. Released in the next year he spent his final years lecturing at a number of places at England, though at the very end he centered his activities at Warwick. Cartwright's ideals were essentially Presbyterian and he had less sympathy for the Brownists than for the bishops.

CASAUBON, Isaac (1559-1614). A giant of classical scholarship, he was a native of Geneva who was given the professorship of Greek there when he was twenty-one years old. His learning made him famous throughout the world of educated men, Scaliger calling him "the most learned man in Europe," and when is 1596 he moved to Montpellier his acquisition was regarded as a municipal triumph. Three years later he moved to Paris where he was tempted with a major post if he converted to Roman Catholicism, but he refused and was in 1601 established as librarian to the king. A contest for his presence was vigorously waged by all European centers of learning and was finally decided in 1610 in favor of England where he was warmly welcomed and became especially friendly with Lancelot

Andrewes, where King James I gave him a handsome pension, and where he lived and studied until his death. Casaubon produced twenty-five separate publications, most of them on classical subjects, and although the Puritans disliked him because of his friendship with the bishops, they relied heavily on him for their own classical learning.

CHAMIER, Daniel (1565-1621). An outstanding French Protestant divine, he engaged in theological and ecclesiastical controversies and was best known for his *Panstratia Catholica* (1646), 4 vols. His works were published in Geneva.

CHRYSOSTOM, St. John (ca. 347-407). Doctor of the Church, he was educated for the law but responded to a call to the monastic life and after some eight years as a hermit came to Antioch where he was ordained in 386. In 398 he became Patriach of Constantinople but carried his reforming zeal to too great an extreme for the comfort of the Empress Eudoxia who arranged his banishment in direct opposition to the wishes of the pope and of the people of the city. When exile in Antioch did not hasten his death, he was moved to Pontus and then deliberately killed by enforced travel in bad weather. His honesty and asceticism constitute one part of his claim to fame, the other being his power in preaching and his skill in exegesis. His *On the Priesthood* was, in Cotton's day, a highly respected description of the responsibilities of the Christian minister.

CICERO, Marcus Tullius (106 B.C.-43 B.C.). His works made up a solid part of the seventeenth-century schoolboy's curriculum; Cotton refers to *De officiis*.

CLIFTON, Richard (d. 1616). Pastor of the Separatist church that met in William Brewster's house at Scrooby, he left the congregation in the hands of John Robinson when he emigrated to Amsterdam in 1608 to avoid persecution. There he joined the Separatist group headed by Francis Johnson and engaged in a number of controversies within that group as well as between that group and the established church, his chief adversary within Separatism being John Smyth with whose denial of infant baptism, among other matters, he differed.

CORNELIUS (d. 253). Elected pope in 251, he was faced with strong opposition from Novatian and his followers who demanded that he be more stringent toward those who had lapsed during the Decian persecutions. Tradition says he died a martyr.

COVARRUVIUS, Diego (1512-1577). A Spanish judge and cleric who was chosen by the Council of Trent to draw up its decrees. He wrote treatises on the Bible, church law, and civil law.

CRANMER, Thomas (1489-1556). Archbishop of Canterbury, he received that post in 1533 chiefly because of his service to Henry VIII in divorce matters; before his ordination he made it clear that his service to the king came before his loyalty to the pope. He acted accordingly, but though he favored the royal supremacy in the church he acted to protect those who could not subscribe to it. He was one of the governing council during Edward's minority, but after the young king's death was drawn into the Lady Jane Grey faction and as a result was convicted of treason in 1553. Though spared on this count he was kept in the Tower and in the following year called to account to a Catholic regime for his heresies as one of the chief framers of the Church of England. After months of disputation, his companions, Ridley and Latimer, were executed, he being made to witness their deaths, but he was spared for another five months during which time vigorous attempts were made to convert him. Though he signed recantations, when brought to the stake he disavowed them and offered first to the fire the hand that had signed them. Since he was archbishop when the English church made its great breach with Rome he was considered a martyr by all Protestants but an incomplete reformer by the Puritans.

CYPRIAN, St. (d. 258). Bishop of Carthage during the stormy days of Decian and Valerian persecution, he was a converted pagan rhetorician whose chief human guides were the writings of Tertullian. He wrote a number of works that gained him a readership through the ages, and he was recognized as an authority on the ministry and the sacraments.

DANAEUS, Lambert (1530-1596). A French Calvinist divine who preached at Geneva and wrote a number of theological treatises.

DAVENANT, John (d. 1641). Bishop of Salisbury, he was a loyal episcopalian in church matters but a Calvinist in theological matters; at the time he was called to examine Cotton he was

President of Queens College, Cambridge, as the result, in great part, of the efforts on his behalf of John Preston, who had been converted by Cotton. His presence at the examination probably indicated to Cotton that the bishop intended to be lenient.

DAVENPORT, John (1597-1670). Puritan minister and one of the founders of New Haven, Conn., he was vicar of St. Stephen's Church, Coleman Street, and an active Puritan when he visited John Cotton hiding in London from the High Commission in 1633 and planning his departure to America. In conferences with Cotton, Davenport concluded that he too was unable to minister profitably in England and accordingly fled to Amsterdam, and, after a period of service to the English congregation there, emigrated on Cotton's advice to New England, arriving in June 1637 in time to take part in the synod on Antinomianism. The following year he rejected offers from Massachusetts communities and with friends founded the colony of New Haven. He remained a lifelong friend of Cotton's and a vigorous writer on behalf of Congregationalism, a form to which Cotton, if he did not convert him, certainly attracted him.

DOD, John (1549?-1645). A Puritan minister in Northamptonshire known to Cotton's generation as "Old Mr. Dod," he was renowned for the moderateness of his temper and the soundness of his advice. In 1633 Cotton, perplexed as to whether or not he should flee persecution or stay to witness against it, visited Dod and took his advice when Dod said: "I am old Peter, and therefore must stand still and bear the brunt; but you, being young Peter, may go whether you will, and ought being persecuted in one city, to flee unto another."

ECEBOLIUS (4th cent.). A Greek sophist who under the reign of Constantine turned Christian, but who afterwards under Julius became a zealous pagan.

EDWARDS, Thomas (1599-1647). An extremely virulent Puritan minister who suffered persecution prior to 1640 and who after that year took a position of leadership in Presbyterian activities in London and turned his sharp tongue on the Independents, in which connection he produced *Antapologia* (1644), from which Baylie quotes, and, in 1646, the harshly severe *Gangraena*.

ELIOT, John (1604-1690). Known as the "Apostle to the Indians," he had become a nonconformist in 1622 as the result of the influence of Thomas Hooker, and did not have a ministry until he came to New England in 1631 and was established at Roxbury. He studied the native Indian language diligently, preached in it, translated the Bible and the catechism into it, and by these activities entered legend as well as history.

ENDICOTT, John (1588-1665). One of the original patentees of Massachusetts Bay, he took charge of the settlement at Salem (then called Naumkeag) in 1628, and retained positions of power in the New England government throughout his life, serving as governor a number of times. His arrival preceded Winthrop's by two years; the Salem church which he helped found was the first nonseparatist Congregational church established in America. Though Endicott in his later years earned a reputation for sternness and orthodoxy, in the early years of his settlement he was sympathetic to the ideas of Roger Williams.

EPIPHANIUS, (ca. 315-403). Bishop of Salamis, was ardently orthodox, and in his *Panarion* attacked every heresy known to him from the beginning of Christianity to his day.

EUSEBIUS (ca. 260-ca. 340). Bishop of Caesarea, he took an active part in the Arian Controversy and in the Council of Nicaea, but is known best for his *Ecclesiastical History,* which is the chief source of knowledge for the history of Christianity from the apostles to his day and earned him the epithet, "Father of Church History."

FERIUS, Paul (1591-1669). A French Protestant minister who preached in his native city, Metz, for over fifty years and wrote many theological works.

GOODWIN, Thomas (1600-1680). Vicar of Trinity Church Cambridge, he became dissatisfied with the terms of conformity and in 1633 sought out John Cotton who was then in hiding from the authorities preparatory to his migration to Massachusetts. Cotton confirmed him in his interest in Congregationalism, and when in 1639 his own position in England became untenable Goodwin fled to Holland. Returning to London in the next year, he took part in the Westminster Assembly and, together with four others, dissented from the propositions on church government, which were Presbyterian. In explanation, he published *The Apologeticall Narration* (1643), the platform of Independency. He was made President of Magdalen College, Oxford in 1650, but was deprived of the office at the Restoration, after which he led an independent congregation in London.

GORTON, Samuel (ca. 1592-1677). A London cloth finisher, he emigrated to New England in 1637 and was promptly embroiled in trouble over his religious views, and fined, imprisoned, and then banished from Boston. In Plymouth and even in Roger Williams' tolerating Providence he continued to raise controversies because of his views, among which were a denial of the Trinity (though he believed Jesus to be God), a repudiation of the ministry in favor of the priesthood of all men, and a belief in conditional immortality. He and his followers proved so troublesome to the Massachusetts Bay authorities that finally in 1644 they were all arrested even though they lived outside of Bay jurisdiction, and, after a term at hard labor, they were deported to England. Under the protection of the Earl of Warwick, Gorton returned to Rhode Island in 1648 and lived peaceably until his death in the town he founded in the Earl's name. Cotton took a prominent part in the proceedings against Gorton and his followers in 1644.

GREENWOOD, John (d. 1593). A London minister who became friendly with Henry Barrow and who was arrested in 1586 for holding Separatist conventicles. He remained in prison for six years and together with his fellow prisoners, Barrow and John Penry, underwent frequent examinations by the authorities. During this time he also managed to smuggle out various books which he and his fellows had written, and after being released in 1592 he was again arrested for these publications and for the Separatist congregation he was conducting. In 1593 he was hanged with Barrow. A report circulated that Elizabeth regretted their execution.

HERLE, Charles (1598-1659). An ardent Presbyterian divine, he was frequently called to preach to the Long Parliament, was one of the licensers of books appointed by that body, was placed on important committees of the Westminster Assembly, and succeeded Twisse as the Assembly's prolocutor. Herle disapproved of the execution of Charles and collaborated with Lord Derby in the abortive attempt to bring Charles II to power that ended at Warrington Bridge.

HIGGINSON, Francis (1587-1630). Apparently a conforming minister until influenced by Arthur Hildersam, he was deprived for nonconformity in 1627 and supported thereafter by wealthy Puritans. In 1629 he sailed as minister to the Salem settlement and there together with Samuel Skelton gave emobodiment to nonseparating Congregationalism. He died a little more than a year after his arrival in New England.

HILDERSAM, Arthur (1563-1632). Although frequently interrupted by suspensions, he had a distinguished preaching career at Ashby-de-la-Zouch where he maintained a prominent intellectual center for Puritans. He was in correspondence or personal communication with almost every eminent Puritan of his day and was one of the most active managers of the Millenary Petition. Cotton wrote a brief introduction to his *Lectures upon the Forth of John* (1629).

HOLMES, Nathanael (d. 1678). An Independent London minister of no great reputation, he became an active Millenarian together with Henry Burton and published works setting forth the movement's views.

HOOKER, Thomas (1586?-1647). Second only to Cotton in his influence on first-generation New England theology, he was a far more practical man and after three years in Massachusetts Bay, whence he had arrived in 1633 on the same boat with Cotton, he led his congregation to settle at Hartford where he was a political as well as a religious leader. His *A Survey of the Summe of Church Discipline* (1648) was a major contribution to New England's defense of its church system, and was, like Cotton's work, a prominent target for the Presbyterians.

HUTCHINSON, Anne (1591-1643). A native of Lincolnshire, she had frequently heard Cotton preach there; her eldest son, Edward, had migrated to Massachusetts with Cotton in 1633 and she followed in the next year. At the root of her "Antinomianism" was a belief that the power of grace in a saved believer so destroyed the creature in him that he was apart from religious law, a belief that had foundation in the Puritan theology of the day. She was banished from the colony and excommunicated from the Boston church after civil and ecclesiastical trials, and in 1638 emigrated with her family and some friends to Rhode Island. At her husband's death in 1642 she moved to the present Pelham Bay, New York, where, in 1643, she and her family died in an Indian massacre.

IRENAEUS, St. (ca. 130-ca. 200). Considered to be the first great Catholic theologian, in his career and in his writings he provided an important link between Eastern and Western Christianity. Irenaeus was among the bishops who blamed Pope Victor I for his severity in threatening with excommunication Bishop Polycrates of Ephesus for continuing the Eastern custom of celebrating Easter on the Hebrew Passover (Nisan 14) rather than on the Sunday following. Though Victor called synods before making his threat, Irenaeus appears to have protested the threat to the Eastern churches rather than, as Cotton would have it, the synod itself. Since Rome continued communion with the Eastern churches even though they kept their traditional Easter observance, it is likely Victor never carried out his threat. Cotton knew Irenaeus best as a heresiologist, his chief contribution to this genre being *Adversus Omnes Haereses*.

JACOB, Henry (1563-1624). A noted Separatist minister who joined the Brownists around 1590 and went to Holland with them when they were banished in 1593. He returned to England in 1597, but because of his writings was compelled again to flee. He settled at Middleburg in a congregation of English exiles; there, influenced by his talks with John Robinson, he adopted his ecclesiastical views. Accordingly, the church he founded in London upon his return in 1616 is generally considered to be the first Congregational church ever gathered in that country. Jacob allowed that the Church of England was a true church though in need of thorough reformation and was thus less extreme than other Separatists.

JOHNSON, Francis (1562-1618). A disciple of the views of Cartwright, he was banished from Cambridge in 1589 for preaching that church government by elders is divine law, and went to Middleburg where he became preacher to the English merchants there. In 1591, after reading Barrow and Greenwood, he turned Separatist, and upon going to London to meet with them shortly before their imprisonment, he founded a Separatist congregation.

This gained him imprisonment from 1593 to 1597, after which he made his way to Amsterdam where he became Ainsworth's colleague until 1610 when those who believed with him that the eldership rather than the entire congregation was the seat of authority in matters of excommunication withdrew from Ainsworth's group.

JULIAN the Apostate (332-363). Roman Emperor 361-363, he was a nephew of Constantine the Great, and a fellow student, at Athens, of St. Gregory of Nazianzen. Nevertheless, as emperor he set about a systematic program to promote paganism and degrade Christianity though he stopped short of outright persecution.

JUNIUS, Francis (1589-1677). Born at Heidelberg and educated at Leyden and Middleburg, he came to England in 1621 as librarian and tutor in the family of the Earl of Arundel where he began his lifelong career as a philologist specializing in the northern and Teutonic languages.

JUSTIN Martyr, St. (ca. 100-ca. 165). After a long search for the truth in pagan philosophers he embraced Christianity and was a vigorous apologist for this faith in Rome. He is regarded as foremost among apologists because he was the first Christian writer to attempt the reconciliation of faith and reason.

LECHFORD, Thomas (*fl.* 1629-1642). The first professional lawyer to come to Massachuetts Bay, Lechford had suffered imprisonment in England for soliciting the cause of William Prynne and opposing episcopacy. After his arrival in 1638, however, he found himself at odds with the authorities and was not received into the church, which meant that he could not acquire civil privileges. In 1639 he was debarred for trying to influence a jury out of court, and in 1641, leaving his wife and goods behind him, he returned to England where he became a supporter of monarchy and episcopacy. Shortly before his death he published *Plain Dealing,* a critical account of Massachusetts Bay practices.

LOTHROP, John (1584-1653). Renouncing his orders in the church of England after some fifteen years as a preacher, he joined a Separatist congregation in London and succeeded Henry Jacob as the pastor in 1625. For this activity he was imprisoned in 1632, and on his release in 1634 he fled to Plymouth Colony where he became pastor of the church at Scituate.

MATHER, Richard (1596-1669). He migrated to Massachusetts in 1634 after his suspension for nonconformity, settling as pastor of the Dorchester church from 1636 until his death. Mather married Cotton's widow, and his son by his first marriage, Increase, married Cotton's daughter, the issue of the union being Cotton Mather, grandson of both Richard Mather and John Cotton.

MAVERICK, John (1575-1636). Minister of the church at Dorchester from 1630 to his death, he was preceded to New England by his better-known son, Samuel, who attained a semi-legendary character in New England history.

MELITO APPOLINARIS, or MELITO, St. (d. ca. 190). He was Bishop of Sardi, and though very little of his works survived he was widely known to posterity through the praise of him found in the writings of his time. His lost writings are primarily in the area of apologetics.

MOUNTAIGNE, George (1569-1628). Promoted to the bishopric of Lincoln in 1617, he was also dean of Westminster, an active member of the high church party, and a strong ally of Laud's. He became successively Bishop of London and of Durham (to make room for Laud at London), and in 1628, Archbishop of York. He was for the Puritans the very model of what was wrong with episcopacy, and John Milton characterized him as a man with a "many-benefice-gaping mouth" and a "canary-sucking and swan-eating palat."

NORTON, John (1606-1663). After a storm drove his ship back in 1634, he successfully reached Plymouth in 1635, and though invited to stay preferred to move to Massachusetts Bay where he became minister at Ipswich. Cotton, on his deathbed, nominated Norton to be his successor at Boston, a post which Norton did not assume until 1656, four years after Cotton's death, because of the reluctance of the Ipswich church to dismiss him. He wrote the first life of Cotton, *Abel Being Dead Yet Speaketh* (1658).

NOVATIAN (d. 257-258). After the systematic persecution of the Christians by the Emperor Decius (250-251), Novatian, a Roman presbyter, apparently disappointed at Cornelius' election as pope, changed from a policy of leniency towards those who had compromised under persecution to one of severe opposition to Cor-

nelius' leniency. He and his followers were excommunicated though
they commanded support from some churches, such as Alexandria.
Novatian was martyred under Valerian.

NYE, Philip (1596?-1672). His nonconformity forced him into exile
in Holland in 1633, but after his return in 1640 he took a leading
part in church politics. In the Westminister Assembly he was a
leader of Independent thought and an author of *The Apologeticall
Narration*. Nye believed in the ultimate triumph of good sense and
saw fanaticism as folly not crime. His opponents as well as his
allies regarded him as a man of extraordinary talent.

OCHINO, Bernardino (1487-1564). Born and raised in Italy, he
entered the Franciscan Order, but gradually became attracted to
Lutheranism and in 1542 fled probable presecution and placed
himself under Calvin in Geneva. In 1547 he came to England at
Cranmer's invitation and was made preacher to the Italian church,
but on Mary's accession returned to the continent where he lived a
mobile life in response to the fortunes of Protestantism in Germany,
Switzerland, Poland, and Italy. He was a prolific author of
theological works.

ORANTES, Francisco (1516-1581). Bishop of Oviedo, he wrote a
prominent confutation of Calvinism.

PAGET, John (d. 1640). Ejected for nonconformity, he went to
Holland where he was chaplain to an English regiment from 1604
to 1607 when he accepted the ministry of a Presbyterian church in
Amsterdam. He engaged Henry Ainsworth as well as John Davenport in printed controversy on church government.

PARKER, Robert (1564?-1614). He fled high commission persecution
in 1607 and settled at Leyden where together with William Ames
he established a moderate position between Presbyterianism and
and Separatism and earned a place in the honor roll of the
Separatists as well as the nonconformists. When he joined Paget's
Presbyterian congregation at Amsterdam he was unable to reconcile
Paget to his views on, among other matters, the limited use of
synods. After two years stay in 1613 he moved to Doesburg as
preacher for the garrison there.

PEMBLE, William (1592?-1623). An accomplished expounder of

Calvinist theology from the pulpit and in print, he remained loyal to the episcopacy while urging greater leniency towards those who dissented from it.

PERKINS, William (1558-1602). A staunch opponent of Roman Catholicism and its vestiges in the English church, he was the greatest of all Puritan teachers and preachers at Cambridge, where Cotton attended his lectures. He exerted a very great influence over the generation of Cambridge students who were to colonize a new land and to lead a revolution in the homeland. His published works came for the Puritans to fill the theological vacancy left by the discrediting of the Scholastic theologians.

PHILLIPS, George (1593-1644). Among his Essex parishioners was John Maidstone, nephew of John Winthrop, who put him in communication with his uncle with the result that Phillips migrated with Winthrop in 1630. He founded the church at Watertown together with Sir. Richard Saltonstall who established a settlement there.

PISCATOR, John (1546-1625). A professor of theology at Strasbourg, he was obliged to leave when he embraced Calvinism. He was best known for his commentaries on the Bible.

POLANO, Pietro Soave (1552-1623). The author of the *History of the Council of Trent* which was the standard work on the subject in its day.

PRYNNE, William (1600-1669). A London lawyer, he first distinguished himself as the author of *Histriomastix* (1633), an attack on actors and the stage which also indirectly criticized the king and queen, for which offense he was debarred, degraded from his university degree, and set in the pillory where both ears were cropped. Because he continued his anti-government writings during his subsequent imprisonment, in 1637 he lost the stumps of his ears and was branded on both cheeks with "S.L.," which, though it was intended to mean "seditious libeler," Prynne chose to interpret as "stigmata Laudis," in view of his enmity for the Bishop. When he was released from prison by the Long Parliament in 1640, Prynne reentered London as a great popular hero, but in the ensuing years he fell out with almost every faction of Puritanism and was finally arrested and imprisoned in 1650, to be released in 1653, and to be made keeper of the records of the Tower on the accession of Charles II.

RATHBAND, William (d. 1695). One of the lesser Presbyterian polemicists, he was an Essex vicar.

RIDLEY, Nicholas (ca. 1500-1555). From 1535, when he was a vicar in Kent, onward, Ridley showed definite Protestant leanings which became pronounced on the accession of Edward VI. He assisted in the compilation of the *Book of Common Prayer,* and, as Master of Pembroke Hall, in the establishment of Protestantism at Cambridge. With Mary's accession he was deprived of the bishopric of London, on which he had entered in 1550, and when heresy was made a capital offense he was burned at the stake at Oxford together with Hugh Latimer.

ROBINSON, John (1576?-1625). The most revered of the pastors of the Pilgrim fathers, he joined the Scrooby group around 1607 and emigrated to Amsterdam with some of them in the following year, but, in 1609, moved to Leyden wishing to avoid the dissension that surrounded the congregation led by Johnson and Ainsworth. When, in 1620, the Leyden group contemplated migration to America, it was agreed that Robinson would stay with the majority though he was sorely disappointed that the majority chose not to go to New England. He preached a famous farewell sermon to the colonists, and in the following years persuaded his congregation to join their brethren in Plymouth, although he himself was prevented from going by lack of funds. Robinson, through letters, showed great pastoral concern for the Plymouth group. In the Amsterdam disputes he sided with Ainsworth and in his last years he came part way back from Separation and agreed that it was lawful to hear the word and pray in the Church of England though not to receive the sacraments there.

ROLLOCK, Robert (1555-1599). Cotton's reference to him is probably ironic because although he was a member of a committee of the Edinburgh presbytery appointed to hold a conference with the king in 1591 on the affairs of the kirk, he was won over finally to the king's policy and, at the insistence of the royal party, he was chosen moderator of the Dundee Assembly in 1597; thereafter he lent his

aid to the king's ecclesiastical polity. The Latin treatise to which
Cotton refers was translated by H. Holland and published in 1641
as *A Treatise of God's Effectual Calling.*

RUTHERFORD, Samuel (1600?-1661). Pastor at Anworth in Gallo-
way, he was silenced for his nonconformity in 1636 and ordered
to reside at Aberdeen at the king's pleasure. At the covenanting
revolution he left Aberdeen and was appointed professor of
divinity at St. Andrews by the Glasgow Assembly of 1638. He was
a prominent member of the covenanting assemblies, a staunch
representative of Scots Presbyterianism at the Westminister Assembly, and an increasingly rigid adherent of that way, so much so that
he was mentioned by Milton in "The New Forcers of Conscience
under the Long Parliament." The work of his with which Cotton
was most concerned is *The Due Right of Presbyteries* (1644).

SAMOSATENUS, or PAUL of Samosata (3rd cent.). Bishop of
Antioch, in 208 he was condemned and deposed by synods at
Antioch for maintaining that Jesus was God only in the sense that
a power from God the Father rested upon his human person.

SCHINDLER, Valentine (d. 1604). A professor of Oriental languages
at Wittemberg, he compiled a lexicon in Hebrew, Syriac, Chaldaic,
Talmudo-Rabbinic, and Arabic, which was first published on the
continent but published again in abridged form in London in 1635.

SHEPARD, Thomas (1604-1649). Forbidden the exercise of his
ministry in London by Laud in 1630, and later silenced by Archbishop Neile, he migrated to New England in 1635, became pastor
at Cambridge, and was one of the founders of Harvard College.
Shepard was an extremely effective writer and his *The Sincere
Convert* (1641) enjoyed great popularity. He was probably shocked
to read in Cotton of Mrs. Hutchinson's preference for him, since
he was a decided opponent of her group and even distrusted Cotton
because of his association with her. Could Cotton have known of
Shepard's distrust (recorded in Shepard's private journal) and here
be twitting him by associating him also with Mrs. Hutchinson?

SKELTON, Samuel (1593-1634). He went to Salem in 1628 and was
the pastor of the first Congregational church in America that claimed
membership in the Church of England. Cotton at that time, however, thought him too close to the Separatists and wrote him a

cautionary letter of which Baylie makes great rhetorical use to demonstrate that Cotton changed his mind after he arrived in New England.

SMITH, John (ca. 1554-1612). A Separatist minister in England, he led a company of exiles to Amsterdam around 1608 where his group fell into distinct and prolonged disagreement with all other Separatist congregations in Holland, primarily because he came increasingly to believe in a Mennonite doctrine of baptism. His congregation is considered by church historians to be the first modern Baptist church.

STONE, Samuel (1602-1663). Suspended from his Essex curateship for nonconformity in 1630, he obtained a lectureship in Northampton-shire where he met Thomas Hooker with whom he emigrated and with whom he served in the church at Newtown from 1633 to 1636. Stone selected the site of Hartford to which his and Hooker's congregation moved in 1636 and he negotiated its purchase from the Indians. In all probability the settlement was named for Hert-ford because the latter was Stone's birthplace. After Hooker's death in 1647 Stone, until his own death, was sole minister at Hartford. His formula for Congregationalism sums up a great deal of what Cotton maintains in the foregoing pages: "a speaking aristocracy in the face of a silent democracy."

TERTULLIAN, Quintus Septimus Florens (ca. 160-ca. 220). A Church Father, native of Carthage, who received a pagan education and became a lawyer. Converting to Christianity, probably in Rome, he returned to Carthage about 196, where he became a priest and where he founded his own church party. A prolific author of apologetic, theological, controversial, and ascetic works, he was the first Christian theologian to write in Latin and is credited with having created the language of Western theology.

TWISSE, William (1578?-1646). Noted for his learning at Oxford, he was chaplain to Elizabeth of Bohemia in 1613 before becoming a rector in Buckinghamshire and proceeding to the degree of D.D. He was a doctrinal rather than a political Puritan and managed to retain the respect of Laud as well as of the more zealous Puritans because of the style with which he maintained doctrinal orthodoxy. Twisse was unanimously elected prolocutor of the Westminister

Assembly. Cotton refers to Twisse's *A Treatise of Mr. Cotton's ...
Concerning Predestination* (1646), in which Twisse read him a
lesson in the shakiness of some of the theological views he had
held during his Lincolnshire ministry. Cotton seems to have
changed to a position closer to Twisse's after his migration and
he did not respond to Twisse because, in all probability, he had
come to agree with him

VICTOR, St. (d. 198). Pope from 189, he ordered synods to be held
throughout Christendom to settle the rule that Easter was to be
kept on the Sunday following the Hebrew Passover date (Nisan
14) rather than on the date itself. Irenaeus, among others, opposed
his threat of excommunication to those who would not follow the
practice laid down by the synods.

WAREHAM, John (d. 1670). Pastor of the Dorchester church after
his arrival in 1630, he migrated to Windsor, Conn. in 1636 where
he lived for the remainder of his life.

WELD, Thomas (1595-1661). Deposed by the high commission in
1631, he arrived in New England in 1632 and became pastor of
the church at Roxbury. He was among the more zealous of those
who attacked the beliefs of Anne Hutchinson's party, and when,
after 1641, he resided in England, first as the colony's agent, later
as a minister, he was instrumental in getting published Winthrop's
account of the controversy, *A Short Story of the Rise, Reign, and
Ruine of the Antinomians* (1644). Weld engaged in polemics on
behalf of the New England way and edited and wrote in part
the first major work of Massachusetts public relations, *New
England's First Fruits* (1643).

WHEELWRIGHT, John (ca. 1592-1674). After being silenced in
1633, he lived privately in Lincolnshire until his migration to New
England in 1636. A party in Boston wished to engage him as a
second teacher in the church, together with Cotton, but when
this plan was abandoned, largely because of Winthrop's opposition,
he settled as pastor at Mt. Wollaston (now Quincy). Anne
Hutchinson was his sister-in-law, and Wheelwright was a supporter of her views to the extent of preaching a sermon in 1637
that was condemned as seditious by the General Court. For this
he was banished from the colony. He settled at the present Exeter,

N.H., but moved to the present Wells, Maine, when Massachusetts Bay extended its borders to include Exeter. In 1643 he sent letters of repentance to Boston and in 1644 the banishment was removed. From 1647 he served in pastorates in New Hampshire.

WHITAKER, William (1548-1595). Noted for his scholarship in the Bible, the commentators, and the Schoolmen, he rose to the mastership of St. John's College, Cambridge. As a theologian he was a strict Calvinist; in matters of church government he agreed with the bishops. Whitaker's scholarly theology earned him the praise of a wide range of contemporaries, from the Puritans, to Scaliger, Casaubon, Bishop Hall, and Cardinal Bellarmine.

WHITGIFT, John (1530-1604). While master at Trinity College, Cambridge, he opposed the Puritanism of Thomas Cartwright; his vigor in this enterprise gained him the attention of Queen Elizabeth, who, in 1583, named him Archbishop of Canterbury. Under his administration the Church of England solidified its position between Presbyterianism and Roman Catholicism, and it was he who commissioned Richard Hooker to write the monumental apology of the Elizabethan settlement, *Of the Laws of Ecclesiastical Polity* (1594 and 1597).

WILLIAMS, Roger (ca. 1603-1683). Arriving in Massachusetts in 1631, he was pastor at Salem, but believing Massachusetts Bay to be insufficiently separated from the established church, he moved to Plymouth within the year. In 1634, however, he was back at Salem, having found even Plymouth too compromising, but when he was called by the Salem church to succeed the recently deceased Samuel Skelton, the Bay authorities began to proceed against his radicalism, and in 1635 he was expelled from the colony. He went to Rhode Island, founded the city of Providence, returned to England (1643-1644) to secure a charter for Rhode Island, and served as governor of that colony four times. He visited England again (1651-1652) and won Cromwell's support. Cotton conducted two disputes with Williams: the first, over the grounds of Williams' banishment from Massachusetts, is to be found in Cotton's *A Letter of Mr. John Cottons . . . to Mr. Williams* (1643), answered by Williams in *Mr. Cottons Letter . . . Examined and Answered*, and responded to in Cotton's *A Reply to Mr. Williams His Ex-*

amination (1647) ; the second, on toleration, began with Williams'
The Bloudy Tenent of Persecution (1644), which attacked a
treatise of Cotton's, first published together with the attack, and
was answered by Cotton's *The Bloudy Tenent Washed and Made
White in the Bloud of the Lambe* (1647), responded to by
Williams in *The Bloody Tenent Yet More Bloody* (1652). In
relying on Williams' testimony against Massachusetts, Baylie is, on
the one hand, using a well informed eye witness, but, on the other
hand, citing a man whose theological and political opinions are
far more opposed to his own than are those of Cotton.

WILSON, John (ca. 1591-1667). After a preaching career in England
frequently interrupted by suspension, he migrated with Winthrop
in 1630 and became the founding pastor of the Boston church.
Cotton, on his arrival, joined him as teacher of that church in
1633. Although Wilson and Cotton disagreed at times, especially
during the Antinomian Controversy when Wilson was roundly
attacked by the dissidents while Cotton was warmly praised, in
the main they were amicable colleagues in what was the most
influential church in the colony.

WINTHROP, John (1588-1649). Educated at Trinity College, Cambridge, and a member of the Inner Temple, he was chosen
governor of Massachusetts Bay by the London company and arrived in Boston with the patent in 1630. He was certainly the
most influential member of that colony throughout his lifetime,
serving as governor repeatedly. As a member of the Boston church
he was a zealous opponent of the Hutchinson group, but as a
magistrate he was judicious enough to recognize Cotton's value and
he turned the prosecution of the opinionists away from becoming
a public examination of Cotton also. His *Short Story* is frequently
cited by Baylie; his *Journal* is the single most importance source for
the history of New England from 1630 to 1649.

ZANCHI, Jerome (1516-1590). An Italian monk who converted to
Protestantism and, after teaching at Geneva, was a professor of
theology at Strasbourg. He was a prolific exponent of Calvinist
theology.

INDEX

THE JOHN HARVARD LIBRARY

*The intent of
Waldron Phoenix Belknap, Jr.,
as expressed in an early will, was for
Harvard College to use the income from a
permanent trust fund he set up, for "editing and
publishing rare, inaccessible, or hitherto unpublished
source material of interest in connection with the
history, literature, art (including minor and useful
art), commerce, customs, and manners or way of
life of the Colonial and Federal Periods of the United
States . . . In all cases the emphasis shall be on the
presentation of the basic material." A later testament
broadened this statement, but Mr. Belknap's interests remained constant until his death.*

*In linking the name of the first benefactor of
Harvard College with the purpose of this later,
generous-minded believer in American culture the
John Harvard Library seeks to emphasize the importance of Mr. Belknap's purpose. The John Harvard
Library of the Belknap Press of Harvard University
Press exists to make books and documents
about the American past more readily
available to scholars and the
general reader.*